MW00562300

GRASSROOT HORIZONS

CONNECTING PARTICIPATORY DEVELOPMENT INITIATIVES EAST AND WEST

Editors

Richard Morse • Anisur Rahman • Kersten L. Johnson

INTERMEDIATE TECHNOLOGY PUBLICATIONS 1995

A CIP catalogue record for this book is available from the British Library

ISBN 1 85339 290 1

Originally published in India by Oxford & IBH Publishing Co. Pvt. Ltd., 66 Janpath, New Delhi 110 001.
Printed in India.

PREFACE

This book, to apply a Hawaiian image, catches two waves that are globally important in the 1990's and beyond:

• The increasing success of grassroots, community-based groups of dispossessed, excluded peoples in asserting, defining, organizing, and acting to create and sustain their own futures.

• Increasing recognition in development thinking of the significance of such participatory, self-motivated action, with awareness by major international agencies that external support to such movements can only be effective when defined, designed, and implemented on people's own terms. This new policy orientation was affirmed by representatives of more than 120 governments at the World Summit for Social Development in March, 1995, in their declaration of the action principle "that empowering people, particularly women, to strengthen their own capacities is a main objective of development and its principal resource. Empowerment requires the full participation of people in the formulation, implementation and evaluation of decisions determining the functioning and well-being of our societies."[1]

The book's purpose, indicated by its title, is primarily to connect and communicate among grassroots groups, and between such groups and external institutions—academic, non-governmental, governmental. It is intended also to be useful to facilitative organizations, including those who are in a position to interpret and adapt relevant sections for use by local groups who do not have direct access to a volume in English.

The book opens in Part I with personalized reports of the 1989 workshop, *People's Initiatives to Overcome Poverty*,[2] presenting fifteen profiles and a synthesis of participatory action in India, the Philippines, urban and rural United States including Hawaii, Newfoundland, Thailand, and Bangladesh. An initial purpose established in Part I is to continue connections and communication among participants of that workshop, and to seek reasons on why and how it succeeded not only in bonding members from widely varied cultures but in generating principles and enthusiasm for new organizing and theory-building efforts.

Authors of the volume are participants of this original workshop. In individual chapters they report and critically analyze subsequent participatory organization, research, and learning experiences in which they have engaged. Many of these authors joined in a followup workshop at Koitta, Bangladesh, in 1990 to formulate a collaborative project on Participatory Learning Resources. This workshop facilitated further exchanges among members. It also resulted in sponsorship of the editorial meetings among Richard Morse, Anisur Rahman, and Kersten Johnson that were needed to shape and produce this volume.

Three themes define the clustering of the authors' chapters. Issues of identity, awareness, and solidarity among local, indigenous populations are addressed in Part II. Part III points to the larger structures—cultural, educational, governmental, corporate—faced by local, widely dispersed groups, and reports measures organized and used by local groups to confront and change these structures. Part IV, building on cooperation among members and related non-governmental organizations at the Rio Conference on Environment and Development, addresses issues of equity in global resource distribution and control, grassroots initiatives in environmental protection, and core values and connections among groups seeking sustainable, just paths of development through participatory means.

Each part opens with a brief preface and contains reflections, crystallized from dialogues among the editors, on the significance and challenges opened by the authors—and their grassroots colleagues and movements—in support of ethical, perceptual, and pragmatic advances to foster and cascade participatory movements locally, nationally, and internationally.

END NOTES

[1] See World Summit for Social Development, *Copenhagen Declaration and Programme of Action*. March 1995. New York: United Nations Development Program. For the concurrent non-governmental statement, see *The Copenhagen Alternative Declaration*, signed by 750 NGO representatives, in *Global Advocates Bulletin* # 29, June 1995, United Church Board for World Ministries, 475 Riverside Drive, 16th Floor, New York, N.Y. 10115-0109.

[2] Membership of the workshop and its summary are provided in *Preliminary Report, International Workshop: People's Initiatives to Overcome Poverty*, March 27–April 5, 1989. East-West Center Institute of Culture and Communication and Resource Systems Institute, Honolulu, Hawaii. May 1989.

CONTENTS

IV. TRANSFORMATIONS THE COMPASS ROUND

ABOUT THE AUTHORS

Richard Morse lives by turn in the United States and Southern Asia, engaging with local and international colleagues in participatory action research and sharing communities' experiences and purposes as an East-West interpreter of social and political change. His applied work includes consulting and writing on community dynamics and organization; small enterprise economics, entrepreneurship, and industrialization policy; farming and rural energy systems research and development; self-determination, federalism, reciprocal rights, and education. His 1965 book, *Modern Small Industry for Developing Countries*, with Eugene Staley, continues as a standard work. He has co-coordinated the Participatory Development Group and Forum with Kersten Johnson at the East-West Center, where he is Senior Fellow Emeritus.

Address: Richard Morse, East-West Center, Honolulu, Hawaii 96848, USA

Anisur Rahman was Professor of Economics in the University of Dhaka, Bangladesh, before he joined the International Labor Office in 1977 and built and coordinated a programme on Participation of the Rural Poor in Development until 1991. His recent publications include *Action and Knowledge, Breaking the Monopoly with Participatory Action Research*, co-edited with Orlando Fals-Borda (New Horizons and Intermediate Technology); *The Lost Moment, Dreams with a Nation Born through Fire* (University Press Ltd., Dhaka); and *People's Self-Development, Perspectives in Participatory Action Research* (ZED Books, London and University Press Ltd., Dhaka).

Address: Anisur Rahman, Eastern Housing Apartments, No. 802, 6 Segunbagicha, Dhaka 1000, Bangladesh

Kersten Johnson is a freelance writer, trainer, and activist involved in community-based initiatives in sustainable development. She holds a B.S. in Environmental Science (1981) and an M.A. in Energy and Resources (1985) from the University of California at Berkeley. As Co-Coordinator of the East-West Center Participatory Development Group she has focused on research, training, and organizing in the field of participatory, community-based development in India, Bhutan, Bangladesh, Nepal, Thailand, and her adopted home in Hawaii. At the Global Forum in Rio, she participated in drafting the treaty on consumption and lifestyle. She has a special interest in promoting alternatives to consumerism, through encouraging the adoption of simpler lifestyles in industrialized countries.

Address: Kersten L. Johnson, P.O. Box 980, Volcano, Hawaii 96785, USA

Christine Tan, a Filipino woman, is a religious Sister of the Good Shepherd, living for 15 years now in the slums of Manila identifying with the urban poor in their life, suffering, and aspirations. Born in Manila, she comes from a loving and wealthy family. Her education was with German Benedictine Sisters in Manila and American Sisters in the United States. She is known as an advocate for human rights, particularly during the Marcos dictatorship when she engaged in the battle for human rights for the Filipino masses. She was a member of the Philippine Constitutional Commission which framed the 1987 Constitution. She was elected the first Filipino provincial superior of her area, covering the Philippines, Taiwan, Hongkong, Guam, and Korea, and has participated in many international conferences. She is a follower of Oriental Spirituality, particularly Siddha Yoga.

Address: Sister Christine Tan, 2172 Fidel Reyes, Malate, Manila, Philippines 1004

Syed A. Rahim, Senior Fellow, East-West Center: I have been a student of communication and development starting with involvement in the Comilla rural development project prior to Bangladesh independence. For many years now my professional life is deeply embedded in a highly contested terrain of knowledge. I have tried to understand the processes of development and deprivation, accumulation and marginalization. One lesson I have learned is that there is no substitute for deep dialogues with the people in understanding the dynamics of poverty alleviation. However, dialogues uninformed by theory are like a fluid without a container—you cannot hold it and keep it. If you ask me, where to start? My answer is, start with dialogues, and don't forget to bring along a theoretical container.

Address: Dr. Syed A. Rahim, Program on Culture, East-West Center, Honoloulu, Hawaii 96848, USA

Sharon Taylor specializes in women's economic development and participatory methodologies for community building. She co-founded Single Moms Against Poverty and the recently formed Women's Economic Network of Newfoundland and Labrador. With faculty and students of Srinakharinwirot University in Thailand she has conducted training in women's community-based economic development, using video with village women to help them identify barriers and solutions to economic and social development. She innovated teleconferencing techniques with native women's groups across Canada; helped plan a Women's Development Program in the University of Dar es Salaam, Zanzibar, and Women's Studies at the University of Indonesia; and was a resource person with the Regional Conference on Women in Development Initiatives in Southeast Asia. As Vice President, Canada World Youth, she is in contact with exchange programs in many countries.

Address: Sharon Taylor, School of Social Work, Memorial University of Newfoundland, St. Johns, Newfoundland, Canada A1B3X5

Owen Wrigley graduated from university at age 19, then journeyed overland via Europe to Afghanistan and Nepal, where he built experimental windmills. He spent most of the next 20 years working in voluntary, non-governmental organizations in South and Southeast Asia, with intervals at Kansas State University, where he holds the Masters in Regional and Community Planning, and the University of Hawaii, where he holds the M.A. and Ph.D. in Political Science. He moved to Thailand in 1981, where he now lives. He has been twice decorated by H.M. the King of Thailand for his contributions to the Kingdom of Thailand in rural development, voluntary organization, and educational development. His most recent book is *Sound Knowledge: The Political Meaning of Deafness*, Gallaudet University Press.

Address: Dr. Owen Wrigley, 110/1 Pradipat Road, Bangkok 10400, Thailand

Laurentino D. Bascug has been a peasant educator and community organizer for the last 38 years. He started organizing sugar workers in Negros Island and in 1959 to 1961 led the first labor strikes which exposed the exploitation in the sugar industry. After realizing that sugar workers alone cannot eradicate the evils of the hacienda system, he forged an alliance with other activist groups to stage a nationwide protest in Metro Manila. Though the protest's failure made a violent alternative more attractive to many activist groups, he remains convinced that peaceful means will ultimately succeed, because the violent strategy will always violate the people's basic human rights and the ensuing dictatorship will undermine human dignity. This belief led him to develop the "Holistic Integrated Sustainable Development Strategy" for liberation, now applied on a macro level in his home province of Southern Leyte.

Address: Laurentino Bascug, President ODISCO Farm Systems Development Foundation, Inc., Block 8, Lot 2, North Ridge Park Subdivision, Santa Monica, Novaliches, Quezon City, Philippines

Varun Vidyarthi turned to development research and action from an early career as an engineer in industry. Based on action research in north India, he examined issues of people's participation in rural energy and forestry as Visiting Fellow at the Institute of Development Studies, Sussex, the East-West Center, and later as Consultant to the FAO. In 1986, with his wife Dr. Amla Vidyarthi, he founded the pioneering institution **Manavodaya**, devoted to community-based training and organization in participatory rural development, with local sponsorship and international support. The distinctive feature of Manavodaya, as in Varun's own life and thoughts, is the importance given to individual awakening and effort in the process of transformation.

Address: Varun Vidyarthi Manovodaya, B-1/91, Sector K. Aliganj, Lucknow, U.P., 226020, India

Russell Fox and **Carol Minugh**, Members of the Faculty, The Evergreen State College.

Russ: As a teacher and community activist I try to contribute to the theory and practice of participatory research. Growing up in a working class ethnic neighborhood in Cleveland, Ohio, studying mathematics, social work and urban planning, living and working in a non-Western culture, loving baseball, raising my children on a small farm and teaching at Evergreen have all influenced who I am and how I work. Strengthening relationships—with the land, work, others and the unknown—is my life work. I don't own a television.

Address: Dr. Russell Fox, The Evergreen State College, Olympia, Washington 98505, USA

Carol; I grew up in a large family on the Fort Belknap Indian Reservation in Montana, members of the Gros Ventre Indian Nation. Community responsibility was integral to everything in my life. Recognizing the two strains of knowledge within my community helped me realize the need for validating the knowledge of the people through academic systems. I believe strongly in the need to build education which emphasizes community rather than the individual, although each individual is important to the overall health of the community. Currently I direct the Reservation Based Community Determined Liberal Arts program at Evergreen. It is my hope to build stronger reservation communities and prepare community members to teach in the program.

Address: Dr. Carol Minugh, The Evergreen State College, Olympia, Washington 98505, USA

Tony Williamson has 25 years' experience in community development and participatory research with aboriginal groups in northern Canada. He is Director, Don Snowden Centre for Development Support Communications, Memorial University of Newfoundland, and was Founding Director of the university's Labrador Institute of Northern Studies and a founding member of the Indonesia-Canada NGO Forum. He has used small format video for social development and technology transfer in cooperation with local organizations in Labrador, Nepal, India, Thailand, and Pakistan and has been a project resource person in Zanzibar and Brazil. His cooperative video productions include women's occupations and production credit, farm and farm family education, and farmer involvement in irrigation and conservation programs.

Address: Dr. Tony Williamson, Don Snowden Centre for Development Support Communications, Memorial University of Newfoundland, St. John's Newfoundland, Canada A1B3X5

Kari Anderson Lende: Completing high school and university education in three cultures—the U.S., Thailand, and Denmark—helped shape my pluralistic, intergenerational, cross-cultural sensitivities to life. Continual engagement in participatory development struggles, starting with refugee crises from political upheavals in Africa, South America, and Southeast Asia, has given me opportunity to serve in a multitude of roles and made me acutely aware of the need to restructure our international and local economic, political, educational, and societal systems. Most of my concentration is on facilitating and coordinating collaboration among grassroots, NGO, and policy making groups. Exposure to many community projects has given me an excellent medium for creating plays and educational street-theater skits, and for writing a chapter in this collaborative book you are about to read.

Address: Kari Anderson Lende, 2228 46th Ave. SW, Seattle, WA 98116, USA

Khushi Kabir, an internationally-recognized advocate of the rights of women and men for autonomy, security, and dignity, was born in Bangladesh in 1948 and graduated in fine arts from Dhaka University in 1969. She was deeply affected by the 1971 War of Liberation against Pakistan which created the new nation of Bangladesh after suffering one of the largest refugee crises in history and almost completely destroying the country's infrastructure. She dedicated herself with many of her colleagues to re-building their new country. She is the Co-Coordinator of Nijera Kori, a national association of landless men and women promoting the needs and rights of the nation's poorest people, and is currently Chairperson of the Association of Development Agencies of Bangladesh, national coordinating organization of NGOs. In her work of mobilization, she is committed to the belief that people are their own development agents, and that harnessing their energies and talents must be central to social change.

Address: Khushi Kabir, Coordinator, Nijera Kori, P.O. Box 5015, New Market, Dhaka 1205, Bangladesh

Penny Levin received her B.A. in fine arts at Colorado College, the M.A. in Asian studies at the University of Hawaii, and her education from more than 12 years' learning, living, and working with small communities in southern Thailand. The **Forests for Life** project has been a long walk with villagers to help build tropical forest resource management strategies from a place of local knowledge and expertise, in a way which revitalized community identity, history, and self-sufficiency. Many years back it all started from a conversation sitting on a floor around fragrant bowls of curry and wild things, celebrating southern Thai food, whose ingredients lay in the forest. At the Global Forum in Rio, she participated in treaty drafting on biodiversity conservation and indigenous peoples' rights.

Address: Penny Levin, East-West Center, Honolulu, Hawaii 96848, USA

Arthur Getz is a community activist, writer, and specialist in agriculture policy, land use, and use of computer communications and information management for environmental and cultural preservation. On-farm sustainable agriculture research is his central professional focus. As a Fellow of the Institute of Current World Affairs, he participated in and documented alternative agriculture movements among farmer and consumer organizations, research groups, and governments. He served in NGO consensus-building and negotiating roles at the Earth Summit in Rio and in consultation with the UNDP and World Bank on grassroots participation in agriculture and water resource issues. With the East-West Center he has conducted policy research and public education projects, facilitating community development in Hawaii including key responsibility for the public participation process of the federally sponsored Resource Conservation and Development Council on Kauai. He is a board member of the Waimanalo Community Development Corporation and President, Hawaii's Thousand Friends.

Address: Arthur Getz, East-West Center, Honolulu, Hawaii 96848, USA

Puanani Burgess is a *keiki o ka 'Aina*, child of the Land, and as such draws her strength, knowledge, values, and compassion from Hawaii. She's a published poet and storyteller who uses poetry and stories in the building of healthy and sustainable communities. As Executive Director of the Wai'anae Coast Community Alternative Development Corporation she has helped establish the Backyard Aquaculture Program in which Wai'anae Coast families are taught to grow food fish in their backyards and the Cultural Learning Center at Ka'ala, a center for teaching children and adults the cycle of life through Hawaiian values and practice around planting, caring for, preparation, and eating of Kalo (Taro).

Address: Puanani Burgess, Executive Director, Wai'anae Coast Community Alternative Development Corporation, Wai'anae, Hawaii 96792, USA

I

A WORKSHOP THAT CONNECTED

CHAPTER 1

WHY WAS THE WORKSHOP SPECIAL?

Richard Morse, Anisur Rahman and Kersten L. Johnson

Editors, Looking Back

Anis: This workshop had a very special way of consolidating, connecting people. That was a very distinct process, gradually moving towards each other, finally connecting in a way that we had strength and felt connected. It has not happened in any other workshop I have attended. I feel we should elaborate somewhat, for the benefit of the readership, first, how the people were selected, people who connected so well, who clicked so well to have developed the desire to connect more deeply, and go on together. And then what was it in the workshop process, and even the struggles with the methodology that changed, that completely clicked with this desire?

Kersten: Those meaningful events, turning points. I think there were several. A: Yes, turning points. It would be very worthwhile to share this with the readers. It will help in thinking, in designing workshops for the future. This is a great learning experience, for many of the participants also.

K: Well, should we be completely honest? A: Yes, absolutely. K: Because really, these sources came from great senses of inspiration, and vision, and consequential small connections with various people, in a sense with the idea of bringing together the elders of this whole process. A: Yes. K: That was the original idea. And that call went out in ourselves, and eventually reverberated and brought back some answers. Entirely through the judgment of people we work with. With no preconceived vision of who was the person. Only with the idea of bringing together a balance of different types of people. Dick: That's important, yes.

A: Still, there was some invisible hand working, to make this selection that would click like this. What was that invisible hand? How did it operate?

WHO AND WHY THE WORKSHOP?

The original idea of the workshop was to enable people deeply engaged in participatory organization with and among marginalized people to share experiences together, reflect on the values and practical lessons of their work, reinforce their efforts, and develop insights and new approaches for policy change. The idea took shape in talks among Deepak Bajracharya, Kersten Johnson, Richard Morse, and Varun Vidyarthi at the East-West Center in October 1987. They had recently completed an intensive project together with communities in Bangladesh, Bhutan, and Nepal in participatory action research for rural development and energy planning (Bajracharya, et al. 1987). Joining in these talks was Kari Anderson, who had worked closely with planning and marketing organizations in Thailand and Japan.

The idea evolved in 1988 with the support of Obaidullah A. Z. M. Khan, invited by President Victor Li as a Visiting Fellow at the East-West Center. A "Working Group on Creativity for Social Change" was formed and, in addition to pursuing its own agenda, undertook formal planning for the *People's Initiatives to Overcome Poverty* workshop. Institutional and budgetary support of the East-West Center and University of Hawaii was received. In an early planning stage, Soedjatmoko, retired Rector of the United Nations University, emphasized the importance of such a meeting, but urged more fundamental attention to structural, global issues.

Criteria of Selection

The core intent in seeking participants in the workshop was to bring together persons who work actively with disempowered, impoverished communities and are seen by them as friends—not their voices, but in trusted roles. This intent was the basis for the workshop proposal that half the participants be from primary organizing groups, either local residents who have initiated their own organizing efforts, or members of voluntary organizations who work directly with local communities as well as with larger alliances or federations (Working Group, 1988). Organizers were sought who interact personally, often daily, with landless families, marginal and smallholder farming/forest/ fishing communities, women's groups, ethnic or linguistic minorities, the homeless and other urban poor, indigenous populations, artisans, small enterprise founders. Participants should include senior and young practitioners, women and men, with functional diversity representing agriculture, forestry, water management, credit, technology innovation and industry, health, and education.

Another third of the workshop members were to be in academic institutions or research centers, and the rest in support institutions including specialized international agencies, peoples' banks, community development corporations, foundations, and so on.

Identifying Participants

The impulse, style, and expected outcomes of the workshop were defined in the proposal as the main avenue for identifying and attracting proposed participants. Apart from inquiries to people known to the workshop designers, nominations were invited from some 50 individuals in non-governmental organizations, universities, international agencies, and foundations. Binational agencies representing the East-West Center in Bangladesh, India, and Pakistan were approached; the former two sent nominations. Persons who had key roles in nominating those who attended included Gelia Castillo, Antonio Contreras, and Edel Guiza in the Philippines, Obaidullah Khan in Bangladesh and the United States, Ruth Lechte in the Pacific, and Niranjan Mehta in India and Southern Asia generally.

ON THE WORKSHOP PROCESS

The dynamics of the ten-day workshop were dramatic. The people gathered represented a mix of personality styles, experiences, and expectations: practitioners and theoreticians, faculty and field workers, poets and professionals, hard cultures and soft. The workshop designers, having sought and welcomed such variety, undertook to create an open decision process in the organization and conduct of the meeting. They were faced, nonetheless, with certain institutional expectations. The resulting tensions, events, and emerging connectedness are worth briefly retelling.

Songs and Opening Style

Important in jelling the process of connecting was the weaving together of the various "cultures" that the participants brought into the workshop. It was proposed on the first day that each day's session should start with participants from one country sharing a song or dance in which all would participate. The first morning, Monday, started with a song from Hawaii, the host land. The second day it was the "Motherland" song from Bangladesh (see page 59), and this went on. The songs were written on the board, so that everyone could join.

Some days a song or dance was introduced in the midst of a day's session when a sense of fatigue or conflict was felt. The process had its own climax on the final day, the weaving of the *lei*.

At the outset, Dick Morse read a message received from Niranjan Mehta in the early planning of the meeting:

> The cardinal rule of ecological agriculture is to let each field "speak" for itself, reveal its **Tao**. This is even more true, in every sense, in a workshop such as the one planned.

Tom Dinnell, chair of the University of Hawaii Department of Urban and Regional Planning, and invited also as head of a charitable religious trust, picked up on the reference to **Tao**, seeing individuals on separate journeys coming together as people, giving life to feelings of oneness and solidarity. In a continuing vein, Obaidullah Khan invited participants "to the search for joint creation of meaning evolving out of action and practice." "Poverty as an exclusionary relationship," he went on, "is unnatural. It is contrary to the humanness of the species. But the crisis of poverty persists...The obvious hypothesis is that in many countries a significant number of human beings has been structurally excluded from access to property and resources, to academic credentials and information, and to cultural identity and spiritual togetherness through subjugation of culture and being and dispossession of the world of the mind."

Each participant, from his or her own field, gave a self-introduction through the rest of Monday morning and early afternoon. Why am I here? Whom do I work with? What do I want from the workshop? In a free and relaxed manner, with considerable humility, windows to personality and social role were opened through the diversity present.

Agenda Review: Divergent Expectations

Real dialogue started at mid-afternoon in discussion on the draft Agenda. Divergent styles and expectations soon became clear. Both practitioners and theoreticians in Participatory Development were present, perhaps more practitioners than theoreticians. The draft Agenda had been designed to focus from the beginning on discussion of issues and principles, to come up with theoretical statements of an academic nature. The practitioners had an urge to share experiences more than theoretical reflections, and to know each other better. They primarily sought in-depth sharing of organizing experiences, struggles, values, unresolved barriers, and resolutions in the building of solidarity and empowerment.

Institutional participants, especially those based at the East-

West Center, were under pressure for the workshop to produce a clearcut report, including policy analyses and recommendations. The President of the Center had stated to staff members, "We don't just want people to talk story." Publication as a criterion for academic tenure and promotion was a related institutional influence.

Although these competing objectives were not immediately apparent, they underlay a vigorous afternoon debate on questions of process and substance. Sequence of topics was a key question. How soon to divide into working groups for analysis of specific issues was another. The draft Agenda proposed that Tuesday morning start with the topic "Principles and values which guide our work." A suggested format to guide individual inputs and discussion groups was presented. Afternoon sessions would then explore "Experiences and perceptions of poverty," also in working groups.

Some Initial Positions

Sanjeev Ghotge: Don't assume a consensus will be reached. Marta Savigliano: It's extremely difficult to decide on this in the abstract. Choice between plenary and working group will change with the topic. Obaidullah: Let the form flow out of the content. Too much of structure or method might hurt the content.

Faruque Ahmed: The sequence is important. Experiences and perceptions should precede discussion of principles.

Puanani Burgess: We are still a community of strangers. We need to create a community of trust. Kapunas are never ready to teach secrets to people they don't know. It would be tragic if we divide up in groups. We need to put our guts on the table, for everybody to hear.

Tony Williamson: In plenary we may wind up giving speeches. We need more time to debate back and forth—a model of real life. If 40 are together, 20 won't get a chance to say much. In groups, everyone would have something to say.

Two hours of lively debate, several people changing their initial positions, failed to resolve these questions of process. A small steering committee was formed to propose the next day's program. This planning process, with different group members, was repeated at the end of each day's sessions.

Experience- or Issue-based Discussion?

Fortunately, Varun Vidyarthi had been requested to initiate the process of sharing experience and practice in-depth late Monday afternoon. He told of the philosophy and working context of Manavodaya, the órganization he and his wife Amla had founded in north India.

This led to active, open dialogue. (See section on Experiences and Principles of Participatory Action). The openness and depth of questions encouraged Varun, and other members, to remove the masks from their experience and practice, and probe deeper into values and organizing principles.

Tuesday's meeting was principally in plenary. It opened, as suggested by Faruque, on experiences and perceptions of poverty. The discussion was wide-ranging, with several people attempting to define major questions for focus. How is poverty to be defined? Why define it? Should emphasis in participatory organization be on self-determination, or material improvement? How can isolation and the destruction of culture be reversed, creating a culture of strength? From local action, how do you engage in structural change? Is there cooperation among NGOs, or in-fighting? How do you relate to government and international donors?

Ways of Knowing

In an attempt to clarify questions of process at midday Tuesday, Russell Fox gave a characterization of the dialogue:

I am seeking, in this discussion, for a balance between values, between two ways of knowing:

Intuition	*Rationality*
Life experience	Analysis
Instruction in cultural survival	Focus on poverty
	Tear down structural creators of poverty
Focus on building community, building replacements	Life-work replaced by jobs
Enchantment/myth	Science to explain the unknown

The second way, the rational, limits my scope. The Native American view of community may help us. In this view, essential relationships are between:

Person   Land   Others   Work   The Unknown.

I live on a farm because I do not want my children to be impoverished. Global, transnational corporations are cut off from the land. Poverty, in this worldview, is the lack of community.

Notwithstanding this holistic comment, the advisory panel

Tuesday evening suggested formation of working groups on Wednesday in an effort to sharpen discussion and analysis. As background, the workshop organizers had prepared a list of specific issues compiled from participants' own statements in their letters accepting the workshop invitation. The panel clustered these issues in five suggested topics for Wednesday's discussion, as summarized in Figure 1.

On Wednesday afternoon, rapporteurs from each working group gave summary reports in plenary. Much solid content emerged, yet a sense prevailed that the perspectives were still too fragmented. The richness of personal experiences—our social and ecological "fields"— was not yet being revealed.

Revolt, Then Bonding

Discussion of this kind had been frustrating to the practitioners, and was tending to alienate them from those more theoretically oriented. Fortunately, the theoreticians, being theoreticians of participatory development and involved in practice themselves, were also inclined to hand the workshop over to the practitioners. At mid-morning Thursday, a group meeting in the women's restroom decided that their feelings should be clearly expressed. Dorris Pickens, with eloquence and vibrancy, voiced the group's dissatisfaction with the structured approach. This "bathroom revolt" clinched the takeover. Thereafter, sharing of experiences became the preferred mode of dialogue.

The workshop designers remained anxious to see some theoretical conclusions emerge to satisfy the East-West Center academics. From time to time they kept pressing for a convergence to a set of theoretical statements. The practitioners were in no hurry about this. Some theoreticians also took a clear epistemological position that theory should follow practice. When they were told by the designers that the establishment had to be satisfied, the "House" asserted that this group had a very powerful set of theoreticians who could take on any establishment and face them on the question of how to build theory. That clinched this question also.

Ka'ala: the Weekend and After

This process of sharing experiences, getting to know each other, and working together to build a theoretical articulation of their work was an important factor that "connected" the participants and has kept them "together" since then even when physically distant. When smaller sub-sets of the group have had the occasion to meet again, the presence of those absent has been "felt." Yet another creative sharing was crucial in this bonding process: a Saturday bus trip and day-long

FIGURE 1

Proposed Working Groups and Discussion Issues

GROUP I: Addressing people's initiatives through structural issues and linkages

  4   Discussion of specific instruments of oppression and ways to overcome, cope with them
18   Ways the poor can address political/structural issues
20   Ability to generalize from local issues and strategies to broader development processes
25   Linkages: village, regional, national
27   Values and ideology, the role of religion
54   Access to resources by the poor

GROUP II: Sustainability of people's initiatives

  2   Funding driven development, effects of funding processes
10   Improvement of management capabilities
22   Replicability
21   Sustainability
54   Access to resources by the poor
56   Support systems (physical, emotional, financial) for long-term activities by poor communities

GROUP III: Partnerships and alliances within and between institutions

  5   Bottom-up work within a top-down organization
  9   Partnerships (as opposed to patron-client relationships) between privileged and less privileged classes
13   Development of a shared sense of purpose among people of various backgrounds and situations
24   Institutionalization
25   Linkages: village, regional, national
54   Access to resources by the poor

GROUP IV: Holistic understanding of poverty

16   Importance of holistic frameworks which link economic and non-economic dimensions
27   Values and ideology, the role of religion
32   Definition of poverty
54   Access to resources by the poor

GROUP V: Nature of participation, facilitation

23 Nature of participation
34 Related to (23) Nature of participation, discuss various definitions of the term and concept
42 Working through community jealousies, mistrust, frustration and fatigue
45 Development communication as part of process for overcoming poverty
46 Role of participatory research
57 Relations between national government and indigenous PVO's
59 Participation at local/community level—theory vs. reality
63 Tools of liberation—research, analysis, vision, popular knowledge, communication
69 How to distinguish between facilitation and intervention
70 How to avoid the use of participation as a controlling and legitimizing mechanism
71 Participation: definitions of the term and concept

immersion at the Ka'ala Culture Learning Center on the leeward Wai'anae Coast. Puanani Burgess, welcoming the visitors, invited them all to hold hands with the community in a circle and sing "Motherland" together, saying "You have come to visit us, please bless us by singing this song." All then took part in community work on the taro farm, with the principle of exchanging and sharing with each other and with nature, nourishing each other as one life.

After several ten-hour days in a room without windows—where only our minds were getting any exercise and our only common experience was sharing words—standing in taro fields in the hot sun and crowding into a community-built meeting hall where *real* community work was conducted was liberating and energizing. From that day on, our discussions were grounded in a common *community* experience we shared.

In the days after the weekend, sub-groups on future collaboration and on theory were constituted. The latter group was given the charge of weaving a theoretical statement out of theoretical concerns and expressions handed in by every participant. The resulting synthesis, or *"lei,"* was fulfilling to all participants, and astonished some of the designers. Apart from its conceptual power, every participant could identify with it as a product in whose construction he/she had an organic part, and was thus a creator of the product. There was no alienation anymore, between the practitioners and theoreticians. All had, together, constructed theory.

Participants' narratives of their experiences and the ensuing critical dialogues are reported in the next section. From these experiences, issues of political economy are briefly summarized and qualities and relationships crucial to participatory development are identified. Forging of the synthesis and the workshop's concluding event, weaving the *lei*, are reported in the chapter's final section.

EXPERIENCES AND PRINCIPLES OF PARTICIPATORY ACTION: FIFTEEN CASE PROFILES

Major experiences in participatory action to overcome poverty were described by workshop members from India (rural and forest, people's legal rights), the Philippines (farmers, fisherfolk, inner city), United States (inner city, rural south, Hawaii, river basin), Canada, Thailand (the deaf, a cultural minority), and Bangladesh (nationwide, women's issues). Holistic, systemic approaches and principles of work exemplified by these experiences of people's organization were enriched by lively discussion and debate. We report these here.[1]

Dharma: Self-discipline and Love

Varun Vidyarthi: The key issue in poverty is the process of getting dependent. Dependence, helplessness are the opposite of freedom, where a person enjoys the bliss of nature, of everything in the world. I am worried when people including my Marxist friends see poverty only in economic terms. Dependence in the person, the family, the community, and the world are interlinked. In the person, dependence arises from attachment. In the family, from estranged relations—often due to men's dominance. Structurally, we are not able to exercise control over resources that are all around us. Economic or military power prevent it. These things are all interlinked. We have to look at them together. In Vedanta style, we have to seek the unity in all things, understand that unity.

This is a very personal statement, not academic. How can the struggle against poverty become meaningful at all levels? Through *dharma*. Pardon me if this is very unconventional. *Dharma* does not mean sectarian religion. It means "self-discipline and love." Self-discipline implies keeping a check on temptations by being aware of the overall consequences of a particular action. Love implies compassion for fellow humans and life in general.

Human awakening (Hindi: *Manavodaya*) starts with individual awareness and action. Self-awakening leads to family awakening, community awakening, societal awakening: by the resource rich as well as the resource poor.

At the structural level, what does self-discipline imply? Access to resources, to rights. We cannot be passive about it any longer.

Many priests talk about change at the individual level. It becomes more meaningful when linked with structural change: greater control over resources, decentralization of authority and power. The struggle means being constantly on the move to understand our relations with others.

In the process of empowerment, gaining greater control over local resources, people usually don't organize themselves. There has to be leadership, methods of taking decisions, shared perspectives. Exploitative structures move from one head to another. How can we avoid this? Strong bonds of trust and relationship, on an equal level, must be forged, with emerging leadership. A long process of dialogue is required. Who are we? What are we trying to do? Whom are we talking to? We have to be selective.

In north India, we observe different types of poverty situations. Extreme poverty, that of a bonded laborer, a divorced or widowed woman, a person living off seasonal labor only, often results in complete despair and resignation. Poverty due to social maladies includes excessive expenditure and consequent debt for a daughter's marriage, or for drinking. It includes the social stigma of lower castes who continue to work in occupations like leather working and are boycotted by their own brethren. Most poverty is associated with structural factors: skewed resource ownership, feudal social relationships, market control by external wholesale dealers, bureaucratic government structures.

People who take the lead in starting new ventures, taking on organizing responsibilities, form the mainstream of struggle against these structural factors. We need to strengthen their hands in developing alternative institutions, practices and methods to move toward self-reliant, *dharma*-centered living.

Specific actions initiated by groups through this process include:
* low caste owners of buffaloes formed societies for collection and collective processing of milk into clarified butter (ghee) and its sale in urban centers.
* leather flayers, outcastes, are organizing to gain the right to lift dead animals in about 100 villages, now contracted for by middlemen.
* members of a weavers' cooperative were trained in producing new varieties of cloth, eventually specializing in handloom products in popular demand in the region.
* women have been assisted in market development in urban areas for handicraft, sewing, and embroidery products.
* villagers have formed a law committee to resolve local disputes.

• to reorient social forestry policies, multipurpose trees (for fodder, fuel, food, timber) fitting an agroforestry pattern are grown in nurseries and made available to families for planting on homesteads, field bunds, and small parcels of unused land.

Where there are oppressors, how can alternative leadership be developed? Not everyone will take part. It is particularly difficult to find leadership among women.

Puanani Burgess: Why should the mother be the only one to take risks? What is the impact on empowerment strategies of changes in the cultural fabric of society?

Varun: Women have to spend a lot of time in the home, caring for children, preparing meals, in addition to outside work. Other cultural factors oppose women's initiatives. In a Muslim community, a woman who went out on an errand found the door locked on return. What does that culture imply? Husbands will not allow their wives to move more than 10 meters. We cannot come with definitive answers, but open up a process of inquiry and introspection. We share our own lives, encourage people to think for themselves. All of us have to facilitate each other. Culture has to adjust.

Anisur Rahman: Is that *your* consciousness? Varun: Men denying women is exploitative thinking. Sanjeev Ghotge: Culture itself is responsible for oppression. The creation of Indian culture was probably by people who are now marginalized. Through language, grammar, culture has been appropriated. Chhatrapati Singh: All conventions or pathologies are not part of culture.

Puanani: Is it a perception among people themselves that they are being oppressed? Hawaii was very matriarchal. Women had an ordered life. The missionaries introduced change. People were made to feel that the culture was oppressive. So I am a person who walks in two worlds.

Tony Williamson: The change agent must already be in that community base. Can you find those people? Varun: We must develop that capacity. Obaidullah Khan: Can you find enough Varun Vidyarthis? Can you develop discipline and love at the structural level? Romola Morse: Love means compassion, for life and the environment. It must develop as a slow infection.

John Gaventa: Commitment at one level will often conflict with commitment at another level. How as organizers can we decide which level to serve? Varun: The decision has to be left to the community. Organization must be democratic.

Chhatrapati: How does the Vedanta philosophy help, when it is necessary to analyze each event? Varun: The fact that you are aware of *dharma* helps make decisions better. Don't force it on yourself. Go outside one's self. Watch one's self. Meditate.

Khushi Kabir: Who constitutes the community? Varun: It depends on how they define themselves. Leather flayers consider themselves a community. Certain village youth groups formed, deciding to oppose unauthorized occupation of lands.

Faruque Ahmed: I have some difficulty with love and unity. Who are the actors in development, and underdevelopment? If you love the poor, do you love the oppressors? All around us we see atomization, disintegration. Unity is a trickle. Anis: How do you generate love? Varun: Awaken compassion for the human. If the structure is wrong, we try to change the perceptions of people too, to change the structure. During the freedom movement, Mahatma Gandhi suddenly said "No" when the movement tried to remove certain people rather than the governing power. In a school run by local landlords, government funds stayed in the pockets of the landlords. The local youth group arranged a cultural program, inviting the Inspector of Schools and District Education Officer. A debate followed on the process of primary education. The funding channel was changed.

Obaidullah: In Bihar, owners who gave land were burned, murdered. The court released those responsible. How do you cope with brutalization? Varun: The community has to decide. The local power structure is often too strong to go by persuasion. Anis: If you say the community will decide, you are intervening with certain values. Varun: We are not deciding. Sanjeev: Can you say the community will decide on the basis of *dharma*? Varun: The community could also go to the court. Obaidullah: When brutalized, people's security is at stake. A buffer zone is needed. We must be ready to stand as a buffer. This needs our attention.

Varun: Certain issues emerge for the process of facilitation. How can self-reliance be sustained? What is the economic base? How can we avoid being drawn into project-based funding? This applies to the East-West Center also. What are methods of being independent? What are sources of core funds, for projects on which the community decides? How can we institutionalize the learning process, but still keep it adaptive and dynamic?

Integrated Farming in the Philippines: The Whole Person
Laurentino: We evolved the ODISCO (organic, diversified, integrated, scientific, cooperative) farming in response to the dependency and sense of hopelessness among farming families. ODISCO is concerned 80 percent with human beings, 20 percent with technology. Farmers experienced soil acidity after repeated applications of

chemical based fertilizers. They were drawn to natural farming methods, using and adapting their own farming knowledge. We add science too, showing the use of the microscope, soil analysis kits, and measuring outputs. Yet the emphasis is human, on the whole person in his/her relation to God, nature, society.

The whole person, body and soul. The nature of man. What is man? Who is he? Why is he holy? Why was man created in this world? Why not in heaven? Using the Bible, we seek as our objective total human development through total liberation in all aspects—economic, political, social, cultural, and moral—of the peasantry.

We can say that at this stage of our development we have yet to show a fully liberated farmer family. To understand this, one must look at the behaviour of Filipino farmers. Negative values and attitudes have been built through the unjust absolutist system of ownership and use of land which impoverished the farmers on small holdings. Living in long years of poverty dehumanized them. Hopelessness prevailed in their outlook in life, breeding lack of initiative and determination to succeed, making them more susceptible to vices. These are the greatest stumbling blocks to total liberation because new technologies, support services, and agrarian reform will amount to nothing unless these factors are first removed from the minds and hearts of the farmers. Even God cannot remove them from their minds and hearts if they will not give their full consent.

Due to this analysis, LAKAS-ODISCO has designed an educational program called Economic and Social Awareness Seminar (ESAS). This is a pre-membership seminar that can motivate the peasants to remove these barriers to development from their minds and hearts. People in these meetings examine together values of love, justice, truth, freedom. We undertake analysis of the problem, the poverty of the mass majority. We examine how productivity can be increased, and equitably distributed. We examine the Philippines number one problem: the land. This is a moral problem, since tenants have developed a landlord mentality. They feel, to succeed, I have to become the landlord, Don Emilio. In discussion, new values emerge: a sense that the land belongs to God. The right to use is more important than the right to own.

Sanjeev: Many religions offer ethical guides, but are just not practiced. Churches find ways of giving absolutions, theological or legal. Isn't God there also?

Laurentino: Yes, but humans have free will.

Sanjeev: This is a theory created by men, Augustine prominent among them.

Laurentino: Religion contributed to the unjust system because it was introduced wrongly. It did not practice or incarnate justice, love.

Kevin: Can you give educational examples of ODISCO's approach?

Laurentino: To motivate the farmers to regain their dignity and to remove their hopelessness in life, we develop examples with the farmers that they are the most important people to God, to the government, to the church, and to the whole society. Example: The seeds of rice, corn, wheat and all the fruits as the source of food were entrusted to farmers and not to the Pope or any religious groups. Hence the farmers are very close to God because practically the survival of mankind is entrusted to them.

Puanani: Hawaiians consider ourselves in the same genealogical descent as the slug, the tree. The Land owns us. We are part of the land. We are in a struggle, fighting for our own land. Christians came saying, "You are heathen."

Laurentino: Christianity holds man most important. The Hawaiian way out may be a cooperative system, land community-owned, used for the good of the members. In Negros, individual households farm, and market cooperatively.

Sanjeev: I don't think Christianity is intuitively able to put man on the same plane as nature, to see life as nature. The Kingdom of God has man and nature in hierarchical relations, though not split. But if people believe in this view, in the Philippines or elsewhere, don't you want to try to change it?

Chhatrapati: Locke held the different view, that property should belong to individuals, that this would "liberate." On this basis land settlement policies were instituted in India and other areas of British rule. Now we face many difficult problems in land reform, and in wasteland development. It is not sufficient to get land to the tiller: management efficiency is also needed. We can't have large chunks of land, as in the Punjab. Yet we also face the fragmentation problem, land held in different places. These land issues demand practical solutions.

Laurentino: We have found in places where five or so families farm 10 to 15 hectares among them, we were able to invent a management course tailored to their farming system needs. The course includes self-questioning: how and by what values do we decide on our pattern of existence?

Anis: In this model, we must introduce the Devil also. God created the devil, and having a sense of justice, gave part of the land to the devil.

Sanjeev: Don Emilio is the head of this attitude.

Faruque: Laurentino is in a good position. God is on his side.

Tonton: He has shown that religion can be used to liberate, as well as oppress. The Church is not a monolith. Liberation can be encouraged within it. We can extend this analogy to the University as an institution, to academe. As educators, researchers, we are implicated in the system. We share shame and guilt. But education is not a monolith. We can search for parallel movements to that of ODISCO, and create equivalent agendas.

Coalitions of Fisherfolk: From the Visayas to Parliament

Angelito: Our community fishing cooperatives formed in the Visayas and other island provinces to resist illegal encroachments in municipal waters, less than 7 kilometers from the shore. Encroachers were both concessionaires, "crocodiles," and commercial trawler operators, "sharks," using large capital and high technology. Government supports these outside ventures, motivated by export earnings and political connections. Through savings mobilization, cooperatives were able to start marketing and build resources to develop a fishing code, restricting outsiders to areas beyond 15-20 kilometers.

Tony: How did you start?

Angelito: Earlier cooperatives were forced to deactivate with martial law in 1972. These organizations were reactivated, and new cooperatives formed, in 1986 when PROCESS, a national NGO, invited us to meet, start analysis, train, and study our legal rights.

Faruque: Facing crocodiles, what strategy did you use?

Angelito: To counter their strength, we needed the strength of numbers. This led to the formation of HUMMABI, the national coalition of fisherfolk, going beyond marketing to protest, to assert our rights to livelihood. Based on our fishing code, we have introduced legislation to enact these rights in law.

Obaidullah: How do you lobby?

Angelito: First we build support through dialogue. Then we received training from legal rights advocates in how to influence legislators. Now HUMMABI has a national lobbying presence. We have eventually been able to build influence through the Bureau of Fisheries and Aquatic Resources. The Canadian International Development Agency (CIDA) has also helped. In some areas, we were even able to persuade the military to neutralize the strength of outsiders. We have formed regional councils to represent us with agencies such as the Asian Development Bank.

William: My impression is you are always fighting.

Angelito: Battles have been won, but there is much still to struggle for.

Sanjeev: Structurally the problems are the same in coastal Kerala and Goa, in southern and western India. Let's share names, so these groups can exchange experiences.

Arthur: Japanese boats are among the foreign exchange earners. This undermines local fishing in Japan also.

Chhatrapati: Under the Law of the Sea, outside the 200 mile EEZ (Extended Economic Zone) there is no foreign exchange earning. You can also argue for a 400 mile zone, and against illegal electronic devices. Has HUMMABI's legal program been taken up at the international level?

Angelito: This is necessary, but we still have other hurdles to fight. In Negros, capital-intensive, not labor-intensive shrimp production is being financed by the United States Agency for International Development (AID). It pollutes the waters too. We must still address this struggle at the national policy level.

Creating People's Institutions in Inner City Chicago

Dorris: Julia and I will describe our experiences together. In many ways they are the same, though geographically and ethnically very different. The civil rights movement of the 1950s gave rise to rapid racial transitions, especially in northern cities. In a 10 year period, there was dramatic disinvestment. Social values, including property values, rapidly changed. The South Shore area of Chicago was formerly very diverse, with 80 percent of the housing units rented. Prejudice and fear became more acute as more black families moved in, and whites rapidly sold out to blacks and moved to the suburbs. Banks left, the hospital wanted to leave, stores left, neighborhoods were filled with abandoned store fronts.

This was a time to reevaluate earlier minority lending programs, and create a comprehensive program for change. First we studied trends in market forces in the economy. Legal action was taken, and supported by the Supreme Court, to require the oldest national bank to remain, an existing powerful institution. A Neighborhood Development Bank, the South Shore Bank, was established, by mobilizing investors—churches, large corporate foundations, individuals. A holistic program was conceived: both human and physical. Credit was a key entry point, both short- and long-term. We looked for sources and lines of employment, and organized relevant training. A major effort was to restore confidence among families, the community, and business. Investors were attracted and oriented to an emphasis on maximizing human capital development.

A clear philosophy was adopted: that neighborhood renewal requires integration among low and moderate income families. For the poorest, a Neighborhood Finance company was created with both equity and debt portfolios, oriented to the small business person, and chartered to provide leverage to South Shore Bank loans. A holding company was formed combining these and other finance entities, a profit-centered engine to provide functional variation and complementation. The Neighborhood Institute, not owned by the holding company but essentially part of the institutional family, was created exclusively for low income programs: advocacy, jobs, training, equal opportunity, equal access, equal ownership.

The Neighborhood Institute was able to mobilize "Program Related Investments" to the amount of $1,500,000 from foundations. Decent housing was a major goal, through cooperative home ownership opportunities. By 1988, low income families owned 20-25 percent of neighborhood housing, including some of the best homes. This contributes to the overall emphasis on motivation, self-confidence building, access, training, and leadership development. Indigenous, bottom-up initiatives are encouraged. If a business operator is illegally working out of his or her home, ways are found to provide support, such as a business incubator program. Vocational education is geared to job creation: through one year's carpentry training, a person can be earning $30,000 a year.

Adapting Asian Institutions in Rural America

Julia: Dorris has not mentioned the learning aspect of our experience, from the Grameen Bank in Bangladesh. Dr. Mohammad Yunus, the Grameen Bank founder and managing director, observed that people who have money can usually get money. Governor Winthrop Rockefeller, in Arkansas, invited managers of Shorebank Corporation to work with local, rural communities in designing an integrated strategy for economic development. It was realized that development needs some large-scale investments, and many small. The result was the development and capitalization of a new development bank holding company, with related Arkansas institutions:

Southern Development
Bancorporation

Elkhorn Bank and Trust	Arkansas Enterprise Group	Opportunity Lands

Elkhorn is a 104-year old bank capitalized at $55 million, with expertise in how to package micro-enterprise loans. The Arkansas Enterprise Group was established as a non-profit entity, to foster entrepreneurial development and provide seed funds. The central purpose of Opportunity Lands is to purchase and develop commercial, industrial real estate as well as develop affordable housing in rural areas.

The Good Faith Fund was created to build on the Grameen Bank example. The philosophy is of group support as a basis for credit, with many social and technical assistance components for the program's customers. In towns, the Good Faith Fund builds solidarity among peer groups, bi-racial, male and female, predominantly black in membership. Most of the people involved are low in literacy. Our opener: "Find four to six other people. Choose peer group people you like and trust." People themselves thus create a screening process for talent and purpose. Groups are encouraged to look for opportunities suited to the market. One year term loans, and more recently three and six month loans, are provided to group members. Loans are often in the $1,000-$2,500 range, perhaps for a sewing machine, or a welding machine. Bi-weekly repayment meetings are held. No collateral is required. We assume: You will pay it back.

The South Shore Bank and the Good Faith Fund both cooperate actively with the Grameen Bank in exchange visits of officers and staff, and in analysis and documentation of program innovations and lessons.

Knowing by Seeing, Confidence by Sharing: Newfoundland Model

Tony Williamson: The people of Fogo Island, off the northeast coast of Newfoundland, became innovators in development communication over 20 years ago. Ten communities, with a total of 5,000 people, mostly fishermen and their families, faced government pressure to locate to "growth centres." Isolated geographically and lacking in basic linkages (newspapers, phones, radio or TV), they perceived themselves to lack the power to negotiate redevelopment on Fogo. There were plenty of problems, but there were also strengths and opportunities, which were inhibited by lack of confidence, communication, and cohesion on the island.

The community outreach goal of Memorial University of Newfoundland, through the Extension Division originally and in its International Development Projects through the Don Snowden Centre for Development Support Communications, is and has been human development. We find each generation must build its own vision, its own confidence. Together, with the people of Fogo, we were provided a challenge and opportunity by the National Film Board (NFB) of Canada: to participate with the NFB in a series of film modules on the communities' perceptions of their own lives, their strengths and weaknesses, their failures and successes, their joys and sorrows. Producing the film modules and screening them back to the communities, though just a tool, became a catalyst for discussion and action, with participation of individuals seeing themselves for the first time as an island community rather than as representatives of five communities with competing interests. The aim was to create or improve communications between people in the same community; between communities; and between such communities and the "authorities." When people saw community discussions on the screen, they became very proud.

To get the full meaning of this, you have to know the strong individuality of the Newfoundlander. The film modules provided a unique mirror to the Fogo Islanders, from which they drew lessons and gained confidence. Seeing the films helped people develop a realization that contrariness was getting them nowhere and that island unity was what they needed. "From mistakes, we learn. We have seen things perish in our midst...we learned from this. Let people know what we know, and what we are capable of." This statement by Andrew Brett at Shoal Bay relates to people lacking in confidence and afraid to speak out because of their perception that they have no "learning." He was basically saying, we must no longer be afraid of ourselves and we must let people know that we know a great deal even though we have no formal education.

When the film was shown to the provincial cabinet, they decided to invest in the redevelopment of Fogo rather than close it down. The communities were linked by an improved road system and a new high school was located at the centre of the island, serving all five communities. A fish producers cooperative was strengthened and expanded to market its own produce, and a ship building cooperative produced "longliners," which allowed the fishermen to expand to midshore waters with access to fish stocks not previously reached by inshore boats and gear.

Film-making used in this manner (and later small format video) is a process of self-discovery, creating new modes of cooperation. It was extended by Memorial University to other communities. At Port au Choix, on the Great Northern Peninsula of Newfoundland, the process became a catalyst for strengthening a voluntary rural development organization and for the creation of a new fishermen's union. This has radically altered the relationship between fisherman and merchant throughout the province, in both the inshore and offshore sectors as well as for the plant workers. In the communities of the even more isolated Labrador coast, this communications process also built self-confidence and helped the fishermen to break free of their bondage to merchants who rented fishing gear, weighed the fish at their own premises, and purchased fish on "open receipt," "squaring up" at the end of the season.

In all of this the extension worker, or animator, maintained trust by placing editing rights and screening approvals in the hands of the subjects of the films or videos. Ultimately the technology has become simplified to the point where the people themselves become their own producers and their own animators in the process. This happened with the Inuit in the Canadian Arctic, where the process was introduced to mediate joint management of the Kaminuriak caribou in the Keewatin (a district of the Northwest Territories). In like manner, rural women from Ramghat in the Surkhet Region of western Nepal, quickly took over the technology from their trainers, set their own agenda, and used the videos they made to negotiate rural development assistance from the Panchayat Department of the Royal Nepalese Government and to provide peer teaching for other rural women wishing to improve their lives.

The Deaf in Thailand: Overcoming Cultural Exclusion

Kampol (in Thai Sign, translated by Owen): The deaf, in Thailand, have not been recognized as a minority group. We are often lumped together with all disabled and those of little use or value to the country. Deaf children have never counted in the development equation. The deaf child leads a lonely life, often a stranger rejected even by the family. Sign was not recognized as a language, and Thai Sign not taught. A foundation existed, but it was a charity group that focused on "testing ears." This was of no interest to the deaf, but did receive government support. Most deaf have no jobs. Through a family connection, I went to work in a company. I didn't like it, and wanted to be a teacher. I was fortunate that I convinced the foundation to support me as an adjunct teacher in the central school, where I was a teacher for many years. I left to join the work to create the National Association of the Deaf in Thailand (NADT).

The earlier efforts to create educational opportunities developed very slowly and from very small seeds. One lady of the royal house-hold took an interest in deaf children and initiated a school. One of her assistants was sent abroad for study at Gallaudet University in the United States, and she devised the Thai finger-spelling chart. She also took interest and learned the Thai Sign Language (TSL) better than any other teacher had, so she has always remained in our memories, even though she is now long retired.

Through the Declaration of Human Rights, we became more aware of our lack of basic rights. As deaf, we were allowed to be issued the Thai national identity card, which is required for many things, but not all deaf people were able to convince officials to issue them one. When an identity card was issued, we found it was an identity that had no schooling and no available jobs.

Interestingly, the American moon landing became an inspiration for us. We saw it as an analogy to our own development. We established a Thai Deaf Club, then a bigger Center for Deaf Alumni. This club was active, but did not really seek out new directions until Charles Reilly, an American volunteer at the main school, became involved. Reilly attended our club meetings and encouraged us to become more active in communal organizing. That is when we met Owen and began our larger program which led to the creation of the National Association of the Deaf.

This did not happen quickly. We first had to teach Owen how to sign! He began slowly, but, in time, we taught him well. Then he became involved in gaining support for our training programs and for building the NADT from the one small club into our national network of regional offices and widely spread Deaf clubs. The *Thai Sign Language Dictionary* project actually began as a very small activity to document useful signs to help parents and medical personnel. It later grew into a major research project of its own.

Varun: In India, the deaf are treated as disabled. How do you feel about this?

Kampol: I don't agree that we are disabled. We are a language minority. But the Government deals only with the "Council of Disabled." So we are working for a new law, guaranteeing basic civil rights to all disabled.

Jan: How do you make a dictionary? What is this going to do for children in Thailand?

Kampol: Using American Sign is colonial. The dictionary is necessary for teaching Thai Sign, and is also proof and symbol of Thai Sign's distinctiveness. It is evidence of our cultural identity. Our NADT membership fee is Baht 90 per year. Our board is comprised entirely of deaf members, all Deaf Thai, who are elected every two years. We created a workshop and small business to give initial job training and employment. It is now an independent enterprise. We began our organizing in Bangkok, then opened association branch offices in three regional centers. Financially, our self-reliance is good, though we are somewhat beholden to one wealthy family who have a deaf son. We do not yet have a permanent home. We have had assistance from Swedish deaf experts, but this is now a source of conflict over their ideas on how we should run the program.

Dick: In working for new legislation, what policy or political resistance do you face?

Kampol: We work directly with members of Parliament. There are many barriers. Our approach is to "keep cool." The Thai way is not to get angry. In our training programs, along with sign teaching, we pursue the need to stand for our basic rights.

Dick: I don't understand what barriers you mean. What entities oppose these rights?

Kampol: There are many within government. They don't believe results are possible. They ask, where are the skills of the deaf? We have to resort to much persuasion to carry a point. In this respect, Manfa Suwanarat is highly effective, working in Ministries and service agencies with those individuals who control the turf.

Kevin: I know the resistance you speak of. In Liberia, the deaf are looked on as "witched," thrown out of families, made work horses. In Sri Lanka they are outcastes, said to be the result of their *karma*, not even accepted in the labor force.

Kampol: We would really like to know where these attitudes come from. We are seeking more opportunities to explain the children's needs and potential to parents. As more adults attain the position of role models, there may be changes. Already the status of the deaf association, and official acceptance of the TSL Dictionary by the Ministry of Education, are making a difference.

Self-determination, self-reliance: these are keys to our approach. We find and develop leadership among those who understand these key ideas early. Participation is at the fundamental level of each member, and brings results. Outsiders who come in to help are fine, if they have awareness of these basic principles. It is essential to build our own organizations. We accept outsiders because we want outsiders to understand us.

I find it valuable to listen to our discussions here, and welcome the East-West Center role. There is much work ahead, in different cultures. The action research method is useful. Much sharing and communication is needed. Video is good as a means of presenting our needs and methods.

Anis: One of the tasks of leaders is to generate new leaders, to encourage initiators, pioneers.

Kampol: We do this through respecting equality of rights, not through charismatic leaders.

Anis: In the *Bhoomi Sena*, the stance of leaders is to merge with the people and be one of them.

Kampol: We have basic rules in the deaf organization that provide for that.

In the Heart of India: Education and Structural Struggles

Sanjeev: We have been speaking of the polarity between experience and theory, but this is not sharp. We have to have patience in learning how to live with this complexity, with the way life really is. In an important dimension, we all live within the hierarchy described by Laurentino. We have to admit that part of each of us recognizes Don Emilio, part wants to see people as equals. We are also in the technologist era, a "middle class" neither here nor there in values, always trying to get to the top. Self-questioning without engaging in action can lead to dead ends, no answers. But the hierarchy is not monolithic. It may make us angry, lead to disagreements, but dialogue is still possible. I agree with Laurentino's position that addresses the moral aspect of this issue. When engaging in political education, if all I end teaching is violence, what have I done?

The experience I have to report and reflect on is of living some seven years with the Shahdol group, in a forest area of central India, spanning parts of Madhya Pradesh. Some members of the Shahdol group have been there almost 20 years, a diverse body, all shades of political thought. The emphasis is on practice, engaging in struggle on people's immediate issues, with long-term objectives of organization, empowerment, development, and political education. Intensive dialectics are continual.

The group originated with a farmer-poet, amongst others, who had worked with Jaya Prakash Narayan in the *bhoodan* (land donation) movement in Bihar. He bought a plot of land near the forest, levelled it, and gave agricultural training to tribal boys. They took to it, produced new, surplus crops, and sold to the market. This gave rise to the first conflict. It alienated a local village group, who resorted to violence and drove out the tribal boys, gained police support, and organized cases against the outsiders.

When this conflict subsided, one of the members of the group started the long process of shifting from the green revolution to organic agriculture. Since information on organic agriculture is far away and scattered, this took lots of time, trial and error. The organic farmer then met with difficulty over agricultural prices and marketing. The "legal" market for the area encompasses 36 villages, but is town-dominated through linkages with groups primarily in two villages. Farmers were not able to obtain adequate prices, or obtain needed inputs. They were illegally taxed while taking products to the market. When they protested, they were threatened by *goondas* (strongarm bands), with support from lower-level local police. Scattered farmers' locations made organization very difficult. Some headway was made on prices, not much on development. This poses an issue for political education. Among households in 36 villages, this is an endless process. Is the way of trying to educate to focus around a common interest? I don't know. This is still an abyss.

Tribals were collecting varied produce from the forest all this time, never considering it work. Observing these patterns, it was difficult to get data on forest loss. Satellite data over a 10 year period suggest reduction of forest cover from 30 percent to 11-12 percent. A transnational company, Lever Brothers, introduced collection of sal seed, a favored hardwood species, employing tribals at a "fixed" wage level, Rs. 2.50 per day, just the subsistence level. Wage conflicts increased. Laborers struck, as the Shahdol farm was paying more. Farmers also opposed the Shahdol rates, seeking to keep wages down. As already seen, the market structure kept prices of their products down, so they had little margin to raise wages. Until farm development yields a surplus that can be sold at reasonable prices, wages can't rise. Labor : farmer conflict, explosion, are inherent in this bottleneck, part of the structure.

Information is lacking on how to raise productivity: part of underdevelopment. Farmers vacillate in and out of debt, varying with the rainfall and drought. Though the district bank has by and large replaced the money-lender, bank relations with farmers have no relation to nature. Bank loans often get used, therefore, for marriages or illness. Debt conflict is thus also part of the structure.

This setting of tribal : farmer : labor interactions gave a framework for understanding man : man : environment dynamics. Major environmental struggles ensued. A paper mill, 100,000 ton/year capacity, was operating in the district, a major cause of deforestation. Policies of government subsidies for this purpose are a case of obfuscating logic. Major water pollution problems resulted. Cattle health was affected, milk yields went down. Local water users protested. We tried to persuade the mill union to support the protest. The union started to take it up, then perceived the problem from the mill viewpoint. A caustic soda plant to meet the paper mill needs was also operating. Tribals were hired for mercury cleaning. Chlorine outbreaks occurred. But the concerned health regulatory agencies were far away. There was no way we could get these issues into the power structure. The nose could smell the excess chlorine, with no need for a measuring instrument, but doctors supported the company.

The press said, we know, but must sell advertisements. The union was influenced by nearby coal mine structures. The coal mines employed their own doctor, who calculated 19-20 percent coal dust exposure, but officially reported nine percent. At a very small cost, this could have been corrected. Public sector control of the mines had effected some "improvement" over the past contractor system, but abuses persist. Miners are afflicted by alcoholism. Bihar mine union leaders have armed henchmen, and are brutal. Unions in new plants are wary of such structures, and weak.

Processes of self-organization were encouraged, but face obvious danger: if we do not succeed in gaining solidarity, the power structure would destroy you. Again, issues of political education, organization. With small groups, or individuals? Groups are better, but one has to earn their trust, to establish credentials.

William: Only through large-scale projects, engagement of labor, can resources be exploited. Chhatrapati: But how will this be distributed? Sanjeev: They distribute suffering. Faruque: Whose development? Laurentino: For the banks. Faruque: A new project in Kerala employed 1,000 people, but displaced 2,000.

Sanjeev: The success of the *dalits* in Maharashtra, whom I spoke of earlier, has been a historical experience of a different magnitude. Ten to 15 years ago, the Dalit Panther movement was violent. Now the movement eschews violence. Their long struggle has symbolic significance, as well as practical. In the late '70s, the movement undertook to rename the Marathwada University as Ambedkar University. There was enormous upper caste resistance. Now, they are trying to start their own university but there are no models, though they are looking at folk schools, and Highlander experience. One emphasis will be on forest development technology. A king several centuries ago had donated 50-100 acres as collective land, in 3,000-5,000 villages. With people on these lands to work with, replanting is being started. What is to be grown? How? What will survive? How are these rural developments to be woven together with urban life requirements of the dalits? These have to be self-reliant processes. This dalit upsurge has helped liberate other communities: women are now free to walk with dignity in the streets.

Sharon: How do you sustain yourself through all this pain?

Sanjeev: In part, we study oppression in other places, Latin America, for example: manipulation, fragmentation, cooptation, repression. We internalize these. At last, only the generosity of the poet, perhaps, can help us.

Laurentino: Poetry is part of our effort too, though indirect. It is a symbol, an element in a new culture.

Claudia: How do you overcome fragmentation? Knowledge and power are fragmented.

Tony: For empowerment, it is often necessary to choose movements in which people can achieve small victories.

Sanjeev: The goal is long-term: total liberation from cultural oppression.

Obaidullah: *Dalit* poetry is an important part of the movement. As to failures and partial victories, Hirschman's accounts are valuable: in Colombia, when a movement for land control was blocked, the people shifted to fishing issues and collective use of the sea, with remarkable results.

John: Many struggles of this kind are winnable, but don't get to the structure. What we don't win, reinforces the struggle.

Anis: This notion of victory is mechanical. At least, you have been able to assert, not be beaten up.

Laurentino: The sense of the ultimate is very important here.

Sanjeev: We need this as individuals. Is it needed socially? The sense of imagining the absolute is not the same for everyone.

Christine: Did any Marxist theories have a positive role in the Shahdol experience?

Sanjeev: Both positive and negative.

Tonton: When you struggle, and feel empowered in local issues, this could be used by dominant groups.

John: In any event, you are building knowledge.

Proshika: Plurality of Approaches in Bangladesh

Faruque: We agree, we are working in the context of structures, a hierarchy. You cannot call a village a community. This calls for a plurality of approaches. We must work with the poorest, because non-participation of the poor is built into the structure. When we advocated forming village *samitis* (committees) in 1975, we were called dangerous radicals. Now the government has its own program for the rural poor.

Varun: Does Proshika have to intervene all the time? Or find local animators, and allow them to take the initiative in their own hands? What is the nature of a group?

Faruque: We have to start with animators. Then spread the process by sharing information. Now that groups encouraged by Proshika are federating, (a) they are organizing other groups, including women's organizations and men's groups, and (b) they say other villages need animators. In these areas we are thinking of withdrawing.

Sylvia: How long does one stay? We thought three to five years. At the end of five years, we felt people weren't ready. But we didn't want to develop dependence. This is a practical problem.

Faruque: We have just been thinking of this. Are the forces of underdevelopment phasing out? If not, why not? What do you as a facilitator phase out? Total withdrawal, and lack of communication?

This would be irresponsible. If local leadership has developed, then we can phase out some activities.

Dorris: Does Proshika have deep philosophical differences with the Grameen Bank?

Faruque: The Grameen Bank has done a marvelous job with credit. But it is monolinear. We didn't start with credit, but were open-ended. The Grameen Bank provides credit to women, but doesn't attack dowry. It doesn't plug the holes that are weak in the system.

Tonton: In the uplands, many people are migrants. Community is invisible. They don't perceive themselves as a community.

Faruque: Community has both physical and psychological aspects. The fishermen described by Angelito did not at first see themselves as a community. When they were brought together to talk together, they developed a common sense.

Puanani: How does one make a community out of a gaggle of people? A school is one path: children learn to dream, and can influence their parents. Organizing around food is another path: production, consumption, quality, marketing.

Laurentino: People's organizations can form at different scales, around different issues. There is value in encouraging basic groups to keep separate from each other, to prove they can do it. We can help motivate, animate, but essentially bring out the potentials within the farmers. The sooner the organization gains legal status, the better. Trust the farmers. The longer you stay, the more dependency. But this is a very delicate matter. It should be addressed directly, explicitly, otherwise we will violate our basic principles.

Faruque: Animators are not running the organization. They are seeing the emergence of leaders, who are helping the people make an annual plan for the area.

Laurentino: It is important to cut dependency on external funding.

Angelito: What are the bases for phasing out? To what extent will groups still sustain their efforts?

Faruque: Training as many people as we can is one important process. Providing fair credit, based on what they have planned. Encouraging new initiatives: beekeeping is a current example. Building legal support: Women in Development in Bangladesh is providing training in how we can prevent dowry, how we can provide legal services and gain the support of the courts to divorced women.

Angelito: Do you inform the organization: you are now strong.

Faruque: We are beginning to do that. Analysis of the situation is critical. We have to realize the role of the organization as a buffer: the forces of underdevelopment have not withdrawn.

"We Do It Ourselves:" Bangladesh Women's Organization

Khushi Kabir: Our name, Nijera Kori, means, "We do it ourselves." Our goal is organization of the landless, people who are selling their labor. Land is stronger than simply the earth: it means people who don't have control over the means of production. It means working with slum-dwellers in Dhaka who are also landless. Poverty is not scarcity of resources, but how resources are controlled. We start by working with women who are in the same class. Gender and class issues are intertwined.

Nijera Kori is an NGO registered with government, permitted to, receive funds from abroad. We are trying to create a participatory, independent organization of the landless. In rural areas, the landless are scattered. We encourage formation of separate groups of women and men. Groups come together, analyze their situation, learn to speak up. Women are starting to speak out in front of men, becoming more assertive. Men are learning to listen, and how to work with women.

We try to build linkages and coordination among groups through formation of committees. At the neighborhood or ward scale, temporary committees are formed. When about 40 percent of the people are organized, they are ready to form committees. In the local community, women's and men's committees are separate. At union and *upazilla* scale (larger units of administration), they are mixed, with adequate representation of women. We have not yet succeeded in going beyond the upazilla scale. When we started to form a national committee, it was hijacked by a middle class group. There are still gaps, though, between the group and the leadership. We are trying to move toward greater group control, groups feeling their strength, able to guide and change their leadership.

Group meetings are our central method: people coming together to analyze, to change, to realize it is not fate that governs them. At five centers, we organize workshops. These address the root, fundamental concerns and structures. Social awareness of the self is encouraged, gender analysis, the need to work together, breaking fatalistic beliefs. Groups engage in in-depth analysis of the national situation, the history of struggles, issues of leadership. They prepare for upazilla committee meetings. Workshop groups produce popular drama, analyze what culture is. Do folk songs, plays strengthen us? What alternative plays can we create? From the workshops, groups prepare to spend four to five days in a village area. In some village workshops, 2,000 people meet, feed themselves, organize their own programs.

Equipping people for legal action is another key method of

organization. Legal literacy, legal aid: giving information on basic rights. Land law: how to claim government land, monitor transfers. Wages: enforcement of minimum wage laws. Women's and children's right and legal status in Islam: enlisting religious leaders to seek contradictions in the law, and in practice, on issues such as rape, violence. Legal strength: how to fight counter-cases framed by powerful groups against the landless to prevent organization. Teaching reading and health are further important activities.

Faruque: You might mention your emphasis on groups raising funds locally, on collective savings.

Khushi: Each person is encouraged to contribute a minimum amount to group savings. Nijera Kori supplements these funds, but no outside resources are drawn upon. A collective mentality is encouraged, collectively planning group production activities. Landless now number 50 percent, the poverty rate is increasing. If *khas* (abandoned, degraded) land is nearby, groups try to get it. Often, landowners organize to seize crops at harvest time, using violence against us. People get discouraged. Now, at harvest, everybody goes to the fields, and women's groups go first to harvest. Culturally, landowners' men recognize that it is not right to beat others' women, or those already at the bottom. They gain respect for the movement, for women. Women in this way are taking on new roles vis-a-vis land.

Social issues are also attacked directly. Dowry has been a big issue the past 10-15 years. Men are learning new attitudes. Care of the wife in pregnancy: men are becoming more responsible. Acceptance of inter-marriage is growing. Women are gaining strength in analysis of these issues, and standing for their rights. They have stood in front of the district D.C. and made their case, and won. "This official was despite the system." The system temporarily prevailed: he was immediately transferred. Supportive forces at the center are too far removed.

It is important to examine how Nijera Kori, as an organization, relates to the landless organization. We don't provide material inputs, don't create dependency, but encourage to fight. This may take longer, but is more staying. We keep assessing the question of when to withdraw. The local organizations still have need for communication. If there is no person, no central place, their continuity will be difficult. We work on linkages, going to people in offices, encourage them to listen, talk. By these steps we seek to diminish the government structure, reduce oppression and brutality.

Faruque: You also keep open contact with journalists, to try to bring issues to public view.

Khushi: Nijera Kori is the biggest university for ourselves. We have 200 full time people, paid. We receive funds from many European agencies. We pay allowances, but not enough to change alliances. Most are middle class. Many staff are in need of a job, but I believe 40 percent would stay on without pay. Once a year, we hold a five-day meeting of all staff. This happened just before I came here. We discuss issues of organization, focus, styles of analysis within workshops, management within Nijera Kori. This year we are deciding among ourselves how units at *upazilla* scale should function, and how units should elect representatives at the Division scale. We encourage each person to feel responsible to all people around.

Kevin: What type of external aid do you accept?

Khushi: We specify what we need. International donors tend to agree with our proposals. The government is more cumbersome. It requires much de-learning. There is learning entropy, functionaries being tired, dispirited, apart from having their own vested interests in present patterns of aid.

Sylvia: Do gender groups stick to their own issues?

Khushi: In training programs, genders are mixed. In the village and in ward committees, individuals need privacy, security. In union and upazilla committees, members are mixed and deal with issues more generally. Here the factor of scale helps. At one remove from the village, representation of gender issues is safe. The woman speaks from her village situation: "I have learned from this," without endangering privacy. Communication, it is important to note, may require opportunities for silence.

Varun: What is your perspective on working toward self-reliance? Should the 40 percent be encouraged to work without money? As a voluntary organization, how much should you expand?

Khushi: These are difficult questions. Some feel that to raise resources, a Robin Hood strategy might work. Some in Bangladesh have tried, but haven't gained support.

Faruque: Landlords and other established interests have monopolized foreign funds for a long time. There is need for international aid reform, empowering not the rich but the poor, and on our terms.

Laurentino: In Negros, some NGOs have used aid to maintain the status quo. We are afraid the "mini-Marshall plan" now being discussed will be used against us.

Tonton: Some NGOs sprout from aid, and are valorizing privatisation, contract forestry.

Kersten: The aid process is itself a result of impoverishment. Where does this aid come from? Isn't it important to be engaging in analysis among the wealthy?

Dick: Khushi, you spoke of collective planning and use of means of production. Can you give some examples?

Khushi: We are trying to get long-term leases of land. We stopped the fishing lease of foreign companies, and are trying to get into shrimp production and marketing. Groups are producing salt from local poulters. Other groups are taking on direct contracts for road-building. In Noakhali, on an area of 1,000 acres, landless are undertaking collective farming.

Living Together: A Base Community in Manila

Christine: Let me try to describe the life of Leveriza, a community in urban Manila, with a density of 25,000 people per square mile in 1979. The picture is of the outstretched hand. Hunger is constant. There is no equal opportunity for work. No role models. Rampant gang wars. No health facility. Three pregnant women on one cot. Family culture is weak, under these burdens. God is called on, but the Church itself is an oppressive factor, preaching of guilt and punishment.

Four Filipina Catholic sisters found space for living in Leveriza, to share this life. The first three years we gave only to living, listening. Then we worked with people to face issues as they rose. When houses were to be demolished in a slum "clearance" project, we helped barricade them to save them. We had no foreign funding, no stars, no five-year plans. Our entry was simply being women, being able to see things with women that men can't. The tenacity of sustaining daily life. How to obtain safe water: we worked with the community a year and a half before they could get water. Only one faucet for 2,500 users. *Living* with a sense of the spirit, its liberating quality, was our most important activity. No labels, but the sense that a good Christian gives his life for his community.

A wholistic way of living was our approach. We sought to link people in Leveriza with farmers, with people in other slums, with elites. People bought rice directly from farmers. They started self-producing industries to meet their own needs: soap, other labor-intensive handicrafts. They studied market demands in greater Manila, and produced to meet these demands through marketing linkages with voluntary organizations that support home and small enterprises.

People engaged in lots of analysis and self-evaluation. What is going wrong? What brings good humor? How should we evaluate our activities? Now, after much self-study during several years, perhaps we can identify some indicators for the eventual withdrawal of the sister facilitators:

- enough rice to eat, even fish
- true sharing
- happy in work
- confidence in work skills and habits
- decision-making without nuns
- no gangs, no prostitution, no communist, no money-lenders
- a fine web of communications among families, neighborhoods, and other sectors.

There are withdrawal pains, too: separation, anxiety, worry over the absence of linkages. What is the image of success? Not the outstretched hand, but the fist, ready to fight for our rights. What are the qualities of the facilitator, the agent of change? Sustained passion. Motivation. Tenacity. Intensity. Ability to face internal constraints.

Sanjeev: To live with pain.

Christine: Awake at 4:00, reflect to 6:00. We received three warrants of arrest. We opposed Marcos as immoral, from the devil. I was called to Rome, told by the Cardinal to stop our activities.

Anis: Your indicators say it is time to leave. The people must now test their capability to carry on the struggle on their own.

Christine: This year they have been able to mobilize themselves. We have made no decisions.

Faruque: You spoke of population crowding. People will say there is overpopulation, blaming the victims.

Christine: The poor are not the problem. Priorities in the country are the issue.

Khushi: What will you do if it all falls back?

Christine: We will analyze, try to prevent the mistakes again.

Khushi: In urban areas, it is difficult to develop dynamics of movement. There is so little work.

Christine: We have to keep searching the demands in the market.

Puanani: Our dreams are fenced by our memories. You have brought our memories forward, reopened our ability to dream. Memories of you and your actions together will remain in the collective memory of the people.

Dorris: Someone has learned from that experience. People in the community have themselves learned the change agent's role. We will never be the same again.

Laurentino: It lifts up the dignity of the people. This is the message: humanist, communist, Christian. Man has dignity. Dignity has been restored. People have been empowered. It is a little victory.

Varun: Most of us have to go through some process of institutionalization: self-organization, committees, representation, assemblies.

Christine: We just walk around, listening to silences behind silences.

Elizabeth: Aid agencies will force institutionalization, structures. The banks, UNICEF will say, "You need this." They reduce people.

Arthur: How has Aquino affected the passion?

Christine: Our people awake at 2:30. They go home from market, burning, finding so many things to be done. They are committed.

Tony: Can it be done without passion?

Christine: I prefer passion over training. But we are trained. In social work, liberation theology.

Sharon: I have been flying high with joy. You have also been grounding us with the pain. Your language leaves me with many visual impressions.

Kevin: Many in Sri Lanka would argue that participation has no meaning. They see their daughters paint sniffers, or going into prostitution. The government, police, are so damn corrupt.

Christine: You have to be ascetic. Go from A, A to B, from A, A to B...not to Z. Passion is never given, it is caught.

Sanjeev: We have philosophical differences, as usual. In space, none of us is going to withdraw from the world. In time, happenings are not linear. Change is happening at the level of *being*. The world is with us. If we see being as this, there is no need to be anxious.

Dorris: Has there been any effect on the church?

Christine: They never answered back.

Transforming the Law to Support People's Rights

Chhatrapati: Law has been described as "the necessary evil." My path started with training in philosophy, including the influence of Nietzche. Studying in Canada in 1981, I saw the law being used to support native rights movements. I don't agree with those who say the causes of poverty are fate, over-population (over what?), laziness. The law is an instrument to do struggle, that I'm engaged in.

Democratic countries can take recourse to the law to reverse colonial law, to "stop the hunters." It is an instrument for unleashing democratic forces. It has symbolic value: Malaysia, Thailand, are looking to India for precedents in legal change. Changing the law calls for attention to moral responsibility. It has new applications in many areas: in natural resources, forest law, energy resources law; in housing, laws now being drafted by the people; consumer law; labor law; finance, including the legal status of International Monetary Fund fiscal prescriptions; laws relating to knowledge.

New kinds of legal research are emerging, for example contract law in studies by the American Law Institute. By and large, legal research has served either lawyers, corporations, or the government. Now it is being redirected to service the people. The Indian Law Institute, as an autonomous body, can engage in this work. Research supports action in several arenas. Litigation in the public interest is undertaken, either directly or on behalf of NGOs. This attracts the press, in some cases, strengthening conscience raising. As Justice Bhagwati said in the Krishnayya case, Call the public to the courts, correct the evil. Fraud can be uncovered. Law reform is guided. People themselves write the law. Advocacy is taken to Parliament.

Training camps are held. These develop capabilities of people and NGOs in devising schemes for land acquisition, for anticipatory bail, for filing counter cases against administrative actions. New avenues for conscience raising are explored. Women's studies centers are organized on Saturdays and Sundays, to explore problems and rights issues needing solution, and to provide legal information. *Lok adalats* (people's courts) are being formed to take up issues that can be settled outside the courts. Recent graduates are assisting their formation.

Some illustrations. In the Doon valley, closure of 50 mines was forced to reverse destruction of the environment. Advance training was given to prepare labor and NGOs for the consequences, and get sufficient compensation. In Kanpur, 50 tanneries were closed for health violations. Dam projects, atomic energy projects have been halted or delayed until corrective plans could be made. Planning Commission assumptions are examined: is the planning process constitutionally valid? Values embodied in the fundamental rights section of the Constitution are studied, for further clarification.

Such research and action has international significance. It contributes to removing ignorance in the First World. People on the whole are morally good. They are not aware or sensible on what their governments are doing to the Third World. The law is a window to fundamental principles: no one can get poor unless his labor value is taken away from him. No one can get rich unless he is taking from some one. This provides tests for World Bank guidelines: are they in keeping with international law? No. For labor, and minimum wages. What is labor worth? The International Labour Organization prescribes equal worth for each person. Attained? No. For multinational liability. In Bhopal we did not yet succeed. The value of life does not yet meet the test. In the Ahmedabad plane crash, Indian victims received Rs. 100,000 ($ 5,000), U.S. victims $75,000. For immigration laws and their administration; with $40,000 in your pocket, you can walk in. For patent law, contributing to the 1988 treaty on transfer of technology in drugs and pesticides. For educational policy: the influence of NASA hiring standards on Indian industrial training institute syllabi. For the nuclear non-proliferation treaty; the U.S., which has the lead in arms trade, says, "You don't make it. I will." For unilateral national action: in the U.S. Congress there are three bills pertaining to environmental rights in other countries, including the tropical rain forest in Brazil. Do they meet the Human Rights Convention? The IUCN (International Union for the Conservation of Nature and Natural Resources) is silent.

There are important constraints on this work. It takes away from the professional interests of lawyers. It faces a lack of women power, and lack of funds. It raises needs for different kinds of legal knowledge, better informed to throw new light on economic factors, social traditions, history.

Some future needs can be projected. There is need to identify national laws in the First World bearing on poverty there and in the Third World. To identify the agencies involved. To fashion viable strategies for change.

Sanjeev: India is characterized by a user-unfriendly legal system. It was designed on how to build a colony. When Ambedkar accepted the interim principle of reservations for Scheduled Castes, he neglected the sovereignty issue, the building of a power base. He should have said, Give the tribals their lands, their water. We tend to confuse the coercive system with the legal system: the policeman is "the law."

Chhatrapati: To change, we must make a basic appeal to the principles of justice, equity, liberty.

Puanani: Using the courts can create binding precedents. What is the usefulness of this in the process of really empowering people?

Chhatrapati: People can be involved in drafting petitions, and formulating the principles of new law. Precedents can be drawn from other indigenous law, for example, Maori law. Law can be used in this way for liberation purposes. In the gas leak at Delhi Cloth Mills, one person died. People's legal action achieved a huge compensation, setting new precedents.

Arthur: What efforts are being made to license rights to the use of genetic resources?

Chhatrapati: A scholar, Rajiv Dhavan, is studying this issue.

Russ: Even though you can use law as a tool, it is still a system based on logic, on reductionism. It is the same epistemology.

Chhatrapati: Changes in the style of thinking are slow, but on the way.

Tonton: All forms of law are dominating. Even radical law.

Chhatrapati: Good theory should be able to help distinguish

between good and bad law, based on the principles of justice, freedom, equality.

Tonton: Once you institutionalize a structure, it becomes an instrument of control.

Chhatrapati: Look at property law. Nehru was able to change it. Law provides a balance.

Varun: Are you collaborating with those who wish to heal the duck, rather than stopping the hunter?

Chhatrapati: Prem Bhai has shown in the Banswani case that the hunters can be stopped.

Faruque: Even if the law is improved, how can you get the government to implement it?

Chhatrapati: Was the act meant to be implemented?

Christine: Thank you for giving us hope in law.

Renewal with Nature: The Restoration of Hawaiian Identity

Danelle: To understand our work at Waipa on the island of Kaua'i, visualize a land base of 1,600 acres from Ka'ala ridge to the ocean. The Hawaiian families involved in the project lived there. As a Hawaiian activist, I lived with Alaskan people for three years. Our tradition of "sharing" makes us reluctant to claim or hold land. When we began organizing to work in this area, we found riverside dwellers blocking the effort. We held committee meetings for two months. Those who came to every meeting became board members.

The land is in the title of Bishop Estate, supposed to be used for the benefit of Hawaiian people. It is fertile. We researched the Bishop Estate plan to build condominiums, and found they would not benefit the people directly. Who were involved? The Mayor, and a certain trustee. We did our homework, then hit at the gut level, telling them, you have to answer to the people. Our purpose is to have our people return to the land, and develop a food base for the people. We applied for financial support to the Association of Native Americans. They refused, saying previous taro projects had failed. They would accept for "tropical agriculture," within which we could grow taro. We are growing taro, and every Tuesday morning we make poi, put up in 5 lb. bags. In the market poi costs $2.49 for 12 ounces. Families went back to fishing, and eat fish. They found the ocean waters being polluted, and gasoline killing the *limu* (seaweed). We are developing information and spreading awareness on these problems.

Miniprojects which we are developing at Waipa include reforesting the mountains. We have a health project. In September 1989 we will start a Hawaiian language preschool. This will be a school in our own tradition, not that of the Department of Education, to attract children. We find we cannot attract youth of high school age. They can make more money selling marijuana. As organizers we are unpaid. We do our Waipa work after hours. Outsiders doubt our ability to keep on.

Julia: Often there are unexpected benefits, when you do one thing, and it leads to another. What did you do when people took up fishing?

Danelle: We acted on it. Our main struggle was with commercial boats. Such efforts are taxing — we have to spread ourselves thin.

Puanani: In our project, Eric drops off taro. He says, "Is this Samoan food?" This is jarring. Taro is not part of land planning or agricultural policy. This is cultural genocide. So we are using food, water, as organizing tools.

Danelle: The food is also our medicine.

Arthur: If one taro project failed, what is the logic in not supporting yours?

Puanani: There is no logic. It is scapegoating, keeping people down.

Danelle: Overlapping of projects is barred. But the problems are deep. We need overlapping.

Khushi: We find taro in plastic bags in the market. Who produces it?

Danelle and Puanani: Individual Japanese farmers grow taro at Hanalei, on Kaua'i. They process and package it in a poi factory. We plan our own poi mill, which will conflict with the Honolulu mill. We plan to use hydroelectric power for the mill, getting back our own hydropower.

Elizabeth: How widely is poi accepted? Health food stores accept Gerber. Poi is not allergetic.

Puanani: But why is poi so expensive?

Syed: Hawaiian culture, as you say, values sharing. Here we have Filipinos, Chinese, Caucasian. Where do you draw the line? What are the linkages, coalitions?

Danelle: We face this question every day. Outside people come in. For example, an architect from the mainland. A whiz. We have helped him. We don't love other people any less, but feel we have to have control.

Puanani: Princess Pupule, who some thought to be crazy, said Give away the fruit, but hang on to the root. This is an incredibly difficult question. Doesn't sharing extend consciousness? Is there a line between being racist and preservationist? Not a line, a sense, a feeling. If I didn't like what is being said, I would leave. For other people there is no line. When you feel respect, you give respect back.

Tony: That is one of the best answers I have heard.

Sanjeev: In cultivation, if you change the amount of organic matter, you may reduce the amount of water required. Ask a person to experiment.

Arthur: There are also ways to make more water.

Puanani: Radical science is often old. Cultural assertions are made through the daily things we do. It is very thrilling.

Evergreen: An Educational Base for Community Action

Russell: We are weaving a beautiful tapestry. I can add a few fibers, making a piece of fabric. This involves students, working with a community, dealing with the U.S. Army. Creating knowledge, facilitating joint action, achieving community sustainability. Facing structural issues of liberation, knowledge, oppression.

Evergreen, a state educational institution, fosters participatory research by students in collaboration with communities. Our students are mostly the haves of the First World, white, upper middle class. Many people we work with are disenfranchised urban residents, Third World people in dynamic change, Fourth World indigenous people. These include native Americans. For some, all generations of their heritage are based on one particular land area. They have faced resource exploitation for decades.

Collaboration in this style creates a potential teaching mission, in which teaching and learning can be personal and collective. Learning includes analysis of contradictions between ideals and reality, the development of skills to act on, and tools of liberation. Who controls it? Students themselves engage with communities in definition of the problem, the parameters of relevant knowledge, the rediscovery of democratic principles.

Democratic principles are at the heart of such education. Any time we fragment knowledge, we foster an epistemology that leads to reductionist information and opens us to oppression by experts. It leads to competition for grades, without processing through the heart of analysis. It perpetuates the power of that kind of knowledge in the world. Evergreen was founded on an alternative educational philosophy, that of practitioners like John Dewey and Paolo Freire. Organizing themes are holistic, built by interdisciplinary teams. Affective and cognitive awareness about ourselves is built from ourselves, in reflection and dialogue. Problem-solving, collaborative study is encouraged, connecting theory and practice, challenging values, empowering students. No grades are given, there is no need for tests. Instead, students and faculty are given help in writing their own evaluations.

Collaboration with communities in problem-solving is a central feature of the program. Students serve as facilitators, animators. Projects are mostly small. I've learned to trust students in this process: they provide their own peer challenges. We've learned to trust citizens. Citizens also enroll for credit; at present, 40 native American citizens are students.

In the Bonneville community relocation struggle, students and citizens faced the U.S. Army Corps of Engineers. This is a body of individuals who take for granted the power of instrumental reason and the importance of specified artifacts. The community learned to understand these values, and to develop in the Corps an understanding of community values and social relationships. The students gained understanding of how to facilitate such cultural and knowledge exchange, finally including creation of a mutually negotiated plan for community rebuilding.

The criterion of sustainability, here, means the community being able to transfer such participatory methods to new and different kinds of problems, for example, to geothermal projects, elections, volunteerism.

The students come out different. Supporting such participatory research, Evergreen curricula areas are strong in:
- Education, including teacher certification
- Ecological agriculture, and alternatives to large scale agriculture
- Alternative energy systems
- Political economy and social change
- Community development and cultural awareness.

Julia: It is exciting to find this in a state-supported college. Can it be introduced in state-funded land grant universities?

Russell: Yes, if the faculty is thirsting to do something collaborative.

Sanjeev: We face similar cases now. In one, 11,000 people are to be displaced by a dam, one of 30. They see no way out. There is said to be no land for their resettlement. Inquiries are often blocked on grounds of the "official secrets act."

Chhatrapati: Russ has told us a case of participatory democracy. Governments based on lines on a map, that negate culture, are not representative. How can election laws reconstitute the true cultural base, with links to representation based on the will and interests of the people? We need to redo this.

Laurentino: Your example suggests a vehicle of seminars for farmers, fishers, using the existing educational system. Recognizing the constraints, we could design these.

Single Women against Poverty: Overcoming Exclusion in Canada

Sharon: Single Women Against Poverty works as a voluntary organization with women whose lives have been, and are, full of fear. We seek to base life on the opposite, love. This helps bring women to confront real life, with balance. The low energy life of fear is brought together with the high energy of love, in a process that results in power sharing.

We work with local groups of 12, in an experiential process. Single mothers, battered women, police women, usually with a ratio of four or five police in a group. Part of the process is educating the advantaged, the police. It enables the police to go back to a strong culture, that of the police, with new understanding.

Workshops include varied, selected elements. Women engage in a whole-day poverty game, simulating choices faced in being on welfare, such as cheating yet facing the need for self-respect. They take part in community forums. I have to be clear on my role as facilitator. It is a low budget program. Techniques include role-playing, connecting through food preparation and meals, dancing — all night long. The social aspect, "giving to, with joy," is balanced with work tasks and livelihood training.

Women explore attitudes, behaviour, and skills called for in decision making and problem solving. Systems that affect you, and how to influence them. Your responsibilities, including mutual aid, to people you don't like.

A spiritual focus is fostered. Creative visualization, light, energy between us, music, collective meditation. Belief in being worthy of self-love. Feeling good about oneself physically, and about each other. Letters are written to each other, and verbal expression encouraged. Changing relationships, or confrontations, are delved through a sandwich process: first giving or receiving a gift, then raising a problem, then again a gift. Silent times foster awareness and experience of the quiet sanctuary within the self.

Action and advocacy are encouraged, social as well as individual. Lobbying the Department of Justice for new policies, and pressing personally for maintenance by one's father, are examples.

Tony: How far is this approach transferable to other contexts? Could it be used in your work in Thailand?

Sharon: I don't yet know. This we must find out.

Reflecting on the Profiles: Issues of Political Economy

These profiles of participatory experience reveal spaces for lots of different agents of change—at middle levels, micro levels.

Pressures from the grassroots can bring qualitative changes. Beyond a critical point, the state can no longer oppress, suppress. It has to make deals, in the public arena, in the streets. The opportunity may be posed as follows. The state is a central actor in accumulation. This leads to unequal distribution among regions, groups. It contributes to the belief that the poor cannot become accumulators. Might not people be animated to ask the question, is there any way we can produce our own surplus? Retain, re-use, control it locally? With demographic factors causing erosion of surplus, such action by the disadvantaged is all the more necessary.[2]

To look systematically at the kinds of opportunity suggested by the profiles, elements of present control and steps for regaining control may be summarized.[3] These include:

i) Control of land resources by large landholders (landlords) in opposition to small landholders and landless.

ii) Dominance of agricultural technology that favors large scale agricultural production as opposed to small scale subsistence farming.

iii) Dominance and control over markets by established entities to the exclusion of small new entrants: mechanisms of control range from physical to "legal" to price.

iv) Dominance over marine resources by large scale capital-intensive techniques to the exclusion of small traditional fishermen.

v) Control of urban market and price information, and political influence, to the detriment of small scale fishermen.

vi) Control of forest resources by industries, multinationals, to the exclusion of traditional groups such as tribals.

vii) Control of social infrastructure (banks, hospitals, stores, property values) by dominant group (or race) to prevent disprivileged people moving in.

viii) Cultural control: exclusion of the handicapped by the "wholes."

ix) Control of women by law, religion, bureaucracy, education, health practices; physical control of women.

x) Regaining control of law away from the interests of lawyers, corporations, government and back to the people: new kinds of legal research to promote justice, equity, liberty.

xi) Regaining control over land, water, food and marine food, education and culture.

xii) Regaining control over knowledge systems: anti-reductionist epistemology, opposition to the power of institutional reason, end to competitive systems of knowledge creation and education.

Qualities and Relationships in Participatory Initiatives

As portrayed earlier by Russell Fox, Native Americans' view of the world is a view of relationships, relationships between:

The person	**Others**
The unknown	
Land	**Work**

The Hawaiian view of qualities and dimensions of life as expressed by Puanani Burgess, and the traditional Fililpino view portrayed by Laurentino Bascug, are very similar to this Native American world view. Workshop members introduced and talked intensively about central aspects of these qualities and relationships. In a larger, detailed portrayal, these are presented in Figure 2. The empowerment realized in the workshop, therefore, was not only in the strength of each member's experience, but in combining and reinforcing strengths among all these qualities that are crucial in participatory action to build community and to overcome the causes and conditions of impoverishment.

SYNTHESIS AND MOMENTUM

Moving holistically, teams were formed in the last days of the workshop to identify issues and opportunities for future collaboration, and to develop a synthesis on fundamental principles of participatory action to overcome poverty. Areas for collaboration were further elaborated in plenary, as stated in the preliminary workshop report (East-West Center, 1989) and cited later in this volume. The process of interactive learning and forging of consensus continued, the last day, in members' analysis and reflection toward a synthesis.

Forging the Synthesis

As a personal statement, each workshop participant wrote a brief note on "your sense of synthesis regarding principles of participatory development (people's initiatives) to alleviate poverty." A team of Khushi Kabir, Sanjeev Ghotge, Dorris Pickens, Syed Rahim, Anisur Rahman, Christine Tan, and Tony Williamson analyzed and consolidated these statements in key concepts and categories. In the final plenary, Sanjeev arrayed these elements in outline form on the wall in a pattern of three sets:

Statement of the problem

Where to go?

How to go there? What are the contradictions and strategies involved?

FIGURE 2

Qualities and Relationships in People's Initiatives As Portrayed in Workshop Dialogues

The person

Life
Identity
Values, ethics
Health, wellbeing
Consumption
Disease, death
Risk, oppression

Others

Love
Aloha
Justice, law
Community
Organizing
Institutions
Coercion, violence
Communication
Exchange, markets

The Unknown

Truth
Spirit
God
Intuition
Knowing
Symbols, culture
Education, research

Land

Nature
Resources
Savings
Capital

Work

Strength
Healing
Production, products
Technology

Each concept was also presented on a 3" x 5" card. Syed invited members to give their own order and pattern of relationship among the cards, to reflect and form their own perceptions of an emerging participatory paradigm.

Quite early, agreement was reached to give the synthesis a sense of direction and purpose by putting **"Where to go?"** at the top. Reflecting this change, Figure 3 shows the conceptual map of key concepts and principles arrived at by the members.

Figure 3

Forging the Synthesis

Where to Go

Creating alternatives	Holistic, integrated	Knowledge:
Passion, commitment,	Self-reliance	- Popular, organic
sharing, trust	Self-determination	- Inner knowledge
Joy	Empowerment	- Intuition, wisdom
Creativity	Organization	Sustainability:
Innovation		- Grassroots
		- Ecological zone

Problem Statement

Poverty, oppression	Inner conflicts	Culture
- Economic	Leadership	Ideologies
- Social		
- Political		

How to Go There

Ownership and	Spaces in existing	Participation at all
exchange question	structures	levels
Rights and entitlement	Changing dominant	Self-identity, dignity,
to resources	institutions	strength
Pluralism, coalition	Nonjudgmental stance	Positive image, collec-
Networking, linkages	Question of withdrawal	tive solidarity
		Decision/policy making,
		accountability

Enthusiasm for the visual presentation was contagious:

Christine: This has great value. Relationships among the three sets are vivid. How to put in English?

Syed: Englishes. We have to go back to your statements to fill in concrete details.

Tony: These make an outline.

Tonton: This is very important and relevant. How different it is, as a counter discourse. How to present it to others? To Marxists, post-structuralists? How operationalize it, link it to collaboration?

Jan: On this map, I locate myself in Popular Knowledge. Local control. Stay long enough. Dig deep enough.

Kersten: This gives a sense of healing: sharing, trust, solidarity.

Khushi: It helps me focus on all the different perspectives. It provides enrichment. But not rigid. Just a framework, not a structure.

Sharon: The pattern shows strength. Weaknesses become visible. One can see a balanced approach.

Laurentino: What is the purpose of the synthesis? To show priorities, objectives?

Khushi: It is philosophic. We share different experiences, values. We need a synthesis as a symbol of linkages. It shows we do not subjugate the ideas of others.

Christine: It is useful to practitioners, to the oppressed. Diarrhea is just in front of me. Use this pattern to think. Light comes on the gaps.

Several members sought deeper content:

Dick: The problem statement avoids hunger, fear, alienation.

Anis: In the writeup, such concrete aspects should be elaborated.

Laurentino: I have some doubts. We need to show a reason why poverty should not prevail. Some cultures accept it as the will of God. We need to condemn it.

Tonton: This might run the risk of making it an exclusionary discourse.

Faruque: How does ideology fit in?

Varun: Should the leadership issue be more explicit?

Laurentino: Social philosophy defines the goal. If we have no ideology, we're not holisitic. Just palliative.

Puanani: We need to condemn wealth. Where does this lead us?

Chhatrapati: We need to condemn impoverishment.

Varun: Condemn dependence. Even the rich are dependent.

Laurentino: We should condemn inequitable distribution of wealth. Concentration in the hands of a few. This is immoral.

Sanjeev: And unequal distribution of power.

Faruque: And unjust structures.

Anis: I have difficulty condemning hunger. If everyone is sharing, the community gives a human response. Condemn oppression. Condemn relative poverty.

Kevin: We need understanding, not condemnation.

Tony: Many of us have made eloquent statements on poverty. We should use them.

Kersten: As Kathy Wilson says, statements of the problem are often part of the oppressive system. We should look at where we want to go.

Laurentino: We need to look at causes, too. Unjust law, as an example.

Kevin: We need to build understanding of what it means to have your child die in your hands.

Tonton: Reflect our burning desire for change.

Julia: We're trying to translate our experiences and perceptions. This is also a manifestation of power. I suggest bringing participation to the first set, "Where to go." The more people who believe something, the less alternative it becomes.

Puanani: Our final statement should combine mind, heart, and spirit. Show one universe.

Synthesis Statement

Syed Rahim, building on this intensive discussion and prior notes, wrote the synthesis statement of "middle level generalizations" for the preliminary report. We repeat the synthesis here, slightly edited to reflect participants' subsequent comments.[4]

A. Goals and Direction

People's initiatives are based on actions that reach for social goals. At the heart of these goals is self-reliance, a core issue of locally directed participatory development. It is important to understand the notion of self-reliance clearly for what it is and for what it is not.

1. Self-reliance means self-determination and empowerment. True development belongs to the people; they are the owner and creator of development. That ownership responsibility involves getting together, creating mutual trust and cultural solidarity, bringing passion, commitment and joy to work, making organized efforts, building local institutions, raising courage to take risks and to sacrifice, and enhancing local creativity and innovations. Self-reliance is demonstrated in the people's own empowered, connected action in everyday life. It is neither personally or socially isolationist. It is not an utopia. It is not a mode of self-deception to escape the pain of poverty.

2. Life-enhancing values form the basis of self-reliance. Enlightened self-analysis by individuals and groups allows the evaluation of existing conditions and the choice of those values which best serve the future of self and society. Social growth drives economic improvement, provided it assures each person's ability to feed, clothe, and house herself and her family. Individual dignity, but not individualism, is considered essential to self-reliance. Community welfare enhances individual welfare; they are not in competition with each other.

3. Self-reliance implies exercising the basic human right to participate at all levels of policy making and planning decisions affecting the communities' life, and to ensure that public officials are accountable to the people. As citizens, the poor have the right to participate fully in shaping national policies of investment and material support, in defining and organizing regional and sector programs to create resources and infrastructure, and in setting priorities for local projects meeting needs that they themselves identify and defiine.

4. Self-reliance is not autarky, totally independent of external support or imports. But dependence on outside resources is contrary to the principle

of self-reliance when those resources carry with them the implicit power relationships through which outside decisions become controlling. Dependence undermines sustainability of local efforts, and cultural values. Since not enough outside resources are available to eliminate massive poverty and deprivation, external dependence makes things more difficult by helping some to get out of poverty and not others. In contrast to dependence, self-reliance is manifested by positive, optimistic expectations for life, family, community, and the future.

5. Knowledge is the basis of self-reliance: the integration of and respect toward different kinds of knowledge—scientific, conceptual, practical, local, organic, intuitive and inner knowledge.

6. Sustainable grassroots development and ecological sustainability cannot be achieved without self-reliance. The great diversity among local ecosystems makes it essential to base technological adaptations and innovations on direct working knowledge of local citizens, assessing and incorporating exogenous information.

B: Analysis of the Problems

The structures of poverty must be clearly understood if they are to be transformed. Economic, political, legal, ideological, and knowledge structures are constructed by society to organize, regulate and control the members' own material and spiritual conditions of living. When the structure is hegemonic, dividing people into antagonistic groups (based on wealth, gender, race, ethnicity and other factors), and one section of society is appropriating power to control and dominate the lives of others, it becomes oppressive. Poverty is not a natural consequence of structuring society, it is produced by structural hegemony, domination and oppression.

1. The political-economic structure determining the ownership, control and allocation of resources, and the knowledge and information structure determining the ownership, control and dissemination of technology have most pervasive effects on all other structures of society. These structures use and create culture to define and legitimize their particular concepts and practices of ownership and control, and the uses and reproduction of resources and knowledge. Therefore, it is important to recognize the critical role of culture in development. Culture is the arena where people ultimately take their struggles for constructing and reconstructing non-hegemonic, democratic structures.

2. Poverty is living in physical insecurity, spatial isolation, political impotence, economic deprivation, cultural alienation and spiritual despair. The complex interplay of economic, political, social, and cultural factors in poverty conditions must be recognized. Reducing the complex problem to only economic or political factors may simplify research, but it also increases mistakes and misunderstanding. A holistic approach, however difficult that may be, is a necessary condition to deal with the problem effectively.

3. A low-consumption lifestyle should not be equated to poverty. To identify poverty, a standard of material consumption having no cultural basis and imposed from outside is inappropriate. Absence of human integrity,

dignity, supportive family/social relations, and spiritual values are very important factors contributing to true poverty conditions. Absence and prevention of access to resources, knowledge, and tools is also a critical contributing factor.

4. Those who are continuously degraded and oppressed are then also collectively labelled as inadequate—complete with stigmas declaring them lacking in ability, or education, or intelligence, or drive. Eventually, the oppressed may internalize the negative self images thrust upon them by those in positions of privilege, and can become mired in traps of factionalism, mistrust, envy, apathy, acquiescence, escapism, fatalism, demobilization and inaction. These consequences are then confused with original causes, and implicate the poor in their own oppression.

5. People's initiatives to overcome poverty often remain only a potential, awaiting to be facilitated by external intervention. A cautious intervention, and its timely withdrawal, are very important in promoting self-reliant development.

6. The struggle against poverty is ultimately fought at the cultural level, by reaffirming and where necessary renovating traditionally valued concepts and practices of ownership, achievement, and socially responsible use of economic resources and knowledge and information.

C: Scope and Strategies for Action

With the rising number of people's initiatives in both developing and developed countries the scope of self-reliant, participatory development is increasing and it is attracting the attention of national and international development assistance institutions. New opportunities for better linkages and integration of macro and micro level policies, program planning and implementation are being created everywhere. The ground is cultivated for enhanced creativity and productivity based on ecologically sound and sustainable use of local resources and new technologies locally developed as well as imported from outside. These will stimulate patterns of decentralized infrastructure, industries, and access to specialized knowledge. Global issues and local issues are converging to form common issues for humankind.

1. Within the existing economic, political, and knowledge structures spaces are available for taking new initiatives and there are informed people willing to help facilitate such initiatives. The scope of such action and support is far from exhausted.

2. The people's rights and entitlements to individual and group ownership and exchange of resources, knowledge and new technologies cannot be asserted without understanding what those rights and entitlements are and why and how the people are at present deprived of those things. Therefore, regular group discussions and analysis of personal, social, and historical conditions, at times assisted by qualified facilitators, are the first steps toward self-reliant development.

3. Flexible organization and innovative leadership for group activities aimed at the mobilization of financial, material and human resources, import of appropriate information and technologies from outside, and export of prod-

ucts to external markets after internal basic needs have been met, are the next most important requirements.

4. Plurality of interests among the poor form the basis for organization beyond local scale. Local struggles and popular organizations are vulnerable to cooptation and repression. Overarching mediation through macro-organizations and macro-policies can help support and strengthen local action. But the nature and form of such overarching systems need very careful scrutiny to avoid the creation of new systems of control that merely replace the old ones.

5. The lessons from people's initiatives need to be examined, evaluated, accounted for, and communicated among both local groups and external supporters. A positive image of strength, dignity and solidarity can thus be created to help translate local experiences and knowledge into public policy at the macro level.

6. Systematic and sustained efforts at creating and disseminating knowledge and information about self-reliant development require closer collaboration among practitioners and scholars through national and international seminars, exchange visits and internships, and joint research and educational projects. Institutions like the East-West Center should take initiative in facilitating these activities.

Weaving the *Lei*

Puanani proposed on the next to last day:

"Tomorrow is our last day, and we want to give you a farewell in Hawaiian style. We in Hawaii love flowers and the *lei*. In the final session tomorrow we shall make three *leis*. I shall bring a basketful of flowers and a thread. The basket will come to each one of you. You will pickup a flower from it, and holding it, will express a thought that comes to you. You will then thread the flowers in the thread, pass on the basket to the friend on your right, and with your left hand hold the right hand of the friend to your left. The *lei* of flowers woven in the thread will be the first *lei*. I shall weave a poem with the thoughts that you will express, and this will be the second *lei*. Holding hands together we shall make the third."

When in the final session on the last day the third *lei* was made, a *lei* of connected humans, a number of the participants were in tears. Puanani then invited the friends from Bangladesh to lead the song on the "Motherland" that they had shared earlier in the workshop. All sang together, holding a verse, in tears and in fulfillment for having connected with a wonderful group of people.

Editors' Reflections

Anis: The *lei* is very important, to give this message, to the whole grassroots movement of the world, that we need to connect. This is one way we did. Kersten: And that's also a message for the institutions of the world. Take some courageous steps for being. It seems the grassroots people know of that message.

A: Also another thing came out, and I have put it theoretically. That to do serious analytical dialogue, you are at your best when you are relaxed. It's like the diver, you know, who plunges into deep water. If he's tense, and then plunges, he doesn't make it. He has to be very relaxed. K: Laughs. A: And for us also, when we want to go to analytical great depth, we have to be relaxed. K: Hm. A: And these songs and dances, and the emotional connections, gave us that feeling, and we really went deep, when we came to the final theoretical stage. Because we were so relaxed. We were confident, every one knew we could do it. K: And to me also that was creative because Puanani modelled this session, where we become relaxed because we become naked to each other. A: That's right. K: And without that, even the songs, or anything else, cannot bring us to that depth. A: So, you know, this is also different from conventional academic seminars, where you are unable to relax, you are tense.

Dick: Then the message of the book has already been substantially achieved, in the sense that the reader is aware that workshops can do this. And that other groups of people can get together and do this. A: And also the message that what we are wanting, is for people of the whole world to make that *lei*. D: Yes. A: And how do you do it? Not by imposing on each other. Not by designing things for the others. But by connecting.

K: I like the way this is shaping. I like this very much. Because in the first thing people read, they'll have a sense of the humanness of what happened. And that to me is the important thing. The synthesis, the directions, later on that we did is all good, but it came out of that humanness. It came out of that restful analysis, relaxed analysis. D: This is people's human reactions together, what they're happy to say together as a group, after ten days of being here.

A: And it doesn't end with the workshop. D: No. Yes, that's nicely put. K: Right, and then it moves on into things like your own effort, the paradigm. A: Yes. It flows on. My effort, the paradigm paper. Your effort, in your writeup. K: And even in the many ways that people have been working with each other, I think, even your recent weekend with Puanani and Hayden, are part of synthesizing. A: Yes. D: That gives it a dynamic, forward quality. It's what we're after. A: That is it. We are moving, and this is what we're experiencing, and in the process we're trying to articulate, conceptualize moving on. Invite others to join in the chariot. K, D: Exactly. A: That is the whole of the book.

A: That's reminding me of the evening of poetry that weekend, where I was quite fulfilled and surprised when Pua said, "This session is the result of a bond that is being forged between Hawaii and Bangladesh, starting with the workshop, the arrival of the Bangladesh colleagues, Anis, Faruque, and Khushi." Very interesting. One of those connections. D: Right. A: It says something really very powerful.

K: In fact, if we can map some of these things out, and show how it has affected our own way of learning, and our own way of working, it would in some sense help to explain and justify the process of gathering, which in many people's mind is just a frivolous, kind of one-time event. And this is a way of saying, No, if you do this right, coming together is not a one-time event. It's an ongoing strengthening. D: People think it's ephemeral. But there's evidence here that it's not ephemeral. K: Right. And then these summaries don't look like just independent, private reports of experience but you really can see the interconnections, and strengthening.

D: And the summaries also are not the end of the story. A: No. D: They're getting some connections recorded and visible, that can encourage more of such ongoing get-togethers where these kinds of struggles are explored together over greater periods of time and in greater depth, and with more building of joint action.

A: Another thing Pua said, introducing the poetry session, was the role of that song that we brought, the Motherland song. K: Yes. A: That was so universal. In that song, everyone, particularly the Hawaiians, but I felt everyone, through that song, were connecting with your Motherland. In a way which we are trying to articulate in rejecting the conventional development paradigm that we rule over Nature, we harness Nature. K: Yes. A: It was a different kind of connection that was being reinforced by that song. And it touched a chord in every participant. K: Yes. A: We need to relate with the Motherland in that way, the Mother, not the horse with a rider. D: Yes. A: The Mother that feeds us.

K: I was thinking back to the question of how the workshop was structured. We sort of moved toward the idea of a synthesis from the beginning, because of the institutional imperative, having an output. And yet the process of going through the discussion toward a synthesis was very meaningful. A: Quite so. K: There was enough time given. It didn't seem to be forcing issues. A: No. K: Or creating false results. A: No. Some of us would have wanted to go in that direction in any case. Forgetting our institutional parts. K: Right. A: Of course we would not have forced it if we found that the flow is going another way, fair enough. But there is in this process a desire not just to do, but also to reflect. With the practice. K: And not just to reflect, but to distill. A: To distill. Yes. And this goes on, dialectically. Sometimes you want to reflect and conceptualize, knowing that this is never complete or final or full, but still useful. And then go into action again.

K: It's natural. A: Very natural. We are always doing it. Doing and reflecting. Some possibly are not. They are not doing it. Many activists, NGOs are not quite doing it: they are doers, not reflecting or writing. I feel there is a gap there. They also sometimes feel that. It seems they then want the help of somebody. K: And often just crave, for a month to spend. Pua's trying to find support for that too. A: That's right. So here it was that two urges met. The institution's urge to give something of this nature. And this process has its natural urge from time to time to reflect and conceptualize.

K: What's interesting to me about this...how to put this? Things that strike me, in something a person might say, or in telling a story, or speaking of a principle, or whatever...If my energy needs to move in some particular direction, it can move that way most quickly if the circuits are connected. And if my thoughts and feelings and experiences are in many directions and don't know which way to flow, then somebody who speaks something can connect them for me. Then my energy can flow more powerfully, in that direction. But there's no way for me to know in advance what that thing is that I need. Except to have some sense of people that have experiences that I expect would have those kinds of connections. So, listening in a workshop, I usually come up with learning moments, even in that discussion, which affect me for years, maybe the rest of my life—as powerfully as anything I've ever read, as powerfully as anything I've ever studied.

A: Yes. K: And it's not because it's some surge of creative experience or because a thousand people said the same thing, and so therefore I can believe it. But because somebody said the right thing for that moment. Now, I tend to extrapolate, and think that's how many people learn. It may not be true, it may be too limited. I guess, because of my own way of thinking, would be to advocate for, how can we begin to more greatly legitimize the very chaotic and context-specific way that people learn? In this workshop everyone learned something different, because everyone had different circuits that had to be closed. And they got that from some different time and place. And perhaps some of the things were mutual, maybe everyone was affected by what Dorris said, by what Pua said, and got the sense of that force and direction. Maybe not. Maybe for others the most important thing—well, you say the most important thing for you was Kampon. So we need to do justice to those many different kinds of learning.

A: Yes, Kampon: "I am not disabled." I think that was the most important statement at that time. K: Yes.

A: Gradually feeling more and more close. Not in terms of the logical articulation of the commitment, but in human terms. K, D: Um hm. A: Retaining our differences. I know that some of the people in the group don't see the whole problem in the same way that I do, but I still felt some affinity to them, to him or her. That was quite an experience for me. In other occasions, I have often felt put off. By what it seems are some differences between us. But here, there was something, that those differences did not come in the way of our still connecting. K: Um, um. A: These differences still exist. Even in the Bangladesh team, for instance, I find great differences between Khushi's work and approach and Faruque's. One could discuss them, in logical terms. They're poles apart. Still, you know, there is no problem in sharing the warmth. D, K: Yes. Laughing. A: That was a very interesting experience for me. So what was it? Was it something unarticulated, that we had in common?

A: I don't feel that we questioned our own or somebody else's commitment. Which is a very hard thing to do. D: Yes. I think you're saying that we reached some plane of trust and warmth among ourselves, that is deep enough so that we didn't feel it necessary to pay that much attention to differences of particular points of view, of stances and styles. K: To me the fact that people were sharing themselves from such an utterly intimate, naked kind of emotional style, making themselves vulnerable. It makes it impossible not to respect a person, no matter how different their opinion is, when they reveal things that are very personal and central.

A: In spite of having differences in our commitments, we still felt such an affinity. K: Hm. A: I don't know quite how to put it. We are not stuck to any rigid definition of our own commitments. D: Um hm. K: Hm. A: You know—we are not fundamentalists. K, D: Agree. A: We see that something is there, the thing that is binding us, something common that transcends our individual commitments. And it converges to a deeper commitment to something that cannot be described or articulated easily. K: Yes. You're right, it's a deeper commitment. And I think it's so obvious that that commitment is there in everybody. It rings like a bell. A: That's right, we recognized it. D, K: Um hm. A: Although the articulations would be different. We were not stuck there. We were not sold to that. You know, you're different, I don't want to work with you.

K: To me the lesson of this is something on the level of trusting your instincts. But instincts aren't all the same. It's part of that question of how to make context for diverse approaches to the world. D: Hm, hm. K: And that's a lesson that everyone's struggling with right now, understanding diversity in culture, understanding diversity in approaches to basic human development, understanding diversity in all these things. And yet having some kind of mutual accountability to one another. And the accountability we can do through judgment, but only if our judgment is highly honed. Both against ourselves, or with ourselves, and with others. And we're willing to hold ourselves up to harsh lights. You know, ourselves as ourselves. Only then can we ask questions of others.

A: There was no desire to impose. K: Um hm. Why not? A. Then what kind of commitment do you have? (All laugh.) D: I think there is a guide. Does it relate to the fact that right on the opening day, several of us said, including particularly those who are most actively engaged with excluded peoples, several said, We are not here to speak for those who are not here. We're not here to speak for the poor. A: Um. D: And so, there is among us, a kind of universal recognition of the autonomy of each person. A: Um. D: The autonomy of the poor, the autonomy of everyone. So that we respect that autonomy, and we're not here to interfere with it, or second guess it, or impose our perception on it. A, K: That's right. D: So maybe we kind of all recognized that in ourselves, and accepted that that was the position we were taking.

A: This is a profound lesson, for me. That: remain open. Here is an example that you have felt that in a very deep sense the other fellow is with you. But the articulations are differing. So don't jump into a judgment.

D: That, I think, is one of the significant paradoxes of the workshop, for ourselves. This openness, this urge, not having decided, implies joy in listening, an attitude of listening. A: That's right. K: Um. D: And, in a way the kernel of animation, when done well, is to give space to the *anima*, the soul of each person...A, K: Um, um...D: Not to come in with a closed chapter, or rebuke. And that was the difficulty you perceived in Mao's *Little Red Book*. A: Yes. Laughs.

D: And so, this openness, this encouragement to the *anima* of each, is one reason that we enjoyed each other. We were happy to listen to each other. But it's also a kind of underlying attitude that makes us comfortable with the human process. A: Yes. D: Rather than with just the logical process.

A: Exactly. And the joy of listening is one part of it, and the other part of it is joy of expressing my urge. Without imposing. D: Hm. A: I want to tell you my *anima*, show you my *anima*. This is what is exciting me. I want to share that with you. But I'm not imposing it on you. D: Very important. K: Yes. A: In doing so I can even challenge you: "Don't you know." But that's also with openness. I don't mean that you have to.

K: That's interesting. Because the challenge posed from that feeling feels completely different from one that is posed from a position of weakness. A: It's fully acceptable, it's just a stimulus, stimulation. D: Um. K: Welcome. Which is why this defies method, or defies codification, because if you tell people to do the same thing, if they do it with the wrong attitude, it's terrible (laughing).

D: I think we're getting at a theme that we hope will emerge in the authors' contributions, as well. This is the theme that people prefer to be open, to be listeners, because they respect the autonomy and self-determination of others. And because they realize that only others in their own circumstances can define the terms of their struggle. A: Hm, hm.

K: This is beautiful. Maybe that was the invisible hand at work. A: Yes, I was trying to understand it. D: Can you say that again? A: Invisible hand. K: Just, in the sense that various of us had the idea of bringing together people of similar orientation, and style of work. And that quality in a person that leads them to respect the autonomy of others is something that we can detect. We know that about a person, very soon after meeting them. And without saying that's what we were looking for, each of the people we asked for advice on who to find, to involve in this process, also knew that. And also identified people who had that quality. Intuitively. Just because, that's what we all know is important, without even being able to articulate it, having to articulate it.

END NOTES

[1] Sanjeev Ghotge, Christine Tan, Julia Vindasius, and Tony Williamson have contributed to correcting and editing the original text of these summaries.
[2] We are indebted to T. V. Sathyamurthy for these insights based on his reading of the profiles.
[3] Sanjeev Ghotge has provided this summary of political economy issues.
[4] Julia Vindasius made especially useful suggestions which we have incorporated.

BIBLIOGRAPHY

Bajracharya, Deepak, Richard Morse, Amara Pongsapich, et al., 1987. *Village Voices in Rural Development and Energy Planning: Participatory Action Research in Nepal, Bangladesh, and Bhutan.* Honolulu and Bangkok. East-West Center Resource Systems Institute and Chulalongkorn University Social Research Institute.
East-West Center. Preliminary Report, International Workshop: *People's Initiatives to Overcome Poverty.* Honolulu, Hawaii, May 1989.
Working Group on Creativity for Social Change. Preliminary Workshop Proposal: *People's Initiatives to Overcome Poverty.* November 1988.

THE MOTHERLAND

Full of riches, rice and flowers
Is this earth of ours;
In it there is a land,
The best of all,
O, she is made of dreams,
Enclosed in memories —
Such a land nowhere else will you find,
It is the queen of all lands,
O it is my motherland,
It is my motherland.

The moon, the sun, planets and the stars,
Where else shine they so bright,
Where else plays the lightning
In clouds so endearing dark,
Where else do they pass into sleep
By the call of the birds
And wake up as the birds call again?
Such a land nowhere else you will find...

Which other land has rivers so serene,
Mountains so dreamlike misty,
Where else do such yellow fields
    mingle beneath the sky,
In whose land does the breeze
Wave through such fields of paddy?
Such a land nowhere else you will find...

The branches—so full of flowers are they,
In the groves the birds singing,
Humming come the bees chasing the flowers,
On the flowers they retire drinking their honey.
Such a land nowhere else you will find...

Where else you have such love between folks,
Such love of mother,
Mother, O mother, let me clasp
Your two feet in my bosom—
Born am I in this land,
Die I wish to as well,
On this land.
Such a land nowhere else you will find,
It is the queen of all lands,
O it is my motherland,
It is my motherland,
It is my motherland.

II

IDENTITY AND SOLIDARITY

Preface to Part II

Identity, awareness, and joint action are unifying qualities in Part II. The chapters show deadening effects when they are suppressed, and life-building strengths when they are awakened and active.

In Chapter 2, Sister Christine Tan recalls to us the uprooting of Filipinos' identity under colonial conquest and the behavior and messages of missionaries. Evangelical arrivals continue in the Philippines in present decades. Her chapter's message to them, to development "experts," to anyone who comes to "help," is profound: "Take off your shoes."

Awakening and solidarity among landless village groups in Bangladesh are demonstrated in Syed Rahim's three narratives in Chapter 3. Voices of irrigation water sellers, "awakening sisters," and forest protectors are presented. The three groups' experiences illustrate the value of communication oriented to collective efforts among the dispossessed and excluded, and the importance of reviving the culture of mutual care and care for nature that people had but which has been eroded. Such communicative and cultural processes are not new, but rooted in the traditional culture of rural Bangladesh where (a) the dialogical and consensual process of decision-making, (b) community cooperation in certain economic and social tasks (e.g., labor exchange, building dams and roads), and (c) community concern and care for individual distress situations were in practice. With polarization of resources and power, these practices got abused and started being dominated and serving the dominant sections, and, therefore, started dying. Facilitated by Proshika, the initiatives described here are reviving these practices in the framework of relatively homogeneous social groupings which preclude these kinds of abuse. They lead not only to poverty alleviation, but to new meaning in people's lives.

Searches for identity and purpose by two minority cultures—single mothers in Canada and the deaf in Thailand—are distinctively described in Chapters 4 and 5. Each group—one defined by family breakup and change in social mores, the other by biological inheritance and cultural "differencing"—suffer handicaps in social status and earning opportunity, with high incidence of poverty. Distinctive in Sharon Taylor's and Owen Wrigley's accounts is that each served as a facilitator in group organization and action. Each moved from the role of outsider to one welcomed by the group, with nuances sensitive to the particular culture and circumstances.

Regaining of self-esteem and vision by Single Moms entailed at once the most outward and most inward practices: teleconferencing and meditation. Sharon actively participated in both. We hear participants' voices, first of despair, then renewal. Development of provincial and Canada-wide support, and frustrating blockages, are described. Participatory processes in recreating community, building meaning and values, are reported. The chapter moves from praxis to concept-building, back to practice, through formation of a community-building model and its testing not only among disadvantaged groups but within academic institutions and social development organizations as well.

The unifying vision of Manfa Suwanarat and her colleagues in building the Thai Deaf Association, and in the major socio-cultural project of elevating Thai Sign to recognition as a distinctive language—with sign, generically—is described with feeling by a sign-learning participant. The significance and effects of the Thai Sign Language Dictionary are explored. The association's hard days following Manfa's tragic death and completion of the project, and the crisis of social mobility and dispersal as members move into conflicted social paths, are recognized. Meanings of this experience for wider social attitudes and practices toward those seen as "different," and for continuing cohesion in group motivation and purpose, are explored.

Evolving parallel, linked expressions of new development paradigms was agreed by members of the 1989 workshop as a promising collaborative opportunity. Anisur Rahman in Chapter 6, concluding Part II, seeks to revalue the term "development" in the face of critics who see its meaning debased by cold war usage. He shows how the dominant practices of donor agencies, and by state institutions whether capitalist or socialist, tend to depersonalize development. In the alternative paradigm he offers, people themselves are the subjects of development. Healthy growth of people's creative faculties, expressions, and social life is central. Reversing vertical paradigms of learning and knowledge generation is crucial in this process. The field of economics, as focused primarily on quantitative measures needs transformation to reflect human impulses of creativity, sharing, and solidarity. A human view, replacing the conventional view of poverty, is offered. Rich instances of such popular fostering of knowledge generation, capacity building, and sharing in Asia and Africa are reported by Anisur Rahman from his direct experience as evidence in validating and articulating the paradigm.

Part II concludes with editorial reflections on self and other, autonomy, and cascading to wider circles of participatory action.

CHAPTER 2

THE FOREIGN MISSIONARY ENTERS FILIPINO SOIL: RECALL THE DISCONNECTIONS

Sister Christine Tan

We the Filipinos were "christianized" by Spanish friars in the name of King Philip II, more than four hundred fifty years ago. We were renamed by them "Philippines," in honor of their Spanish king.

Christianity then meant inclusion into the Roman Catholic Church, by force, by the sword. It meant soldiers and friars, grabbing vast tracts of land from tribal Filipinos who had worked on this land and lived on it for centuries, and making these their own.

I remember a classmate bragging about her grandfather, who according to him, was made to mount a horse, and to ride as far as he could. All the land he covered from sunrise to sundown, was given him, a reward for a noble feat done, in the name of the Spanish throne.

I remember another classmate relating the story of her grandfather, who had the harrowing experience of witnessing the massacre of his family. Spanish soldiers threatened them with death if they did not allow themselves to be baptized. This grandfather hid behind the sofa. There he saw his father, mother, and seven brothers and sisters, stabbed to death, the last one, a baby, thrown up into the air, and caught by the tip of the bayonet.

I also remember this time from my own father, how his parents would be dragged early in the morning to the town proper, there to carry adobe stones, and place them, one on top of the other, to build the church. Decades after, the Catholic Church would boast about the fact that there is no town in the archipelago without a Catholic church—the most prominently located, the most huge, the most expensive in raw materials and in blood.

As years moved on, Christianity meant the mingling of European blood with Malay, through a proliferation of babies produced by friars and soldiers. Most of these babies were named after symbols of Catholicity, such as "Reyes" after the king, "Cruz" after Christianity's cross, "Santos" after all their saints, etc.

Into this kind of Christianity, bastardized, I was born. It was a blind world. Everything the Pope said was considered absolute truth. Everything the Church did was for the good of all people. There was no room for questioning, criticizing. There was no room for non-Catholics.

Even when formal education came through the dedication and tutelage of foreign Sisters other than Spanish, such as those from Germany, France, Belgium, the Netherlands, America, traces of Spanish mangling could not be eradicated by such strong cultures as these.

Through formal education, the spirit of hard work, quality work, love for the arts and music, for the nation, and so on were conveyed. We were very fortunate then, to model our lives after persons whom we thought were perfections of humanity, through the rare Sisters who guided us. Our academic and aesthetic development were assured.

However, while this was true, our own values as Malay, and traditions as Filipino, were swept aside as something foul smelling. English was the official language at home, in school, in government. The spirits of our trees and mountains, our fairies and ancestors were looked on as superstition. In their place, plaster cast images of Italian saints in Italian costumes were hoisted on top of pedestals, while we tried to talk with them, from where we knelt on the ground, through formulae devised by European men.

In this drainingly hot tropics we were made to dress in school like the little German boys, with long sleeved blouses and long white stockings. As a Sister, years later, we dressed like the French nuns with woollen habits and capes. Sometimes I wondered if such decision makers suffered from a dire lack of common sense, but as years passed, and a certain freedom of articulation and analysis developed, I could safely think that this was a case of superiority complex.

We were also brainwashed on false notions of what was right and wrong. Only the Catholic Church was good. Woe to those of other faiths who compose three-fourths of the world, or to the scientist who said something about man descending from the ape. With this kind of education, openness to the rest of the world, to what was beautiful and good but not necessarily Catholic was sadly stunted.

While this formal education progressed, more religious orders penetrated our shores. More started schools, hospitals, first with the poor as their charism inspired, but soon even this inspiration was able to rationalize itself to work more and more with the rich who could send their children to Switzerland for vacation. With cultural control, economic growth followed. The Church, through its religious orders, purchased property, stocks, buildings, eventually making itself a part of the one percent upper crust of the economic ladder of Filipino society.

But the purpose of this paper is not to deal with the past, but to assess as far as one possibly can, the inroads made by the foreign missionary into the Filipino soil, the Filipino soul, particularly through development.

As one who has lived for fourteen years in the slums, among the unwashed and crude, the robbers, rapers, the drug addicts, so they say, the poor, the sick and hungry, my observations may sound harsh. This is not meant.

But this I have to say.

The foreign missionary had a different starting point. He started not where the people were in their customs and beliefs, but in what Europe had to say, particularly, Rome. He also started by "adding," not by discovering what we already had. The missionary added rituals, churches, fears, threats. Perhaps this was the only way because we were never considered equal. And because we were not so, little was spent to find out what treasures we possessed in our hearts and heads, in our traditions and clans, long before the missionary came.

Partially because of this, development was slow and lopsided. Largely through our own fault, we learned to hope that we were like the American—white, big, efficient.

We longed for things we did not have instead of cherishing what we already possessed. While the academic field was the focus of development, other fields such as social consciousness, the great religions of Asia, genuine relationship and family ties were barely alluded to.

Though not intended, "change" to us meant that we must change. It was not two way. We were the target, we had the need. We had to become like "them."

And so, if I were to use the Bible as a measuring stick, to use Jesus who became man, as the model, the missionary's process of integration, and consequently his efforts towards development leave significant gaps.

The past years have made me search for the missionary who has truly integrated with our lives, who developed to be like us, and from this point, has grown together with us.

Rare is the missionary who has left his country, and has taken upon himself the Filipino, as Jesus took upon himself, man. Ordinarily, the missionary keeps his lifestyle, certainly more comfortable than that of the native. He keeps his priorities in the use of resources and of time. He usually does not dirty himself with the mire or language of ordinary persons, and with the dirt, stench of their domiciles. He is not involved in the taut pressures of everyday struggle, with which seventy-five percent of Filipinos cope.

Rare is the missionary who has come poor, who has lived as the majority of the population. More common is the missionary who lives in a building with no problems about the absence of running water, or the hunger pangs of his neighbors whom he does not recognize. While lack of physical space is the primary problem of most Filipinos, the missionary is associated with grounds, cars, free time, sabbatical leaves.

Rare is the missionary who has listened to what we Filipinos say or do not say. Instead, we are deluged with sermons and theology, disjointed from the Christ of our daily lives. When we through sheer hardship can rarely eat meat, the padre sermonizes from the pulpit that we abstain from meat every Friday of Lent, under pain of sin. When we cannot afford to own a single electric light because we cannot afford to pay for the connection with the electric company, the church dazzles with strings of lighted bulbs all over the courtyard and around the Virgin's feet. Rare indeed is the foreign congregation that has not undergone a building spree, as multinationals do.

And when it comes to learning, rare is the missionary who has come to learn, and to harmonize with the Filipino, as the First Asian Bishops Conference articulated, "to be one with the cries, fears, aspirations, dreams of the people."

Today, the pattern is the influx of religious armies from Europe, of evangelists from the States, with the objective of tapping Filipino recruits to increase their membership, as one taps Filipinos for overseas labor. These groups come in droves. In the past twenty years, more congregations have started on our islands, than all the congregations that have come since we were discovered by Magellan in the sixteenth century.

To compound this problem, our women, slowly blooming into awareness on civil rights, liberation theology, women issues, are brainwashed into ultra conservative Western spirituality and values which are neither Asian or poor or freeing. When the Third World cries for liberation, such new congregations scream, "communism." When internal and external conflict threaten nuclear wars and biological warfare, such minds caution charity of judgment. And when one is urged into action on behalf of justice, a reaction is to "wait until I am converted." The tragedy of this is that the Filipino woman usually imbibes all this without a whimper. Such is her development.

Evangelists on the other hand, with powerful voices and deep pockets, equipped with the latest electronic devices, appear like magicians, preaching Jesus and promising cures. Nothing of social injustice is alluded to. Nothing of the falseness of national security, of north-south relationships, of military bases, is touched on. Such indoctrination further numbs the Filipino mind and feet into inaction, into sublime unconcern for her suffering people.

Thus, while this picture of the foreign missionary may seem strongly biased, I am the first to say that there have been some, a striking, inspiring minority, who have stood ten feet tall, who have served well, who have lived simply, who have become as close as possible to us, who have listened to our cries with deep compassion, who have fought our battles together with us, using their internationality as a bulwark and weapon, who have the same enemy and the same source of strength as we do.

Such is the missionary we cry for, we plead to stay with us. This is the missionary who has come and has removed his shoes, because this our soil is sacred, for God has been here long before he has come. This is the missionary who has succeeded in entering Filipino soil and the Filipino soul because he has become little.

CHAPTER 3

GRASSROOTS COMMUNICATIVE ACTION AND CULTURAL RENEWAL: BANGLADESH INITIATIVES

Syed A. Rahim

INTRODUCTION

In South Asia, more than half of the rural population own little or no land or capital, and the number is increasing. This vast population has been marginally benefited from the so-called trickle down effect, if any, of the input supply and service oriented rural development programs for the land owning class of rural population. The massive poverty and related human and social impoverishment of the landless population is a nightmare for national and international development agencies. Politically, it is a hot bed of popular discontent and a potential source of violent movements. The fate of this massive rural landless labor force is central to the problems and prospects of development, democracy and peace in South Asia.

Today, significant rural development programs, particularly among those managed by non-government organizations (NGOs), are aiming directly at this huge rural population mainly composed of wage laborers. For example in Bangladesh, the Grameen Bank, Bangladesh Rural Advancement Committee (BRAC) and Proshika have been able to take rural development to a significant proportion of the landless labor population across the country. These programs have achieved considerable success in organizing different kinds of village level development projects.

These programs use a grassroots-focused development strategy. They start with intensive educational and organizational work at the village level. The assumption is that at the local level group action is essential, because the prevailing economic and social structure of rural society tends to exclude the poorest class from having the necessary social and organizational power needed for local individual initiative. Next, local residents are organized—and organize themselves—into village based small groups or associations to do specific projects for generating income and employment and to give educational and social services to the members.

In this strategy, the task of development communication is defined accordingly to raise people's consciousness and understanding of the conditions of underdevelopment and the necessity of collective action for empowerment. Much depends on how the people define their own problems, assess their resources and capabilities, and set their preferred objectives. Development communication faces a particular challenge in facilitating what Goran Hyden (Hyden 1988) called an emerging *enabling environment.*

An enabling environment is one in which people feel they understand their problem, can deal with it, and make a difference. What appears to be new and strange is not actually so. They can see some connection between what is proposed and their familiar way of doing things. It promotes communication and learning horizontally among groups and communities in comparable conditions facing similar problems. Such communities can be geographically contiguous or far apart but linked by communication media.

In an enabling environment, local knowledge, wisdom, values and norms are respected and given proper recognition. This environment influences the way knowledge, information and resources from outside are interpreted, evaluated and used or rejected by the participants of a development program. The enabling environment is an important factor in the global-national-local interaction in today's world of development.

Development communication at the grassroots, communication from and to and among the participants, produces the dynamics of the enabling environment of a development project. The participants' own expression of what development means to them, how they see their action being meaningful and productive, what outcomes they value and like to talk about and share with others, are important factors influencing the nature and direction of social change. In this context, the participants' development communication is both an agent and an indicator of change.

The main objective of this paper is to identify and interpret the development participants' experience and articulation of change that they themselves trigger and construct by their own participation, action and reaction in the context of specific development projects. In brief, this is a study of development communication and change from the participants' perspective.

THREE GRASSROOTS NARRATIVES

First, I want to present three narratives or texts of development communication by project participants themselves. I have constructed these texts by selecting and translating relevant statements and messages from 30 tape-recorded development discourses. During June-July 1990 I visited rural development projects in Bangladesh and talked with people about their own projects. They told me their stories in informal small group meetings in their own villages. I call these recorded stories the participants' development discourses.

The narratives or texts are my selection, translation and summary of representative statements of the participants in their own words. The 30 projects I visited were of three main kinds: irrigation projects, women's projects, and social forestry projects. Accordingly, I have constructed three texts, in each case bringing together relevant utterances of the participants from more than one project. I did not make any judgement as to what was significant and what was not. Anything they said about their development problems and projects was relevant. The main purpose of my selection was to eliminate duplication and condense the themes and messages.

I have arranged the material in a narrative from, in each case using the most informative story as a model and the main frame to which I added utterances from other discourses of the same category. What I have done essentially is to construct "generalized" texts from specific discourses (Clifford 1988). Common and distinctive themes and messages of the stories are woven into the texts. These themes and messages capture the participants' understanding and articulation of what development is, how they are trying to shape it, and how all that is bringing different kinds of change in their lives.

I present the narratives in the words of people who are at the farthest receiving end of national development programs. These groups are conducting various development activities supported by a non-government organization (NGO) called Proshika Manobik Unnayan Kendra, a development agency working at the grassroots. Proshika calls itself a human development agency (Rahaman 1986). It focuses on training, rural credit, small-scale irrigated agriculture and social forestry projects. One of its more distinctive approaches is the promotion and use of folk and popular cultural activities in raising people's consciousness and understanding of the conditions of underdevelopment and how those can be surmounted (Karim et al. 1986).

Proshika works with organized rural and urban groups of laborers having no or very little land or capital. Such a group, organized as a development association at the village or ward level, is locally called a *samity*. Some *samities* are managing small-scale irrigation schemes and selling water to farmers. Others are protecting forests around the villages or managing small nurseries and planting trees along road sides and embankments. Some of the women's groups are raising poultry and livestock or manufacturing building materials to meet local needs.

The Water Sellers

The people in my village are these ten fingers of my hands. Six out of ten are poor and landless; seven out of ten are illiterate. Those who own five or more acres of cultivated land are rich compared to our condition. They are like the two thumbs, the influential families in the village. We are under their hold. Most of us have only a little homestead. We are poor, illiterate and divided.

Not long ago our condition was truly desperate. In order to survive and to escape starvation, we had to slave for the rich landowners. For all practical purposes we were bonded laborers. We had no voice at all in deciding the conditions of our employment. We were treated as inferior humans. Some of them openly used harsh and abusive language to intimidate us. They called us not by our names, but such derogatory terms as *fakiranir pula* (son of a destitute woman) or *chakranir pula* (son of a maidservant). Their women negligently cooked beggar's chow to feed us at the end of a hard day's work. Boiled broken-grain rice with chili paste and salt, maybe a little fried vegetable, that was all they gave us. The wage was very low, not enough to buy rice for the whole family.

Even that low wage was not paid regularly without further exploitation. The owner would say, "You want your money now, you want cash? Then come with me at once, carry this basket to the market, I've to sell this bag of rice to pay you cash." After selling the bag of rice he would shop around, buying fish and vegetable, ordering me to carry his grocery basket and warning me not to steal anything. Then when the market was almost closed he would start returning home urging me to walk ahead of him with his shopping basket on my head. If I asked, "Sir, what about my money?" he would become angry for my impatience and impertinence.

How did I manage to survive? Well, among other things I managed by *ko-re bo-re*. What's kore bore? It's an idiom we use to make fun at ourselves. It means doing nothing but borrowing a few bucks from this relative, a tool from that friend, a cup of rice or oil from the neighbor; repaying these small obligations in kind by lending them a hand to help in their domestic chores; borrowing from one to repay an earlier debt to another.

Have we succeeded in stopping that kind of exploitation and injustice? Well, we have just built a fence for our protection. We formed this *samity* in 1983. We have 19 members in our group. There are three other groups in our village. First, the field worker from Proshika came to talk with us. He said that we should try to understand our conditions and the particular social and economic contexts of exploitation and injustice. We should meet regularly and discuss and debate among ourselves to sharpen our own collective understanding. If we need information and explanations he would try to help.

One day we went to another village where several Proshika groups were managing an irrigation scheme for rice fields. We asked a lot of questions about the costs, risks, difficulties and actual returns from selling water to farmers in irrigation schemes. We were quite impressed by what we saw and heard. We had seen irrigation schemes before. Our idea was that machine irrigation is only for farmers who have plenty of land. It never occurred to us that we could operate irrigation schemes to sell water to the farmers. We saw something new and promising.

In the evening there was a dramatic performance by local artists. They presented a skit showing how old man Zamir had to sell his land to pay dowry in getting his daughter married and how her husband Aziz again lost that money. Aziz was duped by a city tout who promised him a job in Singapore. He put Aziz on a plane supposedly bound for Singapore. But, actually it was an internal flight to Chittagong (the eastern port city of Bangladesh). There was no job waiting for him there. Except the first plane ride of his life everything else went wrong. At the end there were two bitter poor men—Zamir who lost his land to pay dowry and Aziz who lost that money to pay for his greed.

On our way back home we talked about irrigation and the drama skit. We agreed that we need to be very careful. We must take risks, but we should do better if we work together.

First I discussed the idea with a few close friends. Then I consulted the chairman of a neighboring irrigation group. He said, "Discuss with your people and if you can get 10 or 12 persons interested, invite a Proshika worker to a village meeting."

After many nights of discussions and debates, 16 members of our group agreed to start a scheme with Proshika's help. We started our project in the Autumn of 1985. But it was not easy. The landowners were suspicious of our activities. They were saying, "What the hell are those thieves doing meeting every night, conspiring under darkness? How can they operate an irrigation pump, those paupers?"

We borrowed money from Proshika's Revolving Loan Fund, bought a used diesel pump and installed it over an old inactive tubewell. Four of us attended training courses at the Proshika's Koitta Training Center. We negotiated hard with the landowning farmers. They wanted to pay a low fixed rent for water, after the harvest. They said that the rate could not be higher because of the high risk of crop damage by flood or insufficient irrigation. We wanted a fixed share of the harvested crop. Finally an agreement was reached. We would supply water to their rice plots, taking care of a rotating schedule of pump operation and the digging and maintenance of water distribution channels. In return they would give us one quarter of the harvested paddy crop on the field.

After the agreement was reached, we made a plan for digging water distribution channels and a schedule of operating the pump machine. We knew the fields like the palm of our hands. Yet, it was very difficult to take water to every paddy plot of individual owners because of the highly fragmented and scattered distribution of small plots. Sometimes we had to dig a drain at the edge of land owned by people from other villages who did not join the project. Getting permission from them needed endless meetings and persuasion.

During the first three years we made very little profit. The pump machine gave a lot of trouble. We could not get spare parts in time. The farmers who did not get enough water were angry and refused to pay water rent, our full share of the harvested crop. But we worked hard to repay the loan installments. We really tightened our belt. Then came the great flood of September, 1988, which devastated us. A big sum of overdue loan accumulated. Some members left the *samity*. We thought we were finished.

But we managed to survive and revive the *samity*. We had another round of discussion and debate, advice from Proshika, and finally decided last year to go for a new electric pump. Now we have very few breakdown problems. But sometimes the electric line goes dead without notice. Then we have to run to the engineer's office at the sub-district center, and spend some extra money to get attention and service in time. We don't know how the electric supply system works, it is beyond our control. But it is better than before. This year we have 35 acres under our irrigation scheme. The crop condition is good. We expect to get our share of rice worth at least Taka 40,000. Not a big profit, but enough to repay the overdue loan and the current loan installments and to keep us going and making new efforts.

Finding good drinking water is a problem in our area. Last winter we installed a hand pump tubewell for drinking water. You can see it from here, it has a cement base and it works. Jamiruddin takes care of it; he attended a training class at Proshika.

Our relationship with the landowner class has changed somewhat. They depend on us for irrigation water, we depend on them for our income. So there is better understanding now, and businesslike relationship. No, they do not invite us to their wedding ceremonies, but we attend their funeral ceremony prayers at the mosque, invited or not.

We have committees at the village and the Union (local government administrative unit) to coordinate activities of different groups. If there is an emergency, a few hundred members can assemble in a short notice to deal with that problem. This unity is our strength. We have been able to settle with the employers an informal standard of a minimum rate of daily wage for our labor. The rate changes with market conditions.

We have gained some recognition and respect in the village society. Now they call us by our names. "Manik, I want to fix the roof of my cowshed; can you come tomorrow with another worker?" "Karim, when will you start the pump today? Have you seen that large plot of mine at the end of the first drain? Does it need more water?"

Now, the village *matabbars* (traditional leaders) invite us to *salish* meetings for local arbitration and settlement of disputes. We go and sit down at the back. We keep quiet if we think that justice is being done. Otherwise, we do raise our united voice. And they have started to listen to us. This is a real change.

We meet almost every week, make small deposits in our saving fund of the association, discuss our problems and plans, settle minor dispute among members and decide what to do if a member complains that he or someone in his family has been harrassed or treated unjustly by somebody in the village. We have settled two cases where the groom's father wanted excessive dowry. We talk about our children's education and health; urge every member to send their children to school regularly. Most do.

Our saving fund has now a balance of Taka 5000. We are building our own capital, very slowly now, but hope do better in future. At present this fund gives us some confidence, and a means to meet emergencies.

Last winter my daughter got married. I could not afford to give her a wedding sari. I could not borrow money, didn't want to request the *samity* for help. One day the chairman came to my house and said,"Aminuddin, we talked about your problem. We are concerned about it because it is a matter of prestige for the whole community. So, the *samity* has decided to give your daughter a gift. Here is 200 Taka, go to Manikganj bazaar and buy a sari for her."

We take our weekly meetings seriously. If a member cannot attend he must inform in advance. Every member is free to talk, ask questions, make arguments, criticize the group's work, and be responsible to meet his own obligation. This is how we maintain our group identity. The meetings are not always nice and amicable. People get angry, argue vigorously and shout at each other. One day two members lost control and exchanged blows right in the meeting. But later they apologized to other members.

We talk about what more needs to be done. We also do our day dreaming. Can we save and borrow enough money to buy more pumps and tractors to expand this business? Or should we aim at establishing a small factory to manufacture consumer goods?

During the last election of the Union Council we decided in a meeting to put up our own candidate, Azizur Rahman, this young man here. He is not as poor as we are. But he is our man.

Rahman: I own about three acres of land, actually my father is the owner. I graduated from Manikganj college, three years ago. I can't find a good job. I have been helping the group as much as I can. I think I understand the poor people's problems; I like to fight for their cause.

We supported him, and he won. This is the first time we have our own elected man in the Union Council. Now, anytime the union council receives funds or relief goods from the government our member keeps us informed and fights for our share of distribution. We think now there will be less corruption and misuse of funds. Our next target is the national assembly election. But that will require consultation and agreement among many villages, and a lot of election work.

The Awakening Sisters

Who gets the most delicious serving of Rui fish curry? Please ask my dear husband. He's there, standing at the back, that man with a grin on his face. Yes, he enjoys the delicacy, the fishhead. most of the time. I love to see him feel satisfied.

But it was different before, when he was the only bread earner. He didn't earn enough for our bare survival. Then he was an angry man. When he lost his temper and hit me hard I only cried. I had no place to go, nothing to say. Now I've changed and he has changed. We fight with words only. He'll not dare hit me again.

He is happy because he can indulge in a few things he always wanted, like having more time for fishing. But, he helps me in doing domestic chores.

Yes, I do. When my wife is busy with the project work, I take care of the children, walk them to school. After the flood, when the public health man came I went to him with the children and mother. He gave all of us the needle against Cholera. Yes, I wash the dishes and do laundry, when she is not home. Sometimes I cook, at least rice and lentil. I know that much of cooking.

People ask me, "Ayesha, you're so smallboned and thin. Where do you get the strength to do the heavy masonry work for your project?" This is silly. When you came this morning you saw us five sisters casting a sanitary latrine slab. We're strong enough to do that. We're used to hard labor. Didn't we dig and haul dirt in the road-building project under the "Food for Work" public works program? The Americans gave wheat for that program. We earned that by our labor. This is hard work too. But we're making profit. Who are we? We're the 17 awakening sisters of this project. We're 17 members in this women's *samity*.

We have eight *samities* in this area. Our *samity* is the oldest, seven years old. After the great flood (1988), we got a small contract to make RCC posts used in building flood- and storm-proof houses under a CARE project. We borrowed Taka 111,000 from Proshika, bought two sets of forms, iron rods and concrete for casting reinforced concrete posts. We made 650 posts and sold them at Taka 200 each. Made a good profit. That was a very good beginning.

Unfortunately, now there is no demand for RCC posts, no more house building around here, no government program to continue CARE's lead. We've shifted to this small business of making sanitary latrine slabs. We're told that there is much demand for latrine slabs. We don't know why. Probably, the government or a foreign agency has started a new program. We can make profit so long there is demand for latrine slabs. But we don't know how long it'll last. So, we've started discussing ideas for other projects. We're thinking about the dairy business. Nothing big. Each one of us can keep a few cows in our homes and jointly sell milk to Savar Dairy. We need capital to buy good cows. Of course there's the risk that some of the cows may die from epidemic disease. People die, animals die. We're used to taking risks.

We've learned to walk. Initially Proshika held our hands, like the mother teaching her child how to walk. We don't need that any more. We've learned well how to walk and negotiate obstacles. Now the question is which road should we take? If we want to go to Dhaka, we take the highway. What is development's highway? How do we best decide where to go and which road to take? What kinds of machines can we get? For that we still need help and advice from Proshika. We must continue to meet, to discuss and debate among ourselves, no matter how long it takes to come to agreements. We are illiterate, but we can talk and argue, agree or disagree. For us it is very important to understand things and work together. We should never fight with one another. We must shun violence of any kind.

We've learned how to sign our names. That's useful, but not enough. I'm our *samity's* treasurer, but I don't know how to keep account books. Well, it's all in my head. My memory is sharp, so far I have made no mistakes. But written account keeping is very important. My son who is an eight-grader maintains the *samity's* account book. We've a plan to open a school so that all of us adults can learn reading and writing and accounting. As regards our children, we send every one of them to school. We are very particular about this. If you are a member of our *samity* you have to send your child to school, no excuse. Also, we talk about not having children every year or so; about "planning family," as the lady from Proshika explains it to us. Yes, most of us also practice, more or less. It's not difficult to get the things. It's more difficult to get husband's cooperation.

We the women members do all that's necessary to run the *samity*—attending meetings, making small-saving deposits, going to the brick field and the cement shop for estimating and buying cement and other materials, renting trucks for hauling, transacting business at Kamta bank, attending training classes at the Koitta Center.

I'm responsible for collecting loan repayments due from all the *samities* in this area and depositing the amount to the local office of Proshika. That's a big responsibility. No, I'm not afraid of mugging. There's a danger, but the way I do it nobody can guess I'm carrying a big sum of money. "There goes the little shy woman scurrying, she's scared somebody will catch her." That's what the big men would say. No, this woman is not scared at all. Yes, I try to do my work well. I don't depend on others.

We organize cultural activities. In 1987 we staged a little play— we called it the people's drama. Our member Razia, this young woman sitting right here, she's a sweet voice. She got the part of Renu. It's a singing part. We cooked *Khituri* and invited the village *matabbars*. All of them came to eat dinner. Most of them stayed on to see the drama. It's a hilarious story about how the moneylenders grab land from the poor. How a clever poor man named Raju fooled a greedy old moneylender who's desperate to marry Renu, the village maiden Raju loved. Everybody enjoyed it.

Next day the *matabbars* called us to a village meeting. They wanted to try and reprimand us for our "shameful" behavior. They accused Razia of violating the Pardah and for "her act of singing in public, which is forbidden in Islam." We refused to attend the meeting. We organized a protest. We the members of eight groups, which included some of the *matabbar's* wives and daughters, got together. We said, "Whom are you going to try and punish? Here we are, try us all. You are the village leaders because we accept you as leaders. In return we want fair hearing and just treatment. And don't forget that election is coming. You know that now we cast our votes." Then they backed up and said, "All right, this time you are excused. But you do it again and we'll certainly punish you." Since that confrontation our prestige in our families and in the villages has markedly increased. No longer we're ignored or maltreated as poor labor class women.

This's not the only village having women's *samity*. You'll find them in other villages too. They're groups organized by different NGOs—Proshika groups, Grameen Bank groups, BRAC groups. Some of these groups meet regularly and talk about their work and everyday life. Even if nothing else happens these meetings are very good for us poor village women. It gives us an opportunity to be together as birds of the same feather. When together and united we feel a new sense of identity, of confidence and courage. We know that our children will have a better life than us. May be we're sowing the seeds of that life, God willing. We pray to Allah, please let this thing grow and spread across the whole country to awaken all our poor sisters.

The Forest Protectors

This is the *Sal* woodland we're protecting. We've four more woodlots. In this village we've six groups, six *samities*, a total of 90 members. We're protecting these five woodlots. About 300 acres of forest owned by the government forest department. Here we're 20 to 25 members assembled to meet you. Our *samity* has 15 members, most of them are here. The rest are from other *samities*.

Ten years ago we had few *Sal* trees on these lots, only stumps. The forest was devastated due to mindless cutting by contractors and local fuelwood traders. There are many deforested lots in this area. Not all of them are now protected. You can easily see which ones are protected. Look at this woodlot. The trees are about ten years old. Look, how nice they look. The shade under them is deep and cool. Now we have a place to escape from the harsh summer sun. The birds are coming back. Once there were peacocks, deers, wild boars and even a few tigers in the *Sal* forest of our country. If we bring that forest back the peacocks and tigers may come back. There'll be more rain. There'll be more timber for building our houses, furniture and implements, and there'll be no shortage of fuelwood.

A great deal of forest land had been illegally encroached by both the rich and poor people. The forest department is trying to recover some of that for commercial replanting. They don't want to antagonize the rich and powerful people. Our union council chairman owns a small woodlot, which is actually *Khas* land, government property. But, it's the poor who are under pressure. When the forest was large and there was much cutting by the rich farmers and the contractors, it was the poor laborers who did the actual work. Yes, we helped in destroying the forest.

Our livelihood depended on the forest. It's all of us, both the rich and the poor, who destroyed the forest, but now the poor suffer more than the rich.

The forest officers say that these *Sal* woodlots are degraded. The medicine plants we value so much—the *Amloki*, *Haritaki* and *Boira* trees—they think are useless. They are uprooting those few remaining trees in the new plantation areas. They are destroying our medicinal herbs and plants. But when we go to the Thana dispensary there is no medicine available there.

They brought scientists and experts who made surveys and experiments. Now they have a big World Bank project. They're building big nurseries where new species of plants are available. They want to make big commercial plantations. But will they be able to protect their forests without our help? We don't understand why we can't have our traditional *Sal* woodlots as our community property. We know and can protect the community forests. These lots will meet most of our day-to-day needs. They can have their plantation forests and we can have our community woodlot too. Why not?

Now the forest officials are talking about community woodlots and telling us about the new species. They want to replace the *Sal* specie altogether by digging out the old stumps and planting saplings of the new species. That's much too difficult work, and we even don't know what will be the results. We simply let the *Sal* coppice grow out of the old stumps, do the necessary pruning and cleaning. And then we protect the plants. That's not much investment, not much immediate return. But we get our fuelwood from occasional pruning and collecting fallen leaves. When the forest matures we'll get lumber for house building and furniture making.

Most of all these woodlots are a part of our life, our tradition. We benefit materially. There is also a spiritual meaning. Many spirits live in the forest, good and bad. Then there are the birds and the animals, and the traditional medicinal herbs and roots. The forest department people don't consider all these things. Why do they listen more to the foreigners than to us?

I want to try new species. When the forest department promoted *Eucalyptus* I planted some around my and my brother's homestead. Now they say it is not a good specie. I want to try the new ones. In a year or two we'll know how good are those species. Then, if all of us want to do that can the forest department supply enough saplings?

They've a new scheme of community forestry. They didn't consult us in making that scheme. The forest officer said that the project was funded by the Asian Development Bank. The Bank insisted that the project must plant only approved new species. According to their scheme the participants will be selected by the Union Councils and the Upazila Parisads. The cultivators will get 50 percent of the final forest crops. The problem with that scheme is that we don't know much about the new species and how and where will those be planted. It seems that only a few individual poor laborers can be involved in the scheme and the poor landless community won't have any voice in decision making.

Maybe they are right. Maybe we should listen to them and try out the new varieties. If we do plant new varieties in the woodlots we're protecting now, who'll own the trees? Who'll have the right to use the products? How much of it and when?

These questions bother us. We want to discuss those and make contracts with the local government and the forest department. Before the election, the Union Council chairman was speaking on our behalf. Now we don't see him any more. So we wait for him till the next election. The local forest officers say that they agree with us, but such matters are not for them to settle. It requires policy decisions at the highest level. We hear that the minister and the secretary are in our favor, but most of the top forest technocrats and bureaucrats are against us. What can we poor people do?

We meet every Wednesday, deposit Taka 2.00 per head in our small savings account. Our total savings now is more than ten thousand Taka. We've used this fund to reclaim mortgaged land of our members. We use it to help out our members in emergencies. To buy books for our children who now go to school. Once a year we organize a festival and invite artists from other *samities* to sing songs and stage drama.

I plan our forest protection work. Every member donates time. I organize a team of three to guard the forest for two consecutive days, then the next team takes over. Also, the children are always there, keeping watch. We talk about the ways and means of improving our income and our social position in society. We talk about social norms and disciplines essential to maintain our unity and integrity. We know that we are still dependent in many ways on the rich farmers and on government agencies we don't control. As individuals we're very weak. But our *samities* and the coordination committees at the Union and Upazila level are forging stronger relation among ourselves. We're much less isolated and less vulnerable now. That's our strength in facing oppression and injustice. Not that we spend a great deal of time in those meetings and discussions. We don't have an office or by-laws. But we do it seriously. We try very hard to avoid disagreement among ourselves. Sometimes we fight bitterly in the meeting. Our group leader is a wise and honest person. He patiently guides us to agreement by reason. Because we now know that that's the way to gain some power and prestige in our own society.

The day-to-day forest protection is not a heavy workload, not now anymore. People in this area know that many village groups are protecting the forest. The children keep watch and if they see anything suspicious they run home to report to their parents. Twice we caught miscreants cutting trees. We handed them over to the forest office. The word has spread. The miscreants are now afraid to cut trees in the protected woodlots. But we keep on watching on a regular basis. Once in every year or two we organize labor teams to do the pruning and cleaning under the supervision of the forest officers. We contribute voluntary labor, in return we get all of pruned materials. So far that's the benefit. Occasionally we allow people to cut down one or two trees to meet emergencies, such as repair of a damaged home after a severe storm. We don't inform the forest officer about those cuttings.

Now that we're active groups and more united than ever before we've more responsibilities that go beyond forest protection. In some ways we're also protecting our community of the poor landless laborers. We're protecting our families and friends from exploitation and mistreatment. We're fighting against the dowry system, excessive interest in moneylending, and forced low wage rates. We do come in to conflict with other interest groups and classes of people. That's why it's so important to have those Union and Upazila coordination committees. But so far we've avoided major troubles. We listen to Proshika's advice and seek help from the union council and Upazila council. We know, we have a long way to go and we can't do that alone.

INTERPRETATION AND DISCUSSION

A striking feature of the above narrative texts is that each of them represents a holistic picture of development and change. The common interwoven yarns of that tapestry include economic enterprise, technology, identity, self-esteem, politics, interclass relationship, social conflicts, group solidarity, education, health, social reform, cultural and entertainment activities. It is clear from these texts that the grassroots participants do experience, construct and articulate the meaning of development and change in multiple dimensions and in the context of their own communities. But before any further elaboration of this, it is necessary to address two valid questions.

First, is this holistic feature and its different aspects a result of my asking leading questions during the meetings with the participants? The answer is negative. The only leading question, if any, was imbedded in my request at the very beginning of my meetings with the village participants. I said that I came as a student to learn, as much as they can tell me, about their project and experience. Second, is it not possible that my intervention, the translation of the discourse into text, generated the holistic feature of the text? The answer is again negative. Because, in the original tape-records of my interviews the holistic feature is present in almost all the cases. My intervention did nothing more than accentuate in the text the holistic feature already present in the discourse.

It is then valid to conclude from a reading of the texts that the participants at the grassroots experience and understand development as an interwoven process of economic, social, political and cultural change. How they view the dynamics of that process? What do we see in the sample texts that help us understanding the dynamics of change? The following notes on different dimensions of the participants' development experience may provide some answers to these questions.

A New Identity

The emerging identity of landless laborers, their emancipation from the feudal yoke to free labor, is a dominant theme in the texts. This is highlighted in discourse by frequent use of the we/they metaphor for the rural class structure as experienced and imagined by the participants. In the case of the Awakening Sisters a new gender identity of the poor Bengali village women is forcefully communicated. In the case of the Forest Protectors the nature/culture duality is deemphasized, without invoking the notion of "the noble savage." The new identity is institutionalized in the group organization or *samity*. One member explained this succinctly, "We take our weekly *samity* meeting seriously. If a member can't attend he must inform in advance. Every member is free to talk, ask questions, make arguments, criticize the group's work and be responsible to meet his own obligation. This is how we maintain our group identity."

The new identity comes with a significant degree of self-esteem and empowerment. Ayesha of the Awakening Sisters expressed this well in telling her own story: "Now I've changed and my husband has changed. We fight with words only. Never again he'll dare to hit me."

The formation of groups seems to be a powerful mode of production of self-esteem and empowerment. "When together and united we feel a new sense of identity, confidence and courage," said one member. On the other hand the frequency of first-person utterances in the texts suggests that the group formation does not dominate individuality.

Class Struggle

The economic activities undertaken by the participant groups have been instrumental in sharpening the understanding of their own class identity and relationships with other classes. Out of that an informed strategy of class struggle seems to be emerging. This is a strategy of "defense" and "diplomacy." The "defense" strategy is to protect individuals from exploitation. As one participant said, "We have just built a fence for our protection." Their own *samity*, the village organization, and alliance with other village organizations is the protective fence. The "diplomacy" is for negotiating businesslike arrangements with the landowning class and the government bureaucracy.

The participants are more confident in negotiating business with the local landowners and traders, in fixing water charges, wage rates, and supply of materials. They know these people and their business operations. They have learned how to make credit and training arrangements with Proshika through its field workers who visit them frequently. They can also deal with local officials of the government organizations. But when it comes to dealing with the distant government or corporate bureacracy they are helpless. They need intermediaries like Proshika.

The class struggle has actually improved relations between the landless laborers and the landowners by reducing the scope of arbitrary despotic action and exploitation. The nature of social differentiation has become more transparent to different classes. As one member of the irrigation group said, "They depend on us for irrigation water, we depend on them for our income. So there is a better understanding now, and business-like relationship."

Economic Enterprise

The three examples of economic enterprise—irrigation water selling, concrete slab manufacturing and reforestation—show that the landless laborer class has entrepreneurs. They are willing to take risks and try innovations. What they lack most is capital and supporting services. This is why access to rural credit and managerial and technical support services at the local level are crucial in development programs for the landless laborers.

The credit operation of Proshika (and other NGOs) does not follow the conventional bank credit policy of collateral. The landless laborers have no assets to offer as collateral, hence they are not eligible for bank credit. The NGOs credit programs depend on social responsibility, hence the need for giving loans to a group, not to individuals. The group decides how to distribute the loan money to individuals and for joint activities. The group is responsible for repayment. Actually, the repayment rate of Proshika loan is very good. This is also the case for the other two NGO programs. The credit policy is working very well. The problem seems to be how to create extensive productive investment opportunities. This is the realm of macroeconomic policy.

At present the technological opportunity is very limited. The rural women groups have fewer opportunities. Mostly, they are thinking about projects in the traditional line of growing vegetables, raising poultry or keeping cows in the homestead. At this level it is very difficult to raise productivity. The NGOs' intermediary role in linking the rural groups with scientific and technological resources is weak, partly because those resources are lacking or not oriented toward rural development problems. The low level of literacy and education of the rural groups is a serious constraint. Again here, macroeconomic policy is crucial in dealing with the problems.

The borrowed capital investment can hardly generate, after repaying loans and interests at the market rate, sufficient income to have adequate savings for further investment. Even a small natural calamity can destroy the delicate balance. Yet, the loan repayment record of the landless laborer group is as high as 95 percent, much better than the land owner farmers.

Education and Health

Education is highly valued in rural Bangladesh. People who can afford take advantage of the meagre educational services available in the rural area. The landless agricultural laborers have been reluctant to send their children to school because they need them to work in the informal economy to gather fuelwood, edible greens and roots from the woods and to catch fish from the streams and ponds. These activities require considerable investment of time because those free goods are scarce and there is fierce competition in gathering them.

In all our three narratives we can see a clear indication of a very significant change. Now in these villages the children are going to school, and the practice of sending children to school is being institutionalized through the village association. One of the Awakening Sisters made it quite explicit, "We are very particular about this. If you are a member of our *samity* you have to send your child to school, no excuse." The adults are also eager to get some formal education. This was recognized quite early by one of the main NGOs, the Bangladesh Rural Advancement Committee (BRAC). Now the demand is high and BRAC is expanding its education program. All other NGOs are adopting the same strategy. Their success will depend on the macro education policy and national investment in education in the rural areas.

Drinking water is a primary cause of many health problems, including diarrhea and dysentery, suffered by the rural poor. In the past, the government gave grants to the Union Council for sinking drinking water tubewells. In most cases, the tubewells were sunk near the houses of influential persons, who did not take care of the maintenance of the wells. Now in many villages where there are organized associations, sinking a tubewell for drinking water is one of their priority projects. These tubewells are placed in easily accessible locations and properly maintained. During my visit I saw many of them and drank the water.

The condition of general health service is another matter. There is an acute shortage of modern health services—doctors, nurses and medicine, in the rural areas. Traditional medicine is dead, mainly because the supply of indigenous herbs and plant products is scarce. Since the trade is dying there is no systematic reproduction of traditional knowledge from the older to the new generation of practitioners of medicine.

As regards family planning and birth control, the real issue is no longer the availability of information or supplies in the villages participating in rural development programs. The key factors seem to be employment, changing social identity, and social and gender relations.

Culture and Politics

In every village I visited, a few women, men and children were eager to demonstrate how they use popular culture in development communication. They presented songs, acts of comedy and social dramas. The performances were spontaneous and spirited. The messages ranged from direct development talk to highly poetic expression of pain and hope. For example, one song humorously narrated various steps in the operation and maintenance of an irrigation pump machine. Another song was powerful blue music from the heart of a poor woman abandoned by her husband and society.

Politically sensitive cultural expression, encouraged and promoted by Proshika communication strategy, is an effective instrument of solidarity. It is a means of contesting existing social norms and practices, confronting the power structure with the intent to change those in a democratic fashion by showing popular support. The Awakening Sisters, in their confrontation with traditional village leaders, demonstrated this clearly, "Whom are you going to try and punish? Here we are, try us all. You are the village leaders because we accept you as leaders. In return we want fair hearing and just treatment. And don't forget that election is coming. You know that now we cast our votes."

For a long time, rural people experienced a form of representative democracy through local government first introduced by the British colonial administration. The Union Council is the basic unit of that system. However, the local government has very little local governing power. It is the local instrument of a powerful remote central government. Government resources and relief supplies reach the village level through the Union Council and other departmental local offices. Since the landless population is not directly represented in the local government, their interest is not served adequately by that institution.

Now that is changing. We saw an example in the case of the Water Sellers. They have their own man in the Union Council. The women have started to exercise their voting rights. The Forest Protectors are pressing for direct negotiation with forest department officials. These are signs of real democracy taking roots in the rural sites.

CONCLUSION

The interpretation of texts constructed from development discourse at the grassroots level shows an emerging trend of rural development in Bangladesh. This trend is an emerging holistic pattern of development where economic, social, cultural and political change are interlinked in a dynamic system. There is a clear sign of some environmental consciousness and a strong sense of emancipation among the women participants. The texts reveal how culture interacts with economic and political factors. Textual interpretation makes it possible to conduct a cultural study of development without quantitative analysis.

Coming from the development participants' life world experience, this knowledge of holistic development presents an "interdisciplinary" and nonreductionist reality. It shows that in every case examined the dynamics of development action is sustained by a combination of economic, social, cultural and political forces, not in any complex abstract way, but in specific identifiable instances. The participants are able to articulate that picture in verbal communication in a group situation in their village contexts. Thus, development communication becomes both an agent and an index of change.

If this is at least partly a result of the development program (Proshika Manobik Unnayan Kendra) in which a culturally sensitive communication strategy was used to generate local initiative and collective action, then we could expect similar results in other places and countries where the same strategy is adopted. Verification of this assumption through further research will move us toward a social theory of grassroots development, which is necessary in making sound rural development policies and programs.

END NOTE

Revised slightly and reproduced with a new title, with the author's and journal editor's permission. Original published in *The Journal of Development Communication*, Number 2, Volume Four, December 1993.

BIBLIOGRAPHY

Cernea, Michael M. 1988. *Nongovernmental Organizations and Local Development*. The World Bank, Washington D.C.: The World Bank.

Clifford, James. 1988. *The Predicament of Culture: Twentieth-century Ethnography, Literature and Art*. Harvard: Harvard University Press.

Holloway, Marguerite and Paul Wallich. 1992. "The Analytical Economist: A Risk Worth Taking." *Scientific American*.

Hyden, Goran. 1988. "Preface." In: John Burbidge (ed.), *Approaches that Work in Rural Development*. Institute of Cultural Affairs International, Brussels. Munchen: K.G. Saur Verlag.

Karim, Mahbubul, Shah Newaz and Azizur Rahman Asad. 1986. *An Endeavour: Proshika in Alternative Development*. Dhaka: Proshika Manobik Unnayan Kendra.

Rahaman, Reza Shamsur. 1986. *A Praxis in Participatory Rural Development*. Dhaka: Proshika Manobik Unnayan Kendra.

CHAPTER 4

SINGLE MOTHERS UNITING AGAINST POVERTY

Sharon Taylor

Single parent families have become increasingly common in New-foundland and Labrador. In 1986, 12,640 families in this province were female-led, 47 percent due to divorce or separation and 44 per-cent widowed. Teenage pregnancies are higher in Newfoundland and Labrador than in the rest of Canada, with the highest rate in western Newfoundland and Labrador where, in 1984, 19 percent of mothers were teens. Female-led single parent families are financially worse off than male-led single parents or two parent families. Seven of 10 children in female-led families were below the poverty line in 1986, compared with less than two in 10 children in two parent families.

SINGLE MOTHERS UNITING: ORGANIZATION AND PROCESS

In the fall of 1986, the Women's Division of the Secretary of State for Canada funded a workshop in Corner Brook for 12 mothers from across Newfoundland and Labrador. I began the journey with these 12 women as the workshop facilitator. Our experiences as a group began with the workshop, and we all became founding mem-bers of the organization we called Single Moms Against Poverty (SMAP). I moved from facilitator to group member in the first few years of the group's development. My position was quite different from many of the group's membership, most of whom were living below the poverty line. However, my experiences of having grown up in poverty in an isolated rural community assisted us in overcoming the barriers created by my present advantaged position as professor in the province's only university.

The Founding Workshop

One of the objectives of the workshop for single mothers was to examine the impact of the social services system in the lives of these women. Few of the women had previously participated in any sort of workshop experience. Several were somewhat anxious. Taking this into consideration, the focus was on developing an environment which would diminish anxiety and create opportunities for sharing.

To begin with, the participants were invited to engage in a simulation exercise called "Poverty Game." The Poverty Game was developed by single mothers in British Columbia in an attempt to raise the awareness of the impact of poverty on mothers and their children. The game was composed of two sections. In the first part, the participants are assigned the roles of single mothers on social assistance and are given their life circumstances. As the participants play the game, the demands on their limited resources increase and the choices available to them diminish. Throughout the game, most attempts made to the Department of Social Services for additional funds are met with offers of help in budgeting or child rearing classes. Frequently participants are weeping with frustration, anger, and helplessness by mid-day. While this game is intended to identify to professionals the immobilization and helplessness created by poverty, it is also helpful to the single moms themselves. It validates their experience and allows for the release of tension, anger, hurt, and powerlessness. This is followed by a discussion of their feelings of powerlessness and subsequent diminishing of self-esteem.

In the workshop at Corner Brook, the women moved quickly out of their roles into discussing the reality of their own lives. Women spent the first afternoon sharing their stories, sometimes laughing, mostly weeping.

> The hardest thing is having to go to the Department to ask for anything. They want to know everything. Who is the child's father? You can't get anything unless you tells them who the father is. Well, I told them I didn't know. I said there was so many that I didn't know. I said it hard and tough you know, but I was shaking and sick to my stomach. If I told them the baby's father then they'd have to go after him for money and he don't even know. He went on up to the mainland, never wrote or anything. I dare say his mother or somebody told him I was pregnant. Well I don't want him blaming me and all the harbor getting in a uproar because I named him to the Department. Better to keep my mouth shut and act like a slut. They treat me like one

anyway down there. But what galls me is that he's up there in Toronto away from it all and down here everyone is on my back and I have to do it all. Look after the baby and put up with the people at home and the Department.

Some of the anguish comes from the knowledge that the vicious cycle of poverty has gone on for years and there is little hope for the future. Comments which women make after playing the game:

That's what kills me. That there is no end in sight. No matter how hard I try I can't give my children what they need. Good warm clothes for the winter is impossible. Every fall I try to buy a winter coat for each of them but who can afford what they're asking for coats? And if you go to the second hand store, coats are dirty and worn and the kids are shamed in them and don't want to go to school.

It's like a sickness, I can't stop thinking about money. It's in me head all the time. And they come home from school wanting money for gym shoes and bake sales and fancy books every month that the teacher sends home. Then they are going to see a play or wants to go to borrow fifty dollars for a uniform. How come, they say, how come when I say No! No! No! We ain't got it. There's no money. Not like I had it and wouldn't give it to them. And I got to tell the youngsters, We got no money. I look at their faces then. Why should they have to suffer so much and the other kids have it all? What did they do wrong? They think like that you know. They think they must be bad or no good. And that's my fault too. I knows that. When they ask for stuff I yell and yell. What do you think I am? Where do you think I can get the money? And they don't look healthy next to the other youngsters in their class. Sick and poorly. They look afraid all the time. And the other youngsters picks on them because of their clothes and because they always have peanut butter on their bread in their lunch bag. So they fight. And then I gets a call from the principal. And to tell the truth I don't have anything fit to wear to go and see him. So I don't go. I just sit there and cry. And when the youngsters come home from school, I cries and says to them, "Don't fight at school for pity's sake, don't fight." So what kind of a mother is that, hey? Not fit for nothing. I should go and wring it into the principal for letting them youngsters give my own youngsters such a hard time. I should wring it into the social workers who wouldn't give 'em enough money for clothes and food. Not that I didn't used to but it didn't get me anywhere. Now I'm tired all the time. Go to bed tired. Wake up tired. Where will it all end?

It's the cold weather that kills me. I turn off the heat when the kids are in school so that it'll be warm when they come home. But it's never really warm. These buildings are like cardboard. The wind blows right through them. I just want to lie down and cover up with blankets all day. And the youngsters are always sick—always got a cold. How can they help it?

I tell you what I hates. At the beginning of the month I gets me cheque and I pays for the oil and the lights and a few groceries. I tried to hold on to a bit of money to get us through the next time. But there's never enough. We always run out of stuff. We only have milk when I get the cheque. After that it's that Tang and then water. And if I buy treats for the kids they get so excited. But it's only when I get the cheque, then there's no more treats. Seems like we're always waiting. They wants to go to a movie and I say wait till I gets the cheque but you know even when I gets the cheque there's never enough money for movies. So they're always waiting and I'm always waiting.

We shared a special dinner that first evening and every women received a rose. The thoughtfulness of this gesture touched each woman. Over dinner they talked about the lack of special touches and thoughtful gestures in their lives.

The magazines tell you to have a bubble bath. A bottle of wine. Have a friend over for dinner. Go for a haircut. Treat yourself good if you are a single parent. Well, I bought a bottle of bubble bath at the drugstore one time. It smelled really good. It wasn't cheap either. And young Sherry poured it in the tub. "Come see all the bubbles mommy" she yelled out to me. Well, I smacked her right in the face. There she was, bubbles everywhere, laughing and going on about the bubbles and I smacked her. So help me God. I'll never live long enough to forget the look on her face when I smacked her. She sobbed for hours. She didn't know poor little thing. It was the only thing I had bought for myself for a long time.

My friends are in the same state I'm sure. We don't have enough for dinner ourselves. I sees the youngsters getting up from the table hungry, their eyes watching each other to see if one got more. Half the time I didn't eat so they'd have more. That's why I'm so tired all the time I guess.

After dinner we all went to a disco downtown. Joining hands we danced together as a group. It is unusual for a group of women to dance together in a disco. The more traditional Newfoundland dancing allows for women to dance together in groups or couples but in more recent times this is generally considered old fashioned and unacceptable.

When the disco closed we wandered back to the hotel where we stayed awake most of the night sharing stories:

We never had much when I was growing up. Mom always told me to stay away from the boys. 'They only want one thing and you'll end up like I did.' She always said that. Never wanted me to go out. But I did. And sure enough I got pregnant. But it wasn't because Mom didn't try to beat it into me. I just got caught.

Well, I thought he was 'in love.' He was glad enough to get married. We had a big wedding. Bride girls. Cake. Everything. He took off, though he did call and ask after the youngsters. He says he was too young. We were both too young. But everyone was getting married. We had a lovely wedding. I still got the dress. My sister was married in it too.

I got married to get away from Mom. To tell you the truth I thought I would be in charge for a change. Well, I'm in charge all right.

I always wanted a baby. I thought that was the most wonderful thing you could do. I never knew how much work they are. Day and night. He never stops crying. I can' t go anywhere.

It's all that stuff about falling in love. Falling into sex is what it is you know. You wants to go to bed with him so you think you got to own him and he got to own you. So you have a youngster to show you own each other. Everybody makes such a deal about it. Valentines and stuff. Love forever. Anybody who believes that will believe anything.

Throughout the workshop the participants identified the many concerns and circumstances they shared. They argued that the opportunity to come together allowed them to analyze their strengths, assess the expectations others had of them, identify sources of stress, and understand personal and group empowerment. They also talked about creating self-help groups in their own communities. However, there was general concern about this activity alienating them even further from the rest of the community. They explored ways to meet and realized that the cost of this group meeting regularly was unrealistic, but were prepared to try meeting on the teleconference system if ways could be found to cover the cost for this.

Teleconferencing

The Memorial University teleconference system is a province-wide system consisting of four circuits which allow people at teleconference centers all over Newfoundland and Labrador to attend meetings or engage in educational activities. Each center is equipped with a teleconference kit which consists of a speaker and a push-to-talk microphone. No one can be heard on the system unless they push a bar on the microphone. The system is audio only, which means you can be heard and not seen. There can be up to eight microphones in a center, though there are usually only four which means if there are more than four people at a center, the microphones have to be shared. This is usually not a problem. There is also a speaker in each center which provides the sound.

The teleconference centers are usually located in vocational high schools and hospitals around the province. The teleconference system can also connect with ordinary phones. The teleconference center, which is located in St. John's, can dial up the telephone numbers of as many as four people who live in areas where there is no teleconference center. It also allows for people from outside the province to be connected to the discussion. For example, the single mothers group across Newfoundland have connected with resource people from as far away as British Columbia to discuss issues related to poverty and community organizing.

The teleconference system used by the Single Moms is available seven days a week. The Single Moms chose to meet by teleconference on Sunday afternoons since the cost was lower at that time and the time was more convenient for most participants. Single Moms had a regular booking with the teleconference center and met regularly every two weeks until lack of funding diminished the frequency. The Departmental Secretary of State provided funding for these sessions for the first year. Since then, funding has been provided by PLURA,

Oxfam, the Provincial Department of Social Services, and the Women's center contributions.

The objectives of the group sessions by teleconference were: to provide an opportunity for Single Moms to share similar interests and strengths, concerns, ideas, and experiences; to provide opportunity for analysis and assessment of sources of the difficulties they were experiencing; to encourage each other to take responsibility for personal empowerment; and finally, to raise the consciousness of their communities, professionals, and government about their role in the increasingly greater levels of poverty and alienation of single mothers in the province.

The first series of teleconferences organized by the single mothers were highly structured, partly due to everyone's anxiety about using this new tool. Women were encouraged to visit teleconference centers prior to their first teleconference, to meet staff, see the equipment, and develop some familiarity about its use. A list of the centers was provided to the teleconference center so that these centers were routinely contacted for each teleconference meeting. Child care arrangements were an issue for most women so arrangements for teleconferences were made when mothers were willing to find free child care. Sunday afternoons were consistently good for most mothers. Transportation was an issue for some mothers especially if teleconference centers were in nearby communities. However, these arrangements were generally resolved by the women themselves.

The women had varied reactions to the system during the first few teleconference sessions. Some women looked forward to participating in sessions, and came prepared to talk as openly as they had done at the original workshop. Others felt they were pressured to talk before they were ready, since they were uncomfortable with silences on the system. Generally, women did not actively participate in their first few sessions. Usually, women were encouraged to bring a friend or friends to the session. Otherwise, they would be sitting in their center alone which could create difficulties when women were talking about feelings of social isolation and alienation. It was important that there was someone available on site to offer physical comfort through eye contact or touch. We found over the years that many women were uncomfortable with being alone in the teleconference centers and were regularly accompanied by friends. This had the effect of increasing the size of the group on the system as women who came to provide companionship stayed to participate and later brought other friends.

The length of the sessions varied over time. Generally, sessions were two hours long. Shorter sessions did not allow full participation, and energy levels tended to drop off after two hours. The teleconference centers were brightly lit conference rooms which created some strain initially as many women indicated they felt uncomfortable in this formal setting. However, over time, these feelings of discomfort diminished considerably.

Each teleconference began with an introduction and check-in which allowed each woman to share how she was feeling about herself and her life situation at the time. Women talked of their attempts to begin local groups and supported each other's efforts with information and encouragement.

Meditation

An important aspect of the teleconference session was meditation. One of the forms of meditation used by the Single Moms is a process of stilling the mind and body and creating a sense of calm and connecting with power within or Goddess within. Meditation was introduced to assist women to build an inner sanctuary and to reconnect with their inner strength and wisdom. Women frequently identified that they felt good when they were together with the group on teleconference but that these feelings of empowerment did not last long at home, where they continued to feel that things were out of control. Meditation was introduced as a tool they could use in their own homes without the assistance of other group members.

Meditating in teleconference was awkward at first. We used music and sounds of nature in the background. Lights were turned off in the teleconference centers as women focused on relaxing their physical bodies. The connection was made between the mental and emotional states and the physical reactions. We identified where stress or tension was anchored in the body in response to mental and emotional anxiety, and worked on healing our physical selves. Exercises used to do this sometimes came spontaneously from women on the teleconference. We started to develop skills in strengthening our connection with our intuition. Meditation was practiced on an individual and group basis and served to carry out the inner experiential quest for meaning and provided a method to reconnect with our deeper women's wisdom.

Meditation functioned as well to provide a strong bonding for the group and a heightened awareness of the powerful energy which we were creating together. This energy was strengthening and healing for all of us. We became aware that the process of meditation enabled us to directly deal with group conflict in a loving, healing manner. It seemed clear to us that meditation was not necessary as long as we were content to participate in our lives at surface level. However to live fully, meditation becomes necessary to tap the deepest sources of meaning and energy in our lives and reconnect us with our inner knowledge and wisdom. As time went on we consistently drew upon this inner knowledge and wisdom for our involvement in our families, in communities, and in social change.

As well as using meditation in our teleconference meetings, we also began to practice meditation daily at home. Most of us found this process very helpful in creating an inner sanctuary where we could retreat from the worry and chaos of our daily lives.

Meditation was employed to analyze our daily activities and thoughts to see if they reflected love for ourselves or diminished us in some way. We began to acknowledge that the lack of self-love was a powerful force in our lives and undermined most of our efforts. We began to add techniques to foster self-love. These techniques included creating an inner vision of ourselves which reflected who we truly are. We did this first by using guided meditations which included healing exercises, affirmations, and visioning.

The meditations used by the group essentially took two forms. One form of meditation which we called insight or process meditation, was one in which we went to our inner wisdom (or inner Goddess) to present a question related to a personal issue or an issue facing the group. In time this form of meditation became a tool used frequently by the group in times of conflict or problem-solving. It became routine, for example, for the women who were planning strategies for meetings with government officials to meditate prior to meetings. When the group as a whole reached an impasse on some issue, one member usually asked for a period of meditation to ask for guidance on how to proceed. Always the source of answers was identified as power from within, women's wisdom, and always, we found answers to assist us in moving to a more creative and cooperative space.

As time went on, we sometimes held insight meditation sessions for a particularly difficult situation facing the group or an individual within the group. At such times the women could meditate in silence for several hours. At the end of the silence, women interpreted the images and thoughts which had come to them. Sometimes we focused on the image of the earth as mother or the moon or North Star as sources of strength and power for women. Other women found connection through the sea or water. These images were means of bringing together the wisdom and strength of all women.

The second form of meditation was the meditation on space. Women used a simple *mantra* to release themselves from the tyranny of their minds. They focused on putting their attention on their breathing and simply watching the dance of the mind without interpretation or judgment. Sometimes the mind disappeared for brief periods and it was in these periods that the women said they experienced the true meaning of who they were. In their expressions about these experiences, they have said that at the end of such meditation they felt joyful, full of energy, a sense of wonder, a deep connection with all things—trees, flowers, animals, and each other, and a sense of amusement even about difficult issues that were under recent discussion. There was certainly evidence of deep bonding between the women who shared these experiences.

However, meditation, particularly the second form of meditation, was not always accessible or even desirable by some of the women. Women who did not enjoy meditation were sometimes irritated by those who did. Some said they felt left out of the process, others felt the time would be better spent at accomplishing some task. This was perhaps an indication of a deeper split in the group. The women who had been part of the original group or who had joined with the network or teleconferencing in the first year were much more comfortable with focusing on meditations and group process. The more recent members were more task-oriented, particularly focused on developing self-help groups in their own communities. They saw the teleconference system as an opportunity to share ideas about forming groups and enhancing group process. For this reason meditation became less frequent on the system as the older members began to use other tools to retain the early vision of the group as a source of empowerment.

ARRIVING AT GROUP VISION AND FOCUS

The focus shifted to the reviewing of the vision of the group as a source of personal power for the creation of new realities for individual members. Equal emphasis was placed on the creation of a vision for changing social conditions for single mothers throughout the province. Together the women envisioned a world where there was equality and justice for single mothers and their children. They discussed this vision on teleconference, in local workshops and provincial conferences. They re-affirmed the need to remember their lack of self-love and the impact the lack of self-love had on the group as a whole. They acknowledged that the lack of self-love was a powerful influence in their lives and undermined most of their efforts generally as well as in the Single Moms group. They began to add to the techniques to foster self-love. They used the healing exercises which were mentioned earlier. They also used daily affirmations which reinforced the inner image they had created. They began to analyze their daily activities and thoughts to identify how those activities and thoughts diminished or strengthened their self-image. In the situations where they diminished their self-image, they would begin to replace these behaviors and thoughts with empowering behavior and thoughts.

More and more, women were realizing the importance of discipline to the creation of their new realities. Discipline was required to change the conditionings of a lifetime. Stopping thoughts and actions which interfered with the vision of who they truly were and changing self-directed blaming or angry messages required several steps. First, they had to acknowledge the process as it occurred. Second, they began to realize that they were dependent on the energy created by negative thoughts. They had to consciously change their negative thoughts to positive, self-affirming ones, and find more positive sources of energy. The women began to identify that the chaotic nature of their lives had been helpful in providing a sense of aliveness along with the despair and a source of energy along with the chaos.

In discussions of how to replace the negative sources of energy with more positive sources, these were some of the comments made by women:

> I would be lying in bed, too tired to move, trying to get up to face getting the kids ready for school. Knowing that I didn't have anything to give them for lunch except jam sandwiches didn't help. So I would lie there and say to myself, 'Get up you lazy bitch. You are a rotten mother. Get up and get the children up. They will be late again and it's your fault. You are a lazy, lazy bitch.' And that would get me out of bed.

> God look at the clock. Late again. I have pains in my chest because I know the kids will be late. I hate myself when I let the kids down. They go to school without stuff they need. I feel sick.

Most of the women reported that these kinds of angry messages motivated them to get the things done which needed to be done.

Together the women remembered other kinds of energy and its sources. They talked about the energy they experienced as children when they felt "light" and "carefree". Most said these feelings were rare in their adult life. They explored activities they could engage in which promoted this kind of light energy. Some of the activities they identified and also began to engage in as a group included: playing with the children, tobogganing, sliding, skating, dancing, and singing.

They identified other forms of "light" energy. Energy which came from spending time being creative with the Single Moms group; doing creative visualization; affirmations and meditations; dreaming of the future in a positive way; and thinking of good things in the past.

They also identified ways to bring this kind of energy into their lives, individually, and into the Single Moms group. They re-emphasized the importance of continuing to do activities in the Single Moms group which would assist the group in maintaining a balance between meeting the individual needs of the women as well as contributing to the growth of the group. They engaged in a number of activities at this point to assist them in maintaining the discipline necessary to retain their connection with the inner union. Women came together all over the province for weekend workshops where they examined the source of their present lack of self-esteem and lack of knowledge of how to demonstrate love of self. They went back to earliest memories to identify the messages they had received which had strongly influenced them from early childhood to the present. Most realized that the values and beliefs which governed their lives in the present were not truly their own but those of teachers, parents, religious leaders who were operating from their own conditionings about the role of women in society.

Angry yet elated, the women focused on clarifying the values and beliefs which truly belonged to them. This was a further clarification of the vision of their true inner reality. They talked about how living their lives full of love for themselves would differ from living their lives based on other people's conditionings. They clarified the importance of taking time for personal growth activities as well as ensuring task-oriented and group maintenance activities.

The consensus of the women across the province after the workshop was that priority should be given to personal growth and maintenance of the group for self-help, with the responsibility of social change taking a second place until the groups were further developed. They decided to form a provincial organization which would have social change as its mandate. All of the local groups would contribute to the provincial group which would meet by teleconference. The decision was made that personal growth and self-help would be available to the representatives of the provincial organizations in their local groups. However the provincial organization would make decisions only after input from all groups, using the same problem-solving and decision-making process, enhanced the growth of individual members. The role of the teleconference sessions changed considerably after this as the sessions usually became more task-oriented with the focus on issues such as government policies, housing, and social assistance, all of which impacted on Single Moms across the province.

The focus of the provincial group became the economic empowerment of single mothers. They began to consult with local groups to formulate a plan to enable single mothers to gain control of their own economic situations and to contribute to economic decision-making and planning in their own communities. At conferences, teleconferences and workshops, SMAP members explored the skills and strategies used by their mothers and grandmothers in maintaining and developing families and communities.

Reliving Earlier Roles
They found that modern-day women seemed to have forgotten the instrumental role their foremothers had played in the economic and social maintenance of their families and communities. Discussions with women in small groups revealed that historically women assumed responsibility for the community for long periods of time when the men were away fishing in Labrador or working in Canada. In effect, most of the mothers had functioned as single mothers for long periods of time. These women, of course, continued to be married and their husbands usually returned. However, it was important to make the link between the Single Moms of today and the kind of responsibility, problem-solving, and decision-making of the women who had functioned as single mothers in the past.

Single mothers clearly identified that their status in the communities had diminished over the past 15 years. In fact, they felt the status of women, generally, had diminished during that period. They were anxious to explore with their mothers and grandmothers the reasons for this change.

The Single Moms' discussions with older women in the community revealed some of their ideas about the reasons for the change. Women said they believed that the change in the northern fish stocks and federal policies meant that men were away for shorter periods of time and frequently did not go away at all. Consequently, men were at home for longer periods and with less to occupy them. Agencies who were involved with development work frequently focused on male leaders in the community and incorrectly assumed that women played a role more focused on family than community. The organizing of community councils and rural development associations generally involved men. This may have been due to the fact that most of the development workers were male.

In the past, Newfoundland families had worked together as an economic unit and, indeed, had contributed to the maintenance of community as a unit. Men, even when they were living in the community, were frequently away fishing late into the evening, and, as a consequence, women were left with the tasks of organizing community events—weddings, "times," church suppers, etc. They were also more aware of people in need and frequently organized community response to assist a family or an individual in need. For example, if an elderly woman living on her own needed work done or assistance in shopping, or if a young mother whose husband was away had a sick child and needed someone to assist her, perhaps even spend the night to help with child care, other women in the community would help out.

Single Moms also identified other factors which possibly contributed to the change in the role and status of women. Privacy, for example, became an issue in communities. Whereas people visited each other's homes without prior arrangements or on a drop-in basis in the past, privacy began to be highly valued. In communities where people had not previously locked their doors, new highways brought strangers and a lessened feeling of safety. As a consequence, residents began to keep their doors locked. Previous to this, many communities could only be reached by boat. As well, affluence, in the form of regular pay checks or Unemployment Insurance benefits created secrecy as people became more cautious about identifying and sharing their resources.

The arrival of television brought with it a different set of values. Television was identified by SMAP members as having played a major role in what were appropriate activities for women. Rural women who had traditionally worked in the fishery began to see this role as unfeminine. Television, particularly the afternoon soap operas, provided a distraction from everyday reality, so there was less interest in community dramas.

The young women began to develop an appreciation for the knowledge and skills of the older women: fund raising while promoting a sense of community through having "times," soup suppers, cleaning up, or building structures such as community halls. They talked about the money their foremothers had earned through raising sheep, selling wool, and making salt fish. SMAP members themselves remembered days of berry picking where they would pick enough berries for the family for winter and have enough left over to sell. They said their foremothers lived in a time when nothing was wasted, when people lived off the land, growing their own vegetables, and hunted the moose, caribou and salt-water birds, so that there was little they had to buy from the store. The younger women became more aware of the hard work and long days; of community wells; of families bringing their containers (kerosene cans and molasses jars) to the store to be refilled, reducing the need for garbage disposal.

They became more aware of the role of children in the past helping in the vegetable gardens; tending the sheep or working in the fish plant after school, sharing their energy and resources with the family; older children looking after younger children and the elders.

SMAP members recalled times when food was scarce but people shared their moose, berries, and bread. Now it seemed harder to share things they had paid money for than things they had taken from the land. The younger women recalled the conflicts among the older women, and described how some women had remained angry with each other for years. But they also remembered the older women's descriptions of tobogganing at night when they were teenagers and of concerts where they made up sketches and songs and everyone from the community attended. The older women talked about Christmas; the baking and the cleaning that went on for days; about the mummering where men could dress up as women and women could dress as men; the celebration of each of the twelve days of Christmas, dancing, singing, and performing plays until all hours of the night.

There were many songs that had been written about things that had happened in the communities in the past but many of these songs were being forgotten. The songs told stories of fishing disasters, confrontations with the federal fisheries officers, and courting.

Recovering Community

The gathering of the stories of the older women was a time of joy for the younger ones; however, they experienced a sense of loss, too. Although few would want to go back to a time where there was no electricity or running water, there was a sense that something important had been lost, though they were uncertain about exactly what it was. Discussions revealed that this sense of loss was related more to loss of community than anything else. Single Moms talked about the openness of things today when people routinely discuss once taboo subjects such as family violence and incest, whereas, traditionally, such matters were kept within the strictly private confines of the family. However, the sense of sharing and self-reliance seemed to be missing. There seemed to be little sense of community pride, of belonging to a community, or of having responsibility for the maintenance of community. Some of the overall feelings about the community were similar to the feelings that the young women had felt about themselves—low self-esteem, powerlessness.

The discussions with the older women raised the whole issue of experience of poverty. It seemed to the younger women that the women who had experienced the difficult economic times of the past had a richness of community support, and knowledge of who they were which strengthened and sustained them. By comparison, they felt they had more material resources than their grandmothers but little connectedness with each other and the rest of the community. In response to this, they decided to develop opportunities for single mothers to develop their abilities in creating community, building on the skills of their foremothers.

After a good deal of planning and negotiations, three Single Moms' centers were established in central locations across the island. The original purpose of these centers was to provide a place where the single moms could develop and implement training programs in group process, individual empowerment within groups, economic empowerment, and community development. The funding agency, Department of Social Services, was originally in agreement with the aims of Single Moms Against Poverty. There was also agreement that Single Moms would operate as a collective, and that all decision-making would be done by consensus in the local or provincial groups. Staffing and training were also to be done by Single Moms.

The Single Moms were elated at having received funding. However, their enthusiasm was shortlived. Teleconference meetings focused on decisions related to policies for the Single Moms' centers, rather than on provincial issues. Staffing of the centers created problems which haunted the groups for years. Since most of the membership were receiving social assistance, many were eager to be employed doing the work they loved to do but for which they had been previously unpaid. While there was a great deal of discussion and participation in the hiring process, many women felt rejected and hurt when they were not hired. Some of these women began to withdraw from the group, others began to sabotage the group process. This became identified as a critical issue. Healing sessions were done by teleconference and in provincial workshops. The healing consisted of a reconnection with the vision and a recommitment to the discipline required to achieve the group vision. Creative visualization and meditation techniques were used to release anger and tension. A re-examination of conditioning and social structures which reinforced competitive behavior was an important part of this process.

Educational Support and Outreach

During this process SMAP continued to focus on individual empowerment but also worked closely with the Department of Justice on the issue of child support payments. They assisted the Department of Justice in the creation of a new agency which guaranteed child support payments to Single Moms. They were also actively engaged in discussions with the Department of Social Services, and during this period, single mothers were the only group to receive an increase in social assistance benefits from the provincial group. All provincial corporations, agencies and institutions received reduced funding during this period. As well, Single Moms participated in a government review of post-secondary education opportunities and funding of education for Single Moms across the province. As a result of this review, single mothers attending post-secondary institutions received a small increase in funding.

Also during this period, Single Moms participated in several projects. One project was a teleconference presentation at the Annual Conference of the Canadian Research Institute for the Development of Women in Whitehorse, Northwest Territories. Throughout this process, the members of Single Moms were located in their teleconference centers in small communities across Newfoundland and Labrador. Several people from the group were in Whitehorse to co-ordinate activities there. The Yellowknife organizers had set up teleconference equipment in a large room at the conference center where the participants could listen to the presentation from the Single Moms. The presentations were clearly heard by everyone in the room and at the end, conference participants had an opportunity to talk with the single mothers.

The theme of the presentation was the role of the SMAP in assisting single mothers living in small communities to deal with social isolation. The Single Moms began the session with a healing meditation, one which was regularly used in teleconference meetings. They then used poetry, stories and songs to describe the impact of social isolation and the strength which they drew from each other in the Single Moms groups across the island. One of the groups, the Port aux Basque group, had done a drawing. They described the drawing and as they were describing it, the women at the conference center in Yellowknife reproduced it. The women described their dream for social change and the kind of activities they were engaged in at a personal, community, and provincial level to create these changes.

The presentation at the CRIDW Conference was important for the Single Moms for several reasons. First, they organized and created their presentation together which gave them an opportunity to review who they were now and where they had come from. They enjoyed their creativity as a group. They also demonstrated the growth in confidence of the group members as they presented to a group of academic women at a national conference. It also provided them with national exposure and assisted them in connecting with national women's networks.

The Single Moms were also engaged in a international linkage project between universities in Thailand and Newfoundland. Women from Thailand came to Newfoundland; talked about women's organizations in Thailand; and studied the process used by the Single Moms Against Poverty in Newfoundland. This exchange was stimulating for the Single Moms since the process provided an opportunity for reaction and analysis.

Single Moms local groups were engaged in a variety of activities, for example, reviewing opportunities for small business such as fish farming, bed and breakfast, gourmet items, specifically jams, etc. Some Single Moms groups were becoming recognized by local community organizations and were participating as board members on regional economic development boards. Provincial and national women's organizations were beginning to acknowledge the presence of Single Moms Against Poverty and inviting their participation in provincial lobbying, anti-poverty and housing conferences, family violence, and so on. On an individual level some of the original members of the group were becoming less active as they became students at university or college. Some of them contributed to the development of Single Moms support groups at post-secondary institutions.

Crises of Scale and Governmental Support

The crisis came for Single Moms Against Poverty in the early '90s. Many of the original members have enrolled in training programs, universities and colleges. They play a supportive role, but are unable to contribute the level of energy they did originally. The web of structures created by the Single Moms centers created a human dilemma as well. The maintenance of these structures encouraged active participation. However, the effort required in funding proposals and negotiating with government agencies dissipated and sapped the talents and energies of the Single Moms. Burnout and cynicism were inevitable.

The funding agencies had agreed originally to respect the mandate of Single Moms Against Poverty, however they began to attempt to direct and manage the activities of the three Single Moms centers. Federally, the Department of Secretary of State supported the Single Moms' activities, but would only agree to fund activities which they deemed to be politically correct. The Secretary of State was committed to social action. However, he did not feel that personal empowerment, or training in group formation, process, and structure were appropriate to social action.

Also, Single Moms expended much effort keeping up-to-date with the policies of government departments such as the Department of Social

Services, the Department of Justice, and the Department of Education, which provide funding and support for community groups. They attempted to be kept apprised of programs and resources available to Single Moms and the limitations and barriers to these programs all the while attempting to develop effective working relationships with federal and provincial agencies and programs (CLLOA, CEIC). The end results were disparate and fragmented activities; wasted talent and energy; and again, burnout and cynicism. Women resigned themselves to feeling that nothing will change and their efforts were wasted. This began to affect the general membership in the form of lack of coordination, indifference and poor service. The task of developing ideas into opportunities for empowerment seemed too complicated. Instead, the social assistance system of dependency seemed to be the only support: discontent and bitterness continues to build.

All this has generated anguish for everyone: the single mothers who were struggling against the system; other women's groups who were energized by their original vision; and bureaucrats, who are genuinely supportive but who are trapped in a maze of policies and regulations which undermine the actions of groups focused on sustainable self-reliance and community building. Federal and provincial governments and community development efforts have had a structural approach which is both program and project driven. It has generated further alienation and dependency. There is competition among public institutions such as the university and colleges, private consulting agencies, and grassroots organizations for the same funding sources. There have emerged numerous structures federally and provincially which generate confusion, duplication, and a drain on fiscal and human resources.

Community Meaning and Values for Change

Single Moms Against Poverty has made a concerted effort to involve people throughout the province in the development process. They believe that in order for their status and role to change, they must take the lead in encouraging people to look at what community means and how they plan to engage in the re-creation of community together. They recognize that their communities, like themselves, are governed by past conditioning and behaviors. They believe communities have to be confronted with the devastation, isolation, and alienation that these conditionings and behaviors are having on all community members, not just single mothers. They believe that it is pointless to begin a planning process or even attempt to develop a vision until people have a better understanding of themselves, their interrelationships, and their view of economic realities.

Communities must come to an agreement on common values, lifestyles, decision-making, and problem-solving styles. Only then can they begin to confront government departments and agencies with the destruction created by their competitive nature. Unconventional approaches will be necessary in order to encourage people to enter into open, frank, and sincere discussions about the nature of community. Technical tools such as participatory video and community television allow people to view themselves and their environment from different perspectives, to assist them in understanding who they are, why they are who they are, and who they want to be. Participatory video and community television can be used in nonconventional ways to provide a new dimension: a communication vehicle, and a mechanism for evaluation and constructive analysis.

A commitment to the long term has to be made to allow for the evolution of the conscious creation of community. Community members will have to be encouraged as to the necessity of reviewing the assumptions about community values and their manifestation in community decisions related to the environment, family violence, economic development, local government structures, and so on. Facilitators will need to be competent in teaching communication skills; giving insight; identifying feelings, providing healthy outlets for feelings; personal empowerment; conducting economic analyses at local, regional and global levels; teaching behaviors that demonstrate care-giving at community levels; and building networks that reflect the values that people identify as those inherent in community building.

TRANSFORMATIVE STEPS: FIVE YEARS LATER

Single Moms Against Poverty was unable to obtain funding as a provincial organization, consequently it has been unable to maintain its regular teleconference sessions. The impact of the organization continues to be felt, however, as many single mothers who were participants have gone on to become members of local rural development associations, community futures groups, church committees, and community councils. A number of single mothers have gone on to post-secondary education. We are continuing to work together to change attitudes towards single mothers in these institutions.

We are presently in the process of completing a two-year participatory action research project called "Hoops and Hurdles: Barriers to Post-secondary Education for Single Mothers." Single mothers in post-secondary education made a video and resource book called "Standing Strong" which we are using in community building workshops within academic institutions. This is based on the community building model which began to emerge in the work with Single Moms Against Poverty. The model is presently being applied in Memorial University, and has been applied successfully in other organizations. We are making presentations on the "Hoops and Hurdles Project" to the federal department of Human Resource Development and to universities across the country.

Women's Economic Network

A new provincial organization, "Women's Economic Network" (WEN) has emerged as a result of the application of the community building model. This organization has more than 50 women's organizations from around the province as members and meets monthly by teleconference. Single Moms are very active in this organization and are well represented on the provincial steering committee.

The purpose of WEN is to provide an opportunity for women's groups to share information, plan strategies and support each other. The membership is quite diverse and includes organizations such as church groups, native women's groups, multicultural women's association, women's institutes, farm women's associations, unions, and status of women councils. They have worked together on a response to the social reform package of the federal government, with special attention given to the situation of single mothers in the province.

WEN organized a provincial conference on "Women and the Economy" for late 1994. For many of the women's organizations this was the first opportunity for a face to face meeting. WEN has been also designated as the organization on "Women and Coastal Resources" for the World Conference on Women at Beijing in 1995.

Community Building Model

Every model bases its assumptions and activities on some type of underlying framework. It may be called a world view, which incorporates a vision and perception of the world. It also involves the question of the nature of humanity. From a pragmatic standpoint, no one can maintain these to be mere abstractions. More than any other factors, questions of the structure of reality and the nature of humanity determine relationships to self, others, and nature.

The Taylor community building model assumes that the problem of barriers against women and children is rooted in the larger picture of dominant cultural values and norms. It uses a conscious and systematic approach to understanding gender values and practices. Asserting that compassion and love have been demonstrated by research to be clearly a part of the biological make-up of humanity, the community building model is dedicated to the achievement of commitment, intimacy, and care.

The community building model is based on the belief that the world's finite resources cannot support an indefinite expansion of industrial civilization. It sees the world view of western dominant culture as largely responsible for the barriers confronting oppressed groups, such as women and children. It assumes that the grossly unjust distribution of resources has resulted in oppression of minority groups, in spontaneous and institutionalized violence, and in a polluted environment in which life has often become physically and mentally unhealthy.

The model assumes that society, permeated and controlled by disinformation, is largely indifferent to the rigorous business of raising children so that they flourish and become responsible adults. It supports the belief that all citizens share in the responsibility for children. The model argues that bonding is breaking down in Canadian society because individuals and communities cannot achieve a sustainable, healthy lifestyle through reasonable means. It is increasingly difficult for citizens to be occupied in activities which make the best of their abilities, provide them with satisfaction, and have financial security and some measure of appreciation from their peers. The model perceives that success in the dominant culture is achieved through competition and exploitation identified as individual achievement, usually defined as material gain and careerism.

The community building model takes the perspective that the reality of everyday life is conveyed through social and political institutions. These institutions are made by people and can be remade by people. All knowledge gives access to power of some kind, if skillfully used. Learning how power operates in the old framework is liberating. Such knowledge can be energizing and empowering. The challenge faced, then, is the formation of an alternative society through the conscious creation of safe sustainable communities everywhere, including community building within social and political institutions. The process required is one which enables and mobilizes, which uses crisis and change as a opportunity for growth and renewal, and which is driven by the needs and knowledge of the constituents of community.

The model views community from the mentality of trust and respect. The maintenance of community is conceptualized in holistic terms: time is cyclic, progress spirals, the means are the end. All are embedded in ecological relations. The personal is political, everyone matters, everyone is responsible. The focus of attention is on relationships *between* everything and everyone. Existence in and of itself is reason enough to be awarded respect. Everything is part of an ever-evolving organic whole. Society is composed of intelligent, good-willed people who, when given the chance, will collectively figure out the best course of action. The context is infused with receptivity, fluidity, generosity, spontaneity, idiosyncrasy, negotiation, reconciliation, cooperation, care, patience, synthesis, and belonging. Security is thought to depend on peace, truth, cooperation, participation, flexibility, creativity, diversity, and decentralization.

One of the objectives of community building is to provide the community with a framework to consciously analyze its values and norms. Communities are enabled to trace the evolution of values and norms, to analyze their actual implementation in social policies, community planning, decision making, and activities, and to assess their benefits and limitations on the health of individuals and families in the community. The intent is conscious creation of values and norms which are consistent with the community's vision of its purpose and objectives, and are concretized in its daily activities and strategic planning.

The model uses participatory processes to assist communities in evaluating and building frameworks as systems of ideas, conceptual structures that they can use in explaining, justifying, and guiding their actions. Typically, the framework enables the community to do a comprehensive analysis of the nature and causes of oppression, poverty, and violence within its boundaries and build a correlated and concrete set of proposals for ending it. It assists the community in developing an integrated theory of the community's role both in contemporary society and in the society that is emerging with global paradigm shifts

Characteristics of Community Building

The transformative process developed in the community building model begins with change at both individual and community levels. It promotes an environment where the disadvantaged can meet their needs and are participating in challenging systematic subordination. The marginalized and the advantaged work consciously together to build communities which are based on quality of life values, as well as social system and ecosystem values, which reflect the local morality. In its commitment to enhancing local morality, community building begins with understanding and changing our own conditionings which limit our ability for self-acceptance and acceptance of others.

Gender and Intercultural Analysis

The process of understanding and changing our conditionings is long term and ongoing. The model underlines the importance of learning from each other's experience. In learning to claim the diversity of experiences as an important resource, and to appreciate the various strategies for survival and resistance that come out of individual and collective histories, the concept of community experience takes on new richness and meaning. The same careful listening is given to all constituents of the community.

The change process has to involve both women and men. Both women and men create and maintain the patterns of behavior which enhance or limit their human development. Many attempts to empower women are based on the male model of "power over," and ultimately on intimidation. The gender in development approach develops power based on creativity, shared leadership and decision-making, self-acceptance, and spiritual strength (Taylor 1992).

Culture of Community Building

The creation of safe environment is critical to each phase of the community-building model. The six phases of community building in the model include: (1) Empowerment. (2) History and evolution of counterfeit community. (3) Diversity, exclusion, and conflict resolution. (4) Salient moment of community. (5) Co-creating community contract. (6) Living and governing community.

Each phase has a set of tools which contributes to the physical and emotional safety of its participants. The empowerment process enables participants to understand and appreciate their personal needs and assists them in learning ways to have these met. A major part of this consists of reaching an understanding of how they have learned to give and receive love and caring, the impact these learnings have on themselves and others, the strengths and limitations of these learnings, and to begin to develop new learnings on loving and caring.

All phases focus on the enhancement of skills in areas such as: self-assessment, communication, mediation, conflict resolution, problem solving, decision-making, local morality, gender analysis, impact-assessment, adaptability, intercultural analysis, community-based economic planning, and community-based evaluation. All phases encourage the validation and use of traditional tools and skills. These skills contribute to attitude change, increased knowledge base, increased involvement in community activities and increased self-confidence, and are essentially impact indicators for the increased safety of the community and the effectiveness of the model.

Knowledge, Education, Research

Knowledge is frequently deemed by professionals or technocrats to be privileged, specialized, exclusive, expert and objective. The formally acknowledged and scholarly acceptable conceptions of knowledge as articulated in educational institutions today have been developed and transferred throughout history by the dominant elite culture. Community building promotes an exchange of knowledge. Relatively little attention has been given to modes of knowing that may be specific to cultures other than those of the elite, particularly those relevant to the cultures of women or other marginalized or minority cultures. Research skills must be accessible to marginalized people because they need the opportunity to inform themselves, participate in discussion and policy formation, and advance their interests through political action. Demystifying research skills is a vital component of the community-building model which challenges the current approaches to policy development in which expertise remains a source of power for the few rather than a resource available to all.

Balanced Planning and Redefinition of Work

The community-building model focuses on balanced economic and social planning as an effective approach to removing barriers against women and children, providing tools for this process. It assists the community in creating a new framework for the definition of work, which for the most part has come to mean employment. The model focuses particularly on the sexual division of labour and the need to redefine how work is evaluated in economic analysis. Reproductive work (child care, family and home maintenance, community work, care giving to community members) is not counted in national accounting systems which means it is not recognized and valued as work. Since most reproductive work globally is done by women, this lack of recognition renders this aspect of women's work invisible.

In the recent past, development has consisted of moving more men and women into "productive work," producing goods and services for income, with little attention paid to their reproductive work. It has become apparent that development focused on productive work has an unconscious bias which benefits those who are best placed to exploit resources and are usually male, educated, and financially well off. The community-building model provides an opportunity for participants to explore together the meaning of work for their community, the kinds of paid and unpaid work which are required to sustain community, and to find and reclaim ways of valuing work which sustains, supports and nurtures safe community.

Spirituality

A significant attribute of the community-building model is its holistic approach, especially its recognition of the importance of spirituality in development. The spirituality of the model takes the form shaped by the participants. It draws to some extent upon Buddhist, Hindu, Christian, Wiccan, and aboriginal traditions which see social domination over nature as being on a continuum with human domination and hierarchy, and social justice as being linked to ecological justice. The spiritual component is also drawn from teachings of spiritual leaders such as Jean Crane from Labrador, Swami Shyam from India, Starhawk, Scott Peck and others. The women I met in rural Thailand taught meditation as a connection with the eternal, and used it daily to assist them in the linkage between spiritual and the physical. Healing workshops are an ongoing part of community building as participants learn to draw upon their spiritual strength to empower themselves, and provide healing and direction for themselves and for their communities.

Transformational Leadership

Transformational leadership inspires people to believe in themselves and realize that they already have the capability to bring about change. This kind of leader exudes confidence that everyone is his or her own best judge, evoking people's self-respect so they take their own experience seriously. Autonomy is a necessary condition for the development of critical thinking and for the achievement of a sense of true interdependence based upon a solid and affirmative estimation of self. In this atmosphere one's integrity is a given. Rather than expending energy defending one's status, energy is focused on caring for each other, sharing different perspectives, and learning.

Setting a tone that inspires sharing is the most important task of transformational leadership. Moral maturity depends as much on the cultivation of qualities of empathy and caring as on the operation of critical intellect. At the heart is the need to recognize and transform the patterns of competition that grip individuals and community. Competitive conditioning has penetrated deep into most psyches. Facilitators frequently find themselves entrenched in the same patterns of domination and compliance that they are trying to transform in the greater society. Transformational leadership requires the abilities to communicate and interact effectively and to initiate, develop, and maintain relationships with diverse individuals and groups. These abilities are dependent on an authentic capacity for caring and appreciation of others for their essential humanity without bias.

Respect for persons results in the acceptance, affirmation, and celebration of human diversity.

Conflict Resolution and Self-expression

Conflict is an abiding part of any community, and can be a creative dynamic since it can bring to the community's awareness the ways in which it works, and encourage change and growth. Conflict becomes destructive, however, when it destroys efforts towards a common goal, inhibits participation, and diminishes people. Many conflicts in communities are the result of poor communication or misunderstandings about goals and expectations. The community-building model allows for full expression of the diverse emotions expressed throughout the community through such techniques as psychodrama, participatory video and storytelling. Individuals who have the opportunity to hear and see themselves on video are more likely to be able to identify where and how they are impacting on others and the consequences to their relationships within the community. They are also more likely to hear the videotaped expressions of others especially when the person is telling his or her story as opposed to making an argument.

Participatory Video

Participatory video was developed at Memorial University and has been used as a tool for community development since the early 1960's. It has been described as a "powerful means in a process which enhances self-awareness, self-confidence, and self-empowerment through objective reflection, consensus, community action, structural change, and participation in development which improves the quality of life for those who engage in it" (Williamson 1991). Participants using participatory video have complete control over how and when the video equipment is to be used as well as the final decision on the use of the resulting videos. Academic and rural participants have worked together to create videos on such subjects as the development of cooperatives; reclaiming women's role in the economic evolution of the community; and women's stories of their foremothers. Participatory video has been used to enhance group process in areas such as decision-making, problem solving and leadership styles. It is particularly helpful in monitoring the balance between tasks and relationship building. Videos are also used to transmit knowledge from one community to another, to raise consciousness on poverty related issues, and to enhance communication skills.

Partnerships: Local, Federal, Global

The community-building model is non-hierarchical and self-empowering. It promotes egalitarian decision making between federal, provincial, and local governments in partnership with all sectors of the community. The emphasis is on decentralized rather than centralized decision-making. Local and indigenous knowledge is validated rather than trivialized. The process encourages communicative, open, cooperative negotiations. Local representatives of federal and provincial governments must be included throughout the community-building process so that they have the experience of personal and community empowerment, and are more able to participate in the dynamic partnerings that are a result of this process.

The community-building model supports the idea of global community, a shift toward global citizenry and global values. Muller has described the idea of global time as a global value, emphasizing the necessity of seeing the lifetime of the planet as beyond our own lifetime. He also says that while we are working on a local level to transform community, the impact is global. This is critical to the community-building model, as the thought of having to change the consciousness of the whole planet can be overwhelming, but the idea that the work of individuals, families, small groups, and communities locally can impact globally is empowering.

CONCLUSION

Problems experienced by communities in such areas as violence, sexual abuse, and poverty are frequently labelled as women's issues and are most often being identified and addressed by women. However, the barriers experienced by women must be re-focused to relationships between individuals, institutions, and the community at large, and their influence on each other. The focus on the elimination of the oppression experienced by marginalized groups such as single mothers is one of the keys to the development of healthy and sustainable communities. The sustainability of community has to move beyond working on social and economic concerns in fragmented approaches to include holistically all aspects including the transformation of belief systems which perpetuate poverty, powerlessness, and violence and which appear to be embedded in the structures of communities, especially but by no means only, in western societies.

BIBLIOGRAPHY

Bajracharya, D., Morse, R. and Pongsapich, A. 1987. *Village Voices in Rural Development and Energy Planning*. Regional Energy Development Programme, United Nations Economic and Social Commission for Asia and the Pacific.

Belenky, M., Clinchy, B.M., Goldberger, N.R. and Tarvle, J.M. 1986. *Women's Ways of Knowing: The Development of Self, Voice and Mind*. New York: Basic Books, Inc.

Ekachai, S. 1991. How did we get to this state of affairs? *Friends of Women* 2(1), 16-18.

Freire, P. 1970. *Pedagogy of the Oppressed*. New York: Continuum.

Freire, P. 1973. *Education for Critical Consciousness*. New York: Seabury Press.

Henderson, H. 1981. *The Politics of the Solar/Age: Alternatives to Economics*. New York: Double Day & Co.

Johnson, S. 1987. *Going Out of Our Minds: The Metaphysics of Liberation*. Freedom, California: The Crossing Press.

Leonard, A. 1989. *Seeds: Supporting Women's Work in the Third World*. New York: The Feminist Press.

Levesque-Lopman, L. 1991. *Claiming Reality: Phenomenology and Women's Experience*. Totowa, NJ: Rowman and Littlefield.

Mies, M. 1986. *Patriarchy and Accumulation on a World Scale: Women in the International Division of Labour*. London: Zed Books.

Miles, A. 1991. Reflections on Integrative Feminism and Rural Women. In: J.D. Wine and J.L. Ristock (eds.), *Women and Social Change* (pp. 56-74). Toronto: James Lorimer and Company.

Moser, C. and Peake, L. (eds.). 1987. *Women, Human Settlements and Housing*. London: Tavistock Publications.

Moffatt, L., Geaday, Y. and Stuart, R. 1991. *Two Halves Makes a Whole: Balancing Gender Relations in Development*. Ottawa: Canadian Council for International Cooperation.

Peck, S. 1987. *The Different Drum: Community Making and Peace*. New York: Simon and Schuster.

Phongphit, S. 1988. *Religion in a Changing Society*. Hong Kong: Arena Press.

Starhawk. 1988. *Dreaming the Dark*. Boston: Beacon Press.

Starhawk. 1989. Ritual as Bonding. In: J. Plaskow and C. Christ (eds.), *Weaving the Visions*. San Francisco: Harper and Row.

Stein, D. 1988. *The Women's Book of Healing*. St. Paul, Minnesota: Llewellyn Publications.

Taylor, S. 1990. *Co-creating Community*. Report for the Canadian Research Institute for the Advancement of Women. Ottawa: Department of Health and Welfare and Secretary of State.

Taylor, S. 1992. "Gender in Development: A Feminist Process for Transforming University and Society". In: *Oval Works: Feminist Social Work Scholarship*. School of Social Work, Memorial University of Newfoundland.

Waring, M. 1988. *If Women Counted: A New Feminist Economics*. New York: Harper Collins.

Williamson, H.A. 1991. The Fogo Process: Development Support Communication in Canada and the Developing World. In: F.L. Casmir (Ed.), *Communication in Development* (pp. 270-288). New Jersey: Ablex Publishing Corporation.

Yotopoulos, P.A. and Nugent, J.B. 1984. Orthodox Development Economics versus the Dynamics of Concentration and Marginalization. In: D.C. Korten and R. Klauss (eds.), *People-centered Development* (pp. 107-120). Connecticut: Kumarian Press.

CHAPTER 5

SIGNS OF COMMUNITY: DEAF IDENTITY AND THE PARADOX OF DIFFERENCE

Owen Wrigley

The group photograph for this workshop is remarkable both for what it shows and what it doesn't. Like any photograph, it presents a unity which is merely a moment. Everyone is smiling and relaxed. Yet this was a group which spent ten highly charged days with more than a few highly charged emotions being expressed. There is yet another difference which the photo cannot show, that one of the members is deaf. That difference is not visible from merely looking at the photo, yet this distinction is what makes the community he came to represent so interesting. A community of those who might look no different, but for whom the difference you cannot see is so very significant.

I entered this workshop as regional director of an international NGO and as a grassroots activist with more than ten years of specific community involvement in Thailand. Yet I also had a peculiar duty which defined my personal engagement with the meeting more than for any other participant. As the Thai Sign Language interpreter for the first deaf delegate to an East-West Center event, my role was historically secondary. This felt appropriate, but the duty of repeating what everyone else said throughout the ten days was not always easy. As has been noted, the events were dynamic, intellectually engaging, and emotionally demanding. As both participant and conduit, my own circuitry was challenged more than once during that very full period.

Kampol Suwanarat, founding general manager of the National Association of the Deaf in Thailand (NADT), was very self-conscious of being the first deaf person to be formally invited to an East-West Center workshop. The formality of this distinction was something he carried carefully, as is his wont. He was also conscious that his wife, Manfa Suwanarat, had been invited but had fallen seriously ill only weeks prior. More reserved by nature than his internationally renowned wife, Kampol was an attentive participant throughout, but neither as passionate nor assertive as his wife in such settings. But Kampol was also drawn out by this workshop, and by its end was as deeply engaged in exchanges both in and out of the formal workshop as the other participants. He was eager to share with everyone else his unique experiences of grassroots organizing among a widely dispersed "community."

We did not know it at the time, but Manfa, the charismatic leader and wife of Kampol, would die only a month later, victim of an allergic reaction to medications for a minor condition. Manfa was co-compiler and deaf team leader on both volumes of the widely acclaimed *Thai Sign Language Dictionary* and a globally known expert on disability issues. Manfa, who was deaf from birth, wrote rarely but prepared and delivered from memory detailed formal sign presentations. She was a gifted orator and interpersonal genius who left powerful impressions on all she met, whether heads of state or poor street deaf. Manfa was honored posthumously by the Secretary General of the United Nations, which was only partial testimony to the impact this dynamic and visionary pixie had left in her wake. Much of the guiding vision and perhaps even more of the effervescent energy forging the new solidarity of deaf awareness in Thailand was lost with her death.

A pair of European deaf advisors had also recently arrived in Thailand with an ill-fated project. Without Manfa's strength of will and vision, this misguided foreign aid project would fully decimate the NADT in less than two years. In the week before her death, Manfa conducted a meeting in her hospital room of the core NADT staff, in which she outlined the steps needed to contain the growing problem, steps which included the removal of one of the foreign deaf advisors. The steps were too drastic for the staff to enact without her leadership. A rural club structure survived, but the national body did not. Nearly seven years after this disastrous project, very small efforts are attempting to begin, again, from scratch.

But this was yet to come. At this point, we were coming off a decade of incredible growth of a grassroot effort into a national representative organization. Joining the workshop of people's organizations to share the experiences of these successes seemed only natural. The lessons from the powerful growth have much to offer, as do those of the forces which were soon to tear it apart. But before that story is told, one may be wondering just why a grassroots organization

among deaf Thais is of significance to the broader field of self-representative organizations?

LANGUAGE AND SURVIVAL

The issue of language, sign languages in particular, will seem to
get substantial, even lavish, attention here. Yet, as language is such
a crucial component of identity formation, and as attitudes to linguistic diversity precede and underscore any creation of communal norms,
this must be done. The issue is not an either/or set of choices, between
one language or another or between one modality or another, as is too
often forced in such circumstances. It requires more than accommodation to additional differences, but actual adjustments which make
real space for new forms and modalities of contributions.

In the past two decades, sign language as the means by which
those who are deaf may communicate has come a bit closer to the
status of "common knowledge." Far less commonly known, however,
is just how fragile the formal status of sign language is—as a
language, let alone as a mother tongue that might be claimed as a
"birth right." The formal recognitions of the linguistic status of sign
languages are actually of very recent date.

It is significant to remember that UNESCO, which was the first
United Nations body to address the topic, in only *1985* made the
following statement:

> Language of deaf children is developmental. Furthermore,
> sign language should be recognized as a legitimate linguis-
> tic system and should be afforded the same status as other
> linguistic systems.

The World Health Organization, WHO, in only *1986* began to
include statements noting that "The use of the term 'dumb,' an
archaic form of 'mute,' is both inaccurate and misleading. As the lack
of speech is a secondary result of deafness, [this term] should not be
applied to describe the primary condition."

The World Federation of the Deaf, WFD, at its 10th World
Congress in Helsinki, Finland, in July *1987*, adopted its first-ever
Resolution on Sign Language, overturning years of oralist leadership.
The Resolution was re-adopted at the 11th World Congress, held in
Japan in *1991*.

The Global Meeting of Experts convened by the U.N. Secretary-
General at the mid-point of the Decade of the Disabled in *1987*
presented among the principal recommendations statement, accepted
by the General Assembly in December *1987*, that "deaf and gravely

hearing-impaired people [are] to be recognized as a linguistic minority, with the specific right to have their native and indigenous sign languages accepted as their first and official language and as the medium of communications and instruction, and to have sign language interpreter services."

The dates are italicized to emphasize just how recent such statements are. Prior to these statements, formal policy in the majority of the world's nations had been overtly oppressive of deaf people's right to use their own native sign languages. It is also worth noting that the last two statements were direct results of official Thai delegations, as the WFD Resolution and the U.N. Global Meeting of Experts recommendation were written by myself and Manfa Suwanarat.

Officials within the particular sub-office of the United Nations responsible were initially surprised by an enormous demand for copies of the documents which contained these statements. The reason remains both unfortunate and simple. Institutions which have direct control over or impact on the lives of deaf children and deaf adults the world over pursue policies which directly contradict the principles of these statements.

Identity: Vital Signs

But why are the issues of language so important in the context of organizing among this grassroots community? Obviously, language choices available to minority groups, both in rank status or in terms of overt oppression, are of great significance to a community attempting self-representation. If "having a voice" includes the requirement to deny one's own language, then a sense of devaluation is imposed on the community. The problems associated with low status and, often, the direct oppression of sign language are compounded as those who are deaf cannot "simply learn" the spoken language of the dominant group. Yet these circumstances of those who are deaf make visible just how significant such issues are for any disenfranchised linguistic minority.

Identity formation and the formation of a sense of community are immediately linked in cultures which exist on the margins of more dominant societies. This linkage is made particularly visible by the unique features of Deaf Culture, but is similar to that of other marginal groups in that this link is a product of dominant culture oppressions of difference. As small community participation is often about forming an awareness of shared concern towards goals which require active agency, the mobilization requires communication of shared identity issues. The unique aspects of Deaf Cultures mirror inverted images of dominant hearing culture expectations. Disenfran-chised linguistic minorities confront as a matter of course restrictions and barriers in efforts to gain access to information and achieve participation in decision-making processes which directly affect their lives. These barriers which are often presumed as "natural" can be seen as quite "un-natural" practices of specific social norms.

Cultural Divides

Deafness is a culture whose history is rewritten from generation to generation. The conditions of "naturalization" into this cultural and linguistic citizenry are unusual. Over 90 percent of deaf children are born into hearing families. Fewer than 10 percent of deaf children have even one deaf parent.[1] This means the majority of new members are, figuratively, born into the wilderness.

Nor is sign language their native language in the sense that it is available to be acquired from interaction with their parents from infancy. Nevertheless, sign language is probably the first actual language acquired for those sufficiently fortunate to have access to a residential deaf school. Sign cultures, as well as the social "knowl-edge" of Deafness, are necessarily reborn and remade with each generation.

In a sense, sign cultures are also reborn from and into a "place" of ignorance. The common body of knowledge among hearing parents of deaf children is without a generational transmission of family lore. As most parents of deaf children are hearing parents having the first deaf child to be found in their extended families, the requisite regenerative status of Deaf Cultures is mirrored in the process by which each new generation of hearing parents and experts recreates "knowledge" for their administration of deafness. Each generation of hearing parents seeks out and often reinvents knowledge about the deafness of their children.

But while parents seek this knowledge, deaf children are often left to their own devices to learn language. Contrary to the average transmission of spoken language between generations—passing from parent to child—the primary means of language transmission in the deaf world is within generation, from their few peers with deaf parents, or from those slightly older at school. For the deaf youth on the street, language is learned from the older deaf survivors on the streets. For them, survival is often the only code available.

Organizing and self-representation often seem a luxury when you have no place to go and no income. This remains the circum-stance for many young deaf people in the developing world. The project which Kampol and I came to Hawaii to talk about began among a "community" of those facing such circumstances.

Entering

When I arrived in Thailand in 1981 to take up the position as the regional representative for the International Human Assistance Programs (IHAP), an American non-profit foundation, I knew little of the Deaf world. Certainly my life since has been deeply affected by my Deaf Thai friends and my engagement with the Deaf Thai community, but, as Kampol pointed out, it took them a while to teach me the language and details of the more significant issues confronting them. I was not a passive voyeur into that community, but became an active agent in the collective efforts to build the NADT into a representative organization. I remained in Thailand more than ten years longer than I had planned because of a joint commitment with my Deaf Thai colleagues to our work.

The all-Deaf Board of Directors of the NADT presented me with an Honorary Life Membership in 1985. Much of my actual work within this community, particularly from 1983 through 1991, revolved around the language, both its particulars and the social advocacy for rights. The purpose of this chapter is not an exercise in sign language linguistics—that basic ground is presented with the two-volume work of the Thai Sign Language Dictionary (National Association of the Deaf in Thailand, 1986, 1990)—but is a more careful look at the ongoing ways in which discourse about Deaf Culture remains undermined and is re-inscripted by hearing notions at each level of attempted resistance.

The two volumes of the *Thai Sign Language Dictionary* were published in 1986 and 1990. These volumes were a team effort involving many committed individuals. The research to produce and publish these works gave me an opportunity to know a substantial part of this community—and its language—in some depth. The partisan nature of my perspective was born in the process of this collaborative work.

The Thai Sign Language Dictionary: A Political Statement

The dictionary research should be noted as more than just a project to produce a linguistic reference work. The work was also a political activity, an understanding of which informs much of the perspective presented here. The details of this activity may seem at first unrelated to the grassroots organizational efforts, but they are, indeed, crucial to it.

A particular observation about the dictionary work, one more political than linguistic, regards the decision made to organize the research and the presentation of the final materials around a "Deaf" priority of perspectives, over those of a "Hearing" perspective. What does this mean? The work is still a book, printed on paper and organized in the traditions of publishing. In this sense, it is certainly no different. The same could be said of many of the research and linguistic collection methods, including the modernity of computer generation of research databases. The contentious terrain, however, is both that of the visual positioning of the sign representations and the ordering principles of the vocabulary.

The work contains both written English and written Thai, with English privileged on the title and credit pages, Thai privileged in the main body of the dictionary and index positioning (Figure 1). The sign illustrations are on the outside of each page, whether left or right side. There are generally three illustration fields per page. Thus, as a reader flips the pages, the sign illustrations are located in the easiest or most immediately accessible field of view. This was primarily driven by our perceptions of how to create a readerly convenience for an audience unused to reading, unfamiliar with the habit of flipping through large books and one oriented to the first language of that primary audience. The political intepretations regarding the significance of placing of languages on the page, and the potential for perceiving rank positioning vis-a-vis each other, was basically a luxury of our production team which few others will consciously notice.

The more contentious and deeply political ground, however, was the ordering of the vocabulary. In simple terms, there is a choice:

> Is the book "alphabetized" by the A,B,Cs of the spoken languages, regardless of which spoken language? Or is the book ordered by the internal rules of the sign language, itself?

Interesting question, and very political. The answer can be given in clean terms, but the methods to provide the fulfillment of the implied demand are not yet fully agreed upon. If framed from the external referent of the spoken language, that is by the A,B,Cs of the spoken language, the work is, at best, a glossary. The majority of so-called "sign language dictionaries" are not dictionaries, but really only glossaries as they are organized by the logic and ordering principles of a spoken language.

A dictionary, however, is necessarily not so simple. Again in brief, as these issues are not at focus here, there is not yet a final agreement on the precise principles of ordering of sign vocabulary, although the *Thai Sign Language Dictionary* is the largest to have undertaken to apply these principles. The first volume was organized by a grammatical ordering principle, focusing on verb types. The final volume, consisting of over 3,500 images in a work of 1,500 pages, implemented the alphabetizing by root radicals of hand shapes in a descending order of use frequency.[2] Cross-references, one each for written Thai and English, are in the back of the books for those seeking access via the spoken languages. I refer those interested to the technical notes in the respective volumes. The point here is that both volumes are political documents, both in what is presented and in how it is presented.

Very few works have presented sign languages in any format other than in glossary-like approaches to assist the beginning hearing/outsider learner to learn the language from a perspective privileging their view. The hearing learner may look for words s/he knows in order of his/her own language. Part of the political contentiousness of this revolves around hearing school policies that refuse to allow deaf kids to learn written and spoken language in the same manner: based on their first language.

Thus, presenting a sign-based ordering principle highlights two political fields: one, that the sign is a full linguistic entity, a language in its own right; and, two, that if hearing people find it useful to learn one language from the cognitive foundations of their mother tongue, then deaf people might well benefit from the same way of doing so themselves. This is vehemently contested in some terrains that have administrative power over deaf children. To engage this struggle directly was one impetus to establish the NADT. The dictionary work was one tactic of that engagement.

ORGANIZING: THE NATIONAL ASSOCIATION OF THE DEAF IN THAILAND

The "story" of the formation of NADT and of the nascent attempts to build an awareness of a greater Thai Deaf "community" has several root strands. The central story revolves around the resurrection of a dormant social club of alumni, call the "Center for Deaf Alumni," at the oldest deaf school in Thailand, the Sethsatian School for the Deaf. In the communal lore, this club was formed on 21 July, 1969, the day the U.S. launched the Apollo 11 moon expedition. The excitement of that event inspired the founders of the Center for Deaf Alumni with the enthusiam that they, too, would soar to new heights and accomplishments.

For the next decade, this club functioned much like any other small Thai social club, with small fund-raising activities for the annual Red Cross fair, and other such charity events. In 1978, an American volunteer from Oberlin College, Charles Reilly, joined the Sethsatian School and became increasingly involved with the adult deaf staff and out-of-school deaf youth. In 1981, with assistance from

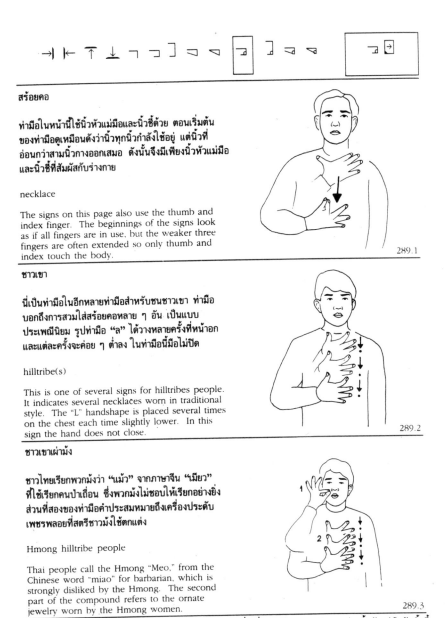

สร้อยคอ

ท่ามือในหน้านี้ใช้นิ้วหัวแม่มือและนิ้วชี้ด้วย ตอนเริ่มต้น
ของท่ามือดูเหมือนดังว่านิ้วทุกนิ้วกำลังใช้อยู่ แต่นิ้วที่
อ่อนกว่าสามนิ้วกางออกเสมอ ดังนั้นจึงมีเพียงนิ้วหัวแม่มือ
และนิ้วชี้ที่สัมผัสกับร่างกาย

necklace

The signs on this page also use the thumb and
index finger. The beginnings of the signs look
as if all fingers are in use, but the weaker three
fingers are often extended so only thumb and
index touch the body.

289.1

ชาวเขา

นี่เป็นท่ามือในอีกหลายท่ามือสำหรับชนชาวเขา ท่ามือ
บอกถึงการสวมใส่สร้อยคอหลาย ๆ อัน เป็นแบบ
ประเพณีนิยม รูปท่ามือ "ล" ได้วางหลายครั้งที่หน้าอก
และแต่ละครั้งจะค่อย ๆ ต่ำลง ในท่ามือนี้มือไม่ปิด

hilltribe(s)

This is one of several signs for hilltribes people.
It indicates several necklaces worn in traditional
style. The "L" handshape is placed several times
on the chest each time slightly lower. In this
sign the hand does not close.

289.2

ชาวเขาเผ่าม้ง

ชาวไทยเรียกพวกม้งว่า "แม้ว" จากภาษาจีน "เมียว"
ที่ใช้เรียกคนป่าเถื่อน ซึ่งพวกม้งไม่ชอบให้เรียกอย่างยิ่ง
ส่วนที่สองของท่ามือคำประสมหมายถึงเครื่องประดับ
เพชรพลอยที่สตรีชาวม้งใช้ตกแต่ง

Hmong hilltribe people

Thai people call the Hmong "Meo," from the
Chinese word "miao" for barbarian, which is
strongly disliked by the Hmong. The second
part of the compound refers to the ornate
jewelry worn by the Hmong women.

289.3

Width of rectangle; distance   ความกว้างของสี่เหลี่ยมผืนผ้า; ระยะห่างระหว่างนิ้วหัวแม่มือกับนิ้วชี้
thumb to index finger

Figure 1

Mr. Reilly, the Center for Deaf Alumni approached an American non-profit foundation, The International Human Assistance Programs, for a small grant to support self-help activities. This grant, called "Reaching the UnReached: Thailand's Deaf Community," was received from USAID through IHAP in conjunction with the U.N. Year of the Disabled Person. It began a relationship which would last until the closing of the IHAP/Thailand office in 1991.

The earliest efforts were not all easy. Many formal channels, such as the Ministry of Education's Special Education Division and the Royal Foundation for the Deaf, were not initially supportive. Some officials were derogatory, others threatened or even threatening, while only a very few voiced private support. The Deaf were not seen as a group deserving of empowerment. Charity and social welfare was what the official channels endorsed. During these early years of organizing, a decision was made to separate from the formal channels, from the schools and institutions "for" the Deaf. This was not easy and hard feelings by some officials took years to subside. It was, however, the only viable option for establishing a valid self-representing organization.

During the years which followed, many other small donors became interested in the activities of the Deaf Thai leaders and support for distinct activities was received. The activities of this self-representative organization received wide positive coverage in local and regional newspapers, which in turn generated a wider support network. The complex history of the relations with foreign donors which followed has yet to be written. Without doubt, the support from these sources allowed for much of the phenomenal output of that decade, yet it also brought tradeoffs which any grassroots organization must face when accepting external aid.

The legal formation of the actual NADT took several years, with key government documents being issued in October, 1983, and final formation requirements being completed in May, 1984. Perhaps more symbolically important than the legal recognition was the fact the organizational management was comprised entirely of Deaf Thais, including an elected Deaf Board of Directors and the all-deaf management of the new offices. A panel of "external advisors" with both deaf and hearing members was formed to provide assistance of their specified expertise.

The many successes quickly began to outrace the minor setbacks and word of the new NADT spread among both Deaf and hearing worlds. With the word of its activities catching interest, more Deaf Thais were showing up to visit the NADT in its newly rented space. Work days often became largely social days, due to the numbers of visitors and duration of their visits. While structures were put in place to facilitate tasks that needed to be completed, this social aspect of the NADT was something the leadership recognized as a value in itself and continued to encourage visitors, often leading detailed tours themselves.

The enthusiam of the staff and the community of Deaf Thais who kept returning caught the eye of several donors, such as USAID, the Canadians and the Australians. Many high level visitors were mingled with the drop-ins. A U.S. Assistant Secretary of State, wives of the Prime Minister and Foreign Minister of Australia, and ambassadors from a wide number of countries came to visit. All of them went away impressed with what they had seen: a grassroots organization being run by Deaf Thais, offering services and conducting research into their own unique language.

Inscribing the Language: A Grassroots Process

Within the NADT, the dictionary research began to generate increasing amounts of enthusiasm. While deaf people have always understood their sign languages to be "language," the official hearing world did not recognize them as language, per se, until only quite recently. The chance to show the full linguistic status of the unique Thai Sign Language (TSL) held great symbolic as well as practical significance to the leaders of the Deaf Thai community. It was hoped that such documentation would lead towards improved education for the deaf in Thailand, and to a use of the TSL as a language of instruction by fully qualified deaf teachers in the provision of that improved education.

The excitement of the dictionary research team was infectious, not only within the NADT but also throughout the broader community as they conducted field interviews and traveled to other parts of the country to interview other Deaf Thais regarding vocabulary and dialectical differences. The draft materials were taken to schools and to the newly formed rural clubs for review and comments. This constant checking of the materials with the grassroots sources was crucial to both the accuracy of the research as well as to the sense of ownership and pride in what was taking shape. The collective sense of the project fed the broader collective sense of a community, itself.

It was also fortunate that the nature of this project caught the attention of several reporters who did a series of articles about the organizational efforts, but often found reason to focus on the sign language research team. These articles, in turn, caught the attention of international organizations and brought support from other international disabled organizations, such as Disabled Peoples International and the World Federation of the Deaf. Presentation of the early draft materials electrified the WFD World Congress in Palermo, Italy in 1983. Manfa Suwanarat received a standing ovation after presentation of the preliminary research findings. By the next WFD World Congress in Helsinki, Finland, in 1987, the Thai Sign Language Research Team was world renowned for this pioneering research and, as noted earlier, took an active role in global political positions in representative forums.

Among the Deaf Thais outside of the NADT membership, reaction to the dictionary project ran the full spectrum from delight to apathy. Nearly all, however, recognized that such works were crucial to improved future opportunities. Individual responses often turned on whether such improved opportunities looked possible for them personally. Advocacy by the membership outreach teams sought to better educate the community about the benefits from collective representation. While some Deaf Thais wanted little more than reduced bus fares and other possible welfare benefits, the broader community was deeply supportive of and excited by the research and advocacy programs of the NADT.

Thai Sign Language research work was not the only activity of the NADT. Beginning from a small handicrafts workshop which sold toys and paintings to the foreign residents in Bangkok, the Workshop for People Deaf was later spun off to create Silent World Crafts as an independent company. The NADT's other main activities primarily revolved around membership outreach, which conducted many program events of educational and social purposes. These were quite popular, and full membership meetings often exceeded 500 people attending. A bi-monthly illustrated newsletter kept the broader membership posted of events and news items. Knowing that even a very nominal membership fee of under US$4.00 per year was too much for many members, the paid membership list of over 1,000 represented far more through shared information. Regional visits by clubs representing the geographical areas of the country were also popular, and official manuals for club operations were developed through field testing of the procedures with each club.

Broader social concerns, particularly about rights of deaf people to vote, to obtain national ID cards and passports, and to marry, gained public attention through advocacy efforts and most—although not all—abuses against such simple rights are now relegated to the past. Soon, leaders of the Deaf Thai community were participating in international research and U.N. sponsored social agenda meetings. The Thai delegations played key roles in a number of events which went into the U.N. Decade of the Disabled Person, and in forging the statements which led to significant policy shifts within the global representative body, the World Federation of the Deaf.

Details of events which marked both the growth and dissolution of the NADT have high interest value in their own right. Yet, while this organizing history is interesting and in many ways remarkable, why is this particular grassroot program of broader theoretical and practical significance? This question returns us to a focus on the cultural identity issues which are both so crucial to self-representation and which, for minorities, are also so fragile in the face of external pressures. The unique circumstances of Deaf cultures and the experiences of individual Deaf communities make visible many issues which confront all grassroots organizational efforts.

DEAFNESS IS A BIG COUNTRY

Deafness is democratic in its occurrence. "Citizenship" cuts across all boundaries of class, gender, or race. But, clearly, deafness is not a country—or is it?

Contrary to how the average individual defines deafness, that is as an audiological impairment, deaf people define themselves culturally and linguistically. The global deaf population is currently about fifteen million, which makes Deafness equivalent to a modest sized nation. Yet it is a "country" without a "place" of its own. It is a citizenry without a geographical origin.

There is a geography of identity, a location of culture, that deaf cultures illuminate. Where one is has a lot to say about who one can be. That spatial dimension is not limited to merely a physical presence, but also to a social location and a logistics of perception. Deafness is often called a democratic affliction, an equal opportunity condition. People who are deaf come from all walks of life and belong to any and all ethnic and national groupings. Nevertheless, in most cases, all occupy lower economic strata in adult life.

As noted at the outset, Deafness is often called an "invisible" disability. As a community with no physical homeland, the Deaf are doubly invisible. Only in their conversations—signed in native sign languages which borrow little from the spoken languages which surround them—is their identity "marked," their "ethnicity" made visible. The search for a "place" of their own is one which is shared with other minority cultures, yet they can never return to a native homeland.

This difficulty of a missing "place," or absent "anchor," is a recurring one. Without claim to a specific "place," and without the juridical and policing agencies by which we know nations in the twentieth century, Deafness cannot be a recognized nation. The medical model of the body inherited from the 19th century has left the common view· of deafness as merely a "condition." But the claims of a distinct "ethnic" identity which have accompanied the resurgence of deaf awareness in the past two decades call for an assessment of this and other identities excluded from the equations of "normal" identity.

Deaf cultures, like other cultures, are not homogeneous, either in makeup or in the diversity of individual or group experience. But an ethnography of deafness is not our concern here. Rather, it is the issue of exclusion and inclusion, of the availability and administration of acceptable identities, and about the construction of perceptions by which particular differences are most effectively excluded and others most effectively included. (For a more complete treatment see Wrigley, 1992).

An Oppositional Ethnography

Deafness, as an audiological condition, imposes few limits on human potential. Deaf people, as the bumper sticker says, can do anything—except hear. The problem, however, is that communication strategies of the dominant world make most information and training available only through channels which require hearing. The distinction in this framing is that if additional strategies made the same information and training available through visual modalities of language, not only would the world be a richer place, but those who are deaf would face fewer exclusions from the economic and social "mainstream."

Deafness is less about audiology than it is about epistemology. Inclusion and exclusion in participatory processes revolve around the practical paradox of identity and difference. This paradox is about belonging to and among those one might call the unusual, a genre currently known as Otherness and Difference. Exploring techniques of inclusion and exclusions in identity formation is not about ethnography in the usual sense. The classic view of ethnography presumes an explorer who enters into a foreign culture or space, who then returns with authentic stories, stories which authenticate both the authority of the story teller and the positions of the "original we" (the empire, community, or academy who are the audience) to validate empirical truth. The economy is one of recognitions of the tales told as evidence of truth, a self-referencing authenticity.

If only to complete that metaphorical frame, the present story is more about a return of the explorer with stories to tell about how the "original we" talk about those we presume available to be explored. It is rather an ethnography of the dominant gaze, particularly as applied to those deaf to its textual order.

The traditional counter-themes of appropriation, domination, exploitation, colonization, and oppression remain useful narrative embellishments by which both structural and ultimately personal relationships with Otherness and Difference might be better understood—possibly a more "honest" goal for an ethnography in any event. An ironic or oppositional ethnography seeks to explore the presumptions such relationships with knowledge require.

As such, this genre is not about centers, but about borders and margins. There are neither simple nor unified theories, as these are about creating centers which will in turn require evasion. Theoretical framings require the exclusion of those outside the borders and margins of their newly claimed centers. The hermeneutical anchors used for framing meaning in late modernity are most often those rooted in surveillance of bodies. As the site for naming distinctions, the body is a recurrent theme in studies of Otherness and Difference. Deafness is about a body surveilled.

Difference and Diversity

Reactions of the common to the unusual, and the practices by which they dominate them, are the best means through which ironic insights into the politics of identities are illustrated. In particular, the uses of the unacceptable, either of body or image, to reproduce and enforce naturalized categories serve to clarify both those identities which are allowable and the interests served.

Deafness is part of the bio-politics of nature, about the politics of being "normal," about the politics of diversity and deviance, about the politics of identity. The politics of difference is about inclusivity and cohesion. The techniques of exclusivity, including the institutional practices bound up within the educational settings, are only part of the ever evolving search to abolish difference toward the goal of a totalizing inclusivity.

My work is in the ethnography of appropriations, colonizations, constraints and constructions by which "we," the dominant hearing, have come to "know" and "make use of" those who are Deaf. I have sought to explore a series of perspectives on d/Deaf identity which each seek "to disclose the operation of power in places in which the familiar, social, administrative, and political discourses tend to disguise or naturalize it." (Shapiro, 1992).

There is a particular politics in such an activity; a dimension of politics which adheres in my writing. The tactics of such ethnography are primarily those of irony and displacement. My intention is a disruptive one, disruptive both of presumptions and practices which derive from and descend upon deaf bodies. This disruptive intent requires me to shift the frame or perspective from place to place. These shifts, in part, show that there is no one interpretive frame; that there is a politics of interpretation which needs to be made more visible. While certain questions about identities available and acceptable will remain constant, no single interpretation of possible answers can or will.

The tension between resistance and complicity is a theme which runs throughout my explorations. Each level of participation denotes complicity at some level, even in the most overt actions of resistance. The questions raised here are about making such tensions, as well as peculiar and long unquestioned forms of oppression, both more visible and accessible to a wider social discourse on interpretive models and on allowable identities for those marked "abnormal." This work is about the political meanings of Deafness, about the politics of Deaf identity and about what it costs to be "unusual."

The institutions of Deafness, including the proponents on either side of the supposed great oral-manual divide, manifest a neo-realism which reflects the western will to truth, the will to interpret the world and then to insist that the interpretation reflects the world as it is in itself. This neo-realism, bound to its positivistic claims of empirical data, is a major component in the policing of diversity.

Diversity has two faces. Diversity is a fact, when placed in the context of the vast extent of biological life on this planet. Diversity is a goal, when placed into the context of human societies. Neither is doing that well as we move into the twenty-first century. Diversity of the biosphere of this fragile planet is losing an ever-increasing percentage of biological life forms to extinction, while diversity in the human terrain is rapidly falling prey to the increasing discipline, surveillance, and homogenizing practices of late modernity.

Yet, an ethic of revaluation of differences, an accommodation in which the social space for such difference is widened, is reached as easily as a view which would construct them as villains or enemies to be vanquished. It is an ontology which creates its own room for ethical debate, but is at least free from the demand to control or cure. A potential is suggested for a way of allowing differences on their own terms. Control over the definition of terms, over the discursive economy in which such lives are placed, however, is the most divisive terrain.

Cultural Triage: Preschool "Failures"

What might a deaf child begin to understand about the world s/he is growing into when s/he is a second round loser, formally labeled a "failure," when only six years old? Will that child consider it to be, after all, a "hearing" world and gather that strength of inner inspiration to take on the heroic endeavor to acquire the competence now held out as required for basic membership? Or, rather, might s/he get the idea that this so-called "hearing world" is simply uninterested in anyone different enough to suggest that choices had already been made and forgotten?

When a child is only just out of pre-school, s/he does not find it easy to present objections strong enough to reopen negotiation on rules of societal membership. When two systems dedicated to the production of acceptable identities have already rejected you, simply because of a difference that interferes with their preferred social ground, rules about how teaching and individual communications will take place, the deaf child, with so few backup support mechanisms either personal or familial, is effectively excluded from any meaningful participation by definition. This happens in educational systems throughout the world. Call it "marginalization by preschool."

How can this happen? (And why are good preschools for deaf children so important?) A curious phenomenon seems to occur within official efforts to establish special preschools for deaf children. The deaf children selected are generally identified as failures from regular school entry groups, or similarly selected out as teachers prove unwilling to give further effort to communicate with—or control—the different child. After gathering these "problem" children, those children named as "deaf" to form a class, a special class comprised of children identified by their hearing loss, a curious shift takes place. Rather than accepting what all the children do have in common, nearly all efforts are focused on discovering which children, if fact, "don't belong"—those who demonstrate any residual hearing. These children, the ones who can almost hear, are then given nearly all the instructional attention. The defining characteristic which brought the children into the class, that they did not hear, becomes, again, grounds for further exclusion.

What is meant here is that all "teaching" efforts are focused on the residual hearing of that part of the group who might still be partially hearing, those children more accurately called "hard of hearing," or "hearing-impaired." Those children who are actually deaf are ignored as "failures" of this further test. Those children whose residual hearing is such that some speech skills are exhibited are the particularly prized and receive special attention. These children are labeled as "successful" while those for whom the special class was originally designed, the children who are deaf, are (yet again) labeled as "failures," reproducing and reinforcing the negative stigma onto the body of the deaf child.

This location of meaning is further reproduced in educational reporting about the achievements of deaf children throughout their school years. In conversations with both officials and teachers, for example, deaf school children are often referred to as "learning impaired" due to their poor achievement records. The circumstances by which such statements could be produced more likely suggest that these children have been "instructionally impaired" by the practices of the teachers, themselves. While the opportunity structures of learning for deaf children may be said to begin from a "marginalization by preschool," such expectations are reproduced in a self-fulfilling manner at each level of educational experience.

The negative marking of the child, thus, becomes inescapable. Having been deprived of early access to sign language, in addition to their "failures" in oral education, many deaf adults, when later attempting to enter into a Deaf social community, suffer the next stigma of "signing like a hearing person." Having learned the language late in life, their articulation skills mark them as "non-native" signers. Their legitimacy for membership in the Deaf identity—even when marked as an "oral failure"—is compromised. They lack the social competency measures, in this case of sign language fluency, required of the "native." They are marginalized, yet again.

The Sign Masters

One of the most valuable locations of cultural production for Deaf communities are the residential schools for deaf children. While part of this terrain remains contested, particularly around institutional practices and structural control over access to opportunity, the residential deaf schools are also places in which positive relationships develop and cultural transmissions occur. Most often these child-created worlds emerge in spite of the school's official intent and are unintentional byproducts of the physical warehousing of so many deaf children together. They are, however, among the most creative engines for the reproduction of deaf cultural knowledge.

Deaf children often create a richer peer society than do "average" children. (See also Reilly, 1994). As deaf school kids receive little stimulus from teachers or other external sources, they create rich worlds themselves. Part of this "richness" is due to the "loaded" nature of the learning experience. The significance attached to meaning production is "loaded" or more heavily laden due to the exclusivity, and scarcity, of its production and audience. The access to any content-laden event, educational or otherwise, is rare. Any source of information is thus value-added due to its rarity.

In this deaf children's world, among the most important sources for learning and self-awareness are the story tellers, those among the children whom Charles Reilly calls the "sign masters." The sign masters are leaders who are not appointed, but simply emerge in each generation of children. Children gravitate to them out of their own desires.

The story tellers are the primary sources of narratives and intellectual stimulus deaf children receive in rural schools. Their styles vary substantially. Some are comedians, some are serious and concerned. The creative reflections by sign masters, kids themselves, some which deeply mirror their social positioning and future prospects, provide among the most significant, if not the only, intellectual and linguistic stimuli in the deaf child's experiential world.

Regardless of style, each sign master finds an eager and hungry audience of younger children who hang on every nuance of their stories. The "hunger" is real. When children are directly asked why they want to sit with the story masters, why they like their stories, why they are eager to participate in their re-tellings, the response is invariably a sign which translates as "desire, hunger, crave." Manfa Suwanarat frequently spoke of her "hunger" to learn. Even in referring to social opportunities to meet new people, she often used a compound phrase which I might metaphorically translate as a "hunger to socialize."

Through sign, the story tellers play a crucial role in the reproduction of Deaf Culture. Satisfying hunger, they recreate and keep alive the language of survival.

DEAFNESS AND POVERTY IN MODERN LIFE

Deafness, in terms of the socially constructed relationship with Hearing culture, is about barriers to communication and to participation. In this framing, it has a great deal in common with poverty. Lack of access to timely information, to basic education, to decision-making processes and a total disregard by those with authority of specific local concerns are shared by deaf and poor people alike. The dreams and desires that have led other disenfranchised minorities, as well as the deaf, to band together in mutual self-assistance are remarkably similar.

The key claim to language rights, the right to distinctive ethnic languages as mother tongues for education and communal life, is also a frequently shared concern with poor minorities. Nevertheless, the overt subjugation of the sign languages of native deaf communities has continued with little change over the past century, while similar such oppressions of other linguistic minorities have been greatly reduced, at least on linguistic grounds. While the total disregard of concerns by formal authorities is shared, the state apparatus which maintain the exclusions of deaf people are both more explicit and rigid than those applied to the poor.

Deafness and poverty are also coupled in a much more immediate way. The experience of Deafness in the developing world, in the absence of family support, is almost always coupled with underemployment and poverty. This is not particularly surprising, but means that the Deaf are, thus, doubly excluded. Self-representation and self-help are often the only avenues remaining.

Unfortunately, the experiential base of such forms of expressive representation is often totally missing from the community as a body. Having been cut off from not only the decision-making processes which have directly affected their lives, but also from the very details and information which may have preceded or informed the decision processes, deaf people in the developing world have had little experience in any public arena. They are both information and process poor, in a very real sense. Self-representation and self-help organizing require both information and skills in public consensus building. In any body of people so long denied access to information and to participation in decision-making processes, such information and skills are extremely rare.

This description suggests the experience of deafness as one of victimization. While this is certainly not by definition, victimization is very much a part of the life experience of many deaf people in these less than ideal settings. The descriptions above are part of the context in which and from which the claims to an ethnicity are emerging. But the stories are not necessarily negative. Skills, talent, and initiative are also part of the deaf experience. As with poverty, the defining criteria have more to do with opportunity structures than with any individual "virtue" or "merit." Both poor people and deaf people are too often on the wrong side of the opportunity structure equations.

In 1982, a training seminar was conducted among the first deaf "employees" setting up a handicraft workshop, under what would later evolve into the NADT. The agreed purpose was to develop a worker-management style of operations. None of the staff initially wanted to participate in management decisions. They preferred to have decisions presented. To them, optimal circumstances meant only that such decisions were explained, not that they should or would be expected to have an active role in making them. When it was made clear that decisions were to be participatory, they initially participated reluctantly and absentee rates were often highest on staff meeting days. Major issues on the agenda often saw an empty workshop. When these meetings became part of the daily schedule, it became more difficult to avoid, but many came late until the experience—and the responsibilities—of participation became more common.

An interesting observation, when the seminar began, was that the staff did not have vocabulary distinctions between "money" and "budget." After the concepts were understood, vocabulary emerged to make these distinctions, as well as many others, for operational purposes. The point is not that the language was impoverished, but that the experience of the workers in having access to such information or processes was so limited.

If only to complete the example, with the basic training of these first workshops, and the assistance of several summer interns from the Stanford Business School in the mid-1980s, the Silent World Workshop became and has remained a freestanding business operating totally on their acquired commercial skills, Deaf-managed and without donor financial aid, since 1985.

Down and Out in Bangkok

Deaf "communities" in the less wealthy nations are mostly found in urban settings, as rural deaf people migrate in search of both employment prospects and other deaf people. Isolated linguistically from the surrounding dominant culture, they focus their attentions primarily on each other. Thus, a village or "small town" attitude and atmosphere is found even in large urban settings.[3] Within these small "towns," bickering, gossip, manipulation, exploitation, jealousy, and spite are the norm. Alcohol abuse and gender violence are common. Funerals and the occasional holiday parties are the few occasions on which intermixing of groups occur. Fights are not uncommon at such events. Money and personal slights are the usual provocation. Scandal mongering is a favorite past-time.

The western notion of "the village" resonates with the romanticist notions of cultural purity and of a time and place of simpler virtues. As with many other romanticist notions, this one has little to do with life as lived in those villages. The city is the village in generalized Deaf Culture. While the backdrop may appear to be that of a cosmopolitan modernity, the interests of the deaf village are generally each other—who's doing what to whom and with whom. The city is merely a backdrop, the "forest" in which this village is located. However, to borrow from classic primatology, it is a dark and nasty jungle.

Certainly the positive aspects of sharing, cooperation, and mutual assistance occur, but it is equally important to observe that lives in which negative experiences dominate produce a focus on negative emotions. The outlets for negative emotions are much more easily available than the opportunities for positive experiences. The Thai sign language, for example, is extraordinarily rich in descriptive and evocative vocabulary for negative experiences, big and small, precisely because the population base has such a rich experience of negative life events.

The urban deaf community of Bangkok is marked by disparate groups, roughly analogous to "gangs," although only a few fit the model usually noted as "gang" in the western urban sense. Groups of disadvantaged deaf gravitate towards leaders, be they those who can employ them, who are charismatic as strong leader figures, or those with resources to lend in time of distress. Loose alliances develop among the leaders based partly on old school ties, financial dealings or simple affinity in style. Intrigues to expand power, influence, or economic control are the stuff of everyday life. In these regards, the elite of the urban deaf communities mirror the elite of the surrounding dominant hearing community, at least in motivation and vice.

In this usage, and in the circumstance of less wealthy nations, the elite generally mean those who have homes, family support, and have had access to education. Unfortunately, this is only a very small percentage. The rest are poor and get by either by living in the servant quarters of larger estates, in sweat shop dormitories, or they get by on their own on or near the streets. Economic options for deaf people in less wealthy nations are rarely adequate to make an independent living. Most deaf people in such circumstances rarely rise above dependency on family or local indulgence for their livelihood. Peasant life in agrarian and fishing communities makes little distinction of hearing status, but the options for fulfillment are circumscribed by birth position within such locales.

Urban settings, while acting as magnets for deaf people seeking other deaf people, offer only a slightly wider range of options. Most deaf men without family connections are laborers of various types. Women have traditionally had slightly more options, but the risks are frequently higher. Cooking, sewing, and domestic skills have often allowed deaf women to gain employment outside the home, although stories of exploitation and physical abuse are common. As education has become available to an increasing number of deaf people, employers are still more likely willing to employ deaf women than men, simply because deaf females more readily display docility in the face of poor communication.

Sold on the Street: Vendor Life

Several perceptions of Deaf Thai life and opportunity avail themselves. Part and parcel of the time frame in which the growth of the self-representative organization occurs is Thailand's phenomenal growth in both physical and economic measures, and of Bangkok as the sole urban node of the national "economy" in particular. Tourism has been only one part of this growth, but has actively fueled the growth of "local culture" industries. While other economic sectors offer interesting turf for analysis, the growth of the street vendor economy is noted here as a voluntary terrain on which deaf people found some form of "equal footing" with their hearing competitors.

Vending from baskets on poles, pushcarts, or small store fronts are part of all trading societies. The tourism industry has built periodic agricultural and holiday festivals into a daily chorus line of displays piled high with any consumer good that looks to be going well this season. They vary little from any other tourist destination in the world but in tacky colors or thematic overlays.

The influence of petty capitalism among the urban Deaf population in Bangkok, primarily through street vending to tourists, has produced powerful social changes. Street vendors, selling a typical range of tourism trade goods, compete vigorously with each other. Deceit, malice, and greed are the primary social virtues developed in this setting. While the income is remarkably good during high tourist season, even the most successful lament the mind-killing attitudes and environment in which they work. The best and brightest of the educated, the most motivated of the uneducated, and the street deaf with no other choices are drawn onto the street to deal with corrupt police, street thugs, thieves, weather and the incredibly thick air pollution as they work alongside some of the world's worst traffic jams.

In Thailand prior to 1981, vending by deaf people was very unusual. Only three or four deaf individuals were visibly engaged in the tourist trade, and these were from families of vendors. The exceptions were two artists who had begun selling their own art works near a major tourist attraction in central Bangkok. In 1985, a government "clean-up" campaign aimed at clearing the footpaths of vendors and hawkers brought the attention of a few deaf individuals to the money being made by vending. As the overall government campaign backfired in general, bringing an increase of street vending and public support of vendors rather than a reduction, deaf people also joined the ranks of vending in droves.

Bangkok, widely promoted as an exotic destination with more than slightly naughty allures, has seen an active vendor culture of petty capitalism fill the streets in both tourist and local shopping entertainment centers, most particularly amid the night life areas surrounding the well-known Patpong Road, somewhat erroneously labeled Bangkok's "red light" district,[4] and the stretch of Sukhumvit

Road between two other such "entertainment districts," Soi Cowboy and the Nana Entertainment Complex. Patpong Road, itself, opened a night bazaar down the middle of the street, transforming a tawdry go-go, strip bar and prostitution district into a tawdry go-go, strip bar and prostitution district with its own brazen market display of counterfeit watches and fake designer clothes. It has proven a huge financial success, if not exactly an aesthetic or cultural improvement.

This addition of the night bazaar to the bar district is only a few years old, but fortunes have been made in that period, both by the "landlords" and renters of each parcel of approximately one square meter. Rent for such space can be well over $1,000 per month, depending on precise location and arrangements with the local officials. This includes electricity for lighting, but no protection from the elements. The elements include pimps, pushers, prostitutes, and police, in addition to the polluted air and acid rain.

More than a few vendors know they are working in horrible conditions which are affecting them both physically and psychologically. One girl spoke of the desire to "wash the tacky contamination of the street from her [entire] body" at the end of each day, while making the further observation of how difficult it was even for her friends to avoid changing under the steady onslaught of visible corruptions of the surrounding bar-zone of Patpong Road.

Still, income is good, and deaf vendors are now a very substantial and visible percentage of the vendors along Patpong Road, the adjacent streets, and over along Sukhumvit Road. These deaf vendors include some of the most educated and most well-traveled of the Deaf Thai community, as well as hired labor with no formal education at all.

Financially, vending has been the first major entrance into the economy for many urban deaf. The non-profit financing of the self-representative body, the National Association of the Deaf in Thailand, or NADT, paid wages that were higher than ever available before and comparable to modest civil servant wages. These involved a smaller number of individuals, however, and were very modest in comparison with recent vendor income. The NADT wages ranged between Baht 2,500 and 7,000 ($100-280) per month, mostly at the lower end of that scale. The street vendors range from about 4,000 ($160), for a paid assistant, to 12,000 to 15,000 ($480-600) per month for individual stall holders. Several multiple-stall owners are clearing in excess of Baht 100,000 (US$4,000) per month in high season. They dress and talk quite poor, however, to fend off the malice and revenge of their competitors. The two immediate past presidents of the NADT are also stall owners on Patpong Road. The current president is a stall owner down from Patpong on Silom Road.

The deaf vendors have also found a qualified form of equal footing in competing with hearing vendors for the tourist trade. With so many languages flooding down the street with each group or individual, establishing clear verbal communication is often a slow and laborious process.[5] Gesture and use of calculators to cut straight to numbers as a simple effective technique employed by deaf vendors is now more often emulated by the hearing vendors as a manner of conducting business. This is not by faking deafness, which is hard to do for very long, but simply by use of the same broad gestures and calculators to lead their customers' attention more immediately toward the products and their prices.

The issue or story here is the impact this sudden avenue to wealth has had on the social bond. Key to basic street capitalism is, surprise, capital. The few Deaf Thais with family wealth or other connections to funding hold positions of dominance to which lowly employees act in serf or very subservient relations. Several of the best and brightest of the school products are now peddling tourist trinkets as sales assistants on daily wage to make their meager livings.

A Displaced Community

The up-side, if you will, is that many more Deaf Thais can, as the first of a generation to have such options, pay their own way and are not left living back at home or in worse conditions of servitude. More Deaf Thai couples have married in the past decade than in the past known visual/oral histories of the Deaf in Thailand. Two major factors provided the circumstances by which this could take place: the broadening of the social network by the organizing efforts which produced the socializing opportunities crucial to the expansion of sign language communities; and the expanding economy into which the Deaf could enter, if not by invitation, then engage on terms sufficiently favorable to earn incomes unheard of only a few years earlier.

As the "community" grew in these aspects, it began to contract in its perspectives and articulated concerns. With only a few exceptions, vending on Patpong or in other vending zones has been a one-way ticket out of community involvement. As the vending phenomenon grew in the late 1980's and early 1990's, the best and the brightest, even of the research and organizing staff, turned to vending as their only activity and concern. This included those who had traveled to numerous other countries as representatives of the "community"— those seen as the highest "beneficiaries" of the foreign donors.

Many of the more successful vendors admit that social interaction skills with foreigners were honed through their participation in activities with the National Association of the Deaf. Yet, today, very few have time to contribute back to that organization. More than one admits that the "elements" noted above have a stronger influence than they initially suspected, and are not happy with what they see happening to themselves and to their friends. Bickering, greed, and jealous fights over wholesale prices found for the same tourist art and trinkets have become the acknowledged life of several of the most highly trained during ten years of multi-donor programs and successful projects. Thus, while vending has been the first major financial entrance into the economy for many urban Deaf, it has not been without ambivalence and some regrets.

Today, the remaining members of the once world renowned research team work as street vendors and sheepishly admit they have all but forgotten the linguistics training which had made them famous. The leading male has two minor wives who run adjacent vending stalls, while he lounges in a beach chair in the shadows, gambles with his buddies, or heads for late-night entertainment spots. The description holds true in several minor variations with other former staff and members.

These brief comments about everyday street life are less about the details of Deaf Culture than about the available options and position of Deafness in a world insistent upon denial of its existence, and some of the paradoxes inherent in inhabiting an identity so denied.

Such limitations on life options circumscribe "community." Like the triage that takes place in preschool, the "options" for adult life are delimited by discursive definition. The escapes or leakages through the borders serve to make more visible the socially constructed nature of such limitations. Deaf Thai culture, as with other Deaf cultures, has more than one center. Yet this work is not about the cultural center of any Deaf culture, but is rather about the ambiguity of their borders, too. The circumstances of Deaf life in Thailand, as in other countries, provide little option for change from within. Those described above are driven to seek escape from a place that is no "place" for them. In a framework of cultural politics, Deaf people are refugees in hostile territory.

Give More, Take Less

Circumstances are rarely as ideal as we might desire. This chapter emerges with the notion of "working with what we have." This is less a statement than, rather, an approach that I attribute to H.R.H. Crown Princess Maha Chakri Sirindhorn of Thailand. Princess Sirindhorn's ability to call forth extraordinary efforts, whether to physical challenges or to overcome entrenched attitudes, is rooted in a dedication that her subjects actively seek to reciprocate. Following in the footsteps of her father, she encourages all around her to "give more, take less," (see Gray et al. 1988). While calling upon all Thais to assist one another, members of the royal family are visible symbols of such responsibility.

The requirements of those responsibilities are not always easy. In a conversation about the difficulties of deaf Thai children in the more remote areas of rural Thailand,[6] the princess spoke of her own experience only several days prior while traveling in rural Thailand where a poor mother presented her young child to the princess saying the child was deaf.

What was the princess to do, with no direct knowledge of this child's actual situation? The clear evidence of a poor child in a remote rural area who needed special attention could not be ignored by the princess, neither in her position nor in her known personal compassion. On the other hand, was the child deaf? Were there other or additional concerns regarding the child's circumstances? Certainly she was able to direct official medical examinations be conducted. Yet, the princess felt required to wait upon medical doctors' examination, while even then worried of how to deal adequately with so many such children presented to her during such rural visits, and equally worried whether strictly medical concerns should prevail.

Should the child be diagnosed as merely deaf, the question still remained: should the child be removed from the rural family to be raised in an urban residential institution? Or should the child remain with the family? As in urban industrial nations, there is not one simple answer. The "best" interests of either the child or family are not determined easily. Yet the family has come forward seeking royal intervention. Simple neutrality or inaction in such circumstances are not options available to the princess. As this work makes clear, no perfect answer is available. As also in the older community, the opportunity structure produces sharply reduced horizons of possible goals. The former and the potential leaders all ask what other options might be possible. The question seems almost rhetorical. Yet a response is expected, perfect or not, and the princess lets you know. Regardless of rank or station, we are left to working with what we have.

END NOTES

[1] In Thailand, there has been only one documented case of a deaf child of deaf parents. Hence, nearly 100 percent of deaf Thai children come from hearing families.
[2] The principles of ordering used in both these volumes represent the pioneering research work of Dr. Lloyd Anderson.

[3] These examples draw primarily from Thailand, particularly from Bangkok, a city of over 8 million.

[4] The naming is erroneous not because ago-go, strip bars and prostitution activities are missing, but because the neighborhood has only the public claim to a sanitized version of what exists in more localized places in the city. It is featured, albeit just briefly, in nearly every government tourism presentation on the country. The image is thus "promoted" by formally disapproving glances accompanied by winks to the bankers and police.

[5] Particularly over the din of pimps and bar hawkers.

[6] On 11 April, 1991, five representatives of the project team that produced *The Thai Sign Language Dictionary* presented copies of the final work to H.M. King Bhumibol Adulyadet, which were received by H.R.H. Princess Sirindhorn as the representative of the king. The audience ran substantially over its allotted time, as the princess engaged the group in a detailed conversation on language policy and deaf education. Any additions to or comments on that conversation are entirely those of the author.

BIBLIOGRAPHY

Gray, D., J. Everingham and O. Wrigley. 1988. *The King of Thailand in World Focus* ("Give More, Take Less," interview in *Leaders*, April–June, 1982, and "The Princess Who Descended from Heaven," Die Zeit, 2 March 1984), Siriwattana, Bangkok, pp. 126–29, 136–36

National Association of the Deaf in Thailand (1986, 1990). *The Thai Sign Language Dictionaries*, Bangkok. Thailand: Thai Watana Panich Press.

Reilly, C. B., 1994. *A Deaf Way of Education-interaction among Children in a Thai Boarding School.* Ph.D. dissertation, University of Maryland.

Shapiro, Michael J. 1992. *Reading the Postmodern Polity: Political Theory as Textual Practice.* University of Minnesota Press, page 1.

Wrigley, Owen. 1992. *Sound Knowledge: The Political Meaning of Deafness.* Ph.D. dissertation, University of Hawaii.

CHAPTER 6

TOWARDS AN ALTERNATIVE DEVELOPMENT PARADIGM

Md. Anisur Rahman

INTRODUCTION: DO WE WANT DEVELOPMENT ?

What economists need to do most urgently is reevaluate the entire conceptual foundation and redesign their basic models and theories accordingly. The current economic crisis will be overcome only if economists are willing to participate in the paradigm shift that is now occurring in all fields.

—Fritjof Capra, *The Turning Point* (1983; ch. on "The Impasse of Economics.)

It is a great privilege for me to have been invited to give this address to the Bangladesh Economic Association biennial conference. The privilege is all the greater because I left conventional economics about fifteen years back and have been working since then in a field in which economics is not necessarily considered to be the primary motivation. The fact that I have nevertheless been invited to give this address indicates an openness in the economic profession of the country which is truly healthy and encouraging.

Last March I attended a seminar in Cartigny, Geneva on "Towards the Post-Development Age".[1] In this seminar I listened to an all-out attack on the notion of development from a set of scholars and scholar-activists of both north and the south. The attack included a vigorous plea for abandoning the word "development" altogether. In starting my address I wish to share with you the substance of the discussion and debate in that seminar.

It was observed that the idea of "development" was born as part of the "Truman design" of 1949 in response to the emerging cold war between the two great rival ideologies. The threat of the Bolshevik Revolution inspiring social revolutions in the so-called "Third World" was sought to be countered by a promise of "development" and "development assistance" to help "underdeveloped" societies catch up with the "developed." Development was exclusively defined as "economic development," reducing the degree of progress and maturity of a society to be measured by the level of its production.

Development was considered possible only by emulating the ways of the "developed" nations—their aspirations, values, culture and technology. And financial and technical assistance were offered with a patronising assumption of superiority in the march to civilization. The attraction of massive external finance and thrilling technology generated client states in the "underdeveloped" world where oligarchies able to capture the organ of the state could enrich and empower themselves as a class relatively to the wider society, to whom "development plans" one after another at the national level, and, subsequently, "development decades" at the global level, were offered as a perpetual hope for prosperity.

The result: The economic benefits of such development have not even trickled down to the vast majority of the people in most countries honorably referred to as "developing." But the most fundamental loss as identified by the Cartigny seminar has been *the obstruction of the evolution of indigenous alternatives for societal self-expression and authentic progress.*

The vast majority of the people were classified as "poor," and therefore as objects of sympathy, paternalistic intervention and assistance. Many of these peoples, under the blinding light of compassionate observation which was flashed upon them, have internalized this negative self-image. Perceiving themselves as "inferior," they have sought to be "developed" by the "superiors," surrendering their own values, cultures and their own accumulated knowledge and wisdom. Others have been forced to do so by the sheer power of "development" effort which itself has concentrated power, privileges and wealth in a few hands with the ability to subjugate and exploit the broader masses, and which has often uprooted vast masses of people from their traditional life and life styles to become inferior citizens in alien environments. Thus they have suffered not only economic impoverishment but also a loss of identity and ability to develop endogenously and authentically with their indigenous culture and capabilities—*a deeper human misery* which as economists we were not trained to recognize.

I had no problem agreeing to this critique of "development." But I was struck by the intensity with which the very notion of "development" was attacked. It was asserted that the notion of development is an "opium for the people" which legitimizes the exercise of power by dominating structures and creates dependence of the people and societies upon them, and which destroys the vernacular domain in which the people could evolve authentically. (The term "people" is used to refer to those sections of the population who have no economic or social status in the society by the standards of the dominating structures—those whom Adam Smith referred to as workers and "other inferior ranks of people.") Granting this, I argued that we should have the right to give and assert our own conception of the term development. I submitted that I found the word "development" to be a very powerful means of expressing the conception of societal progress as the flowering of people's creativity. Must we abandon valuable words because they are abused? What do we do then with words like democracy, cooperation, socialism, all of which are being abused?

The debate was inconclusive. But it was a revealing indication to me of the fact that at least in some societies pro-people forces do not assess that they have the power to use the word "development" to their advantage even by redefining it. This is perhaps not an universal phenomenon yet, and we know of authentic popular movements which are using the notion of "development" as they conceive it, as a motive force in their initiatives and struggle. This throws to us, social scientists, the challenge to understand and articulate what development might mean to people who have not lost their sense of identity and are expressing themselves through authentic collective endeavours, and also to understand how such sense of identity and collective self-expression could be restored to others who may have lost them. In other words, to articulate an alternative development paradigm in which the evolution of popular life is not to be distorted and abused by paternalistic "development" endeavors with alien conceptions but may be stimulated and assisted to find its highest self-expression which only can make a society proud of itself.

POPULAR INITIATIVES

In November last year I visited a number of organizations of landless workers in Sarail Upazilla in Bangladesh in the program of a rural development agency. Every year that I visit such organizations in Bangladesh as elsewhere I learn a lot. In Sarail in particular it was profoundly inspiring, seeing the kind of development some of these organizations of economically depressed classes are initiating.

The organizations of the landless in Sarail are managing, first, group-based saving-and-credit programs, and the best of them compare well with the best such program anywhere. Priority is given in these programs to internal resource mobilization over external credit. External credit is given only against an equal contribution from the base groups' own saving fund. The repayment schedule is tailored to the nature of the activity for which loan is advanced, and unlike some other credit-to-the-poor programs in the country there is no bias here against long-yielding projects by way of requiring repayment to commence immediately. Each credit application is endorsed by two members of the concerned organization who undertake to follow up the use of the credit and general financial condition of the debtor and to alert the organization of any unforeseen problem that may arise which might affect timely repayment. The group discusses such a situation with the debtor in its weekly meetings and seeks to assist the debtor overcome the difficulty, sometimes extending the repayment period if the difficulty is considered to be genuine. The approach to the credit operation is thus *sociological, humane and self-educational* rather than the approach of a credit bank with rigid procedural rules insensitive to specific human circumstances. The internal supervision procedure reduces the overhead cost of supervision as well. All this, with a repayment record claimed to be nearly 99 percent in recent years—a worthy illustration of *people's self-management.*

What was furthermore impressive was that a number of these organizations explicitly assumed a responsibility for the welfare not only of their members but for all "poor" in their respective villages. Cases of unusual distress of economically depressed families, whether they are members of an organization or not, are brought to its weekly meetings and distress loans, grants and other kinds of assistance are extended. This is a value which some of the organizations that I visited were proud of and wanted consciously to preserve. Candidates for new membership, in these groups, are not taken in immediately but are asked to attend the weekly meetings of the organization to be exposed to the issues and concerns of the members, and are admitted only when the organization assesses that the candidate wants to join not for selfish interests only but would also be concerned about the welfare of other poor in the village. Otherwise, they explained to me, "our organization would be disoriented."

Some organizations have gone further and have initiated development work involving and benefiting the village community as a whole. They have convened meetings of all villagers and proposed large projects in irrigation or flood control which would bring more land under cultivation extensively or intensively, or land would be protected from flood, and land-owning farmers as well as agricultural labourers would be benefitted from greater production and employment. The groups have offered their own contributions from their saving fund and their labor to such projects and have invited other villagers, rich and poor, to contribute in cash kind or labor. In a number of villages such projects mobilizing the resources of whole village communities under the leadership of organizations of the landless are underway. In one village I had the privilege of witnessing a mass meeting discussing the proposal for one such project—the construction of a dam which would save crop land from flood water as well as add land for habitation. It was being proposed that the extra land to be obtained from the earth work would be allocated in mass meetings to those who had no homestead at all. To me, such constructive and humane leadership in social development coming from the downtrodden was one of the most hopeful signals about the promise of social progress that I have seen anywhere.

In recent years such popular initiatives, spontaneous or "animated" and "facilitated" by social activists, are growing in many countries. Conventional development agencies have started recognizing them in a participatory development rhetoric without necessarily understanding their basic aspiration and message—such movements cannot be "coopted" in the conventional development paradigm without being disoriented. Radical thinkers now disillusioned with the great experiments with "socialism" are also looking at such movements with new hope. However, these grassroots movements and associated animation and facilitation work as a whole have matured sufficiently today and exhibit convergent thinking among significant trends through networking, exchanges, mutual cooperation and joint articulations in terms of their philosophical orientation, to provide the basis for outlining some key dimensions of the alternative development paradigm to which these trends belong.

POVERTY AND HUMANHOOD

In a forum on Participatory Development at the East-West Center in March 1992, I repeated my development philosophy, i.e., that the development problem should not be seen as one of solving the problem of poverty. It should be seen instead as one of inspiring the people to give their best human response to their situation. I added that I have no sympathy for the poor—I have only respect for them. A graduate student in the forum asked me what was the meaning of such philosophy in a condition of such extreme poverty as hunger. In response, over the several days of my stay at Honolulu, I shared with colleagues and friends there the following experience of a relief team during the devastating flood of 1974 in Bangladesh.

We were two teachers and twenty students in a relief team of the Dhaka University Economics Department. We collected some relief materials from Dhaka residents—wheat flour, some clothing, match boxes, medicines, etc. An advance team of five students went to Brahmanbaria district in the northeast region of the country and identified a cluster of villages deep inside the district where normal relief operation was not reaching. We went to Brahmanbaria town by train and from there took country boats to go to those villages with our relief materials.

Approaching these flood-ravaged villages we realized that what we had brought with us were drops in the ocean. Village after village was submerged in water. People had started dying by starvation; in many families male members had left days ago in search of relief and had not returned. In this situation, how were we to distribute the meager relief materials that we had brought?

We decided that we did not have the competence, nor the right, to solve this problem—the villagers alone had the competence to handle this, and they alone had the right to shoulder this responsibility.

As we approached to land on one village, hundreds of people, old and young, men and women, small children, rushed toward us, shouting "relief has come, relief has come." We alighted from the boats and introduced ourselves, and told them that we had brought very very little. And we were seeing such devastation all around that we could not give to this one village all that we had brought; perhaps we could help only three or four families in this village and then we should move on to other villages. But we did not know which three or four families they should be. Only the villagers knew them.

Could they tell us unanimously to which three or four families we could give some little help and then move on?

It took some time for us to communicate our question. Perhaps the villagers did not even have the patience to listen what we were trying to communicate. Many parents pushed their naked and half-naked children toward us and keep on saying, "Look, sir, my son, my daughter, has been starving for two days."

We replied, "It is indeed very painful to look at them. But there may be a family in this village whose children are starving for three days or for four days. Thus you would talk of them first—wouldn't you?"

After some efforts we were able to communicate what we were asking of them. We were seeking their help to solve a very difficult problem. We were inviting them to accept the problem of distributing the relief materials that we had brought, among so many people who needed relief, as their own problem, and we were challenging this with the trust that they would give their most human response to this challenge.

Gradually the clamor started changing its color, the villagers started discussing, debating which family was starving the longest.

We sharpened the question, "If we can help only one family in this village and then move on to other villages, which family should it be? You know that family—couldn't you identify that family to us, unanimously?"

The clamor now got focused and more disciplined. They played with the names of a few families and then told us: "You can help this family and go—we are all agreed."

We announced, nevertheless, the name of that family to the crowd: "This is the proposal—if we help *this* family and leave, you will not have any grievance against us."

"We agree."

We gave that family a slip to go to the boat and get a ration, and then said: "If we can help another family, which one is it?"

The villagers discussed and debated as before, and pointed to another family.

In this way we gave rations to four families only in the village and then said, "Now we absolutely have to go to another village. Would you show us another village in the neighborhood whom the flood has struck like this, or even worse?"

The villagers pointed in one direction, "Go to that village—thither."

They all followed us to our boats. And they said, "You are a different kind of relief team. May Allah bless you."

We left most of the villagers in starvation and pulled our boats toward the next village.

We did our relief operation in this manner in seven or eight villages. We went through the same experiences in each of them. Flood-devastated starving villagers. First everyone rushes at us saying, "relief has come, relief has come." It takes some time for them to understand our challenge. Parents push their children or lift them up toward us vying with each other in the hope of attracting our sympathetic eyes. But we cast on them eyes not of sympathy but of respect. When they understood the challenge the focus of the clamor started turning. They all identified unanimously which families had been ravaged the most, who needed relief most.

In one village we called the women separately. We had only

seven or eight sarees with us, and in this village we could at most
give two sarees. To whom should we give them?

The women lifted the free parts ("anchol") of their sarees,
drenched in flood water with a hundred holes, to show us. Big holes
through which the bodies showed. We had to turn our eyes.

"Your saree is indeed in a very sad state. It is embarrassing to
look at you, mother. But is there some grown up girl in some hut
who cannot come out to show even this, because she has nothing on?
If there is one, you are her aunt. Won't you talk of her first?"

Slowly the aunt lowers her head. With the fingers of her two
hands she twists the hem of the anchol, once in one direction and
then in the other. As if she was looking at her own self, once turning
this side, once the other. After a while she said slowly, still twisting
the hem of her saree, "Yonder in those two huts there are two grown
up girls who have nothing on—they cannot come out. Give the sarees
to them, I do not want a saree."

Even in abject poverty give people this respect due to a human,
and the best human being that is inside all, comes out.

THE CONVENTIONAL DEVELOPMENT PARADIGM

A development paradigm is an agreed school of thinking
about how to view development and how to investigate and assess
reality for development policy and action. In broader terms, how to
generate knowledge relevant for development. The basic premise of
the conventional development paradigm is a conception of *hierarchical human spectrum* in which some quarters are "superior" to others
and are therefore qualified to guide, control, determine the latter's
development. In this view, some nations are more developed than
others. Classes within a nation are superior to others in terms of
achievement, education, culture. These superior quarters create, or
occupy and control already existing structures, to exercise organised
domination over the "inferiors"—globally, nationally, locally—and take
responsibility for their development.

A professional class of intellectuals serves these structures
by assessing reality and constructing knowledge that are addressed
to and supposed to guide policy and action of these structures.
Educational and training processes are developed to transfer such
knowledge to members of the wider society through a hierarchical
teacher-student, trainer-trainee relation. Such processes not only transfer the concerned knowledge but also deepen the hierarchy. The
degree holder, the professionally or vocationally trained, are "superior" to the non-graduate or the untrained, and are part of the
structural "cadres" of development.

The generation of knowledge in this paradigm is a specialised professional function that is discharged by prescribed methods of the profession which require *observation from a "distance"* as opposed to getting "involved." The premise is that from one's "superior" vantage position it is possible to look down and assess what an inferior life lacks and needs, for the purpose of formulating development policy and action to help such life move up.

This paradigm, finally, gives *primacy to economics*—the management of scarce resources—as a part of its ideology, reducing the notion of development to economic growth which in recent times is being tempered with a concern for "distributional equity."

Needless to say, it is the development policy and action of the hierarchical structures dominating society which are responsible for the dismal state of so many individual nations today and of the world as a whole. The ordinary people have not had the responsibility for their own and society's development. In some of the most "developed" societies we are witnessing social disease formations which are going beyond human control. On the whole, the economic, social, moral and ecological crises which we are facing today, coupled with the diversion of resources from productive uses to create means of mass destruction, are ample testimony to the inherent incapability of the dominating structures which have appropriated the responsibility for social and world development, to steer society and the world toward a course of healthy progress. Instead, these structures have lent themselves to malignant interests whose growth and power are now threatening the very survival of the human race.

TOWARDS AN ALTERNATIVE DEVELOPMENT PARADIGM

The emerging paradigm of development represented by converging trends in grassroots movements combines several formative qualities, explored here.

Endogeneity of Development

The alternative view rejects the notion that development can be "delivered" from "above". Development, meaning development of peoples and of societies, is an organic process of healthy growth of creative faculties and their application. This process may be stimulated and facilitated by external elements, but any attempt to force it toward one's own standards from the outside can only result in maiming it. *Development is endogenous*—there are no "front runners" to be followed. One can be impressed, inspired by others' achievements, but any attempt to emulate could at best produce a carbon copy in which the originality of a creative social life and evolution would be lost. In reality, even a carbon copy would not be attainable without its necessary historical preconditions, and an attempt to become such a copy can only yield gross distortions.

If development is endogenous, then in people's development the *people are the subject*. This has profound implications for the categorizing of people as well as for the relations of knowledge in the society.

Non-hierarchical Human Relations

In the hierarchical scheme of the conventional development paradigm the broad masses of the people are the objects of development and most of them, with economic "entitlements" less than standards defined by the dominant structures, are categorized as "poor." In fact, the development problem is widely viewed today as overcoming the problem of such poverty, thus reducing human aspirations to the attainment of a bundle of economic goods. This problem of poverty has not been overcome and remains intractable for many nations after three "decades of development." In my lecture to the Asiatic Society of Bangladesh last year I elaborated the argument that even such poverty cannot be overcome by identifying this as the problem to be solved, as this creates negative motivations. Subsequently, I was struck by the following story in a paper presented at the Cartigny seminar:

> I could have kicked myself afterwards. At the same time, my remark had seemed the most natural thing on earth. It was six months after the catastrophic earthquake in 1985, and we had spent the whole day walking around Tepito, a dilapidated quarter of the Mexico City, inhabited by ordinary people but threatened by land speculators. We had expected ruins and resignation, decay and squalor, but our visit had made us think again: there was a proud neighbourly spirit, vigorous activity with small building co-operatives everywhere; we saw a flourishing shadow economy. But at the end of the day, indulging in a bit of stock-taking, the remark finally slipped out : "It is all very well, but, when it comes down to it, these people are still terribly poor". Promptly, one of our companions stiffened: "No somos pobres, somos Tepitanos !" (We are not poor people, we are Tepitans). What a reprimand! Why had I made such an offensive remark? I had to admit to myself in embarrassment that, quite involuntarily, the cliches of

development philosophy had triggered my reaction. (Wolfgang Sachs, 1990).

I have myself been a victim of this received culture of thinking and have called the people "poor" in many of my writings. Nor are all people themselves able immediately to assert themselves as proudly as the Tepitans since many have internalized, as suggested before, the "gaze" of the rich upon the poor (Rahnema, 1990). *The development problem starts precisely here: there can be no development (which is endogenous) unless the people's pride in themselves as worthy human beings inferior to none is asserted or, if lost, can be restored.* The human quality of a people is independent of their economic condition—even more, it can shine and can inspire under the most trying conditions. The people need this self-esteem to give their best, most creative and humane response to their situation, thereby to develop. They must, therefore, be invited and empowered to relate with anyone and with any structure horizontally and not vertically, as equals.

Generation and Relations of Knowledge

Together, the above two premises—the endogeneity of development and a non-hierarchical concept of human relations—lead to a third premise which concerns the vital arena of knowledge relations and the generation of knowledge relevant for development. Development being endogenous, it is not possible with somebody else's thinking and knowledge. Nor is a relation of equality possible if one feels that knowledge essential for one's development rests with others.

I once visited a village in Bangladesh with an agency which went there to open a credit-for-the poor program. I was introduced to the people as a very wise man, thereby doing damage immediately to the possibility of a dialogue as equals between me and the villagers. I tried to undo the damage by telling them that they had seen "wise" persons like me before, and they knew that they had not benefited much from listening to such persons. If I were thrown now to make a living in their village, I would not be able to survive without their help. Maybe I knew something about international structures and linkages that they did not know, but they knew so much about their own environment that I did not know. Would they, therefore, let me learn from them? I did not succeed much in making a deep-rooted perception of vertical relation change in a few minutes of such smart talk (after all, this "wise" man had come with and had been introduced by agents of a program to give them money!)

Let us look at this claim of wisdom a bit more closely. We spend in the order of, say, twenty-five years of our early life in classrooms and studies shut off from active life, to become "educated"—wise. Life moves on meanwhile, struggling and moving through challenges and odds. Those who survive the odds must be very able and wise, and among them must be some who are the ablest, *resourceful* even if "resource"-less, wisest and most creative of all human beings. Yet we have the audacity after these twenty-five years of existence isolated from people's life, to stand above this life with our educational certificates in our hands, and tell it how it should move, not caring even to learn from it how it has come so far and what its own thinking on issues of concern to itself are.

The "educated" have not proven to be any more "enlightened" or capable of wise and responsible decision and conduct than the "uneducated". While we "wise" persons have been responsible for the sad plight of the world today, there are numerous examples of ordinary, "uneducated" people devising responses to problems confronting them which show great wisdom, sense of responsibility and morality. But the myth remains that it is professionals, and the "educated" generally, who are the repository of the knowledge and wisdom necessary for development. And that it is they who are the only qualified agents to generate knowledge and construct reality for developmental action. The myth is not only factually false; by perpetuating a *vertical knowledge relation* it also vitally obstructs development.

Social reality does not exist "out there" in an absolute sense to be observed by standardised techniques. Reality is constructed by the observer, whose own perceptions and values as well as the method of observation determine what is observed, what is abstracted in distilling the observation, and what is finally constructed. Reality, in other words, is constructed within a given paradigm, i.e., of a particular epistemological school. Its validity therefore rests on the premise of designing policy and action within the given paradigm. The logical validity of educated professionals constructing social reality— knowledge—by standing apart from people's life and observing this life from their own vantage point, for the purpose of prescribing policy and action addressed to hierarchical structures (and to make great mistakes in doing so) is not in question. But the value of such knowledge stands and falls with the paradigm which premises structural subordination as the basis of development. If the people are the principal actors in the alternative development paradigm, *the relevant reality must be the people's own, constructed by them only.*

I was educated in this epistemological theory when in 1976 I visited a "shibir" for "Lok Chetna Jagoron" ("awakening of people's awareness") in the Bhoomi Sena movement in India. In that shibir attended by about 40 acutely oppressed adivasis from a number of villages, the leaders of the movement and a few external "animators" who were also there did not seek to transfer any knowledge external to the endogenous creativity of the people. Instead, they invited the people to create their own collective knowledge about their own social reality—their own social science. The central invocation in this "animation" work was to invite the adivasis to assert their self-perceived life's experiences as *their "truth"* irrespective of the "truth" being spread by the dominant structures or by the professionals (social scientists). This the participants were first invited to do individually, to assert their personal (subjective) truths; then to discuss the common elements in these personal truths and thereby to move to their collective (objective) truth. They were invited, after this, to take collective action to promote their interests on the basis of their own social knowledge thus generated, and engage thereafter in a systematic collective praxis—cycles of reflection-action-reflection—of their own, to keep advancing their objective knowledge as well as their overall collective life of which the generation and advancement of self-knowledge is an essential organic component. Thus, to keep developing, endogenously.

Popular movements in many parts of the world are today using variants of such an approach for the construction of social reality by the people themselves as a basis of and an organic part of their collective self-development. The Freirian movement for "conscientization" first started in Brazil and today spread in many countries of the world, and the "participatory research" movement pioneered by the International Council for Adult Education and now also a global phenomenon, are overlapping movements with the same epistemological premise as Bhoomi Sena's "Lok Chetna Jagoron". The International Labor Organization's program on Participatory Organizations of the Rural Poor (PORP) has played some role in helping the sharpening of this approach to social knowledge generation and people's own praxis in both theory and practice.

The central premise in this approach is social enquiry by collectives of the people themselves. A strategic task in such people's self-enquiry is the *recovery of history* by people's collectives, to "rewrite" history with the people as the principal actors having taken initiatives of their own, having responded to action by external or hierarchical forces, and having formulated and implemented collective policy and decisions to promote their own interests. It is of critical importance for the people to take inspiration from history thus "rewritten," to view and assert themselves as the subject of their destiny—reversing the negative self-image that we have given them. Another critical task is the recovery and reassertion of the core *values and cultural elements* of the people themselves which are being threatened or are eroding as a result of the operation of the development paradigm which the dominant structures have imposed upon them. Finally, the results of such popular inquiry are the property of the people and are to be documented and disseminated through means of communication of the people themselves in accordance with their level of literacy and cultural development.[2]

"Building" and "Sharpening" Each Other

In people's development, thus, reality will be constructed by grassroots social formations and not by "top-down" professional investigation. This does not deny the role of professionals to contribute to the construction of specific aspects of reality—e.g., macronational or international aspects to which the popular forces may not have immediate access. Specific skills of professionals may also be of value to popular forces in assessing specific aspects of reality. A constructive interaction between the two has the possibility of enriching popular construction of their reality—always granting, however, the right of popular forces to consider, adapt or reject any external input to their own effort at creating their own reality. Needless to say, from such a constructive interaction the professionals themselves have the opportunity to learn and be enriched immensely.

This brings us to the question of what is conventionally called "education," and "training," and to the idea of "transfer of knowledge."

There is need in every individual to improve one's intellectual capacity, breadth of knowledge and specific skills. The conventional methods of "teaching" and "training" administered in a hierarchical relation and aimed at a "transfer of knowledge" are a dull, depressive approach to serve this need. The "student" and the "trainee" go through such processes mainly because the dominating structures require them to do so for entry into the job market. Such processes have very little to do with real learning, and actually invite the recipients of knowledge to seek ways of acquiring the certificates without necessarily putting in even the prescribed efforts.

Knowledge cannot be transferred—it can be memorized for mechanical application, but learning is always an act of self-search and discovery. In this search and discovery one may be stimulated and assisted but cannot be "taught." Nor can one be "trained" to perform tasks which are not mechanical but creative. Institutions of teaching and training which seek to transfer knowledge and skills serve mainly to disorient the capacity that is in every healthy individual to creatively search and discover knowledge. It indoctrinates them, furthermore, in the value of hierarchy which they then tend to pursue with vengeance—the humiliation of being subordinated is passed on to one's own subordinates.

For some time in recent years I have been looking for a language to replace words like teaching and training. I got it in March this year from a workshop of African and Caribbean grassroots activists held in Zimbabwe on the training of field animators to promote participatory development. In this workshop I raised my question on the notion of training which I said is a hierarchical notion that creates both hierarchy in personal relations as well as institutions for "training" without an organic relation with and standing above practical life. I asked the participants in the workshop to search whether in the vernacular language of the people with whom they had been working there was any word which expressed an alternative, non-hierarchical concept of learning.

The participants searched, and came up with two words in the Bantu language of South Africa: "uakana" meaning "building each other," and "uglolana" meaning "sharpening each other." I invite you all to reflect deeply on the power and richness these words have in expressing both the concept and practice of non-hierarchical learning in which no one teaches or trains anybody, but instead knowedge is sought and created through mutual dialogue and collective enquiry. I would also invite you to reflect upon the power and richness of such popular conceptualisation as an organic part of their urge for collective self-development in a non-hierarchical framework—a power and richness which we are trying to destroy by imposing upon them concepts of education and training derived from an altogether alien scheme of values—i.e., the values of structural domination.

Economics

I come, finally, to economics.

A distinction needs to be made between economics as an ideology and economics *as a tool for rational calculations*. As an *ideology*, as I have said before, economics puts economic development as the central concern for development, as part of the conventional development paradigm in which the dominating structures and the professions serving them presume to decide what the people's aspirations and needs should be. As a tool for rational calculations economics remains an important discipline, and quantitative calculations with which economics is chiefly concerned are also very important in sizing up some major dimensions of the economy. However, it cannot be claimed that economic calculations are necessarily the prime considerations in the life and aspirations of individuals, communities and societies.[3]

While most economically depressed communities would want to improve their economic condition, most would also have a finite trade-off between higher economic disposition and such treasures as human dignity, indigenous cultures and self-determination if such choice were sharply put (Rahman, 1989b). At a more fundamental level as I have stated in the Asiatic Society Lecture, since the distinctive human faculty is the faculty of *creativity*, every human being must have a fundamental urge to fulfil this faculty; hence the opportunity for creative self-expression—a synthetic representation of all the above treasures—must be the primary "basic need" of human beings as distinct from animals. Whether this is quantifiable or not, economics cannot drop this primal human need from the desired "bundle of goods" and yet claim to be talking of the development of humans rather than of animals. The development problem is, thus, not of delivering a material bundle of goods to the people, but of facilitating the maximum scope for self-creativity of the people with which they could create their self-chosen bundle of goods including cultural and intellectual pursuits according to their indigenous urges.

The landless groups in Sarail about whom I talked before, and innumerable other self-mobilised grassroots groups and communities all over the globe, teach us more. They talk inevitably of solidarity among themselves, and many such groups talk of solidarity with other economically depressed or socially oppressed people in their respective neighbourhoods. The economics that we have learnt—the economics of private "utility" or to put it more crudely, private greed—reflects the value orientation of dominant structures of the West whose interests the mainstream of its economics has been serving. Another economics has been serving the interests of structures seeking to exercise domination over the people in the name of "socialism" invoking the value of "bureaucratic collectivism." Neither of these two economics recognises the concept of solidarity which self-mobilized grassroots groups are asserting—to share and care with and for others, to work together not just as a means of enhancing private fortunes but also to develop together, to extend a helping hand to others in distress or lagging behind, and to ensure that development of some does not take place by retarding the development of others. Talk to such mobilised grassroots groups and you will find these to be natural, spontaneous values which guide their collective efforts.[4]

It is unfortunate that economics has not recognized this *rationality of solidarity*, which is observed in popular behaviour, premised as it (economics) has been either on the rationality of private greed or on the rationality of bureaucratic, hierarchically managed, collectivism. The concern for distributional equity in modern economics which seeks to temper the rationality of private greed is not a response to the popular urge for solidarity which is a value concerned with daily relations among persons rather than with the distribution of social wealth for private pursuits. On the other hand, such solidarity which existed in various measures in pre-socialist societies may actually have been suppressed if not destroyed by the introduction of bureaucratic socialism, in countries where this brand of socialism was introduced, with accountability to hierarchical structures which was not conducive to the forging or retaining of independent bonds of solidarity among the people.[5] While solidarity as an authentic human value has been disregarded in the economics of capitalism as well as socialism, both of which have been premised on hierarchical social relations, it is unfortunate that we have also allowed ourselves to be mesmerized by such economics of exploitative structures rather than rooting our economics in the authentic value of our own people.

People's indigenous behaviors are governed both by the rationality of individual interest and the rationality of solidarity with, let us say, "social neighborhoods"—family, kinship, group, community, and the like. This solidarity is not only a means of distribution of resources but is also a resource itself which "augments" the totality of resources by bringing individual resources, talents, ideas, at the service of a collective as well as by stimulating in a synergic way the creative energy of such collectives. If grassroots groups are exhibiting this value, it is the responsibility of economics to redefine itself to recognize, and serve, this value.

There is evidence, further, that solidarity can be stimulated and strengthened by appropriate policy and action. The relation between individual interest and solidarity is dialectical, the two combining in a unity with its tensions, a unity which may show one face relatively more than the other under specific historical circumstances. Policy and action can and should be addressed to constructing a healthy synthesis between the two. (The argument extends to the question of inter-group or inter-community relations.) In the indigenous cultural evolution of the people such a synthesis is observable in the fabric of mutual support characteristic of traditional livelihood. The economics of both capitalism and socialism have denied and sought to destroy this synthesis by championing the motivation of private greed or of bureaucratic collectivism.

Economics as the science of the administration of scarce resources is a potentially valuable science to serve human aspirations. But its presupposition of the devaluation of culturally-determined behavior has made it an alien science to popular efforts for authentic development. In order to serve authentic development, economics needs to know with what values people administer their scarce resources—in particular, when the people mobilise to assert their own consensual values and take collective initiatives to promote them as part of their own concept of development—and what implications this has for the very concept of resources and for assessment of the resources at the disposal of a society.

Finally, an economics that asks the people to surrender their pride in themselves and to queue up under the "poverty line" is an economics to serve not the people but domination over them. The people (as well as nations), like the Tepitans, must feel proud rather than poor, as a human spirit facing challenges—none can develop otherwise. The corresponding economics, of necessity, must be the economics of pride (creativity) and not the economics of poverty (consumption).

In my Asiatic Society lecture I have contrasted the creativist view of development with the consumerist view. The two corresponding economics will be radically different. In the creativist view the social optimization calculus will not be the maximisation of the time stream of consumption but of creatively engaged labor—i.e., "unalienated labor" in the Marxian philosophy, a concept which got grossly abused by bureaucratic socialism. The concept of employment will be different accordingly—employment to serve hierarchical structures saps one's creativity and is to be minimized. Saving and investment (in real terms, e.g., making a tool or constructing a dam) will not be considered a sacrifice of "consumption" but a positive way of channelling one's creativity with a direct fulfillment or "utility" of its own in addition to increasing the scope for creativity in future. Such fulfilment is the ultimate act of consumption, a concept which also, therefore, calls for a review.

To construct this economics of creativity which is implicit in so many popular initiatives for collective self-development is the challenge to economists if this profession is to serve the people rather than structures which dominate over them.

CONCLUDING COMMENTS: THE ROLE OF THE STATE

I was asked by some colleagues in Dhaka last year what is the macro-counterpart of such thinking—in essence, what is the role of the state in this paradigm? I had responded that they should form a "study circle" to examine this question in interaction with popular forces. Let me, to conclude this lecture, say a few more words on this question.

The machinery of the state is constituted by structures which have enormous power over the people; such power inevitably invites bids to capture these structures or control them in some way or other to promote private interests. This is the central lesson of the present century's experiments with social governance through the instrument of nation states which has systematically undermined the people's own governing abilities and imposed social orders—e.g., capitalist, "mixed," socialist—which have predominantly served the interests of elite minorities in the society.

It was thought that there was a persuasive case for some "guardianship" of society at least as a "trustee for future generations." Alas, what most nation states are bequeathing to their future generations are not very worthy, with massive destruction of nature to satisfy present greeds, mortgaging the future of societies to the humiliating mercy of foreign creditors, malignant social diseases and a chilling sense of insecurity among our children about the future that they see before them.

The role of the state, in order to facilitate and coordinate popular initiatives rather than to dominate over the people, therefore, needs indeed to be redefined. But I suggest that we should not put theory too much ahead of practice. For then, as in the case of democracy and socialism, theory would be abstract and would end up being used by forces with contrary commitments as a ploy to continue domination. The task of social science at the moment is to work with popular movements, and assist them articulate their own social visions and link with each other to develop broader popular forums for such articulation. The theory of the state, and a theory of how attempts might be made to bring about a desired form of state, should emerge from such processes rather than precede them or be developed independent of them.

END NOTES

This chapter has been adapted and expanded from the inaugural address at the Bangladesh Economic Association biennial conference, Dhaka, January 1991. In developing this address the thinking of Gustavo Esteva (1990), Stig Lindholm (1977), Jean Robert (1990) and Wolfgang Sachs (1990) have been found to be particularly useful. Philippe Egger and Ajit Ghose provided some useful comments on a previous draft.

[1] Organized by the Christophe Eckenstein Foundation, Geneva.

[2] As against the concept of "copyright," as part of a culture of "knowledge capitalism" of professional researchers who research upon the people using the people's time and sell the product for private gains.

[3] To quote from an earlier paper of mine: "It is perfectly natural and valid for parents to want to see one's child develop as a wholesome human personality, making a

comfortable but not necessarily lavish living, able to handle life's tensions without cracking, develop creative faculties of social value and engaged in their application, emotionally content with life, loved by family and friends and held in broad respect by the wider society. Most such indicators of personal development are not quantitatively measurable but may nevertheless be at the core of enlightened human aspirations, for oneself as well as for one's near and dear ones. There is no reason why, for society or communities of people, the notion of development should be very different, and should take a narrower, predominantly quantitative view, leaving out important, some vital, considerations which can be assessed by analytical reasoning if they cannot be measured by numbers." (Rahman, 1989a)

[4] For many indigenous communities the idea of solidarity has extended to nature as well. The concept of "owning" and "harnessing" natural resources is relatively recent in many societies, imposed by alien elements after colonial conquests. I was told, e.g., by colleagues in the workshop in Hawaii in 1989 that they never had the concept of "owning nature" (e.g., land, forests, the sea). To them nature was a living being to relate with and not to exploit. The same is true of many indigenous communities all over the world. From this we may begin to see the cultural root of the destruction of nature and the ecological crisis that "development" is causing.

[5] One would have thought that socialism was premised upon such solidarity. Last year in July, I visited a village in Hungary where animation work had been initiated under the ILO's PORP program to stimulate the villagers to get together and collectively review their experience under socialism. The animator, a professional economist of the country, reported to me that he was finding it very difficult to make the villagers come together and talk about their problems. The culture of sharing personal problems had been destroyed by "socialism"—the hierarchical control of society had generated mistrust of the villagers in each other and fear of offending the hierarchies by horizontal dialogues.

REFERENCES

Capra, Fritjof. 1983. *The Turning Point: Science, Society and the Rising Culture.* Bantam Books.

Ekins, Paul. 1990. *Economy, Ecology, Society, Ethics: A Framework for Analysis—Real Life Economics for a Living Economy.* Paper for the Second Annual International Conference on Socio-Economics. George Washington University. Washington, D.C., USA March 16-18.

Esteva, Gustavo. 1990. *Towards the Post-development Age?* Paper presented at the Fondation Christophe Eckenstein Seminar "Towards the Post-Development Age?" Geneva.

Frank, Andre Gunder and Marta Fuentes. 1988. *"Nine Theses on Social Movements."* IFDA Dossier 63, Jan/Feb 1988.

Friedman, John. 1979 "Communalist Society: some Principles for a Positive Future." IFDA Dossier 11, September.

Lindholm, Stig. 1977. *Paradigms for Science and Paradigms for Development.* Paper presented at the second meeting of the phased seminar "From Village to the Global Order." The Dag Hammarskold Foundation. Uppsala.

Rahman, Md. Anisur. 1989a. *Qualitative Dimensions of Social Development.* Paper presented at the Workshop on the Evaluation of Social Development Projects and Programmes in the Third World, Swansea, Wales, U.K.

Rahman, Md. Anisur. 1989b. "People's Self-development." National Professor Atwar Hussain Memorial Lecture, Asiatic Society of Bangladesh, Dhaka, 16 October. *Journal of the Asiatic Society of Bangladesh (Hum.),* XXXIV(2).

Rahnema, Majid. 1990. *Poverty*. Paper presented at the.Fondation Christophe Eckenstein Seminar, see op. cit.

Robert, Jean. 1990. *After Development: the Threat of Disvalue*. Paper presented at the Fondation Christophe Eckenstein Seminar, op. cit.

Sachs, Wolfgang. 1990. *On the Archaeology of the Development Idea. Six Essays*. Paper presented at the Christophe Eckenstein, op. cit.

Editors' Reflections, Part II

Issues of facilitation, insider-outsider relations, autonomy of local groups, and wider expansion of participatory action emerge in these chapters. Editors' comments address these questions.

Self and Other: The Insider-Outsider Relationship

K: I think I might understand the source of my discomfort. A: Yes. How? K: It has to do with sort of interrelated dimensions that I've been struggling with for years. Change occurs because people who are an integral part of something change that something, they are connected to it, they're part of it. Now, we're all integrally connected to everything in the world by virtue of being inhabitants of the planet, but then there are also ways in which we have a more natural inhabitance in certain communities than in other communities. And in certain parts of the world than in other parts of the world. I am outside of the experience of the daily life and struggle of groups like...blacks in Harlem. This really comes down to ethnic, class, national differences. I feel when I go too far outside of what is my place in which I have in a sense a natural right to be, then I feel I'm impinging on someone else. I'm arrogant, even by going there and saying, Let's talk. It's like what Jan calls the invitational. Somebody invites you because they think you have something to share, then fine. You are there by nature. You have been invited to be part of that group. A: Hm.

K: So for me, especially being a middle class white American, just about anywhere I would go is patronizing. And, I've had to confront this for myself, in terms of what is my natural role. I feel I'm in two different parts of a power struggle, which I really cherish, because on one hand being female I'm in a certain power struggle in which I feel one down, struggling for voice. And being middle class white American I'm in another power struggle in which I'm one up, trying to figure out what to do with all this power I got, by virtue of my birth. And I've been observing how I feel in different parts of that struggle.

When I visit Hawaiian groups and they say, Oh you haoles, leave us alone. We don't want you here. You shouldn't be here. Even your desire to help us is aggravating. Go way. And I feel hurt, and I feel sad because part of me is saying, well I have this desire to connect. And part of me is saying, leave these people alone. And then I go and sit in groups of women who are talking about our mutual pains, and somebody might come in, for example, a man might come in wanting to be a part of that, to help it or in some way... and we find that totally infuriating. We want no part of that. And in fact the thing that comes up is usually, the best way you can help us is to go to your natural group, which is a group of men, and ask them to contemplate their role in this dance of power. Not to help us in our little part of the dance of power. We have to work on our own empowerment. You go work in disempowering those people who try to lord things over us.

So by analogy, I kind of figure, in living and struggling in my own community, then I have a right to speak with people in other communities who are making their own struggles in their own ways. And so this idea of animation, whereas I see groups that have similarities being able to do that with each other, there are so few places where I feel I have a right to do that. It's confronting that desire to be an *animateur* that many people of my background often feel, which does not have a natural application except in our own community, which may be a community of power. A: Yes.

D: You know, in some measure there is that tension with respect to any external facilitator who is not easily defined as being naturally of that same situation. Although it very much depends on the personal attitude and quality with which one does this. But it's a generic feeling, and a generic question. 'Cause I think, in many situations there is a sense in which an external person is not part of that natural community. But many of the circumstances we're talking about are of such external people. And we're really trying to create connections that are human connections, but they're among humans who are comfortable in a certain orbit, but when they move into another orbit are easily distinguishable as different, and may be regarded as intruding.

K: And also not coming with the wisdom of that place. D: Yes, that's extremely important. So where the chapters are connecting, they're connecting people on these different planes, in these different spheres. A: Hm. D: And so in some ways the book has to bridge those different spheres.

A: Well, you know I have examples that a complete outsider has become a great animator. K: Yes. A: We have done these experiments in the Philippines. Complete outsider meaning not from another country, even that has happened, we have examples, but from within Philippines in a project, animators have been recruited, who have gone to a village where they have never gone before, to work as animators. And have been able, because they belong to a common nation, you know, it depends to some extent on your personality, but you have been able to break that ice, and make this fully acceptable to you. And then, become an animator and excite these people to mobilize, solidarity, and collective action. This has happened.

Help and Autonomy

A: I remember that when we three had been discussing, last time possibly; we had been using words like "help," and you had reacted against that. K: Right. A: And yet when Puanani came, she was talking a lot using the word help. K: I noticed. A: Yes, I also noticed. And I know that you noticed, naturally, so that was very interesting. I think Pua was not only using the word, she was saying that outsiders can help a lot. How do we reflect on that?

K: I think for myself, it's again not so much the word as it is the stance. I know Puanani a bit. I've been able to talk with her and watch her a lot in the last year or so. Something that seems to be an absolutely core quality that she has is to never, ever affront the dignity of another person. She challenges people, constantly, but she never affronts the dignity of a person. Given that, knowing that about her, and about you, the word "help"... I don't object to what people do, as much as how people use the word help. It's just purely, the language, because most people in this country, the U.S., use "help" in a very different way. A: Um hm. K: It's very patronizing, it's oriented toward charity. So it's just the charity quality of the word that I don't like, not the act of contributing. That is very important.

A: Yes. Helping in the sense that an animator stimulates. K: Um hm. A: That is also a help. If they get stimulated, they will tell you, your coming here has helped us. K: Yes. A: We are autonomous. You can now go away. But even then it has been helpful to us.

K: Or beneficial. Yeah, beneficial, and helpful. A: Yes, OK, language. The cultural context. D: Right. A: I don't know what language to use, then. It has been useful for you to come. K: Useful. A: You stayed with us a few days, and we have, as a result, formed this little group. Most of these efforts have in some sense or other been helped by outside activists. Who have intervened in certain communities, who have thereby in some sense been helped to wake up, and take action themselves. K: Um hm.

A: Well, then I think we are much closer. When you seemed to be rejecting the word help, I was myself recollecting a lot of ways in which outsiders have helped. Without being patronizing. K: Exactly. And that attitude of making a contribution, that's very cool. I have no trouble with that.

A: Yes. You'll find it in Bhoomi Sena's dialogue also. Intensely self-reliant, but at the same time admitting that outsiders can help. Helping us understand our questions, articulate them better. Then to help us find answers, ourselves. There also they seem to be needing help. And they have told us that initially, they did not know how to connect individual experiences. In terms of a structural understanding. K: Um hm. A: And there outsiders help them, to understand the structure, without theorizing. But guide them about how to search. Then you search, and you find out, and you have your own understanding, but that guidance was still a help. And they acknowledge it.

K: I wonder, is it really necessary to sever one's connections completely? A: No, it is not necessary. You know, certain roles you can hand over. Certain others you may still retain. And progressively you hand them over later. Or people link up, so there is a federation. You work at that level, you're still there. Visiting them. K: Still there. An interconnection.

A: And from time to time you find they need some help from you. That is okay. But what I would like to see is progressively, they take over more and more. But I find that many are not even facing this question. That is where I am unhappy. K: It's not even being raised. A. Not being raised, and progressively assessed. K: And if it's not raised as an issue, there is a tendency for one to feel somewhat subordinate, because there isn't the opening to no longer be supported.

A: We were discussing yesterday this question of going and working in other places. It seemed to us that different NGOs have taken certain villages as their constituencies, kind of. They work there. They will go on working there. The question of withdrawing and going to other places doesn't come up. I feel that is wrong. You are keeping them dependent on you. They like you so much. They won't let go of you. Then you are a continuing influence, and so on. Until you build up that kind of relation, that they finally stand up, that we want you to be with us, but we are absolutely equal.

K: Yes, Then it becomes a partnership, friendship, as opposed to a patron, client. A: That I have not yet seen. K: Hm. I don't see any objection to keeping that friendship, that strong connection. A: Sure, of course. There is no objection. But after a time the dependence disappears totally. Should. Now I would like to see that. Then you are just, you know, friend. You reflect together. That is perfectly all right. That can be enriching, still go on learning from each other. K: Um hm.

A: But I don't need you, any more. It's wonderful that you're with us, we are enriched by dialoging. But if you have to leave and go and work somewhere else, we'll go on too.

Challenging, Cascading
A: We have to move in that direction. We have not yet done so. We have to take this challenge for ourselves. Very few of those who

are actually working are identifying the deeper challenges which they have not yet started facing. K: Yeah, those anxieties.

A: Those anxieties. Are you contented with what you are doing? Community participation, is it fine? That's a good way to ask it. D: Yes, because it brings out the inner vision, motivation. A: Yes, Then I will be very disappointed if you reply yes (laughing). No one should be contented. K: We should all be contented, but we don't have to be completely contented.

A: I'm not satisfied with that. Within the space, would it not have been possible to do something more? D: Um. A: Would it not have been possible to do the impossible? But then we may expect a legitimate reply: is it necessary for us to do the impossible? Why do I have to inspire it? I'm doing fine (laughing). It's a very legitimate answer. It's just, you know, my urge. This may not be shared. I also may be, you know, talking from our social context, specifically of the kind that I belong to, Bangladesh, where the problem is so very acute, hard. That you have to do a lot more. You have to get to the depth, dig out that spirit, if at all there is any hope of transforming the society. Just by doing certain things, people participating, sharing poverty...this is not getting us anywhere. This may be our context, from which I am speaking like that. I don't know if it will find an echo, elsewhere.

K: To me, you know, this is a question of language, because part of what's going on in this country, I think, is that the drive to do more is misdirected, at *more*. I'd like to see people asking the question, can we become deeper, rather than bigger. A: Yes. K: Or more active. A: That is true. K: People are active, to the point of losing all sense of perspective.

A: But this is not yet becoming a question of life and death, here. As it is becoming for us. K: It seems like this question is both a personal question, and a broader social question. As people reveal what they feel are the challenges of the world's dynamics, the patterns which are external to ourselves, against which we have to be more clearly organized, will become more visible.

D: And you designated certain inner kinds of challenges as ethical, conceptual, practical. It's on those different chords or dimensions one can examine oneself, and report. K: There's one that's articulated well in *The Chalice and the Blade*, by Riane Eisler. That people experience over and over, but often we don't talk about it. That's the really direct, blatant, violent backlash against efforts by people to break out of situations that are opresive to them. Whether it's women taking on roles, and entrenched male backlash, or ethnic groups that are encountering great upsurges in bigotry, you know, all these kinds of things are really organized, angry, violent backlash in society. D: Yes. Some people may have experienced this in the past three years. How have they coped?

K: There's are you contented with what you are doing, and are you contented with what's happening in the world? They're almost two different planes of questions.

A: Yes, that is also valid, but I was not quite saying that. If you think you're doing the kind of work that should be done, given the world situation, then it is not enough for you to do it but you want to see others also do it, elsewhere. Some kind of general action to improve participation, participatory efforts, community efforts. These should spread. K: Um hm. A: Now, are you giving some thought to the contribution you, your work could make, in that direction? Or are you just satisfied that we are doing it, so we are happy. Don't you feel you have an obligation to contribute towards the spreading, also? Beyond your territory.

K: And what is the way to share that contribution without pre-empting the autonomy of other people? A: No, I'm not talking of curbing autonomy. It's the spreading of autonomous initiatives.

K: Isn't that kind of an oxymoron?

A: No, but then, why are we sitting and talking here at all? If we leave it to everybody to do what they want, that kind of autonomy, then we have no business even to discuss that. K: Right. A: We're doing it because we feel this should spread, and this experience itself has had something to contribute to its spreading. Spreading not in the sense of replicating, but stimulating, inspiring others also to take charge.

K: I guess what I'm saying is that if we want to share those experiences, what is the best way to share those experiences that isn't preempting the other's creativity. A: *Share* the experiences. I want to tell you what I'm doing. That doesn't mean you should do the same thing. You may decide to do something much better.

K: Maybe in that respect it's sort of an impulse for people to find, as part of their imperative work, that time to stop, and tell the story. Maybe that telling of the story should be as important as the doing.

A: Exactly. And also having experienced some great values of what we're doing, we want to go to the next village, and tell them our story, with the expectation that they might also be stimulated to, you know, form solidarity groups, do whatever they want to do. If they want any help from us, we are available. K: Um hm. A: Why are we trying to link and connect? To make it a larger movement. So that it keeps growing, and gets strengthened. Because the structure, the dominant structure is still...K: Much bigger. A: Much much bigger than us. K: Um hm.

A: We don't want just in one little village, to see some progress. We want to see it worldwide. And we can't see that happening if everybody sits and says everyone is autonomous. Actually I've possibly told you before, I have one question to me and to everybody. If anyone is going to assist a grassroot community, like an NGO, she's helping some community to stand up, and so on. I think it is her obligation to the world, to the world's oppressed, to tell this community, look here, why should I help you at all? I'm in a privileged position to help you. Why should I help you if you would not then decide to help others, in the same way? Then I'm not interested in helping. Am I communicating? K: You are.

A: Sister Tan is an outside activist. Not for any tangible, material assistance, but for that awakening to which Sister Tan has contributed, they can say, Thank you Sister Tan. It has been useful that you have come. Sister Tan can in turn tell them, and challenge them, Look, why should I have helped you (whatever the language is) if you would not in turn also take the responsibility to help others, the way I have helped you. This has to spread. If it was all right for me to want to see it spread among you, then you must think that you should try to see it spread amongst others. I cannot do it alone. K: Um hm. A: You must be a participant in that process. This is my challenge.

K: How about, why should I be useful to you if you won't be useful to others. A: That is right, OK. K: Um hm. K: Useful, gives the power to the person who's taking it on.

A: This question I shall ask everybody. If anyone says, we are content with what we are doing, and we don't want to relate to others, I'm very unhappy.

D: The implication is that people among whom Sister Tan has lived and worked have experienced her intervention, her presence. If they were to relive that, and identify whether at some stage they had some resentment and felt this was an intrusion, and if they passed through that and saw some reason to begin to trust Sister Tan and appreciate the spirit, and share the spirit among themselves, people in that community have a larger commitment. A larger equipment to do the same, because they've gone through the process of having an external person come in. They can say to themselves, well, if I now propose to go to another community, I've had this happen to me. Can I be sure that my behavior in this new community is as unobtrusive as possible, is as empowering as possible, because it happened to me and I've gone through that process of organizing, collecting myself. So really the potential for spread is quite rich, if that process occurs.

A: For me it is very important. Otherwise I'm not interested in even coming to you. This is after we have developed a mutual trust. You want to listen to me, I want to listen to you. Well, I have gone there to listen to them. But we have to break the barrier, that they should really want to listen. After we have broken that barrier, then the first thing I want to tell them: I have not come to you just think-ing of you, a little village. But because this is the problem, a big country, and there are all little villages in the same situation. You are the first village, I have come to you to see if we can catalyze some-thing. But not just with you. It must be a first step in a process. Now if you consider that a value, one should thus come as a catalyzer. If you don't, I get out. You have the autonomy (chuckles). But if you think that is valuable, then can we discuss together how then we go on to the next village. I can't do it alone. If you say no, we just want to get what you can give us, we don't want to think of the next village, then I take my train. I am not interested. K: Um hm.

A: Somebody may have come from outside, or may have been from inside. Outsiders have also contributed. I have not. I'm a re-searcher, I'm not an activist. So I myself have not. But I'm talking of somebody who has actually catalyzed action. K: Right. A: Now, is his interest to catalyze action just in this community? Or is he seeing this as part of a process of catalyzing all communities? So that the whole thing turns over. If he is concerned for the wider society, then he will see this as a step, and he will share this concern with the community and discuss the wider problem. Look here, we have to resist this. It's not just we in this community, we want the whole society to resist the structure that is oppressing everybody. And in that process we want to experience something for ourselves, for our own benefit, and also for that experience to become an experience for others, for their ben-efit. And then go over to the next village. So that we can try to see this go on moving. That's what I'm talking about. I don't know if that communicates now. I am not talking of you or me, I am also nobody, I'm not an activist. I have not done it anywhere.

D: Well of course in the sense that you've challenged. A: I go on challenging. But then, I was talking as a challenger. D: Yes. A: Even challenging this animator. This natural animator, who is fully accept-able to the community. I am challenging him, are you thinking only of this community? Or of the whole world? And what your wonderful experience could contribute to the whole world. K: Yeah. I see nothing wrong with that challenge.

A: If you are not interested in that, then I am also not inter-ested. I have gone there, completely an outsider. I have gone and challenged them. What right have you to hold on to this animator? Then you are thinking only of yourself. But 80 percent of Philippine people are poor like yourselves. And you are saying he's a wonderful fellow. Which means he is very scarce. What right have you to hold on to a scarce person? You should release him, so that he can go to other poor. I ask them to discuss this and I'll come back to you after two days. After two days I have gone and they say, we fully agree with you. We want to release him. We are not fully ready. He should come to us twice a month. Someone else says, no, once a month will do. This I have done. Why are you so afraid to impose (laughing)?

There are many other examples. In Bangladesh I go every year. This village I went to, Proshika Comilla. They were telling me, among other things, they have taken a loan from Proshika. For a project that failed totally. It was three or four lakh takas loan. They were very genuine people. It was not their fault. The technology, it was a brickmaking process, the bricks got washed away, or something. So they said, we cannot repay. But we can contribute our labor, if you have any use for it. So Proshika then discussed it in their board, and they decided to forget about it, write it off.

They were telling me this story. I told them, Proshika has written it off. I am not going to write it off. You have to repay it. K: (Laughs). A: You cannot stand with your heads high and tell an outsider like me, very proudly, that we're doing this and that. You have to tell Proshika that we want to repay it. We cannot repay it in cash. OK? But you tell Proshika, can we repay this by sharing some of the work you are doing? Your task is to organize in different villages. We want to take over that task, for the neighboring five villages. You have that experience, several years experience. So you can do that. That will be much greater value, to the whole society, than repaying in cash. If you can do that, then you know, you call me, I'm going to come to you again, and sit with you, and then I'm going to write about it. And go over to all villages in Bangladesh and talk about it (chuckling). They agreed. They did not throw me out.

So I cannot get away from the responsibility or the reality that we are not leaving it to spontaneity. We are wanting the world to turn over, the alternative development paradigm, we are not content to leave it to spontaneity. D: Hm. A: We are intervening. Because we are so concerned. There are different ways of intervening.

K: I'm intervening in a community which considers itself superior to every other community. And I think part of my personal feeling of obligation is to try to overturn that feeling. So in that sense an analogy would be to go to other academics or other institutions that are making these kinds of questions, like the World Bank, and making sure that the people that are taking risks ask themselves if they're taking big enough risks.

D: Well, in that sense, you're in a place somewhat similar to Tony, when he described that what he wants to write is some of the difficulties and obstacles of breaking through. K: In institutions. D. In making universities meaningful to grassroots movements. K: Right. D: So in a sense you and Tony and I are part of that ambience. K: Um hm.

A: This urgency. This is what I have been trying to say in about human development issues. D: Yes. A: The UNDP's Human Development Report has a concern that there be human development, not just economic development. But it does not put this concern in terms of seeing other human beings also have that concern for each other. K: That's a profound message. It's really very very crucial. A: That does not appear in that Index. So I'm a better human being, I don't want them to be as good. You all think of your individual selfish motives. K: Yeah. A: And I will think about you. K: And that goes on.

A: If they are not interested, then I am not interested. K: Um, hm. A: No, they'll say Fine, we didn't ask you to be interested in us. I'll tell them, I'll not write about you. I'll write about *them* (laughter). Tell the whole world, this is a more exciting community, because of this reason.

K: This is like the concept of cascading. I once was very upset, because a professor was doing a lot to support my job searches. Writing off lots of letters. There was nothing I could give. And so I said, Look, I'm very uncomfortable with you, putting all this effort in, what can I do? And he said, it's not about you doing something for me, it's about you giving the same thing to someone else. It's good that you feel that disquiet. But the important thing is that this cascades through you, then on to the next person, so each person is in a position to share that with another person.

A: Cascading, a very good word, cascading. D: Yes. Spreading. A: In that context the challenge that *every* community must take: What are we contributing to the empowerment of others, not just to ours. K: We don't hold the power to ourselves, but let it flow through. And that takes away the idea of being patronized, because if the whole point is that you then agree from the moment of engagement to pass on, then there is no sense of charity. A: That's right. Contributing to others' empowerment. Much better. K: I like it better.

A: Sometimes you can do it by not doing anything. Let others start. Not interfering, sometimes, you can be just as effective. But there is another operational reason even for them. That they have to realize, in certain kinds of structural situations. Certain things pertaining to their empowerment they cannot have unless they have wider strength. Unless the next village also gets organized, and then they move together. To fight the power structure. This is very real. And then my question is, Who will contribute to this process? This spreading. Will this animator alone want to? Also join? This is in their very selfish interest, if they want things from the much broader structure, which they cannot fight alone. This is objective, not spiritual. It is very objective.

K: Well, it can't be objective without being spiritual. A: Well, I don't know. It's again a matter of language. But objective in the sense that, I'm not asking a value from you. That, as I am concerned about your empowerment, you should be concerned about others' empowerment. That's a kind of value, I'm not calling it objective, I'm calling it spiritual. I'm calling objective, you want to fight the structure. But I think we have done a very useful discussion. Cascading, contribution to others' empowerment, concern for contributing to others, not just being satisfied with your own empowerment, desire to see that concern in all, this is all good.

K: Hm. That in the whole process, whatever the process of growth is, that there's an implicit understanding that those who begin to come out of a situation of oppression become part of the healing of the next group.

III

BUILDING SPACES TO
TRANSFORM THE STRUCTURES

Preface to Part III

The Workshop Synthesis highlighted structural constraints, setting goals that include changes in structures. Part III opens with editorial consideration of this agenda. Is transformation of structures a realistic goal? Or are we limited to seeking spaces to work within structures, gradually expanding the spaces? Indeed, are there circumstances where the help of structures is needed? The editors address these issues in the context of institutional, knowledge, and power structures. This trialogue provides a background to the four chapters of Part III.

To open Chapter 7, Laurentino Bascug analyzes the causes of poverty. Land as a moral issue, wrong concepts of ownership, attitudes to work and social status, and aspects of technology and market structure are among the causes he details. Conflicts and violence in the Philippine countryside are directly related. To address the magnitude of these issues, the family farm movement founded by Laurentino and his colleagues is oriented to basic values and religious principles among farm families and communities. Diversified, organic agriculture is the livelihood vehicle developed through the program. The chapter details the ecological features of family-size farms fostered by ODISCO. Descriptions are given of training programs orienting farmers, families, and rural community members in this holistic, non-violent approach.

Not long after Laurentino returned to the Philippines from the Hawaii workshop, the ODISCO training center and tenant-farmers organized through the movement were fired upon by landlord agents. In recognition of ODISCO's continuing efforts facing such adversity, the organization received the annual award of the Asian NGO Coalition for Agrarian Reform and Rural Development (ANGOC). In a brief dialogue with Anisur Rahman, concluding the chapter, the kinds of opposition faced by the movement are discussed.

In his comments in final preparation of the chapter, Laurentino Bascug stresses a continuing problem as of 1994: failures of local and international funding agencies to enter into effective dialogue with such people-based, ground-based initiatives. He recommends a workshop-seminar, regional or international, where representatives of funding agencies would engage with grassroot organizer-educators in creating new modes of support to such family, community-based organizing efforts.

In Chapter 8, building on **Manavodaya's** experience since the *People's Initiatives* workshop, Varun Vidyarthi critically reports and assesses organizing and learning processes that seek to strengthen self-reliance among the rural poor. Among newly created base institutions in this north India region, savings and credit groups have achieved some stability and moved beyond strictly economic functions to broader social, conflict-resolving action. Village *satsangs*, reviving a traditional cultural gathering for songs and discussion, are an innovation that achieved initial success in collective decision-making and action, but have not been widely sustained. Other base institutions considered are functional economic groups, artisan groups, youth clubs, and the local governance body, the village panchayat.

Documenting and reviewing experiences in individual villages, Varun analyzes local and external dependency relationships that present challenges to the strengthening of self-reliance. He points to the inevitability of struggle in such efforts, and the dilemma of how to meet violence, which often arises. Measures to meet such challenges include sustained group discussions to clarify objectives and build solidarity; information sharing and development of an economic base; and striving to build alliances and federating opportunities. Participatory reflections on life goals, values, and behaviour are encouraging in advancing this deep-seated process.

Voluntary associations such as ODISCO and MANAVODAYA seek to expand local spaces for change through non-formal, innovative educational and organizing processes. A new dimension in formal knowledge creation is contributed by the pioneering approach to community-based, community-determined education of The Evergreen State University and Native American nations. Innovative partnerships between indigenous communities and the academic institution are described in Chapter 9 by Russell Fox and Carol Minugh, a member of the Gros Ventre Nation.

Empowering indigenous communities to create knowledge and have it validated as equivalent to knowledge generated in other academic programs of the university is a fundamental goal of these partnerships. This objective builds on Evergreen's founding mission of participatory, action-based combining of theory and practice, actively exploring different cultural paradigms of knowledge. This gave rise to creation of the "Learning Triad" approach by a faculty member of the Lummi Nation. The approach brings together the student, the student's community, and the institution/faculty as sources of knowledge and learning relationships. It thereby seeks to bridge the gap between oral and written traditions, while supporting indigenous students in pursuing a university education. The curricular structure which takes

the classroom to the community and community members to the
faculty is described by Fox and Minugh. The process emphasizes community definition of learning priorities and community empowerment
through action-oriented attention to real-life issues. Educational and
institution-building principles are derived.

An analogous though more program-oriented process for widening spaces for local education and decision-making is represented in
diverse experiences with participatory video. Tony Williamson
assesses strengths and lessons of this communication process in the
Addendum to Chapter 9. He draws on experiences in Pakistan and
India that demonstrate video's potential in ensuring that all stakeholders in projects gain early involvement in their planning, design,
and implementation.

The process of moving from local spaces of empowerment to
larger social change arenas, enabling parties motivated by diverse
interests to build effective coalitions around a common purpose,
presents a complex and familiar challenge to participatory organization.
Kari Lende Anderson has undertaken the arduous mission of becoming
a "volunteer professional" in this realm. Starting with her early
personal history in Thailand and Laos as an American exchange
student, she reports in Chapter 10 a learning process both in Asia and
North America, in networking and coalition-building.

The examples and lessons she draws are multi-dimensional. An
early experience was among community health organizers from 10
Asian countries, cross-culturally contrasting and then synthesizing
their approaches. In selected U.S. cities and regions, cross-fertilization among different movements—labor, gender rights, environmental,
trade—has been undertaken through annual, substantive visits. In
the post-Earth Summit period, a larger networking function among
North and South organizations focusing on sustainable agriculture
has experienced both successful and frustrating stages. Kari closes
her account with two characteristically varied self-assignments: working with an environment education coalition to mobilize community
self-study and cooperation among 79 out of 81 neighborhoods in
metropolitan Minneapolis/St. Paul; and writing/performing a one-act
play on values and concepts of sustainability for the 21st century, as
the basis for participatory dialogue and education.

Part III closes with editorial reflections on issues of autonomy,
scale, coalition-building, violence, and nonviolence raised in these
chapters. This makes a transition to the concluding chapters of the
volume.

Editorial Opener

Creating Spaces to Change the Structures

D: The book should perhaps show that when institutions are concerned, one needs to give at least passing attention to the constraints the institution itself has. In the sense in which the institution is the fertilized egg from which a chicken is to emerge, the need to find a process that will transcend those constraints and yield a chicken, yield the larger result that was inherent in the process. The Synthesis refers to structures. Institutional structures are an important part of the constraints that we face. How are we, three years later, in a stronger position to relate to the structures? To size up the institutional barriers and constraints, and maybe work more effectively?

A: Can you really claim that? That you have sized up, that you are able now to work more effectively? It would be interesting, perhaps you may. But I was telling earlier of my experience in the ILO. I could work effectively for certain reasons, certain forces that helped. Which disappeared after a time. I mean, you don't really make fundamental progress. You are able to use the institutions temporarily. How long this will last is very difficult to say.

K: In a sense, too, how one can make use of this sort of opportunity depends on how courageous and definite one can afford to be in any given situation. We were stretching the institution quite a long way, at that time. The forces against this kind of creativity softened temporarily. But we were still hearing that drum they were beating in the background. Trying to figure how to dance both dances. If we were slightly stronger placed, or more forceful ourselves, perhaps we could have made the case up front for saying, We cannot impose this kind of structure on this type of learning.

D: I point to this in the sense that the Synthesis is a call to action. A: Yes. D: Several of us are responding to that. The Goals and Directions says, "Self-reliance implies exercising the basic human right to participate at all levels of policy making and planning decisions affecting the communities' life..." I'm striving to assure that I exercise that basic human right, and see where I can displace barriers that prevent others who legitimately have that right from exercising it. I see this as a call, a call to action. As the authors' contributions come forth from where they are, what their experience has been, I suppose each will in some way be reflecting that call. As exhibited in her or his own action. If there is a resonance of that call in the book, that resonance goes forward. It builds on the striving that has been sought.

K: It's a call from action, as well. Not just created out of ether. D: Right. A: That's important. D: A call from action, transposed to dialogue. The book is continuing the dialogue. The parts of the book will also be calls from action. They represent the action people have had.

A: Going back to the concept of transforming the structure, I feel this is a very important concept on which there should be some editorial reflection. The question of transforming structure. Is this a good question? Or, is what we are after... We don't know if we can transform the structure. If we could, that's very good. But for the time being what we are after is to expand the space within the structures. Even if it is temporary. We don't know how long the space will last. But for the moment we may decide there is a value in trying to expand the space within the structures. Say within the East-West Center. So the question itself is getting transformed. Not the question of transforming the structure—that's a very big question. Even if we want, we just can't transform. Then we would have to take a lot of the negatives it has. We cannot throw it all out. Would we transform? (Laughing). I don't know the resultant.

K: Seems that it would be very difficult to change the structures without changing the people. If in our dialogues with each other we become different, gradually the institutions will follow. A: Exactly. K: It's analogous to the idea we discussed of revolution. Without personal change it's just temporary. A: Quite so. But if we think in terms of trying to expand the space, in that context there is a role for this Synthesis message. K: That legitimizes, if nothing else, this whole process of our own work, and these kinds of meetings. A: At the same time the Synthesis meets some of the demands from the structure and some of our urges to articulate. Otherwise it would have been much more difficult, if we had not felt ourselves fulfilled, by going through this process of synthesizing.

D: We've been talking about institutions as a particular organization. What I've been sensing is the effort to transform on a different plane, the plane of culture and knowledge. You, Anis, have helped recreate the sense and significance of knowledge derived from action. What Kersten and I have been exhibiting in our own ways is a learning process which is not satisfied with the received positivist notion of knowledge. So, when I'm speaking of Goals, a call is coming forth that includes this deeper effort to enrich the process of knowledge generation, and to use that in changing the knowledge setting in which particular institutions operate. There are passages that lead toward that. In Goals: "Knowledge is the basis of self-reliance: the integration of and respect toward different kinds of knowledge—scientific, conceptual, practical, local, organic, intuitive and inner knowledge." K: I like that.

D: Previously: "Knowledge structures are constructed by society...to organize, regulate and control the members' own material and spiritual conditions of living. When the structure is hegemonic...it becomes oppressive." Many of us were resisting the received hegemonic nature of knowledge. We felt the vital nature of action and solidarity as sources of knowledge. K: Um hm. D: Because we find that it greatly enriches our lives. It has the deeper sense of connecting us to the earth, new bonding with people, introducing excitement even in academic learning processes. Several authors are very consciously in that realm, anxious to contribute to that kind of transformation. We're concerned to enrich learning processes and help universities open their windows, gaining more from direct experience and life as people are living it, the struggles people are having, and communicating without barriers of discipline. These are some of the calls people in the workshop are following through on.

A: Absolutely. We have come there already—the role of knowledge and culture. Sure. D: This will help readers in their own self-reflection and also create a new testing ground for institutions like the East-West Center. A: Hm. D: If we're thinking of knowledge in that deeper sense, it is part of what the East-West Center is supposed to be doing, but doesn't always validate itself on those criteria. It tends to validate itself more on publications. What we are trying to reinforce is an admiration for knowledge that is whole, not simply logical and cognitive, but derived from life and its richness, its aesthetic and emotional qualities. A: Yes.

CHAPTER 7

SUSTAINABLE DEVELOPMENT IN THE PHILIPPINES: THE LAKAS-ODISCO APPROACH

Laurentino D. Bascug

INTRODUCTION

In 1969, the centuries old struggle of the peasants to be free from the bondage of the soil threatened to explode into full-scale violence. This led to the most massive attempt thus far to solve the socioeconomic ills associated with the semi-feudal structure of the Philippines' agrarian system. It was during that year that the government distributed around 90,000 hectares of land to the landless farmers who believed then that their poverty and misery were at an end.

Yet, five years into the land transfer program 60 percent of the beneficiaries sold back their farm lots to the landlords; 30 percent subsequently hired tenants and virtually became landlords themselves; and the rest who persisted as owner-cultivators were in the depths of poverty.

Touted as the centerpiece of the government's development program to eradicate the poverty of the masses, land reform fell far short of its goal to emancipate the farmers. Landlessness in the countryside had worsened. Around four million agricultural families, or roughly 20 million Filipinos, representing 35 percent of the entire population were just as poor as before, or worse.

It is against this grim background that the LAKAS-ODISCO movement was planted as a germ of inspiration to two farmers with a strong sense of mission. Messrs. Laurentino D. Bascug and Glicerio Tan who had been educating and organizing farmers since the late

1950's felt that the time was ripe for a vigorous peasant organization genuinely committed to wiping out hunger and misery in the farms. Drawing the lessons from the failures of the past and their own vast experience, the duo concluded that conventional solutions apparently didn't work. The economic, social and political liberation of the Filipino farmers will require a drastic redirection and reorientation of attitudes and values, specially of the farmers themselves. The two, therefore, sought to innovate. LAKAS-ODISCO is the product of this innovation.

LAKAS-ODISCO is a simple, innovative movement, as the following pages will attempt to show.

ANALYSIS OF THE PROBLEM

Through painstaking dialogue and discussion with the peasants, the underlying principles that lead to poverty were identified as the Satanic principles of greed, pride, and envy. These principles, which are disguised or hidden within fiery demagoguery and deceptive rhetoric, are the foundation upon which are erected the godless absolutist concept of ownership and use of land, and the wrong concepts of leadership and power.

Living in a prolonged state of utter poverty has created an anti-developmental culture that dehumanizes. The landlord mentality of both the landowners and the tillers of the soil, and the negative values and attitudes such as the loss of self-respect, lack of determination to succeed, and a generally pessimistic outlook in life are but a few of the examples. Since values and attitudes are ingrained in the hearts and minds, development and progress to improve peasants' lives are much more difficult to achieve because the individuals themselves resist change or reform. Under this condition, the peasants are perpetually trapped in poverty.

Poverty in turn feeds fodder to other social problems like deteriorating peace and order, rampant graft and corruption, inadequate basic services to the people, huge unemployment and underemployment, large uncollected taxes, lack of capital for industrialization, and diminished purchasing power.

Specifically, the direct causes of the poverty of the peasants can be properly identified as follows (Figure 1):

1) *The land problem as a moral issue.* The land problem is not just a legal, but also a moral issue. It involves not just the maldistribution of land (as a limited societal resource) to a privileged few, but more so the moral right and responsibility over the land by those who directly till it and make it productive. At the root of the

program is the godless, unjust "Absolutist concept of Ownership" by people who have gained control over the land and have proclaimed themselves as its rightful "owners." A tenant tilling the land for many years has no bigger dream than of becoming a landlord himself. Hence, the need is for total value transformation, especially among the farmers themselves.

Unless people realize that they are merely the land's "stewards" or caretakers, human exploitation and destruction of the land for profit will continue.

2) *Technology problems.* Many so-called "modern" farming technologies have proven to be inappropriate. The necessary support services have either been lacking or are beyond the reach of small-scale farmers. While it is true that modern technology has increased the volume of farm harvests, it has also increased production costs, heightened dependency on foreign technologies and corporations, and reduced farmers on small holdings to the status of mendicancy.

3) *Marketing system.* Farmers are easy prey and victims of the law of "supply and demand." They buy expensive inputs and sell their products cheap. The traders dictate the price of their products.

4) *Wrong thrust in cooperativism.* Small-scale farmers have not been organized into effective cooperatives. This is mainly due to the unbalanced thrust of the government and private sectors in promoting the cooperative movement. Heavy emphasis is placed on the organization and development of consumers', credit, and marketing cooperatives, while the development of farm production cooperatives is practically neglected.

Moreover, the successful cooperative is judged more on profitability rather than on the material and spiritual benefits of the members. In fact, many of the successfully managed farmers', consumers' and marketing cooperatives have low membership levels. Some have less than 15 members although their cooperatives' net worth has already reached millions of pesos built-up from the profits of non-members who do not usually receive any patronage refund. Thus, the real purpose or objective of the cooperative, i.e., to serve its membership, has been relegated to the background.

5) *Unsustainable agricultural systems as an ecology problem.* Unlike their forebears, present day farmers do not practice efficient soil conservation and environmental resource management techniques due to ignorance. Soil erosion and depletion of natural soil nutrients have reduced yields so that farm harvest is now insufficient for the basic necessities of a typical peasant family of six. They are thus driven to engage in illegal logging, dynamite fishing and kaingin farming.

FIGURE 1

Holistic Analysis of the Root Causes of Poverty

Root Causes of Poverty	Greed Conceptualized (Justification of unjust economic systems)	Greed's Concepts Systematized (direct cause of poverty)	Poverty of the Vast Majority of People and its Effects (direct cause of the social problems)	Present Social Problems	Present Specific Causes of Poverty

SATANIC PRINCIPLES:
1. Greed
2. Envy
3. Pride
	1. Godless "Absolutist concept of ownership and use of the land"
	2. Wrong concept of leadership
	  a. Dictatorship
	  b. Hero Type
	  c. Politician type
	  d. Philanthropic type
	  e. Genius type
	3. Wrong concept of power. "Might is Right"
		1. UNJUST ECONOMIC SYSTEMS
		  a. Feudal system
		  b. Landlordism
		  c. Unbridled capitalism
		  d. Multinational corporations' control of vital industries
			1. DAMAGED CULTURE
			  a. Landlord mentality of all sectors of society as number one obstacle to fully develop our agricultural land.
			  b. Negative human values
			  c. Negative mental attitudes
			  d. Lack of nationalism
				1. Rightist and leftist rebellion
				2. Rampant graft and corruption in government
				3. Diminishing purchasing power
				4. Inadequate basic services to the people
				5. Huge unemployment and underemployment
					1. Land problem as a moral issue
					2. Technology problem
					3. Exploitative marketing system
					4. Wrong thrust of cooperativism
					5. Unsustainable agriculture as an ecology problem
					6. Damaged culture
					7. Individualistic tendency
					8. Wrong concept of farm work
					9. No access to credit
					10. Moral problem

2. DEHUMANIZING EFFECTS
a. Dependency attitude
b. Developed hopelessness in life
c. Loss of self respect
d. Loss of self confidence
e. No more initiative
f. Lack of self determination to succeed in life
g. Pessimistic attitude

6. Large uncollected taxes
7. Lack of capital for industrialization
8. Secessionist rebellion
9. Natural calamities

Note: The above presentation shows the series of causes and effects from the root causes of poverty to the present social problems which are always the headline news. And poverty, as the direct cause of the social problems, will always remain unsolved unless the wrong concepts, damaged culture and the dehumanizing effects of the poverty are first removed from the minds and hearts of the poor. The effective solution therefore, should also be holistic in its thrust.

6) *Damaged culture.* Unjust economic systems—feudalism, landlordism, unbridled capitalism—imposed by colonial powers have adversely affected the human values and mental attitudes of the peasants. The dehumanizing effects of poverty meanwhile put the peasants in a state of hopelessness and dependency.

7) *No access to credit.* The Philippine banking system works in ways that leave the poor to scrounge for scraps. Hence, the peasants are forced by circumstances to borrow from private sources at usurious interest rates.

8) *Wrong concept of farm work.* Most farmers consider farm work as a lowly and undignified profession. It is wrongly regarded as poor man's work, an occupation of last resort. This has resulted in their lack of self-confidence, and an attitude of subservience. This also douses their enthusiasm to develop or improve the farm.

9) *Moral problem.* Farmers, no matter how poor still cling on to vices such as smoking, drinking, and gambling. They even borrow money and overspend just to celebrate town "fiestas," birthdays, baptisms, and weddings as a way of escapism.

THE TURNING POINT

In the belief that only the farmer can lift the yoke of a fellow farmer, Messrs. Bascug and Tan joined forces and returned to actual farming in search of solutions to the farmer's problems.

From 1981–85, the duo conducted agricultural experiments in a family-sized farm in Victorias, Negros Occidental. They completely shunned external assistance and relied heavily on the wealth of information and knowledge they had acquired through their constant interaction with farmers nationwide. Eventually, they organized a local farmers organization, the Small Farmers and Workers Service Cooperative, Inc. (SFAWSCI) whose members started validating and replicating the findings learned in the farm. This period signified the beginnings of the ODISCO (Organic, Diversified, Intensive, Scientifiic, Cooperative) farming system.

The objectives of the ODISCO farming system are:

1) To establish owner-cultivatorship in a family-size farm of a maximum of three hectares if irrigated, five hectares if non-irrigated, and seven hectares for upland farming.

2) To achieve maximum production through intensive but sustainable land use.

3) To lay the grounds for agro-industrialization, especially in the rural areas.

4) To seek solutions to the unemployment and underemployment problems both in the rural and urban areas.

5) To provide an alternative to a violent revolution.

6) To unite the rural and urban poor in general.

7) To bring about the liberation, cultivation, perfection, and salvation of human beings—body and soul.

8) To make the farm a paradise on earth.

As the small miracles experienced by ODISCO "convert" farmers spread among the peasant, NGO, and government sectors, the proponents of ODISCO established the ODISCO Foundation. The main thrust of the Foundation is to systematically promote the ODISCO farming system in the Philippines.

With the establishment of the ODISCO Foundation as the vehicle for economic liberation, LAKAS was also organized as a sociopolitical confederation to consolidate ODISCO's economic gains. With a solid organizational and financial base, LAKAS is then in a position to effectively achieve the economic and political empowerment of the small farmers, fisherfolks, rural and urban workers.

The objective of LAKAS as a national people's organization are:

1) To strongly organize the cooperatives and unions of the peasantry and urban workers for their economic and political empowerment.

2) To federate all the local cooperatives, peasants' organizations, and workers' unions into municipal and provincial organizations.

3) To establish a strongly coordinated, closely knit, cause-oriented and cohesive national confederation of cooperatives, peasants' organizations and workers' unions.

4) To source local and national funding for economic projects for its affiliates.

5) To represent the peasants in its advocacy for a genuine agrarian reform program and other related laws for the betterment of the peasantry.

6) To establish better coordination and cooperation with government agencies serving the peasants like the Department of Agriculture (DA), Department of Agrarian Reform (DAR), Department of Environment and Natural Resources (DENR), Land Bank of the Philippines (LBP), Department of Trade and Industries (DTI), and local governments.

To maintain the strength and effectiveness of LAKAS-ODISCO, it shall remain purely sectoral in nature, in approaches and main thrust. The LAKAS-ODISCO Movement will participate meaningfully and forcefully in the democratic political processes that will shape policies and programs beneficial specially to the poor. This will entail the formation of a broadly based political organization that will enlist the help of all sectors of society. The organization will be controlled, managed and principally directed by the small farmers, fisherfolks, rural and urban workers. For this purpose, the LAKAS-ODISCO Movement shall be organized with the following objectives:

1) To establish a National Movement that will accept membership from all sectors interested in the unity and liberation of the peasantry.

2) To establish a multi-sectoral national movement that will initially organize a nucleus of a peasant-workers' party.

3) To establish national and international linkages with other political parties here and abroad.

4) To develop a political agenda that can maintain the unity of the leaders, officers and member of LAKAS-ODISCO in the initial struggle to establish a political base and influence.

5) To develop a peasant-workers' party platform for the economic and political development of the whole country.

LAKAS-ODISCO's Philosophy

The ODISCO farming system puts people at the center stage of development. ODISCO considers the human being as the most significant factor in achieving success in farming. Since ODISCO primarily promotes the family-size farming system, it focuses on the individual farmer.

In the Philippines, where majority of the population come from the countryside, ODISCO traces the problems of society to the problem of the peasantry. The increasing gap between the rich and poor can be traced back to the problem in the rural areas. The solution is found in the rural areas. The solution is the farmer.

ODISCO relies principally on the creative talents of small-scale farmers who actually till the farm, and capitalizes on their native resources as a starting point of development. Farmers understand themselves more than others and so they hold the key to their own liberation. The farmers therefore, are their own saviors through their strong organizations.

Previous initiatives by government and private institutions have produced the so-called "miracle" technologies, seeds and plant varieties with spectacular, but short-lived results. However, a methodology or process to develop "miracle farmers" to plant the seeds and properly care for the land was never found. In the depths of their poverty and misery, the farmers were never around long enough to enjoy the benefits of the miracle technologies.

The main ingredient of ODISCO is its training program. The training program draws heavily on Christian theology because of the basic religious orientation of the Filipino farmer. The program strikes at the core of the farmer's frailties. ODISCO espouses the moral obligation of the farmer to his Supreme Creator. The farmer is reminded that he is a co-worker of God in the management and utilization of his resources, so that he is motivated to transform his farm into a paradise. The belief in God helps catalyze a revolutionary change in values within the farmer.

Through long years of working with the owners of the land, the farmer not only develops a certain affinity with their landlords but also assimilates the attitudes, perceptions, and values of the landowners. To illustrate, a farm boy who toils in the farm dreams of the day he will become a landowner himself—one who has a house in Manila, drives flashy cars, eats in plush restaurants, and wears signature clothes. Gradually, the farmer develops a mind set like the landowner. Eventually, "The exploited absorbs an exploiter's mind."

ODISCO's Technology

The philosophy of ODISCO is complemented by farm technology, appropriately designed and geared for farmers on small operating holdings. These technologies are developed to make the farmers self-reliant. In a way, the ODISCO technology represents the farmers' response to the inadequacy of institutional mechanisms and service support systems intended for the farmer.

The thrusts of **ODISCO** as its name implies are as follows:

Organic. One of the main causes of farmers' poverty is the high costs of chemical fertilizers, pesticides, and herbicides. ODISCO eliminates the utilization of all chemicals through the "no-throw-no-burn" policy regarding animal wastes and plant cuttings. ODISCO strictly practices the "law of return" in farming—animals fertilizing plants and plants feeding the animals. Also, it teaches the production of local pesticides using mixtures of certain plants and natural ingredients.

Diversified. ODISCO grows a wide variety of fruit trees, vegetables and rootcrops, cereals, freshwater fish and shellfish, and different species of livestock in the three hectare farm. Annex 1 presents the sampling of crops raised in the farm.

Intensive. ODISCO engages in multi-level, high density cropping system of cash and plantation crops.

Scientific. The farm is designed and structured in such a way that the symbiotic relationships between animals and plants are maximized (Figure 2). This arrangement enables the farm to increase production and maintain its ecological balance at the same time.

Co-operative. As ODISCO discovers the abundance of possibilities within the three hectare farm, the use of family and cooperative

Figure 2

Approximate Layout of ODISCO Farm Systems Development Foundation, Inc. Demonstration Farm in Victorias, Negros Occidental

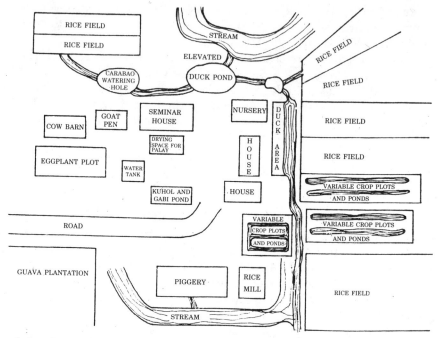

labor is promoted in all farming operations. The principle behind this labor arrangement is that farming is a 24-hour activity and that mutual help also strengthens the traditional Filipino culture of living and working together.

ODISCO technology has also drawn systems, procedures, and standards for the proper selection and care of farm animals. Implements, equipment and tools are vital to farming. ODISCO has developed user-friendly farm tools and equipment that are manufactured locally, and cheaply. They are also designed very simply so that farmers can do repairs themselves.

ODISCO is individual farmer-oriented as much as it is family- or community-centered. Every night, for about an hour, members of the cooperative meet after dinner for Bible study and to report on the individual assignments in the farm. This becomes the basis for discussing the plans for the next day. The meeting relieves the farmer of the full burden of planning and operating the farm all by himself. It also enables cooperative members to express their views and concerns and contribute other resources in the farm operation. The nightly meetings encourage farmers to get involved in all aspects of farm operations.

The successful experience of ODISCO shows that a family can earn an average annual gross income of US $3,000 from a three-hectare plot. Expenses on education, housing, and clothing are shouldered collectively by the cooperative. Most food requirements are provided for by the farm.

The experience of ODISCO technology in Victorias exemplifies the main strategy of ODISCO, that is, to produce first to satisfy basic needs of food, clothing, shelter, health and education; and only later on engage in commercial crops for local sale or export.

LAKAS-ODISCO's Holistic Development Approach

The failure to solve the problem of poverty of the vast majority of the people has caused the downfall of many governments regardless of their ideology. The Soviet Union is the most recent example. Here in the Philippines, the eradication of poverty remains a critical priority of survival, but until now no effective solution appears to be on hand.

It is in this context that the LAKAS-ODISCO Movement offers the Holistic Development Approach as a viable solution to the social problem of poverty. LAKAS-ODISCO'S proposed solutions are a product of its many years of experience and leadership in the field of peasant education and organization. The ultimate objective of this holistic approach is the total liberation of the peasantry in all aspects (economic, political, social, cultural, and moral) of their lives.

Its main strategy of development is to apply solutions to all aspects of the problem of poverty simultaneously, rather than applying solutions one at a time. Central to this strategy is the definition of man's relationship not only to the society in which he lives but also to his Creator and the adoption of Christian beliefs and precepts.

The Holistic Development Approach aims to reorient the small farmers, fisherfolks, rural and urban workers so that they are able to shed negative human values and mental attitudes. With a strong moral framework as basis, the approach simultaneously applies sustainable agricultural technology to increase production and encourage the organization of production-based, multi-purpose cooperatives. The economic and political gains produced by this approach will then be consolidated and institutionalized through a strong peasant-workers' party, initiated and organized by the LAKAS-ODISCO Movement and effectively participating in governance.

Training and Education Programs

Over a thousand farmer leaders and government officials and staff have undergone ODISCO training over the past few years. These persons have thus become the major promoters of ODISCO technology in their respective areas. ODISCO technology is spread through this process.

Indeed, the strength of ODISCO lies in the intensive conduct of its training. Training is done mostly in the ODISCO farm site in Victorias. Training is held usually under Spartan conditions familiar to the farmers. The live-in seminars follow the farmer's schedule—bedtime at 9:00 p.m. and wake-up hour at 4:00 in the morning.

The principal training programs are:

• *Economic and Social Awareness Seminar (ESAS, five days).* The ESAS is a pre-membership seminar that highlights the relationship between God, nature, the farmer, and society in the Philippine context. It also introduces the thrust of ODISCO technology, philosophy, the concept of cooperative, Godly concept of ownership of property, philosophy of organization, and the philosophy of leadership and fellowship. The ESAS is designed to correct the wrong concepts of ownership of land, leadership and power.

• *Management and Educators Seminar (MES, 15 days).* The MES is designed to train lecturers of the ESAS on how to organize people, register their organizations as multi-purpose, production-based cooperatives, and obtain production credits from the Land Bank and other financial institutions. It also introduces initially the ODISCO Farming Technology to the farmers in their respective areas.

• *ODISCO Training Course (OTEC, 30 days)*—The OTEC is designed to train educators as organizer-technologists to propagate the bio-dynamic sustainable agricultural technology. The participants are expected to manage and operate ODISCO demonstration farms for the propagation of the technology.

• *Bookkeeping Seminar (BS, 35 days)*—The BS is designed to train the participants to record the daily transaction of the Multipurpose Production-Based Cooperatives and prepare a simple financial statement regularly.

• *Management Seminar (MS, 3 months)*—The MS is designed to train managers of all types of cooperative ventures. The participants are all graduates of the ESAS, preferably MES or OTEC graduates as well.

EPILOGUE

ODISCO's success is clearly evident in the phenomenal rise in the number of its converts and supporters. More and more requests for training are being received from the peasantry sector. Government itself is undertaking a careful study of ODISCO, and is even poised at a proper time to replicate the technology on a nationwide scale.

However, this tried and tested farming system needs assistance to facilitate its replication. Moreover, ODISCO is not in a hurry to plunge headlong into the raging river of hurried program implementation. Countless government and private programs have failed because of over-eagerness to expand programs at a macro-level in a short period of time.

In eight years of persistent farm experiments, the ODISCO farming system has amply demonstrated that to alleviate poverty in the rural areas, development assistance should primarily focus on the farmer. ODISCO has found that human reform is a prerequisite to a successful agrarian reform.

Human reform is attained only when continuous value education—on proper mental attitudes and the moral obligation to the community and God—is emphasized and related to the daily life of the farmer.

Hand-in-hand with human reform, farmers should be provided with cheap and appropriate farm techniques, tools and implements that are readily available and accessible to them. Moreover, farmers should be motivated to become as much as possible farmer-toolmakers and tool owners. The recycling of plants and animals and the full utilization of all indigenous resources in the farm enable farmers to make full use of this natural capital that is often overlooked and taken for granted. The practice of natural farming guarantees the full achievement of self-reliance and human dignity.

Finally, what may be considered a radical sweeping alternative for farmers in the Philippines—the philosophy and technology of ODISCO—may not be new, after all. ODISCO may have been a forgotten and discarded but effective traditional farming system practiced by Filipino forebears that has been brushed aside by modern farming technologies espoused by various interests having little regard for the small farmer himself.

ANNEX 1

Crops raised in ODISCO farm

Trees

    mahogany
    falcata
    kapok

Plantation Crops

herba buena	bamboo
coconut	madre de cacao
black pepper	ipil-ipil
coffee	cacao

Fruit Trees

mango	pomelo	soursop
sugarapple	calaansi	star fruit
papaya	chico	tamarind
avocado	starapple	
jackfruit	*santol*	
banana	guava apple	

Vegetables/Cereals

onion	watermelon	sorghum
taro	yellow corn	mungbean
squash	lady's finger	cassava
sponge gourd	peanuts	yam
eggplant	stringbean	bitter gourd
sweet potato	soybean	
tomato	horse radish	
rice		
swamp cabbage		

Herbs

artamisa	*mansanilla*
aloe vera	*lamponaya*

A DIALOGUE WITH LAURENTINO BASCUG

Anisur Rahman had a dialogue with Laurentino Bascug, one of the founder-leaders and President of the LAKAS-ODISCO movement. Laurentino presented Figure 1, summarizing his Holistic Analysis of the Root Causes of Poverty which he said is the synthesis of his more than 30 years of experience in the movement.

A: You have written your account as if everything is moving fine in your movement. This cannot be true, and you must be experiencing problems and moving through resistances of various kinds. For example, when you start work in one barangay, not all villagers immediately respond to your philosophy. How do you actually proceed?

L: What you say is very true. When we start work in a town,[1] we recruit at least three potential educators from it, persons whom people trust and respect and who can lecture to the people. Thirty such persons from different towns are taken in a 15-day seminar—the Management and Educators (MES) seminars mentioned in the paper. In this seminar they are trained to give the basic course to the villagers. It is a combination of workshop and practical work.

Yes, not many in a barangay respond at first, and our strategy is to start with one cooperative in a barangay and work to make it a success. We help it to initiate some economic project with a production loan from the Land Bank, without any physical collateral.

Once a cooperative is successful, it acts like a magnet, to attract others to join or to form their own cooperatives. In this way we move forward.

A: Do you face resistance from rich landlords?

L: Yes, in many barangays. They discourage the people to attend meetings; sometimes conspire against the leaders and have them jailed on various false accusations.

A: It seems you have a problem with the legal concept of land ownership which grants ownership of land, while you are advocating the concept of something like "trusteeship" rather than ownership of land.

L: What we are advocating is a concept of limited ownership rather than absolute ownership. Absolute ownership of land belongs to God, but He allows limited ownership to humans for the purpose of its proper use. Some property you can use without owning—e.g. air. Other properties you cannot use properly without owning—e.g., toothbrush. In between falls land. Residential land should be owned by the family. Agricultural land you will own, but only so that you can use it properly, by preserving its qualities. Thus right to ownership is secondary to the question of its proper use. Also, ownership of agricultural land should be limited by area—you have to share it with others. You cannot own a lot while others have less.

We, moreover, give them the value that you should not have a landlord mentality but should till the land yourself. The tiller is a co-worker of God. When the roots of a plant go down inside the earth not man, but God is working there; when the leaves grow up and take nourishment from the air, then also God is working. When a farmer is ploughing then he is putting in his contribution, and becomes a co-worker of God. Thus there is no shame in becoming a farmer. The landlord is not a co-worker of God because he does not physically work.

A: What is the role of women in the ODISCO movement?

L: Women also attend the seminars and become educators. In the cooperatives all members of the families attend the seminars. Otherwise there will be conflicts in the house with different values. This is what makes the difference between success and failure of the cooperatives.

Our educational program is unique—we aim to remove from the mind of the poor the wrong and unjust concepts, and at the same time to remove from the minds the damaged culture imposed by the colonialized system. And the dehumanizing effects of poverty—e.g. dependency, pessimistic, negative attitudes, lost sense of dignity, lost drive to improve one's situation. People cannot be liberated from poverty unless you can liberate the mind first.

A: What are your sources of funding?

L: This is where we have to do better. There is the indignity of dependence on foreign funds. We have to try to raise funds from the villages themselves. If we help them to get bank loans, and if their economic condition gets better as a result, they should contribute to our finance—its only fair. We have not yet insisted this, we have been too soft with them in this respect, undermining the dignity of the people unwittingly. Come back after four years, and I hope to show something more than what we are doing.

END NOTE

[1] A number of barangays make a town.

CHAPTER 8

SELF-RELIANCE AMONG THE RURAL POOR: LEARNING PROCESSES IN NORTH INDIA

Varun Vidyarthi

INTRODUCTION

Self-reliance implies self-esteem and vice-versa. This holds special significance in the lives of the poor for whom basic living needs are at stake. Development efforts by various agencies, both governmental and non-governmental, have often contributed to a loss of self-esteem and self-reliance among the poor instead of their enhancement. Lack of their participation in such development efforts is a direct consequence, and can be attributed to shortcomings both in program design and implementation. Alternative participatory approaches are a difficult challenge to most development practitioners given the various social, economic and political forces that seek to promote dependency instead. Yet, the biggest obstacles are perhaps not external but internal, i.e., in the attitudes and beliefs of people that lead to inertia and inaction. Promotion of self-reliance is thus like promotion of life itself.

I have been associated with a variety of experiments to promote self-reliance among the poor in Uttar Pradesh, north India. The process of experimentation has been very intensive, full of pitfalls and very uncertain—perhaps again like life itself. I venture here to extract some relevant experiences of initiatives by people, with facilitation by Manavodaya, that throw light on the various issues involved in self-reliant development of the poor.

Base Institutions for Self-reliance

Looking back to the past, we find many traditions where people got together to perform economic activities that enabled them to be self-reliant. These traditions were based on sound principles of sharing of tasks and benefits and a system of decision making that provided for equal participation by all.[1] Such traditions now being almost dead, community decision making is a rare phenomenon. For an average villager, this implies considerable loss of opportunities for self-reliance. We need to build alternative base institutions through which people can collectively decide and act on issues of common interest.

In our attempts to develop base institutions among the poor, we worked through several different options: promoting and strengthening youth clubs recognized and supported by the administration; revival of the *satsang*, a cultural tradition of evening songs and discussions; creation of different functional groups based on immediate needs identified by the people; formation of artisan groups to facilitate rehabilitation of artisans who tend to give up their traditional occupations due to various economic pressures; savings and credit groups. In every case, the principal idea was to enable people to decide and act on their own, with minimum intervention from outside. Village level dialogues and group formation were facilitated through a team of trained workers. I shall critically analyze the experiences of formation and working of such village groups and their role in promoting self-reliance among the poor. These were supported through the involvement of Manavodaya in district Sitapur, Uttar Pradesh from 1988-89 to 1992-93.

ALTERNATIVE BASE INSTITUTIONS AND THEIR CHARACTERISTICS

The Village Panchayat

The Panchayats at the village level and their federated body at the cluster level (Nyaya Panchayat) potentially offer good scope for democratic decision making with participation of the poor. Panchayats often have important resources like common lands, ponds, orchards, and grazing lands that could be turned into instruments for self-reliance. It is unfortunate, however, that this important institution has become so affected by outside intervention—both political and bureaucratic—that its own function of mobilizing people and resources has been reduced to naught. Besides, the poor have little voice in the proceedings of the Panchayat and most decisions are taken by a few influential persons living in the village.

The institution of Panchayat, however, has constitutional sanction and will continue to be the basic unit of decision making in rural areas. Reforms in election rules, procedures, and supervision will be necessary, however, if the Panchayat is to become an effective base institution for the empowerment and self-reliance of the poor (Mukarji and Bandyopadhyay, 1993; Acharya, 1994). Meanwhile, one has to seek alternative institutional mechanisms for the purpose. Once the people have developed alternative institutional mechanisms to voice their problems and act on them, reformed Panchayats can be a ground for them to test their strength through fielding of their candidates in Panchayat elections.

Youth Clubs

Youth clubs, known by the name of Yuwak Mangal Dals or Nehru Yuwak Kendras in Uttar Pradesh, have a constitutionally sanctioned role at village level. Every Gram Sabha (revenue village) is supposed to have a youth club to encourage the youth to take part in sports and developmental activities. There is an apex body at the block (area) level to coordinate their activities and to channel funds for purchase of sports goods and the like. The club has to elect office bearers every three years through a secret ballot. The chairperson of the club is nominated to the village Panchayat too. The club has to be formally registered at the district level to become eligible to receive funds.

Most of the youth clubs we came across were actually functioning like defunct sports clubs. Most members were inactive, meetings were scarcely held, and no one really understood the objectives of a youth club. There were few registered clubs and in most villages people were unaware of the process and the eligibility criteria for the formation of such an institution. When we initiated discussion on the formation of new youth clubs with broader developmental functions, the response varied, but in some cases was enthusiastic.

Tikauli

In village Tikauli, when the Manavodaya facilitator suggested formation of a youth club in a village meeting, there was immediate rivalry for nomination of the office bearers. After a few meetings, people decided that the best option would be to take up some work of public interest and allow the leadership to emerge thereby. Soon after there were only a few contenders left and a club was formed. A *Shramdaan* (voluntary work service) was organized for building a 200-meter long road at the entrance of the village. There was very enthusiastic participation by all members. The club also hosted a cultural program which was attended by the Chairman of the Youth

Welfare Program in the Government who promised to arrange sanction of government fund for metalling the road.

Encouraged by the initial successes, the youth club decided to improve the educational situation in the village. As the government primary school in village was not running properly, the club lodged complaints to higher authorities. These had no effect. Later, it raised funds to build a shed for a private school to be run by the club committee. In the initial stage, Manavodaya provided assistance in school management, training of teachers, and installing a hand pump at the school. The school has been running successfully for the last four years. However, the club has become defunct after considerable bickering among its members.

Tikauli's social structure is a principal factor contributing to the club's demise. The population of the village is composed of Scheduled Castes, Other Backward Castes, Upper Castes and Muslims. The youth club had representation primarily from the Upper Castes. Its activities also coincided with their interests. Though people from the Scheduled Castes did attend meetings, their priorities remained undiscussed. At one stage, members of the youth club raised their voice against the village head for improper construction of apartments for the Scheduled Castes under a government program, Indira Awas Yojana. But it appears that this was primarily motivated by political considerations. The village head belóngs to the Backward Castes and had won the elections because of the support of Scheduled Castes. In any case, the youth club did not in any way help in the process of empowerment of the poor in village Tikauli.

Anwarpur

In village Anwarpur, however, a youth club was formed among the Scheduled Castes and that too among the poor. In this case, the initiative was taken by a well-educated Scheduled Caste youth, who organized the people for a *Shramdaan* for cleaning of an irrigation drain, and bringing to book people involved in illegal felling of trees on village common land. Several discussions were held on ways of enhancing incomes of the members. It was decided that the club would take the village pond on lease from the village panchayat and do fish cultivation there. The village head also supported the resolution. However, the club could not pool together resources to take the pond on lease. The youth leader took little interest in following up the proposal with concerned authorities. In a later meeting, people wanted a change in leadership of the club. The educated young man was perhaps more interested in getting a job than in working for his less advantaged brethren.

Villages Pirthipur and Mau had similar stories with some variance. A youth club was formed in those villages among the poorer Scheduled Caste population. There was an early enthusiasm that waned over time due to both problems of leadership and inability to pursue a common social or economic activity that could sustain people's interest in the club.

Satsangs

Satsangs are village gatherings based on tradition where people take part in religious and topical discussions and sing devotional songs. With facilitation by Manavodaya, these meetings evolved into forums where people also sought resolution of disputes and decided on joint action based on consensus. Such forums were organized in several villages as part of an effort to develop people's institutions and initiatives for identifying problems and working on them (Morse and Vidyarthi, 1990). Satsang meetings became very popular in some villages for information sharing and decisions leading to community action. Produced below are extracts of some relevant experiences and a critical reflection on their importance for self-reliant development.

Devipur

During one of the Satsang meetings in village Devipur, one participant raised the issue of a lowlying road entering the village from the canal side. This often led to entry of water inside the village causing floods and accompanying misery. The Satsang members decided to do *Shramdaan* with participation of one member from every household to get rid of the problem. With the enthusiastic participation of almost all households, the road was completed in a few hours. Five men, however, had cultivated land without authorization. When this land was taken over as part of the new road they became angry and decided to file a complaint with the police. They included some of the powerful landholders of the village. The whole village got together and approached these men to desist from filing a complaint, saying that they would then have to face social boycott—specifically, such as refusal to perform traditional community work like replacing and repairing each family's thatch roof. The men had to withdraw.

Other Villages

In a more constructive spirit, a resident of village Tilokpur who had occupied land that was part of a village road voluntarily gave up his possession when the issue was raised in a Satsang meeting. This dispute had had its settlement pending in the court of law for a long time. In other Satsang meetings, people shared information on malaria, and prevention and treatment of water-borne diseases. The book *Where There is No Doctor* was used in the readings (Werner). Elsewhere a revolving fund was started, tree plantations organized and vaccinations arranged for animals.

Satsang meetings were, therefore, seen to be a forebear for various types of activities based on collective decision making. Since they were based on a traditional institutional setting, the meetings had good attendance and participation of villagers. It was noted, however, that Satsang gatherings in some villages were marked by absence of the poorer Scheduled Caste community. Issues raised in Satsang meetings were those of general interest, not necessarily representing the interests of the poor. Besides, as later observed, the gatherings discontinued in the absence of the Manavodaya facilitator. Thus, while Satsang meetings did serve a useful purpose, they could not be sustained and could not effectively contribute towards the self-reliance of the poor.

Functional Groups

We have had several experiences with associations formed by people with a specific function or goal, with either a short or longer term perspective, but linked to the achievement of that function or goal only. Pronouncements regarding formation of such associations or committees are popular among policy makers and administrators in the government who seek people's participation in their programs. Thus the education department organizes village education committees, the forest department would like to form Forest Management Committees, the Irrigation Department would like to work with Water Management Committees and so on.

Such pronouncements of policy and their execution at village level usually make a mockery of people's participation, being completely out of tune with sociopolitical realities in the village and surrounding countryside. In almost every case the village head is the chairman of the committee. The members are usually hand-picked by the head. Often their names exist only in registers. Most members do not even know that they are members. Meetings are never held. Any resolution required is prepared quietly and signatures or thumb impressions obtained easily.

Notwithstanding such practices, genuine functional groups formed by people with clearly defined functions or goals can achieve a useful purpose benefiting the poor as indicated by the following examples.

Water Management Groups

For several years, poor farmers of villages Bakhatkhera, Tikauli, and Mau had been getting little or no water from the minor irrigation channel passing through these villages. This had seriously affected crop production of the poor farmers. Others had pumpsets installed in their fields. The principal reason for the unavailability of water was the inadequate desilting and removal of mud in the irrigation channel by the government-appointed contractors. This resulted in very little water flowing through the channel which was, therefore, often blocked by the influential farmers at the head of the channel and diverted to their own fields.

In 1991, Manavodaya volunteers initiated several meetings in these three villages to enable the people to take a collective decision for resolving the problem. Poor farmers from village Mau, situated at the tail end and hence most seriously affected, took the lead. They joined in meetings with farmers from the other two villages too. It was finally agreed that the whole channel would be properly desilted with or without the involvement of the contractor. When the contractor arrived, the farmers did not allow him to bring outside labor. They did the work themselves for the contractor and worked overtime voluntarily to desilt the channel. As a result, farmers up to the tail end of the channel were able to irrigate their fields for the first time in several years.

Handpump Groups

A large number of deep-bore India Mark II handpumps are often lying idle in villages for want of simple repair or maintenance. Being considered public property, no one feels individually responsible for the pump's repair, while the government repair mechanism does not often work. In the absence of an alternative arrangement for repair, even the loss of a nut and bolt leads to pump dysfunctioning. The poor families are the worst sufferers as they do not have other safe sources of drinking water.

In some villages, Manavodaya volunteers encouraged people to contribute to a revolving fund for hand pump maintenance. In many such villages, the accumulated amount, usually around Rs. 200, was kept in a local bank under the joint signatures of two members. Funds could be withdrawn with signatures of both members and used for minor repairs and maintenance.

Gur Making

In village Tilokpur, the poor farmers producing sugarcane in their fields generally purchased *gur* (partly refined sugar, or jaggery) from the market. This prompted Manavodaya volunteers to form a farmers' group for sugarcane crushing and *gur* making. The group raised a small loan and rented the cane crushing and gur making equipment from the market. After considerable discussions, the group set hiring charges of the equipment to individual farmers. This was based upon the quantity of juice extracted. Members of the group were charged a lesser fee and given priority in using the equipment. The installation attracted a large number of poor farmers in the region and the loan was completely repaid by the group.

This functional group was based on a tradition of community *gur* making that had collapsed since several years. Such a tradition can be revived through proper understanding of its features, especially those which enable development of institutional mechanisms for collective decision making among the poor.

Artisan Groups

Artisans form a separate category of the rural poor faced with common economic problems associated with competition from large-scale manufacture and changing product tastes. Illiteracy, traditional age-old skills, lack of risk-taking ability and inadequate information on new technologies and markets compound their problems further. Manavodaya has worked with two different artisan groups: animal carcass flayers and handloom weavers. The experiences associated with these are briefly described here.

Animal Carcass Flayers

The carcass of a dead animal is flayed by a section of the Scheduled Caste community for processing into leather. Both the flaying and tanning operations which were earlier done by this community are now in the hands of people or institutions outside the community. The processing of hides into leather is done in large tanning factories which receive their raw material from middlemen who engage traditional artisans for lifting the dead animals and flaying the carcass. The artisans get a lowly 5 percent of the total value added from an operation which carried out traditionally is both unhygienic and cumbersome.

In 1988, Manavodaya organized the flayers of block Sidhauli covering about 100 villages. It assisted the flayers' group financially in bidding for a contract for lifting of dead animals and selling the hides to the tanning industry. The group had only one literate member who was nominated Secretary to handle the financial transactions and keep accounts. The hides were sold to the tanneries directly without intervention of the middlemen. The group thus received an added ten percent of the value added on the product. This improved their economic gains considerably and the entire amount loaned by Manavodaya to the group was repaid by the year's end.

Encouraged by the success of the operation, the group made a strong bid to obtain the same contract the following year. This time, however, the middlemen were well organized. They had combined in pooling resources and controlling information to raise the auction bids to levels beyond the reach of the flayers' group. That year the group had to remain content with a sub-contract from the middlemen at great economic disadvantage. Some members of the group also complained of mismanagement of funds by their nominated Secretary, and broke away taking a smaller sub-contract themselves. The other members, mostly illiterate, could not verify the funds' position and lost interest in the group activity. All the flayers have now reverted back to the earlier position of working for the middlemen.

Handloom Weavers

Handloom weavers in village Albada Chiraunji had been struggling to keep their looms running with the production of traditional men's cotton wear, the dhoti. For this too, they had to go to another village 30 km away to do the warping operation. The warping drum required for the operation was not available in the village. These weavers were enabled to form a group and to obtain a warping drum on loan for use by group members. The weavers were trained by a master craftsman in producing new varieties of cloth like shirting and bedcovers in tune with modern tastes. The yarn for this had to be brought from a wholesale market at Kanpur more than 100 km away.

Despite efforts to make the group self-reliant, the weavers continued to depend on Manavodaya for purchase of yarn and marketing the produce. A further change in products to suit local tastes was attempted, but marketing continued to be a problem. Again with fluctuations in the price of yarn, the members could not rely on handloom weaving for their sustenance and the members shifted priorities to growing cash crops in agriculture. Presently, most of the weavers have discontinued weaving. Some have gone back to weaving of the traditional dhoti occasionally.

Savings and Credit Groups

A group of poor villagers, usually around 15 in number, pool their monthly savings together regularly to form and expand a common fund. The group frames its own rules regarding use of this fund. This usually begins with small credit to members of the group at rates of interest decided by the group. As the pooled money grows, the uses generally diversify into, say, purchase of commonly used items by village families like big cooking utensils for use in marriages, or kerosene pressure lamps. The money can also be used for loans to small business, depending on the amount of money available with the group and the priorities decided by the group.

Group members meet regularly—usually once a week—to deposit their contributions and to discuss alternative uses of the money. These meetings are also occasions to discuss local problems and group initiatives to resolve them. The meetings thus become forums for collective decision making and action by the poor. Such group formation has been found to be practical and acceptable among both men and women in very poor living conditions. We are finding that it is an important potent force in mobilizing people and developing institutions that grow in strength over time.

What is it that attracts the poor to form such a group? A major attraction is easy access to credit and hence freedom from the local moneylender. Most poor villagers still depend on local moneylenders for long- and short-term credit at exorbitant rates—usually 10 percent per month, going up to 50 percent depending on circumstances. Members of a savings-credit group can then borrow from its own pool at interest rates decided by the group itself. These rates need not be uniform. For example, usually no interest is charged for emergencies like an accident. Low interest (1 to 2 percent a month) is charged for other medical contingencies like illness, and 3 to 4 percent for trade and commerce. As the fund grows, its use usually changes from distress requirements to trade and business requirements of members.

The other benefit that the group members understand and appreciate with the passage of time is solidarity, that brings with it a new sense of joy and also helps the groups in moving towards self-reliance. I shall describe here the experiences of some savings-credit groups, including the manner in which they have helped in transforming individual and social lives of villagers.

Madnapur

In Madnapur, a small interior village seldom visited by outsiders, the Manavodaya worker was informed on his first visit that no meeting can take place there. Nevertheless a meeting did take place and lasted for three hours with participation from all sections of the village community. The group first formed had 10 members and included the village head who belonged to the Upper Caste. The members, however, excluded the head after considerable discussion among themselves.

At an early stage, a new group emerged with a larger membership, 16. Strict rules regarding individual habits were made and weekly meetings which were not taking place earlier became a regular feature. Group members started questioning unauthorized felling of trees and use of government funds in an employment generation scheme, the "Jawahar Rozgar Yojana." This action resulted in threats from local moneylenders and vested interests. Then, a poor village resident, a non-member who had taken a loan of Rs. 200 from a moneylender seven years back, came to the group to seek justice. The moneylender who had remained silent all these years, wanted Rs. 14,000 calculated on the basis of a monthly interest of 10 percent. After several negotiations with the group, the moneylender brought down his demand to Rs. 6,000 of which Rs. 4,000 was paid up soon thereafter.

Land disputes for some other villagers were also resolved. A poor tailor from a neighboring village whose tailoring machine was stolen was assisted by the group which raised funds for the purpose. Sanitation issues were often discussed in meetings. Members took part in cleaning operations outside their houses occasionally. Four members constructed soakpits. Some members gave up liquor consumption. A training program for manufacture of detergent soap powder was organized at the village. Production was organized and initiated, while on behalf of the local groups Manavodaya arranged printing of labels for packaging and marketing.

As group members continued to be under threat, the local police were informed. Members vowed not to take up arms like spears which were in possession by most and were earlier brought to all the meetings.

Misirpur

Misirpur, a village comprising mostly poor Scheduled Caste families, showed a poor response in the beginning. Villagers indicated that a bank employee had run away with their deposits in the past, hence any activity involving savings of money would be unpopular. A savings group was later formed, but deposits continued to be irregular. Many members worked as laborers outside the village, and therefore could not find a suitable time to meet. Meanwhile, small savings continued and loans were also given out. After considerable discussions, some of the members resolved to hold night meetings.

A school was started by this group to improve the level of education. A member of the group worked as the teacher in the evening from 6 to 9 p.m. Students paid a fee of Rs. 2 to Rs. 3. The school faced considerable problems due to non-payment of fees. Every time this happened the group had to call a meeting of the villagers and start a collection drive. Solidarity among the members of the group gradually grew. Once an Upper Caste villager tried to take away a male goat belonging to a member of the group for servicing his goats without payment. The member resisted and raised an alarm. All the group members assembled and forced the offender to pay.

The group continues to have problems, nevertheless. Most of the members, being very poor, are always looking for a loan. The group has not been able to keep a tight discipline on recovery. As a result there is little money in its kitty at any point of time. Members say they will have to stop credit for some time, and emphasize timely recovery.

Laxmanpur

When a savings group was first formed in this small interior village having Scheduled and Backward Caste families only, an influential member of the Scheduled Caste community wanted all meetings to be organized at his doorstep. Others soon realized that he could not be an equal member. Meetings became irregular and people wanted their savings back. At this stage, a proposal for a new group was mooted. With exclusion of some members of the earlier group, a much larger new group was formed.

The first major advantage of solidarity in the village was a check in dacoity. A gang of dacoits had parked in the region and was regularly committing acts of crime and dacoity. The group was able to organize night vigils that ensured protection and removed the fears from the minds of the villagers. Electricity wires connecting the electric tubewell in the village had been cut and stolen. The group exerted pressure on the administration by making a collective complaint. Although a new line was sanctioned, the actual installation could not take place without bribing a large sum to the working staff. The group made efforts to lower this sum to a manageable Rs. 1,000. That was contributed by group members and passed on to the relevant authorities. This ensured timely connection of wires for energizing the tubewell for irrigation. This would have been unthinkable without an active group.

The Laxmanpur group members continue to face problems from influential Upper Caste families of a neighboring village who had been their dubious benefactors earlier. There are continual suggestions to the members to stop the savings-credit scheme. However, most of the members are determined to continue at all costs.

Other Groups

Savings groups in other villages have assisted members in getting back their mortgaged land, in purchasing productive assets like bicycles, in resolving disputes of various types, in getting literate, and so on. Short-term credit for agricultural inputs like fertilizer has been popular among many groups.

Savings groups are not without problems. Many groups have been observed to bend under pressure of vested interests and break up. Some groups break due to mismanagement of funds. Many others are not able to maintain the discipline of savings regularly and discontinue their meetings. However, it has been seen that once the teething problems of a savings group are over, there are good chances of the group achieving stability and performing various kinds of social and economic functions enabling the poor to move towards self-reliance.

CHALLENGES IN MOVING TOWARDS SELF-RELIANCE

Self-reliance calls for building of effective base institutions among the poor to enable collective decision making and action. From the examples cited here, we note that there are various pitfalls in this process that restrict the participation of the poor and, also, the sustainability of such institutions. These pitfalls are not incidental phenomena. They are characteristic responses of existing relationships and structures that affect the lives of the poor.

Dependency Relationships

Persistent relationships of dependency are among the forces constraining participation by the poor. We analyze these dependency relationships in the context of the given examples before examining opportunities and measures that could help the poor in moving towards self-reliance.

Local Dependency Relationships

The initiative to form a youth club in village Tikauli came from members of the Upper Caste who then undertook programs of immediate interest to them, viz. an access road and a private school for children. The problems of the poor sections of the population remained largely undiscussed. In village Anwarpur although the club was formed by the poorer Scheduled Caste group, the leader was chosen on the basis of his higher education. His interest did not lay with the group. Ultimately the people sought his removal. A similar situation is seen among the carcass flayers. Their literate leader was accused of mismanagement of funds that ultimately led to breaking of the group.

Clearly, it is not easy for the poor to find local allies in their struggle. It does not matter whether the persons taking initiative to form a group or those chosen as leaders of a group are from an Upper Caste or the same caste. If leaders have a different level of aspiration, whether it be due to higher economic status or a special skill or education, their leadership could become useless to the poor and in some circumstances counter-productive. These unequal relationships within the village and neighboring area can be described as local dependency relationships.

As we see, local dependency relationships are based on visible inequalities and social barriers at the local level, and are marked by distinct attitudinal and behavioral differences among people. Inequalities associated with the dealings of local vested interests, i.e., money lenders and landlords hiring labor, belong to the same category. They are more visible and difficult to handle. In village Madnapur, for example, the group had a difficult time trying to resolve the problem of payment of a seven-year-old debt of Rs. 200. The moneylender, who was bent on charging interest at the rate of 10 percent a month, brought down his demand from Rs. 14,000 to Rs. 6,000 due to group pressure. What is astonishing, however, is that this ridiculous amount was ultimately paid up by the poor farmer. This speaks of the conditions and the constraints faced by the poor in the process of self-development.

Local dependency relationships are a constant threat to the solidarity of the poor and the existence of any base institution formed by them. Groups like those of the carcass flayers will collapse, despite a good market for their products, if measures are not adopted to remove or reduce the dependency on one person. Groups in Madnapur and Laxmapur could reorganize and sustain themselves only because the members decided to remove the persons with differing interests from the membership of the group. The process of building solidarity and self-reliance among the poor thus has to begin with persons of similar social and economic positions. Can there be a local benefactor belonging to a higher social and economic position who could assist or patronize the process? Maybe, but the experiences with which Manavodaya has been associated suggest "No" as the answer.

This viewpoint was contested by participants of a recent workshop on participatory development hosted by Manavodaya (GOI and UNICEF, 1994). According to them, it is important to develop relationships with all sections of the population in working towards self-reliance, without excluding anyone from the process. After a long debate, the participants concluded that alliances should be developed only to the extent that the poor are not crushed by them. Empowerment of the poor is a basic condition for any equal negotiation. Thus people from all backgrounds can come together and work on a common platform like a Panchayat, but for such a platform to be truly democratic the poorer sections must work towards nullification of their dependency relationships.

External Dependency Relationships

In the examples cited, we note that handloom weavers of village Albada Chiraunji could not sell their products despite a shift in their product mix from traditional cotton dhotis to terene-cotton shirtings. The principal reason was their inability to cope with a very competitive market. Their scale of operation was far too low to collect raw materials from a distant market and sell the final product at a competitive price. This is a tragedy that afflicts a large number of small producers at village level and constitutes an important external dependency: the market.

In the case of carcass flayers, the market was readily available but the obstruction came from the mafia of middlemen, the small controlling group involved in the trade. The economic strength of this mafia forced the organization of flayers to remain contented with a subcontract only. Such controlling groups exist in all sectors of production and trade, making it difficult for the poor artisans to exist.

Coping with such external dependencies is no simple exercise for the poor. A long valiant struggle appears to be the only way out. It is unfortunate that policy makers in the government have not been able to develop mechanisms to cope with this situation. Why should there be, for example, a restriction on the right to lift dead animals? Again the whole system of contracts and auctions makes it difficult for the poor to enter into relationships or agreements that could enable them to move towards self-reliance. It instead creates avenues for operations of parasitic middlemen who thrive at the expense of the poor.

In the case of the Water Management Groups formed in the three villages Mau, Tikauli and Bakhatkhera, the origin of the problem of desilting lay in the mischief of the outside contractor. He bid for the job of desilting, but was not interested in doing the work properly as it did not affect him. Only when the people from three villages organized themselves and were able to put pressure on the contractor was the problem finally resolved.

Opportunities and Measures for Countering Dependency Relationships

The experience with savings-credit groups shows that local dependency relationships are best countered through effective base institutions of the poor at village level. Such institutions, however, are very fragile. They break up easily or tend to become ineffective in the long run. How can one promote sustainability of such institutions? We shall briefly discuss this in light of the examples given earlier.

Clarity of Objectives: Solidarity and Group Consciousness

Most experienced social activists agree that people come together and organize only if they see an immediate personal benefit. The longer term advantage of solidarity is surely understood by most. Yet, it takes time to appreciate and observe the direct benefits of solidarity. Till such a time the group can be said to be immature regarding clarity of objectives and hence in developing a clear understanding among its members.

Several groups have achieved this degree of clarity and strength. In village Laxmanpur, for example, despite continual suggestions from influentials in the area, the group was not willing to stop its savings-credit program. They had observed the advantages of solidarity in keeping off dacoits and also in getting the irrigation system revived. This was also true for villagers of Madnapur. Such a "group consciousness" on longer term objectives is a key to the survival of a group.

How did these groups achieve this in practice? While the skills of the animator were important, a necessary condition for such group consciousness was holding of regular meetings among its members. The savings-credit groups had a system of weekly meetings for deposits and discussions on local problems. Other groups, i.e., Youth Clubs, Satsangs, Artisan Groups had a system of monthly meetings only and those too were irregular. The saving groups had evolved rules that also included simple fines for non-attendance in meetings. Group regularity and self-discipline are, therefore, important constituents for developing consciousness and solidarity among the poor for waging a struggle to overcome dependency relationships.

An Expanding Economic Base

A gradual transition to economic self-reliance fosters and strengthens other processes of self-reliance too. In the absence of economic progress, other processes tend to fall apart. Perhaps this is what Kautilya had in mind in the 3rd century B.C. when he wrote in *Artha*

Shastra "Economics is at the root of Dharma (religion)." This is certainly evident from the case studies described here. Despite meaningful results from Satsangs, the institution could not sustain itself due to lack of an economic base. Other institutions like the Youth Clubs became inactive for the same reason.

On the other hand, the savings-credit groups did relatively well. One important reason was the economic strength provided by the pooled savings that grew with time. A further strengthening of the economic base requires gradual development of production units, controlled and managed by the groups enhancing the economic gains of its members. However, such a system must not be dependent on a single person for accounts, management, market development, and so on. As noted in the case of carcass flayers, this provides opportunities for funds mismanagement that can eventually lead to collapse of the group. Gradual building up of capability of all members, strict accounting procedures, and systems of monitoring by members are as important as the economic activity itself.

Federating Structures

Local mafias and middlemen controlling trade and markets, contractors of various development projects, and their nexus with people in administration constitute forces and dependencies that cannot be tackled by small groups of poor people at village level. The problem of siltation of irrigation channels, for example, could be tackled only when water management groups in three villages Mau, Tikauli and Bakatkhera came together and demonstrated solidarity before the contractor. For countering such external dependencies, there would be a need to build area level federal structures having village level groups as constituent members.

A federal structure can provide the much needed political strength to guard against injustices, and can turn to larger scale economic activities for competitive production and marketing.[2] This would provide the much needed fillip for intermediate scale production based on low energy inputs and a larger employment base.

It would be important for such federal structures to maintain an autonomous outlook, independent of larger political influences. However, the key to their effectiveness would lie in democratic decision making within its ranks and a system of leadership provided possibly on a rotational basis by its constituent member groups.

Alliances and Support

Solidarity, economic and political strength among the poor are not easily achieved in an environment that is marked by greed, jealousy, competition and apathy among most people. It is important to look for alliances or support from different sections of society: people in administration, banks, and other development agencies.

For example, funding bodies like the Rashtriya Mahila Kosh have been created at the national level for providing credit to women's groups. The National Bank for Agriculture and Rural Development has come up with a program of supplementing the pooled savings of people's Self-Help Groups. Some banks have a Gender Issue Program whereby special loaning facilities are made available to Women's Savings Credit Groups. These funds are inevitably channeled through NGOs working in the area.

Despite relaxation of norms and procedures by these funding institutions there are several operational problems in their effective implementation.[3] One major stumbling block is the continued apathetic attitude of the banking personnel at the local level and their nexus with the vested interests. A process of sensitization, dialogues, and empowerment of people, especially women, shall perhaps gradually pave the way in overcoming these bureaucratic impediments. People's groups must be enabled to make effective use of the policy and program support available.

Process Challenges

Some basic process challenges that need to be recognized in the quest for self-reliance are presented here in the context of the examples just discussed. The attempt here is to provide certain insights from experiences, without claim to any definite answers.

Inevitability of Struggle

Struggle is almost inevitable whenever the poor assert themselves and make efforts to move towards self-reliance. This is because the authority and convenience of the local elites are immediately threatened. Thus, for example, if a person is freed from debt or has an alternative source of cash for emergency needs, he or she need not work for a large-scale farmer at low wage rates. In the Sidhauli region described earlier, the wage rates continue to be between Rs. 12 and Rs. 15 per day, less than half of the minimum rates prescribed by the government. All attempts at creating people's organizations therefore come up with stiff resistance from the elites.

In village Madnapur, for example, the Manavodaya worker was told in clear terms by the local elites not to come in that area, threatening him with life. In village Misirpur, when the leader of the men's group started visiting a nearby village, Gularipurwa (all inhabitants of this village were poor), and started teaching children, the local elites made sure that no children attended the classes, threatening the people with severe consequences if they did not comply with their wishes.

In Laxmanpur and other surrounding villages, innovative methods are being practised for drawing people away from their solidarity groups. The elites have described Manavodaya intervention as a game plan to take away their savings and ultimately buy off lands, making them slaves. It is astonishing to see many poor villagers gullible to the extent of believing in such stories. The clear-headed ones understand the tricks being played on them and they usually resolve to counter the propaganda. Nevertheless, the going does become difficult.

Another aspect of the struggle which is inevitable is the ability to deal with markets. The market acts as an indirect and almost invisible force that controls the destiny of the poor. Most economic programs for the poor fail due to the inability of people to develop this forward linkage. In an age of increasing competition, only those having a high risk-taking ability stand a chance. People trained in detergent powder making, in village Madnapur for example, were faced with a demand from the local village market that was not easy to fulfull, i.e., good packaging, a brand name, and supply on credit. Some people were preparing to meet this challenge. Most others, however, were unsure.

The Question of Violence

The leader of the Madnapur group was known for his notorious behavior. He gave up violence, however, in favor of constructive groundwork, after coming in contact with Manavodaya. This transformation was made possible due to a newly felt mission in his life that came up as a challenge before him, namely, to run the group, achieve social justice and the like.

Violence is often the result of a chain reaction. If we are able to keep tempers under control, violence can be checked. We have learnt to do this by suggesting inner meditation, a long-term outlook, and consolidation of strengths. A quote by Acharya Vinoba Bhave, the famous *Bhoodan* (land gift) movement leader, is apt here: "A movement's success implies proper build up of *Bhakti* (faith), *Yukti* (strategy), and *Shakti* (strength)." Violence is clearly a short-cut route for achieving any goal.

We recognize that a holistic approach helps in winning over the adversary too, at least in keeping the tempers in check and hence in containing violence. Thus adversaries in Madnapur were themselves disarmed by the group's resolve to keep the spears away, to organize a village cleanliness program, and the like. A focus on values including evolution of individual and collective consciousness is an important constituent of a holistic approach. This is discussed separately ahead.

Information Channels

Most people would agree that ignorance contributes to the vicious cycle of poverty. Self-reliance, therefore, also implies development of an information system that enables people to keep abreast with new developments, debates, and happenings that affect their lives. This poses a special challenge in the context of poor illiterate villagers living in remote areas and maintaining links with the outside world perhaps only through the market.

We find that weekly meetings facilitated by a regular economic activity, as in the case of Savings Credit Groups, provide a useful platform for information exchange. The special advantage of information sharing in such groups is mutual reinforcement among members, discussion, and feedback: important constituents of a useful learning process. As the process evolves, it is usually possible to organize meetings at cluster and area levels with the involvement of banks, people from various development agencies, and the administration.

The response is usually overwhelming in the beginning. The challenge, however, is to maintain a match between people's information needs and that made possible through the information network. A two-way information flow through people's groups is, in fact, a true beginning of the process of decentralized planning, yet a distant dream in most bureaucracies.

VALUES AND SELF-RELIANCE

An overriding factor contributing to the success of base institutions and the process of self-reliance is anchorage to values cherished by all human beings irrespective of their background: a purposeful existence in life, love and respect for human beings and the potential inherent in them, faith in the power of positive thinking and action. These are constituents of a spiritual, creative urge in every person that is usually suppressed or relegated to the background by the immediate living environment and its challenges.

The process of conscientization and empowerment bears social meaning and strength in the collective context, but a successful process also implies parallel evolution of individual consciousness that is inherent but dormant in every person. Awakening of this consciousness is a key to the development of self-esteem and consequent effort towards self-reliance.

This is a process that cannot be imposed or transplanted through lectures or preaching, as it depends entirely on the effort of the individual. Here lies the dilemma of the development worker. Does he/she wait for the individual evolutionary process to take place? If not, what is his/her role? I believe that the answer lies in being honest to oneself, enabling others and oneself too to perceive the truth of the situation. There are potentials existing in all human beings—poor or otherwise—to perceive the truth. Simultaneous reflection can, therefore, become an equal, participatory process. This can also turn into a group process reinforcing the effort of the individual.

This process of evolution is not a steady phenomenon. It needs constant reinforcement through regular introspection by the individual, supported by suitable societal or group response. A process of group reflection is, therefore, important both for evolution of consciousness, individual and group, and for achieving associated economic and political strengths.

At Manavodaya, we have begun conducting sessions on participatory reflection with leaders and members of various groups with encouraging results. Sessions include reflections on goals and values in life. As people begin to rediscover a meaning and purpose in life and the need to regularly introspect—individually, in the family and in the group—the truths about present existence (living, attitudes, and so on), including the discomforting irregularitie- begin to unfold. Important changes begin to take place in the individual leading to changes in attitudes and beliefs regarding development.

Achieving self-development and self-reliance is clearly a long and difficult struggle both within and outside, in the individual and the group, and the larger network of people. However, the process can be made joyous by making it collective and by knowing that there are partners elsewhere struggling similarly.

END NOTES

[1] One such tradition was community cane crushing and *gur* (jaggery) production. Many areas boasted of a community system of water sharing for irrigation.

[2] I am aware of instances where this has happened in practice. An enlightened banker in Sri Lanka, working through the Regional Rural Banks, was able to form more than a hundred people's groups in a district. These groups formed federations for marketing of their agricultural produce. The mafias controlling the market sensed the price variations, came to understand the process, and got this banker transferred from the district. Nevertheless, the process did lead to empowerment and enhanced self-reliance of the poor.

[3] See, for example, "Critical Review of the Working of the Rashtriya Mahila Kosh," paper presented at the workshop on Emerging Issues in Savings and Credit Groups of NGOs, July 28-29, 1994, Hyderabad.

BIBLIOGRAPHY

Acharya, P. 1994. Elusive New Horizons: Panchayats in West Bengal. In: *Economic and Political Weekly*, January 29, Bombay.

Government of India and UNICEF. 1994. *Report of Training Workshop on Participatory Development.* Program on Community Based Convergence Services, Lucknow, May 9 to 14.

Morse, R. and V. Vidyarthi. 1990. *Values in Development: the Village Satsang as a Means of Promoting Participatory Learning and Development.* Manavodaya Working Paper 2. Lucknow.

Mukarji, N. and D. Bandyopadhyay. 1993. *New Horizons for West Bengal's Panchayats.*

Werner, David. *Where There is No Doctor.* Palo Alto, California: Hesperian Foundation.

CHAPTER 9

COMMUNITY-BASED COMMUNITY-DETERMINED EDUCATION: NEW PARTNERSHIPS BETWEEN UNIVERSITIES AND INDIGENOUS PEOPLE'S COMMUNITIES

Russell Fox and Carol Minugh

Is access to formal educational systems essential for the survival of indigenous and oppressed people? Our response is yes, BUT... Underlying questions, which must be addressed first, are:

Who has a right to create knowledge that is validated by schools or universities?

Who controls the content and learning processes—the curriculum—of formal educational systems?

Can universities created and supported by First World societies contribute to the formulation and implementation of new development paradigms where community knowledge and experience, rather than Western scientific analysis, form the epistemological framework for development and social change? Again we answer yes, BUT...

This chapter highlights an example of how a fully-accredited state-supported college in the USA is forming innovative college/community partnerships with Native American communities to address these issues.

HOW KNOWLEDGE PARADIGMS DEFINE COMMUNITY AND DEVELOPMENT

All societies have mechanisms for teaching their young the patterns, norms, and roles of their culture, of training youth for their roles in society, and for on-going adult learning and development. Indigenous populations of the world don't need to rely upon formal educational institutions to "teach" the knowledge and skills of their culture. Families and communities build this learning into their patterns of daily life, relying upon stories and traditional practices passed down through generations of people living together on the land.

Most of the rest of us have, to a large measure, given this responsibility to a professional class of people who create and define what is valid knowledge and how it is to be taught and learned. We have broken our traditional relationships with the land, with work, with others and with the unknown. The power to create and validate knowledge, and to control its dissemination, has been given to those who by birth or training have accepted a certain paradigm of knowledge—variously called "western," Cartesian, scientific, and so on. Popular or vernacular knowledge may be studied as an intellectual curiosity, but not validated as an equivalent way of knowing the world, the unknown, or oneself.

What does the dominance of one model of how knowledge is created and disseminated mean to the existence and survival of our communities? Are communities the source of our reality and of our knowledge of the land, of social relations, and of the unknown? Or are communities the objects of academic and professional analysis and of development programs?

Global political and economic webs of interdependence and exploitation, fueled by modern communication technologies, do not allow communities of people to live in isolation, or peace, in the contemporary world. Knowledge of one's own cultural world view, language, norms, skills and ways of being are essential for cultural survival. But, perhaps unfortunately, so is knowledge of how forces external to our communities are working to dominate and control our lives, relationships to the world, and values. This knowledge, particularly in its contemporary forms, may not be included in traditional educational systems. Yet, gaining access to formal educational systems—if possible at all—at present requires abandoning or replacing traditional values with modern (i.e. "western") ones.

We believe that the answer to this dilemma lies in two arenas of work to be done. One is to encourage, assist, and allow indigenous communities to create and control their own educational institutions that would supplement (add to, not replace) traditional patterns of teaching and learning. Another strategy is to encourage, assist, or force existing colleges and universities to give equivalent validity to knowledge, skills, and learning processes controlled by the indigenous or other oppressed members of their societies.

Worldwide, there are many examples where communities have created or control schools for their children's education. Also, thousands of people's organizations have built strategies of adult education and human/community development from the philosophy and work of Paolo Freire and others. Examples of colleges and universities supporting and validating this learning with certificates and degrees, however, are almost non-existent.

NEW PARTNERSHIPS BETWEEN UNIVERSITIES AND INDIGENOUS COMMUNITIES

The case study presented in this chapter represents an attempt to create a Native American community-controlled educational curriculum within a state-supported university in the United States. The status of Native American nations in North America is similar in many ways to that of indigenous people on every continent. Modern "states" have taken land, natural resources, and the power to determine individual and community destinies, imposed legal, economic, educational, religious, and social service systems, and, in general, both overtly and covertly tried to destroy traditional cultural ways of living and thinking.

Yet, at least one university—The Evergreen State College in Washington State—has been willing to initiate a new and different relationship with Native American communities in its region. Currently in its fifth year, this program could be a model or inspiration for other colleges or universities to establish new partnerships with the indigenous communities in their region—giving these communities the power to create knowledge and have it validated as equivalent to the knowledge created in other academic programs of the university. In addition, it could provide a basic framework for the establishment of new, community-controlled institutions of post-secondary education.

Participatory Research and Native American Studies at The Evergreen State College

The Evergreen State College was created in 1967 with a mandate to design innovative curricular structures and pedagogical strategies that may be more appropriate for the 21st century than the

16th century models that still dominate the world of higher education today. At Evergreen, teaching and learning is organized into interdisciplinary, full-time, year-long, team-taught "programs." Knowledge is pursued collaboratively rather than competitively, interactively rather than passively, holistically rather than fragmented and specialized, with different cultural paradigms of knowledge actively explored and recognized as equivalently valid. Theory and practice are interwoven, with discussion and projects emphasized rather than lectures and exams.

Within this general college-wide approach to education, two particularly unique experiments in academic-community relationships were established in the early years. Incorporation of community participatory research projects in academic programs across the curriculum and the establishment of Northwest Native American Studies as a curricular "specialty area" both laid the groundwork for the Native American Community-based Community-determined program presented in detail in this chapter.

Participatory Research

Evergreen's pedagogical philosophy and curricular structure prepares and enables students and faculty to include significant community projects in their year-long studies. Students can learn how to put their participatory learning skills to work in the community as well as the classroom. They can integrate theory with practice, help community groups learn how to address issues of locally-controlled community development and, in general, combine their research and analysis skills with community knowledge as experienced by local residents. Over the years, Evergreen has become a model of how universities can work with communities in participatory research and advocacy projects.

Examples in academic programs taught by Russell Fox have included a multi-year project where students and faculty lived in and worked with a community faced with relocation by a federal government hydroelectric dam project. More typical have been the dozens of four-to-six month projects where two-to-ten students have assisted community groups, non-profit organizations, or small local governments learn how to conduct research and become advocates for social change efforts. An early, year-long study of "Sustainable Community Systems" included community-student participatory research projects addressing issues of housing and homelessness, economic development, waste reduction and recycling, natural resource protection, local control of land use planning, and proposals for sustainable cities.

Northwest Native American Studies

The Evergreen State College is located in western Washington State, an area rich with Indian Nations working to strengthen their cultural and economic identities. There are thirty-one federally recognized tribes in the state, and many other groups who identify themselves as Native American communities. In western Washington, the tribes are primarily fishing people with long and deep relationships to the land and waters of the region.

Strongly influenced by faculty member Mary Ellen Hillaire of the Lummi Nation, the Northwest Native American Studies program was established in 1973. The program's goals were to bridge the gap between oral and written traditions and to support individual Native American students in pursuing a college education. Mary Hillaire's model was based on the following concepts:

* Hospitality—an absolute trust in students' learning motivations and abilities;

* The Learning Triad—the sources of knowledge and learning relationships that include the student, the student's community, and the institution/faculty;

* Personal Authority—the student chooses how to best utilize personal, community and college resources to pursue learning goals.

Until Mary Hillaire's death in 1982, this model was effective in allowing individual Indian students to achieve their educational goals while living in their own communities. After her death, the Native American Studies program maintained its popularity, but primarily served non-native students. Then, in 1988, a two-year study of the program resulted in "...an institutional commitment to a planning process that will develop a model and proposal for how the college could and should respond to the needs of Native American students and communities."

THE NEW MODEL: A NATIVE AMERICAN COMMUNITY-DETERMINED PROGRAM

The 1988 study led to the hiring of three additional Native American faculty (currently totaling nine in a faculty of 175) and a commitment to establish a new community-based and community-controlled academic program. Faculty member Carol Minugh, of the Gros Ventre Nation, took the initiative to establish and coordinate this new effort.

The Native American Community-based Community-determined Liberal Arts Degree Program combines resources and commitments from tribal governments, reservation communities, students, and the college in a strategy to build strong Native American communities. Self-determination, individual and community empowerment, community participation, and community responsibility are the philosophical foundations of the program. The program allows local tribal people, individually and as a community, to identify and develop their own priorities of learning. Weekly classes are held in the reservation communities, with monthly weekend classes at the main campus for additional access to college resources.

Building upon the Hillaire-model Learning Triad, responsibility for the program develops as a partnership. The Tribal Council initiates' the process by adopting a resolution inviting The Evergreen State College to work with the community in establishing a program. Classroom space and assistance in recruiting, obtaining financial aid, and enrolling students are arranged with the tribe and the community. The development of the curriculum begins with community involvement. Questions such as "What does an educated member of an Indian Nation (one who wants to function within the Native American community) need to know" are examined. Students work as a group to identify the curriculum topics. The tribe and/or other community resources may provide specific training programs if needed.

The Evergreen State College provides faculty, develops a syllabus to address the community's learning goals, coordinates speakers and seminars to facilitate the learning process, emphasizes and teaches the skills of analysis, research and communication, provides access to campus resources, identifies appropriate consultants and community resource people for students, insures a rigorous educational program, evaluates and validates the learning process pursued by the students, assists students with financial aid and enrollment procedures, and seeks additional financial support for the program.

Students who do not qualify for admission to Evergreen, or who choose to complete additional community college credits prior to entering Evergreen, may enroll in Northwest Indian College, established by the Lummi Nation, but attend the community-determined program with the Evergreen students. When these students complete their two-year degree or choose to transfer, they enroll at Evergreen.

Students help determine and prioritize the community educational needs, determine their personal learning goals, participate in community-based seminars and projects, describe and evaluate their individual and collective learning, and help evaluate and modify the program as it develops.

Planned during the 1988-89 school year, the program began in the summer of 1989 with twenty students from the Quinault Nation. The Quinault Nation was selected as the site for the first community-based program because of the active support of the tribal government and the number of individual requests for additional studies beyond those available at the local two-year community college. Initial students included teacher aides in the tribal school, social service workers, tribal management employees, fisheries and forestry managers, and other adults seeking either specific skills or a liberal arts education. The Quinault Nation is one of ten tribal governments actively creating alternative self-governing relationships with the United States federal government. Aggressive and effective tribal leadership over the past 20 years has resulted in substantially increasing their land base and strengthening their economy.

In 1991, a second program was established on the Skokomish reservation and a modified version of the local programs was started with the Salish-Kootenai Federated Tribes in the state of Montana. A program with sixteen students from the Makah Nation began in fall 1992, and a second community on the Quinault reservation initiated a class in January 1993. Currently over 50 students are enrolled. Twenty-one have graduated with their Bachelor of Arts degrees. Two Evergreen faculty teach in the program full-time; they are assisted by two part-time faculty provided by Northwest Indian College, interns, and student program assistants.

Not only do students select the themes and topics to study, but the materials are selected to present the knowledge and issues from the Indian point of view. The first year, the general direction given by the students for a curriculum was "Quinault: Past, Present and Future." The second year, they chose a list of "courses" they wanted to cover, such as "Natural Resource Policy," "Alcoholism and Drug Abuse," and "Communities." Realizing a need for a more unifying theme, in 1991-92 the students picked "Cultures" as an overall topic, with Northwest Indians, South Africa, and Cultures in the US as sub-themes for each quarter.

During the 1992-93 year, students studied colonialism, democracy, manifest destiny, Federal-Indian Law and their own tribal laws and governance. In 1993-94, an examination of the concept and meaning of "relationships" was the organizing focus, with child-parent bonding, community concepts of health, relationships with the natural world, human relationships in administrative and work settings, mathematics, and natural history included in the curriculum.

Students hold classes either one or two evenings a week. Faculty rotate travel to the different communities, so some weeks' classes are run by students themselves or with the assistance of local facilitators. When visiting one of the communities, faculty also meet individually with each student to review progress, critique writing, and support students' individual learning goals. Every three weeks, students from all communities come to the Evergreen campus in Olympia for guest speakers, sharing of ideas and learning among groups, special workshops, and time to use the library for their research assignments.

Academic credit-generating work includes formal classes, individual projects and studies, group or community projects, participation in educational offerings sponsored by other organizations or agencies, documentation of prior learning experiences, and new job-related work skills. For example, teacher aides enrolled in a school district-sponsored teacher training class on the "Psychology of Cognition" for credit.

Collaboration with other colleges and universities is another important component. For example, Evergreen and Northwest Indian College share resources when the needs of a student can best be met by the other. Students can obtain a two-year technical degree through Northwest Indian College and an additional two years of liberal arts education through the Evergreen program. In addition, the faculty encourage students to find the best institution for a specific program of study when the Evergreen program is not appropriate. This is particularly true in the area of vocational training and professional programs such as nursing or engineering.

OBSERVATIONS, SUCCESSES, AND EDUCATIONAL PRINCIPLES

In the United States, educational programs provided by most colleges and universities are not designed for people who do not wish to share or buy into the "American Dream," and especially not for the people who are native to this country. The curriculum content, regardless of the philosophical orientation of the authors or teachers, is approached from the western civilization/colonial/pioneer point of view.

In these institutions, the Native American Indian is subjected to an education which is opposed to the existence of their tribes, not only as political entities but as cultures with spiritual and economic relationships with the land we now call the United States. The "melting pot with no lumps" self-identity of Americans, promoted throughout the literature in all academic disciplines and in the popular culture of Euro-Americans, leaves no room for other world views and definitions of education.

Sources of Knowledge

Within this context, the only sources of the knowledge needed to preserve Native American cultural paradigms are tribal communities and governments. If Native American communities are to survive as nations, they must build and maintain knowledge of and loyalty to those nations and their institutions. While knowledge about external and foreign philosophies and practices is useful in communicating with and relating to the rest of the world, if the tribes are to survive as a people and as self-governing nations, they must build and control their own educational processes.

The Native American Community-based Community-determined Program seems to be directly addressing these needs. Adults, who need and want to stay in their communities, who are raising their families, working or trying to hold their lives together in the only supporting environment they know, can pursue a college degree without relocating to another city. Examining subjects and issues from the Indian point of view is, for most, the first time these students have ever been in an educational setting where their culture, history, and values have been acknowledged, supported, and celebrated. Few have ever been able to play a determining role in what, and how, they would learn what they feel they need to know to better their community and themselves. Most, when they enter, can't believe this program is real.

Community Empowerment

The program and its curriculum have an even more important goal, however—building and empowering communities rather than individuals. There are several indications that this may be happening. First, all curricular materials brought into the classes (videos, articles, texts, and so on) are quickly circulated around the community. For example, teacher aides take their readings and videos to their classrooms, extended family members read and discuss class materials, and tribal agencies ask for copies of articles, videos, or other reference materials. Of course, each week's class discussions are the topic of several other conversations over coffee or lunch with family, co-workers, or friends during the rest of the week.

Second, the class itself becomes an element of community dynamics—a new political force in the community. A cross-section of community members, some of whom may be at serious odds with each other over some issues in the community, discuss topics relevant to their community, sharing and learning about each others' viewpoints, building a sense of group identity and togetherness, and gaining confidence and knowledge that could, and in some cases already is, impacting the community. For example, the Neah Bay (Makah) class, meeting in the school, noticed signs telling the school children that if they didn't throw away wrappers, the candy/gum machines would be taken away. They also noticed that there were no receptacles in the area. Seeing their children set up for failure and punishment one more time, they posted a note calling attention to this fact. The next day, waste receptacles appeared. A small, but not insignificant, example of taking responsibility for how the school treated their children.

Personal Growth

Third, and as a further confirmation of the significance of the program, individual students are finding their community-identity transformed—achieving recognition, taking leadership and making significant contributions to their communities. One student, who never graduated from high school, was recently sent to a national conference to present his marine research and is having his way paid to graduate school by Battelle Research Labs because of the success of his internship and the development of his thinking, research, and writing skills. Two of the program graduates have taken the initiative to initiate several community betterment projects and have organized (and will help teach) the new class at a second community on the Quinault reservation. Several tribal leaders and employers have told faculty about the increasing confidence, articulateness, and effectiveness of class members.

Educational Principles

Of course this program cannot be replicated in its entirety in other cultural and institutional settings. Perhaps it can, however, serve as an inspiration and model for those trying to build the education and knowledge paradigms needed to support new theories, policies, collaborations, and community-based social action in international and community development.

From our experiences to-date, several fundamental principles underlying The Evergreen State College's Native American Community-based Community-determined program seem to be important in thinking about establishing new relationships between universities and indigenous communities. These are:

1) A willingness to accept indigenous people's knowledge about the world and their relationship with it as **equivalent** to scientific or "western" knowledge;

2) A willingness to let indigenous **communities determine** the learning they need both to strengthen their traditional community systems and participate or interact effectively with the rest of the world;

3) The establishment of **partnerships** involving the community, the university and the students in the definition and operation of community academic programs;

4) An absolute **trust** in the students' learning motivations and abilities;

5) A **pedagogical philosophy** that considers every human being as a source of knowledge that merely needs a supportive, interactive learning environment to enable them to fulfill their personal and community goals;

6) A **curriculum** taught from the **point of view** of the community's experience, perspective and reality (historical and contemporary);

7) Formation of and support for a **group of students** working together as a class, rather than only working with students and their learning goals as individuals;

8) Classes located **in the community** where students and their families live, work, play and struggle for survival;

9) Learning that is defined by the group's **discussion** of syllabus materials, where different students' knowledge and perspectives are shared, respected, negotiated, and integrated into understanding generated by the group itself, rather than defined by teachers;

10) A learning environment which fosters **cooperation** rather than competition, **respect for differences** in life-style, values, knowledge and perspectives on issues discussed, **collective problem-solving** and conflict resolution, **relationships and connections** rather than specialization and fragmentation of knowledge, **community applications** and relevancy of knowledge, and **individualized recognition** and assessment of student growth and development;

11) **Faculty/teacher support** through providing syllabus materials and instruction in group facilitation, critical analysis, research, writing, and speaking skills;

12) **Academic standards** of thinking, research, and effective communication equivalent to those in any other university classroom experience;

13) Group as well as individual **community-building projects** incorporated as part of the curriculum.

Other strategies and models that: (a) validate community knowledge and experience, (b) facilitate community ownership of both their own and others' knowledge, and (c) empower village, community, or neighborhood people to define their own history and reality and control their future "development" need to be created. We hope that this chapter stimulates not only thinking, but action in establishing new relationships between universities and communities, including the creation of new community-controlled universities.

WIDENING SPACES THROUGH PARTICIPATORY VIDEO

Tony Williamson

In recent years, the Don Snowden Center for Development Support Communications has applied the Fogo process successfully in several South Asian countries, through Canada's International Development Agency (CIDA). In India, the Center worked with the Extension Directorate of Orissa University of Agriculture and Technology to use video and participatory development methods with farmers and their families. Not only did the villagers gain confidence and enjoy seeing themselves on video, but their relationship with the extension workers changed also. The extension workers listened as people talked about the things that mattered to them. They began to deal with farmers more holistically, not just as purveyors of seed, pesticides, and fertilizers.

In one remote tribal village, the farmers discussed and illustrated on video the problem of threshing a new strain of wheat which had been introduced by researchers to improve the yield. The video allowed the farmers to communicate directly with researchers and government policy makers whom they would normally never have the opportunity to meet. As a result, the wheat program was changed. This process enabled information to be transferred to decision makers and officials and also to be transferred to farmers elsewhere, who could relate more easily to their peers than to the experts.

In Pakistan, a multinational mega-project is attempting to reclaim waterlogged and salinated land in the Sindh, through a project called the Left Bank Outfall Drain (LBOD). After five years and nearly a billion U.S. dollars, drainage channels and tube wells are in place, but the system is not yet operational. Although the farmers are generally aware of LBOD activities, there has been no institutionalized communication program to inform them about the benefits of the project. The shortage of information is seen as a serious impediment to the flow of benefits to the farmers. In this context, CIDA funded a pilot project through the Sindh Development Studies Center (SDSC) to test the application of participatory video in bridging the communications gap between the farmers, engineers, and other LBOD personnel. Staff members of SDSC, who had already established a relationship with the farmers through a socio-economic research study related to LBOD, were trained by the Snowden Center to use participatory video to engage the farmers in a discussion of the LBOD project. In particular, farmers evaluated on video the usefulness of a tube well called a scavenger well, which drained the saltwater, but returned fresh water from lenses over the salt water back into the fields. The farmers expressed a divergence of opinions on the usefulness of the wells and on other aspects of the project, which were videotaped and shown to farmers in areas where project activity had not yet taken place. This in turn stimulated discussion on the potential for scavenger wells in new areas.

Videos showing the responsibilities and benefits of water user associations were also effective in generating constructive discussion with peers who had not yet formed associations. In this pilot project, however, there was not effective communication with project managers, engineers, and policy makers, because there had not been sufficient time to include them equally in the process from the beginning. When the farmers' videos were shown to project personnel, they reacted negatively to critical comments by the farmers towards officials and believed their assessment of the wells was simplistic. There had not been adequate time in this project to appraise all of the officials of the objectives of the video communications nor to include them sufficiently in the process. Consequently, they appeared to be threatened by the frankness of the farmers' taped statements rather than to view the videos as an opening for dialogue and constructive discussion leading toward effective water users' management of the system once it became operational.

Nevertheless, the project demonstrated the potential for participatory video as an important tool to inform farmers and their families of the nature of a large project and to provide a sense of "ownership" or involvement in the operational phase of the project once completed. It also pointed out the real need to establish good communications and participation at the very inception of projects, so that all stakeholders are beneficiaries and so that costly errors in project design or implementation can be minimized.

CHAPTER 10

COALITION-BUILDING IN DIVERSITY

Kari Anderson Lende

MY PERSONAL FORMATION OF SOCIAL CHANGE

In order to incorporate the interrelated dimensions of coalition-building with diversity, it is necessary for me to bring forth my personal history in joining the process of participatory development. "Coalition-building" and "diversity" have become celebrated components of social change in this last decade of the 20th century. These elements have been points of focus for my work. My own life course has integratively coincided with the evolution of participatory development.

My relationship to this field has been and continues to be highly unconventional. In fact, as of 1994 many people and groups consider me to be a pioneer and innovator in promoting collective grassroot initiatives to redesign the cultural, political, and social paradigms of our times. For me to admit or accept this role as a pioneer is truly vulnerable. It has taken me over 15 years to come to terms with it. My hesitancy in acceptance stems from the realization that immense responsibility comes with those who find themselves pushing the boundaries of thought, action, and realities of their particular generation. What motivates me to move forward in uncharted territories of social change is that I walk in concert with so many others across the planet who are daring enough to forge new paths for institutional and structural change.

I consider the people who are contributing to this collaborative book to be an excellent representation of the innovators I believe exist within every local community and neighborhood. It is just a matter of encouraging all of us to become the architects of our own future sustainable communities.

My own architectural formation began while attending high school in northern Thailand as a foreign exchange student. It turned out to be quite a transformation for me in that this experience would guide my actions and conscience for the rest of my adult life. It was 1976 and I was located on the Laotian border in the middle of a guerrilla war zone. My exposure to the Laotian refugee exodus into Thailand radicalized me from an a-political 16-year-old into a woman committed toward furthering the consciousness of peoples' struggles.

I witnessed first-hand the devastation of a people's culture and their geographical uprootedness. A century of colonialism dominated by France, followed by the U.S.A.'s war involvement in Laos, left this small nation ravaged by destruction. Consequently, the majority of Laotian people were relocated or forced to flee their country. By living in the midst of refugees and their scattering of camps, I received my first in-depth introduction of East/West, developed/developing, First/Third World distinctions with their divisions and power relationships.

Being in my youth, my understanding was minimal regarding "super-power" nations and their politics in relation to economically poorer nations and indigenous peoples' struggles. The Thais and Laotians asked me: "You come from such a "super-power" country with access and privilege to so much education, science, and technology. Why is it, then, that your ignorance is so great concerning the world beyond the U.S.?"

It took my education in Thailand at school and with the Laotians in their movement for cultural survival for me to begin comprehending the magnitude of how ethnocentric and arrogant my country, the U.S., really was. The U.S. has acquired so much economic and military power through the West's 500-year pursuit of global imperialism. At the same time, our citizenry has become increasingly ignorant of the world at large. This overdose of ignorance and patriotic arrogance greatly concerned me as a 16-year-old and still does 18 years later.

It was imperative that as a U.S. citizen I begin to reduce my own ignorance. Simultaneously, I had to heighten my understanding of my preconditioned social and cultural values. A reconstruction of my value system was required. It has been an ongoing process of reorientation. Unfortunately, to date, I feel the U.S. has not moved much from its false sense of global superiority. The arrogance of many in this country soars higher with our illusions of invincibility. Our need to stay hooked into our overconsumptive lifestyles makes it compulsory for us to pursue domination over other nations and peoples instead of embracing more equal partnerships.

It was from this personal background that my involvement emerged with research and participation of peoples' movements and their strides for participatory and sustainable development. The terms "participatory and sustainable development" were rarely used when I professionally began my interdisciplinary and cross-cultural comparisons of popular participation in 1982. A multitude of non-government organizations (NGOs), peoples' movements, and practitioners then began infusing popular participation principles throughout their individual community projects. As implementation of these newly defined principles took place, it became necessary to create a common vocabulary. Since the conceptualization of participatory development was still in its infancy in the early 1980s, international agencies and governments often discredited this budding field. The lack of legitimization of these concepts made it difficult to sustain local participatory efforts.

It was during this infancy period that I decided to gain experience at both policy making and grassroot levels. In addition, I wanted to study popular participation comprehensively from global to local contexts. Throughout the years I have served in a variety of capacities such as: mediator for international refugees and U.S. communities; lecturer on rural development, comparative/development education, women issues; consultant in economic and socio-cultural change in East and Southeast Asia; researcher of Thailand's agricultural land reform struggle and national development planning.

The more experience I acquired, the greater need I saw for increased communication and coalition building among individuals and communities. Direct interaction with so many diverse international and domestic groups has enabled me to learn the fundamentals of six human languages and some 60 professional languages. Access to a large assortment of vocabularies has prepared me to communicate and translate interests among a cross-section of people and their issues. Since North America and Asia were my original geographical regions for promoting networking and coalition-building, it was natural to continue focusing in these areas where I had previous working relationships and a cultural understanding of the geographical and political contexts.

HISTORICAL AND PRESENT SOCIAL CHANGE CHARACTERISTICS

Historically, if one traces the types of peoples' movements that have occurred throughout the past two centuries, a pattern emerges which intricately connects the struggles of the past with current dilemmas. It is evident that popular participation has been and remains a consistent theme within each particular movement. To list a

few examples of previous movements that utilized collective participation as their primary strategy, we could include the following:

a) anti-slavery and women's suffrage movement in the U.S. in
the 1800–1900s;

b) independence from colonial domination in most "developing"
countries (e.g., India, Vietnam, African nations);

c) Chinese Communist Revolution in 1949;

d) U.S. Civil Rights struggles achieving prominence in the 1950s
and 1960s.

These historical movements as well as recent surges of social
change share important characteristics. In order to gain momentum
and legitimacy, leaders and visionaries have had to identify a reason
to mobilize. Thereby, they create a strategy for action and organizing
which makes it possible to involve a critical mass of people to implement the new ideas for change. Invariably, social movements have
originated from a core of individuals who have established a "safe
space."[1] This space is crucial for the formation of ideas and strategies.
Often these new avenues for change may appear too radical or threatening to the existing dominant culture or status quo. Hence, until
these concepts have had an opportunity to mature, the circle of
participation remains quite limited.

Once this core group moves beyond the conceptualization stage,
the participation process eventually expands as others are invited to
engage in further dialogue. As more individuals partake with the
implementation of concrete social action, a common frame of reference,
a recognizable vocabulary, and a practical strategy become necessary
ingredients for a successful peoples' movement. Orchestrating an entire
movement via popular participation principles requires years of
painstaking commitment from everyone engaging in its process.
Fortunately, we have had a significant range of historic and recent
examples of peoples' movements from which we can learn. As each
generation takes part in their own specific struggle for positive change,
successive generations thereafter benefit from these past lessons.
Through careful oral history and documentation of our collective
attempts, we are able to adapt previous approaches of social change
to our present cultural or organizational situations.

Each peoples' movement has relied on its own collective energies.
However, as we enter each new decade, our societies become more
and more ridden with complex political and bureaucratic structures.
These complexities make it more difficult for our joined energies to
hold together in achieving consensus and common action.

Fragmentation's Crippling Effect on Collective Initiatives

The western-based value system of "specialization of knowledge" has become so internationally pervasive that most professional fields and educational institutions readily accept it as status quo. The rapid acceptance of science and technology has tended to intensify our obsession with specializing ourselves and our realities into fragmented bits of information. Specialization reinforces fragmentation. In turn, fragmentation induces disconnection of knowledge and people. Consequently, any society today can be susceptible to severe fragmentation. A clear consequence of this is when people speaking the same language can no longer understand one another, because its meaning has become convoluted with technical and specialized jargon.

Furthermore, we have disengaged ourselves from the sense of responsibility towards our communities. Fragmentation implies isolation and reduction of thought. We become further distanced from our relationship to land and our natural environment. The effect of this has emotionally and structurally separated our efforts to link. The degree to which fragmentation has confronted most active social change groups is profound. In some cases, it has paralyzed interaction, severed linkages and contacts while increasing distrust among ourselves. Consequently, peoples' political and collective strengths have not been nurtured. Hence, our community-based programs have been weakened.

Community-based projects attempting to overcome fragmentation and separateness have often lacked the necessary moral and financial support to maintain them. This reality can lead many groups to a sense of burnout and defeat. Characteristics of burnout are:[2]

- periods of introversion/introspection/reflection;
- questioning and doubting of values/goals;
- fatigue, illness, and depression;
- frustration and disillusionment;
- withdrawal or "dropping out" from a group or movement;
- decreased reliability among members;
- activities shifting away from the original vision of the community.

The paradox we find ourselves in is that we experience constant conflict with two completely different paradigms. The present accepted paradigm of specialization and fragmentation continues to compartmentalize, categorize, and minimize virtually every sphere of our lives as vibrant human beings. Until only recently, we allowed fragmentation to literally cripple our collective initiatives. Meanwhile, there is a new explosion of fresh energy and concepts which starves to accommodate an entirely new way of relating. What makes participatory and sustainable development so attractive in the 1990s is that they encompass multi-faceted, inter-cultural/generational, qualitative, and holistic modes of knowing and being.

Germinating Collaboration Dialogues

Noticing how systematically fragmentation affects us all, I began concentrating my own collaboration with social change groups by attempting to get them to transcend beyond isolation and burnout. I started identifying channels for strengthening our networking capabilities from community levels to global contexts. My first objective was to coordinate collaboration and alliances among alternative social change groups. My interpretation of "alternative" is: "Those movements bound by shared values of solidarity, trust, respect, and partnership, in preference to a dominator mode of interaction with others, blended with progressive and innovative styles of transformational change."

My second goal was to expand the opportunities for cultural and organizational dialogues among local grassroot initiatives. This is an arduous task because most community leaders, advocates, and activists are swamped with an overload of organizational responsibilities. Lack of sufficient staff and financial support also bogs them down.

An effective way to thwart stagnation has been to multiply one-to-one exchanges among community leaders. Dialogues which have been most successful have highlighted some presumed barriers and stereotypes we historically construct about one another especially in terms of:

- professions
- economic/social classes
- ethnic, indigenous groups
- political ideologies, theories
- cultural identities
- educational disciplines
- structural frameworks and paradigms.

These barriers, our assumptions, and our cultural ignorance of one another seriously hamper our ability to reach intimate partnerships. Our assumptions and attitudes of how people and the world relate ultimately form our individual planetary view. Usually, these assumptions are validated and strengthened through cultural agreements concerning "the norm." Most nations have honored "norms" which are extremely dysfunctional and non-sustainable. For instance, many countries have adopted the "norm" that the more one consumes of natural resources, the better it is for the economy. This type of norm will not enhance the quality of life for future generations. It is time that we reevaluate our norms and start designing healthier ways of relationship to the earth and ourselves.

A Case Study in Cross-cultural Partnership in Community Building

One cogent illustration in which community leaders challenged themselves to stretch beyond current "accepted norms" and assumptions took place in Japan. This endeavor convened in Nagoya, Japan in 1988 at the Asian Health Institute (AHI). The Institute provided financial support for community health organizers from rural areas throughout Asia (Bangladesh, Sri Lanka, India, Thailand, Philippines, Malaysia, Indonesia, Japan, South Korea and Peoples Republic of China) to partake in cross-cultural dialogues pertaining to participatory development. Their collaboration primarily focused on community health. My role was as a facilitator in several dialogues.

These organizers vigorously defined and elaborated the differences and similarities among their own country's development paradigms. They described their respective research methods, philosophies, and styles of practicing participation. They also highlighted what values and goals guided their local projects. Moreover, they compared their different world values and translated them into feasible programs that could be compatible for their individual localities. As their sharing intensified, their collective networks across Asia encompassed an interdisciplinary set of issues. Essentially, the group jointly discovered mediums for mobilizing cultural change, moving from within their districts to regional and national realms as well.

Whether the peoples' movement occurred in Sri Lanka, the Philippines, or elsewhere, a very distinctive pattern wove itself throughout each of their community initiatives. It did not matter if the realm of change involved health, sustainable agriculture, or education. Ideas for implementation of popular participation in each of these cultural cases originated from small clusters of people. Their ideas flourished within the established "safe space." Intimacy and clarity of vision were obtained more readily within a small group. This is the core group where the seed for change usually resides.

An example involving these AHI organizers was deciding on the objective to expand the availability of community health facilitators to the largest population possible within a specific region. Once this was the designated goal, the emphasis became: (1) How to accomplish this task? and (2) What are the core values which can activate the community also to work towards this end?

In order to carry out this effort realistically, the small core group's function turned to:

- providing ideas and suggesting who in the community can be ready to take on leadership responsibilities;
- highlighting the underlying values, beliefs, and assumptions;
- identifying the parameters for logistical action;
- articulating a base for common understanding so that consensus-building can be applied;
- honoring the sense of solidarity;
- finding leverage points to lessen the impact of present major negative forces (i.e., market exploitation, hierarchical domination over others, urban elites' neglect of rural realities, and deficiencies of services);
- opening niches of social interaction between the innovators of the proposed ideas and the rest of the community;
- enabling all concerned people to voice their opinions;
- determining the degree of government intervention (if any) appropriate for the participatory process;
- connecting the various community, regional, and national groups that are involved with the conceptualization and implementation stages;
- expanding the circle of decision-making and making the process available to the largest diversity of people.

Needless to say, these objectives and tasks demand a substantial undertaking of commitment. What is impressive about these listed characteristics, however, is that all the AHI organizers reached consensus. These are goals and functions which can apply to each of their communities.

These health leaders compiled a set of guidelines for organizational and community reflection that could be used with their peers back in their respective rural areas. A list of questions regarding an individual's personal value system was also devised. This working set of guidelines and questions (Figure 1) was designed as a practical learning resource for other community and grassroot leaders to share within their own constituencies. Its main purpose is to serve as an impetus for community members to become clearer with one's personal values in relation to broader cultural dimensions of change. The personal and community contexts can then integrate themselves.

FIGURE 1

Guidelines for Reflection

Your work   Your organization/profession   Your community situation

A: What goals are your projects/organizations attempting to accomplish?
    Are the goals clear or vague?
    Have these goals been explicitly defined?
    Do the programs and goals match?
B. Whom do you think most of your programs serve?
C. Is your organization's activities leading to the empowerment of the people
    you intend to serve?
D. Does your organization focus on tasks and targets or on the process of
    change itself?

Your Personal Value System

1. To what degree do you think the mass media has influenced your percep-
    tions of other people and nations?
2. What are the origins of your present thoughts, perceptions and beliefs?
3. Can you identify the actual parameters to your value system?
4. How do you see your own moral value base manifesting itself through your
    life choices?
5. What values does technology destroy or weaken?
6. How large is your concept of "community"?
7. How would you define development?
8. In which ways do you perceive the direction of your nation and the world
    at large is changing?
9. How is that direction being decided or determined?
10. Where are your life values, aims, and priorities taking you in the future?

CROSS-FERTILIZATION OF STRATEGIES SHARED AMONG MOVEMENTS

What has transpired cross-nationally in the past decade is that
forums similar to the one in Japan have grown at a spectacular pace.
More coalitions and partnerships have galvanized throughout every
corner of the world. Concurrently, participatory and sustainable development models have received heightened attention. Conventional
academic and economic institutions are gradually considering these
new paradigms of change. Interdisciplinary discourse, documentation,
and disseminating of popular participation methods are unfolding.

However, the convergence of this knowledge and its actual practice remains fragmented.

My relationship to these catalytic movements has been that I have either engaged in or facilitated numerous dialogues. Observing the serious gap between knowledge and practice, I envisioned bridging this by fostering cross-fertilization of strategies across our movements. Different participants of social change could then become further sensitized to what has been tried in one region and apply it to another. This cross-sectoral knowledge of grassroot movements reduces the sluggishness, stagnation, and overduplication that results from our isolated efforts.

Many groups in Asia with whom I worked to cross-fertilize visions and strategies were notably curious about the present status of popular participation and collaboration in the U.S. They wondered to what extent successful linkages were being made between U.S. grassroots and policymaking networks. After a ten-year international focus, I thought it was time for me to see for myself how civil rights advocates, labor organizers, environmentalists, educators, and others in the U.S. were weaving their efforts for social change.

It was upon my return to the U.S. that I was introduced to colleagues working in collaboration through the international workshop entitled "People's Initiatives to Overcome Poverty." This workshop included people from the wide spectrum of fields and perspectives described in Chapter 1. We explored the interdependence among our own participatory development experiences. It was acknowledged that "poverty" is a term that affects each of us. We all face spiritual, emotional, physical, environmental, and economic impoverishment. We are linked to impoverishment through our exploitation of people and natural resources as well as the oppression of cultures, races, and non-human species. Impoverishment is so prevalent and inclusive in our lives that its existence can serve as an educational tool for expanding one's consciousness-raising process.

Being an active part of the poverty workshop provided me with a solid foundation of trust and faith knowing that the honesty and vulnerability we dared to share could be replicated in eclectic settings across our movements. I decided to free myself, institutionally and organizationally, so that I could travel around the U.S. and monitor the level of cross-fertilizing occurring in our communities. I used the AHI organizational reflection questions in Figure 1 and the concept of poverty as my entry to conversation with approximately 500 people.

After six months of extensive interviews I discovered how poorly and inconsistently we were integrating our issues and coalition-building efforts. I asked each interviewee what the consequence would be if we did not cross-fertilize our initiatives. Each person responded that the consequence of our inability to link our social change groups would be devastating. If most of us realize our need to interconnect our struggles, why then, are we not pursuing strategies to deal with our persistent fragmentation? This is our challenge in the U.S. All interviewees comprehended the necessity to connect our scattered stories and turn them into a synthesized thread of action.

Challenges of the 1990s

We acknowledge our desperate need to consolidate and coordinate the emerging U.S. coalitions and alliances. Yet, do we have the collective will to bridge our inherent gaps in knowledge, practice, and outreach? Our intellectual discourse and rhetoric is filled with nuances concerning sustainability and the need to restore our environment. Our hearts, however, stay in denial as to the severity of our planetary situation. We prefer to work from our outdated paradigms because of their familiarity. The personal shift in consciousness we must make to accommodate 21st century realities is unknown.

By 1992, enough countries were ready to convene for organized talks through the official venue of the United Nations Conference on the Environment and Development (also known as the Earth Summit) held in Rio de Janeiro, Brazil. Finally, governments and their delegates were willing to admit that environment and development issues had to be inclusive of one another. This collective acknowledgment was an enormous first step in actualizing what measures we need to implement for truly restoring our communities and ecosystems.

By 1994, international treaties, regulations, trade pacts, government plans, the revival of indigenous peoples' values, and sustainable development congresses have multiplied significantly. Even with all these advances, it is amazing to realize how many U.S. citizens still remain ignorant of such major events as the General Agreement on Tariff and Trade (GATT) talks, the North American Free Trade Agreement (NAFTA), the Earth Summit and others. The implications of these kinds of negotiations will critically affect our lives, yet the majority of the U.S. population has not begun to engage itself in dialogue about these matters.

Of course, the national media often decides what will be covered and to what degree an issue will be explored. I believe that the media's lack of coverage and discourse about the Earth Summit is the key reason why so many U.S. citizens are still uninformed about its occurrence. For example, most people have never heard of Agenda 21: The Earth Summit Action Plan. This agenda includes over 40 treaties that will impact our local communities. Pollution, the role of women in development, biodiversity, and an array of other complex issues are just a part of Agenda 21's challenges.

How do we become better informed citizens? Without an informed citizenry, we can not make wise choices about our collective future. We can no longer rely on our present forms of media to provide us with truthful accounts of what is and is not happening across our country (not that we ever could). The dominant media sources will consistently keep us tuned-in to drugs, crime, and domestic violence. Their negative and corruptive bent on current events permeates itself through our living room TV screens. No wonder despair, powerlessness, and fear have their grip on this nation's soul. I seriously doubt we want to continue being a country that makes personal and national choices based from fear.

After five years of full-time participation in community and organizational cross-fertilizing in North America, I observe a vicious cycle of fear playing itself out in our movements. The cycle begins with:

>> our individual arrogance, which leads to
>> ignorance, whereafter
>> our curiosity about each other disappears
>> our learning potential diminishes, whereby
>> dialogues with one another become stifled, and
>> we end up in a state of spiritual dormancy and social inaction.

Breaking this cycle requires us to take risks, transcend our fears, and dare to reach new frontiers of relating with one another. One peoples' initiative that is bursting these chains of fear is that of the People of Color Environmental Justice Movement. They are passionately taking back their communities from the spoils of toxic dumping. The southwest and southern regions have been the nation's hazardous waste pit for decades. These people can no longer tolerate their toxified water systems, or the rise in cancer and other life-threatening diseases. They intimately know the urgency of building diverse coalitions. They cannot afford to work in disjointed, disconnected, and disunited habits of the past. Multi-racial and intergenerational alliances are proceeding cautiously in developing trust. These forerunners in risk-taking are exemplary pioneers of what is possible when we honor collective brilliance.

I have the good fortune of being associated with movements like that of environmental justice. My freedom from institutional and organizational constraints has enabled me to acquire an overall perspective concerning the greatness of peoples' initiatives which are taking root exponentially within every one of our regions. It is exhilarating to see people taking more responsibility for changing their social environments. The mystifying factor, however, is that many of us still have very little access to one another's stories of struggle and triumph. If only the media could refocus its attention towards the multitude of positive individual and community endeavors being created every day. We are ultimately each our own innovators for the restoration and sustainance of our local and global future.

Crossroads of Choice and Action

In the mid-1990s, many of us are beginning to comprehend how impoverished we all are becoming in our relentless neglect of sustainable practices in environmental and economic management. Fortunately, the cross-over between alternative and mainstream dialogues has begun to enlarge. More of us have accepted the actuality that we are at the crossroads of action in humanity and planetary terms. A global recognition is awakening in which we intuit that we will soon be making one of the most momentous choices in our collective history. This choice is: "Which value system will we embrace as we go forward into the 21st century?"

We know we must transcend our current social, cultural, and political constructs. This requires quite an imagination. To spark our imaginations, I have asked this catalytic question: "What is the next step, and who dares to make it?" After raising this question with hundreds of citizens, the responses have been surprisingly similar. Most feel that the motive, direction, and strategies for us to achieve our next step as a nation and globally *must* be clear and precise. Further procrastination will only imply more destruction, loss of species and irreplacable ecosystems. We may permanently be tampering with a very delicate balance of technological and natural forces.

What makes our future course of action so awkward, however, is that we are not sure what our destination will be and how we want to get there. We lack a new vocabulary. We are still in the process of defining the umbrella term, "sustainability." Our new modes of mobilizing popular participation are not yet crystallized or mapped out for systematic change. We still have not created a *coherent framework or mechanism* for interlinking our knowledge and practice.

Each social change group is presently at a stage of determining the parameters of its own agenda. Much of the best work aimed to tackle social ills results from the collaborative efforts of small groups. But these circles persist in operating in isolated, disjointed partnership. In fact, we must often *compete* for the same pots of scarce funds. At times, this underlying competition induces groups with the same or parallel objectives to feel antagonistic toward one another. Another less obvious challenge is that issues which appear different on the surface are closely related by the structural barriers they share. Monopolized political power, rigid educational systems, lack of resources to bring social change agents together are common.

Our limited understanding among groups and the basic lack of awareness regarding "who else is out there to connect with" has made networking very burdensome, with difficulty in maintaining any sort of continuity. Our competence to "reinvent the wheel" has become extraordinary. For the art of networking to be more relevant and functional, we need to circumvent our incessant skill of redundancy.

A NETWORKER'S STRATEGY IN COORDINATING COLLABORATION IN THE U.S. FOR CITIZENS' PARTICIPATION IN CHANGE

A type of link which is often overlooked or not utilized is that of direct human contact. Historically, this was a central consideration. In the busy times of modernization and technological advances, we tend to forget such a simple practice. This particular style of contact involves intermediary networkers. They gain direct knowledge of related social change efforts while sharing this input with like-minded groups both within and across regional and sectoral boundaries. Such bridge-builders can enhance coordination of collaboration among peoples' movements. By traveling to and working with many groups, trust can be established between these groups and the networkers. This trust enables people to feel comfortable in intimately sharing dreams, perspectives, and practical working methods.

There are many individuals who are keen on pursuing this kind of networking. Unfortunately, this type of arrangement is almost non-existent. It requires the networker to be freed from most institutional responsibilities. The primary obstacle to expanding such possibilities, however, is our current funding structures. In present thinking, we channel funding to specific issues, disciplines, organizations, or businesses. The likelihood of receiving funding greatly diminishes if one works beyond such conventional categories.

To move toward the 21st century, we need to invent financial structures that can complement pioneering, innovative, unconventional, non-linear, and non-hierarchical modes of work. Until that happens, anyone who contemplates this type of intermediary networking must contend with limited or non-existent financial support. I believe we cannot wait for the future to build this type of linking. Among citizens I have worked with, there is general agreement that we need thousands of such facilitators. Until these people can receive financial backing, most of those interested in serving this way for social change will fall by the wayside.

It was with this realization that I personally decided to push an old boundary and open a new door for intermediary facilitation and collaboration. It has been a five year experiment of consolidating methods by which to coordinate integrated collaboration among our national, regional, and local peoples' initiatives. The amount of cooperation I have received through my travels is enormous. A collective recognition that we need to coordinate our coalitions and information is the basis of my ability to weave in and out of different groups. Since I work through so many issues and regions, my colleagues are usually very open to providing updates on their projects. This feedback consequently spreads to peers in other organizations and their programs.

Originally, I compiled a range of focus groups and larger alliances who would be likely candidates to work with. Examples include: sustainable agriculture, socially responsible investments in business, multicultural education, religious/faith/spiritual, peace, environmental justice, feminist (ecofeminism), alternative health practices, fair trade, indigenous peoples, scientific, media, arts, theater, film. The next stage was to concentrate within a particular group. I learn their community agenda and the parameters of their issues. I also sensitize myself to their political circumstances and their professional jargon.

Here I use sustainable agriculture as an illustration. This movement has its own collection of working subgroups and different programs to be implemented (e.g., pesticide control, organic standards, soil erosion, animal husbandry, water management). I start by conversing with at least three to six members from specific parts of the movement. They may be from subsets such as the Land Stewardship Project, League for Rural Voters, the Institute for Agriculture and Trade Policy, legislation, or organic farmers. I ask to meet those who are the conceptualizers, strategist, visionaries, or pace-setters. Most communities know who embodies such qualities. I engage in a one-to-one dialogue with the recommended conceptualizer. We try to locate areas where their program is stagnant and compare their situation with the overall sustainable agriculture movement. As this process progresses, the "You need to meet so and so" syndrome transpires.

All linking is based on trust. One-to-one exchanges are essential for trust to evolve. From the trust I have built with the first set of people, I am able to acquire access to other related groups. After listening to the various perspectives and concerns from participants or leaders in their movment or community, we attempt to uncover common themes that are occurring within their own work. I then synthesize emerging patterns from the different groups. I look for areas of concern where there is consensus. These points of consensus become the starting point for further dialogue.

Expanding the conversation is the next step. It is imperative that larger circles of dialogue occur systemically throughout their movement. Inevitably, individuals surface from the first round of dialogues who are willing to volunteer in commencing multiple discussions with their counterparts. It is exhilarating for us to be able to innovate strategies and connections with other peers who are also ready to expand their own network base. I try to keep continually connected with the personal and community.dialogues, and constantly share the fresh perspectives and information with other movements. We do not want to perpetuate the plague of isolation. We pursue vision-sharing and cross-movement interchange. Participation is encouraged to those working in sustainable agriculture to extend their internal dialogues with colleagues in different fields.

In most cases, people who take part in these interactions are personally motivated to participate. The feeling of *urgency* to alter our course of action is the impetus that gets these people involved. The *passion* I see exhibited from so many diverse people (whether they be democrats, republicans, activists, or legislators) signifies to me our genuine *yearning* to unleash our creative energy. Major events such as the Earth Summit have energized enthusiasm for citizens and policy makers alike to join the "sustainability" discourse. In the past two years, the sustainable agriculture community has pushed for more extensive follow up in enforcing Agenda 21 recommendations. For example, advocates of sustainable farming systems recently designed a standard declaration of their movement entitled "The Asilomar Declaration of Sustainable Agriculture." The following gatherings give an idea as to the level of networking taking place:

Building North-North and South-South Bridges: Creating Opportunities for Sustainable Agriculture Networking among NGOs, universities, governments, and farmer. Held in Berkeley, California, August 1993.

"Bringing Rio Home": Using Agenda 21 to Promote Sustainable Agriculture. Held in Mulheim/Ruhr, Germany, September 1993.

International Conference on Integrated Resource Management for Sustainable Agriculture. Convened in Beijing, China. September 1993.

Conceptualizers, strategists, and visionaries from the working subgroups of the sustainable agriculture movement are very much part of these national and international gatherings. Besides the three meetings just mentioned, we attempted to host a follow-up symposium for gauging and monitoring Agenda 21 action plans through an International Sustainable Agriculture Summit in 1994. This particular summit was to take place in the U.S. Its objectives were multifaceted. We intended to include the following areas for review: agricultural policy, plans, and programs; production systems and natural resource management; people's participation and human resource development; ecological criteria for sustainability; marketing systems, processing, consumption patterns and trade; biotechnology, biodiversity, seeds and genetic resources; national plans for sustainable agriculture; international funding agencies' role in enforcing Agenda 21 recommendations; new partnerships and resources; networks and information sharing.

After two years of intense preparation for this Summit by practitioners worldwide, the entire event crumbled because of disparate regional expectations, leadership issues, and eventual lack of funding. Northern partners moved more rapidly to bring in new multinational actors than southern partners were prepared to accept. A lesson from the experience is the need to recognize the strength of geographically and politically varied perceptions and goals, and their influence in slowing moves to globalize too fast.

Being a part of this entire scenario, I feel we lost a great opportunity in promoting sustainable agriculture awareness at an international level. Currently, we are concentrating our efforts on regional issues. Until our regional networks are more integrated with sustainable agriculture initiatives, the national and global realms of dialogue remain fragmented.

As we make inroads of progress in our individual movements, documentation of new alliances and projects gets distributed to kindred organizations. The momentum generating within the sustainable agriculture community is just one example of a movement beginning to collaborate more intentionally. The coordination and networking mature with each additional year we engage in this participatory process. Obviously, other movements are seeking similar courses of action in their respective fields of social change.

Each time a movement documents their work, my own networking and educational outreach gets easier. Many people need to *see* a movement's results in writing. Having it in print seems to boost the legitimacy of the movement's existence. Until these movements published their results, I could not convince other citizens of the magnitude these initiatives actually encompass. Most of these community-related projects remain generally unknown, since we have only minimal access to media sources. Beyond community bulletin boards and electronic communication nets, not yet fully activated, we have yet to find a way quickly and tangibly to create awareness of these movements and their programs.

A Metropolitan Area's Attempt to Unite Neighborhood Environmental Action

We best learn and adapt pioneer ideas from realistic models. We need to see a new paradigm in action before we are convinced of its feasibility. Because of this, I continue to partake in endeavors which serve as exemplary case studies. From such experience, I want to hone in here on the neighborhood level of collaboration. Working nationally is one thing, but ultimately needs to be grounded within the community itself. This metro-urban model, I believe, succinctly contains the necessary ingredients for activating neighborhood and community outreach.

This engagement in collaboration has been with the **Urban Environmental Education Coalition** (UEEC) in Minneapolis/St. Paul, Minnesota. The UEEC was formed in 1991. Its mission is as follows:

> The Coalition is a network of people and organizations devoted to promoting formal and non-formal environmental education to culturally diverse urban communities and to assisting neighborhoods in improving their living environments.

The UEEC wanted to find ways in which neighborhoods and districts could work together on local environmental issues. We designed and undertook a two-year community survey (Figure 2). Had we had financial resources, we might have completed the survey in a shorter time.

Everyone volunteered their time in making this project materialize. We invited each neighborhood in Minneapolis and St. Paul to participate. Out of a total of 81 entities, we were able to engage 79.

After the two-year survey and coalition process, there was a collective acknowledgement that we needed to invent a new kind of position to coordinate neighborhood environment networks. Our recommendation involves the creation of environmental advocates, to facilitate increased education, action, and collaboration across communities. Such a person would be an educator, a resource, an organizer, and connector among groups needing assistance, and an advocate for pro-active environmental planning and management. The UEEC suggests that each city should host at least one such advocate,

FIGURE 2

Assessing Neighborhood Environmental Projects and Concerns in the Metro Area

Neighborhood Organization _____ Date _____

Contact Person _____

Address _____

Phone (day) _____ (evening) _____

What geographic area served(boundaries?) _____

Is your organization currently addressing any
environmental issues?   Y _____ N _____
(If yes, what are they?) _____

Please check those issues which you feel need to be addressed in your neighborhood:

Pollution/Problem Control

Water: _____ surface (lakes, etc.)
          _____ ground water

Air: _____ vehicle emissions
          _____ industrial emissions
          _____ offensive odors

Noise: _____ traffic
          _____ industrial
          _____ airplane

Soil: _____ chemical
                contamination
          _____ lead/heavy metals
          _____ erosion control

Other: _____

Urban Horticultural Needs

_____ boulevard plantings and
      beautification
_____ neighborhood parks
_____ community gardens
_____ flowers vegetables
_____ resp. use of lawn/garden
      chemicals
_____ selection/care of trees/shrubs
_____ home landscaping/gardening
_____ vacant lot projects

Waste Disposal

_____ household garbage
_____ household hazardous waste
_____ large (appliances etc.)
_____ waste reduction methods
_____ recycling
_____ yard waste reductions/
      composting

(Contd.)

Preservation/Use of Natural Areas

_____ wildlife/plant preserves
_____ bike/hiking trails
_____ handicapped accessibility
_____ educational programs
_____ other

Energy/Convervation

_____ mass transit
_____ energy conservation (home, etc.)
_____ alternative energy source
_____ water conservation (home, etc.)
_____ other _____

(Please elaborate on those neighborhood problems indicated.)

_____

_____

_____

What are the obstacles to your organization's involvement with these issues?

_____ technical   _____ publicity   _____   funding/grant writing
_____ education   _____ organizational   _____   other

What other groups in your neighborhood are you aware of who may be interested in the same issues and may work cooperatively?

_____

_____

Would you be interested in providing/receiving information about current issues for your community through:

_____ classes
_____ issue-oriented research
      project
_____ printing or distributing
      materials

_____ hands-on demonstrations
_____ articles in community papers
_____ a listing of environmental resource
      groups
_____ not interested

What facilities are available in your community for use as a meeting location or demonstration site? _____

_____

Thank you for your assistance!   Interviewer _____

_____

Additional notes and description of organization surveyed (avg. mtg. size, frequency of meetings, location and time):

_____

accountable to neighborhood groups. Optimally, there could be several advocates for clusters of neighborhoods in each city, housed within existing organizations or with a yet-to-be-defined group. These agents would seek to accomplish what no one else has been able to do, namely, focus full-time on the environmental needs of neighborhood residents.

As of September 1994, the UEEC is holding public gatherings to have community input on establishing such a position for environmental advocates. The majority of citizens appear to support the idea. However, there is the irony that our present financial structures do not appear able to rise to the occasion. Since this type of position is not accountable to any specific fiscal entity, but rather is available for service to the community at large, we have not yet been able to carve out a new arrangement to enable this work to manifest itself.

Despite this financial bottleneck, I was very excited that a community exists in the U.S. where we could push the limit for what is possible. The Minneapolis and St. Paul experiment, as it struggles to materialize, can serve as a model for us to consider in our own neighborhoods.

Using a One-Act Play as a Tool for Participatory Dialogue

In 1994, I wrote a 25-minute play, *Future Wisdom Passed*, about how future generations may look back upon the collective choices we have made during the 20th century. The play's message is intended to spark lively discourse with community audiences. I ethically challenge my country's present preoccupation with overconsumptive lifestyles. In the play I place myself first as the 16-year-old girl in the forests on the Thai-Lao border, then in an urban, concrete landscape in 1994, and finally in 2045 at age 86 looking back on the choices made between destruction and restoration. This gives content, feeling, and a sense of time to the concept of sustainability.

I currently perform this mini-play in neighborhood centers across the U.S. It has succeeded in generating an average of two hours' intense audience participation. Each audience is invited to create a set of dialogue questions to be used for future groups. The synergistic effect of these conversations is far-reaching. Essentially, most audiences get my underlying point, which is to encourage and invite others to begin writing and sharing their experiences of what it is like to be alive in this last decade before the next millennium. What choices and actions will we make to ensure that the next generations have a sustainable place to live?

Audience Questions
* In a word, how would you describe your initial reaction to this play?
* How do you feel this play relates to your individual life?
* Are you able to internalize how your actions in 1994 will directly affect the lives of those born in the year 2045?
* Do you feel the play exaggerates the current state of the world?

Values
* Which values in this culture do you embrace?
* Which values do you reject or question?

Sustainability
* To what extent do you understand the term "Sustainability?"
* In what ways do you find this culture living sustainably?
* In which areas of this culture do you see we could work on ways to live more sustainably?

Forging Ahead

If we took a national community inventory today, what other innovative initiatives stay disconnected from each other? How can we find out who is forging ahead with new strategies for community revival?

Until we realize that we are ultimately each our own innovators and architects for the restoration and sustenance of our communities, we may not answer these two questions for a long time. I continue with this kind of networking in hope that I will see sustainability and participatory processes honored as the new cultural norms. I am sure that sustainability will become the value system we will need to live by if our communities in the future hope to be vibrant, passionate, and healthy. May we all find the strength within us to carry out our personal responsibilities of this planetary transformation.

END NOTES

[1] Safe space: creating a place among ourselves where we establish a network of support. The support consists of people doing what they do best: catalyzing groups; gathering and disseminating information; working within the dominant culture while planting seeds to prepare the way for systematic changes; and generating new concepts. Once this network is stable, outreach and education occurs. (Kari Anderson and Susan Bowler, St. Cloud, Minnesota, 1991).
[2] These characteristics were compiled from a case study in burnout after the Persian Gulf War in 1991 in Minnesota, where many original peace activists dropped out from coalitions (Susan Bowler).

Editors' Reflections, Part III

Structures, Scale, Coalition-building

D: One of the enigmas revealed in these chapters, and their response to the workshop's call for action, is the enigma of retaining the solidarity that is face-to-face, but building coalitions on a larger scale that still retain the essence of that trust, of those purposes, and can therefore really be empowering against the larger structures.

K: Yes, if in fact that aggregation has a purpose that is complementary to the purpose of face-to-face exchange. If it doesn't substitute for it. D: Right. Aggregation is a central theoretical question that runs through many different aspects of what we're talking about. Maybe what we're saying is that we need to begin to articulate some sets of criteria relating to coalition-building, or to aggregation at different scales. There's the question whether face-to-face relations can build together to constitute a larger whole, or go forth in parallel forms to build a larger whole? Taken from another standpoint, the structures that exist in international finance and trade, and the agents of those structures in local regions and nations, are massively tilted against sustaining community initiatives. K: Sure are. D: Unless face-to-face community efforts, through communication and selective, judicious combining of efforts, can work consciously to overcome those barriers, how will they be overcome? K: Um hm.

D: Trade is only one feature of structures that is important. The question of scale is always a factor that may inhibit local action. In an irrigation system, for example. If the local group reach a level of decision to organize to resist bribe-taking by canal contractors and engineers, and they do it in one area, but that area is surrounded by five other canal divisions in which the engineers and the officers refuse to give up that practice, then those five will submerge the one. That happened in the area where Varun is working. They had to start from scratch. Here the question of scale is one of horizontally building that strength. A: Um. D: And also penetrating the structure in the legislature and in the bureaucracy so that the iron-clad irrigation department is somehow modified. This coalition-building, this outreach, is one of the reasons for connecting. A: Yes.

K: Anis, you were speaking about organizing. How in your own self-interest it may be necessary to join together with other groups to make sure you have access to land. You were talking about it being objective, rather than spiritual. A: The idea of cascading. Seeing the concern for others' empowerment shared. Not my concern alone, others' also. I was calling the desire to see a value cascade a kind of spiritual thing. But then I was saying that even apart from this kind of spiritual desire, there may be objective reasons for which you would want to see others also get empowered. You will join them, to fight a bigger battle. The structure which is oppressing you is too big for you to take on alone. You need to mobilize on a bigger scale.

D: Operational reasons. A: Yes, I was giving the example, suppose I cannot get land back alone, with a small community. But, if like Bhoomi Sena, 125 villages join in a land reclaim movement, that may succeed. Then, Kersten was implying she would hesitate, with the possibility of violence there. But I see violence going on. It is not always physical beating. But to deliberately create a condition in which people will starve and die. This is violence, of an extreme form. K: Sure. A: And this violence is going on, all over the world. Continuously. Thousands and thousands of people are victims of this violence. K: Um hm. A: So why are we stuck with just physical assaults as an expression of violence?

K: I don't think people are. That's certainly not what I'm talking about. I'm talking about the sense that social transformation is a transformation of motives. Transformation of power and wealth is part of transformation. But to me, it's very superficial. Unless the motives change, there'll be constant jockeying for this distribution of wealth and power. A: I agree fully, except I want to say that without this you cannot have that also. If you are saying that we don't ask that... K: Don't ask what? A: Transformation, the redistribution of assets... K: Oh, no. Of course not. I think that comes naturally from the motive, the transformation of motive. But, unfortunately, the time scales are so incommensurate.

A: Well, the dilemma you are pointing to is my dilemma. The dilemma is very real. Without this transformation of the control over assets, I don't see society transforming, in terms of values. That is necessary. At the same time, if the process of transformation brings in violence, then I see the transformation which we want, in terms of human values, may also be blocked. That is the great dilemma. But we have to face the dilemma. And not just say, we don't want to see violence. That doesn't answer my question. That doesn't solve the dilemma at all. K: Um hm.

A: I don't have an answer. First of all, I think we ought to share this dilemma with the communities, with the people. K: That's true. A: This is an insight we are getting. We are becoming aware of this from historical experiences, that revolutions which have involved violence, have in a way already transformed men towards violence. D: Yes. A: From which it is difficult to get them back towards becoming human. K: Um hm.

D: When you say the time scales are different, that's very germane. The transformation of motives may take a long time. That creates an impetus to give a lot of attention to that soon. Address the dilemma soon, so that parties concerned who are engaged in that kind of violence without physical attack, but the violence of the injustice and inequality of the asset distribution, begin to face that dilemma, begin to reexamine their motives. Processes might be created by which that introspection can be increased, and interaction between them and others increased, so that examination of motives is accelerated.

A: In our kind of situations, the structural situations in a Bangladesh village, most times the oppressed people have no chance of making a solidarity group just by themselves. They will just be killed. They have no power. K: You mean no political opportunity. They don't have the political strength, though they have the will to do it. A: That's right. They'll be immediately crushed. They are dependent every day. Every family is dependent for its survival on some or other of the elites. K: Yes. A: Then you need some outside agency, belonging to that structure which is oppressing them, derived from that structure, to come with some strength. K: Aha. A: Like Khushi comes, and when they start organizing there is resistance from the elites. O.K. Then Khushi shows them her card. I am a registered NGO. It is legitimate for me, and the State has approved me. To come and work. K: Yes. A: That helps. Without that there is no chance.

K: That's very well put. There's the kind of help in which one's experience is focused on people organizing for their own self-direction. Then there's also the element of reducing the opposition. A: That's right. This whole structure is much stronger than you. You cannot confront it by yourself. Even to understand the operation of the structure, someone from the structure has to come with full understanding of the structure but on your side. Has to come and help you. In which there is a worry, that you become dependent on that. That is a question we are continuously worried about. K: Um. A: But we don't see any way to begin this process of struggle without help from the structure. This is the big dilemma. We don't see anything being promoted, starting at all without helping.

K: Without that. Again the question of time. If someone is there two years, or five, even 10 years, compared to the millenia that have been taken to create that structure, it doesn't seem too long, doesn't seem dependence. Maybe if it was a generation... A: Yes. But at least I would like to see an attitude, that we want to reduce dependence on you. Can we together keep discussing that, strategizing. K: At least it should be a subject that's up for discussion. A: Yes. In periodic assessments you bring that question in. But I myself am dissatisfied. I'm not seeing that attitude. K: I see.

A: But there's another danger that you can't avoid, coming from outside to help in this kind of social formation. That also gets into trouble. The elites still won't let you go easily. They bring false police cases, court cases, against the oppressed. K: Um. A: To neutralize their leaders, or just finish them. Then you need those outsiders, with their status. Khushi has gone herself to the police, with her standing, with her connections. When she shows that card the police get neutralized. So we have to go on, assisting in that way. Otherwise there is just no chance. It is not like Hawaii, where Puanani decides to form a group.

K: Even in Hawaii, Puanani and I think many other activists have the quality of having legitimized themselves with the structures that have power. She did that through getting a law degree. A law degree is one of the best legitimizing titles in this culture. Even though it has very problematic roots, it's very legitimizing.

A: So basically what we have to recognize is both. The need for outsiders, in certain kinds of structural situations. I don't say everywhere. The need for outsiders to come and help in generating these kinds of processes. K: Yes. A: And then, the dilemma. When, then, can you, can they become self-reliant? The dilemma remains. We have to recognize both.

Counterviolence or Nonviolence?

A: I'm calling objective, you want to fight the structure. They have exploited you. You cannot get back the land unless you mobilize on a broader scale. You don't have the strength to reappropriate it. In that sense I'm calling it objective.

K: This can lead to a different conversation. It poses the question of the role of force and violence in social change. Social change ultimately has to be at the level of awakening people's desire to cascade. Not charity, but contribution. To me, force is only useful to the point where it awakens a person, forces them to confront tension. When it destroys them, then you've defeated your purpose.

A: Well, I may not fully agree with you. But first let me say I am not talking of violence as a necessity. It is quite possible that if there is an awakening and mobilization on a wide scale, they will just yield. They may not need to come to physical blows. K: Right. That's the kind of thing that I'm more at ease with. A: But if this does not happen, if they do not yield, we have to face that question. Some may withdraw. Some may not. And I have a very interesting story.

D: Please tell the story. A: I went to visit the work of an NGO in Bangladesh. One of the first things they told me is, they believe in non-violence. They are Gandhians. With great pride. I said, I'm very impressed, but I want to tell you a story. I'm just now coming from another place. I had gone to a coastal area where there were some organizing efforts. Landless, who were getting organized. There was a college professor who was helping. K: Contributing.

A: Contributing. He did not belong to any NGO and did not want to. He said, I cannot handle an institutional organization. I do not want any money. He used to go to the village, to these landless groups, and just work as an animator, spending his own money. To the point that the landless once told him, we find it very useful that you come and help us in this way, advise us, guide us. We want to pay for your bus fare. He was that kind of a professor. Quite exceptional. He took me to one of these organizations of the landless. There is a government administrative law that land belonging to nobody in the village belongs to the government. It's called *khas* land. *Khas* land will be given on a priority basis to organizations of the landless. It's a policy. So the landless formed an organization and applied for the land.

Now what happens is the elites, the landlords, their son is also landless. (Laughter.) So they also formed their organization, to get the *khas* land. Sometimes the landlords just get it by force, or by connections with the administrators. This is the practice. Most of the *khas* land is controlled by the landlords already. It's very difficult. Here the landless applied for allocation of *khas* land. According to procedure, an inspector comes and visits, to make sure this is a genuine organization of landless. Of course there are many instances where you pay him a service charge to certify that it is genuine. In this case it so happened that the inspector was genuine, a good man. He came to inspect, and was satisfied. He certified that they deserved the land. And the land was in principle allotted to them by a high authority, whose signature was there.

But in practice to actually possess it, you still have to go through about 21 bureaucratic desks. In every desk they had an obstacle. Some want the kind of service charge you cannot afford to pay. Some are in link with other interests in the same land. They found it completely impossible. No way they can actually possess the land. Then they go back to the inspector. You were very kind, generous, but we are still not getting it. We don't see how. The inspector tells them, I have done what I could. The rest is up to you, your strength.

When I went there with that professor they reported that they were now preparing to face musclemen of the landlords who were interested in the same land. Actually, they were operating so that the landless wouldn't get it. Those 21 desks. K: They had their network. A: Yes. And there is a custom that if there is a dispute over a piece of land, if you can take the harvest you have a very strong claim. The harvest time was near. I think they told me that they had already gone and planted a crop there, but they didn't have the official entitlement yet. Those landlords were sending their musclemen. K: To harvest. A: To take the harvest. Yes. And they reported to me, we are preparing now to fight the musclemen.

I reported this story to those people in the NGO who told me very proudly that they believe in nonviolence. I said, I don't know how nonviolence would work there. This is the situation I have just come from. They are going to meet violence by violence. I don't know what to advise them. They replied, You have given us a very difficult story. (Lightly laughing.) That's all. That's all on nonviolence. I don't know what I would advise them. To be non-violent, just go and sit there, do nothing, if they beat you up, sit there. Don't get your land back. I couldn't say this to them. It's their decision. This is very common. In Khushi's work there are a lot of this kind of stories. They just fight, physically. And the police come and take you. In some places they win. In some places they're harassed.

D: This is very common in many parts of South Asia. It certainly is one of the major dilemmas. I remember Sanjeev being very explicit about this in the workshop. He said, If in that situation I advocate violence or preach violence, what have I done. A: Yes. D: And he would refrain from advocating violence, as you also refrained. A: Yes. But shall I advocate nonviolence. D: Yes, he's also not saying that he's advocating nonviolence.

A: It's people's own decision. D: Right. A: Bhoomi Sena also land grabbed, reclaimed their land. They fought with slingshots, not with guns but grassroots slingshots. D: There are other cases where people have succeeded in gheraoing a piece of land, occupied it long enough, maintained it, so that in time they get the coercive force of the district magistrate to support them. A: Yes, nonviolence has worked in many cases, by mobilization, sometimes even by negotiation. D: But it may not be without any physical activity. The gherao itself. A: This is a form of violence. D: It's organized coercion, which is a form of violence, though not expressed in actual hitting. A: Yes. We don't let this fellow get out to the toilet, or eat. K: Um hm. D: Of course in some instances if the members are great enough, their coercion can work without... A: Without actual physical violence. Yes. But it doesn't work always. D: No. A: They bring their guns, they actually shoot you. That example of Khushi's...and the woman died.

D: The action and play of the struggle at this time. These kind of stories get removed from the question of the facilitator, the stance of the facilitator, because these are instances of people's own mature action in which they face the decisions. Those stories need to be communicated. More widely shared. A: Yes, you share them, and you get tremendous insights. But I would not generalize from them. D: No, you can't, absolutely. A: The violence question, it has to be answered in its context. We fought the independence war. We met violence by violence.

D: That's a larger question. It opens ways in which individuals and groups in many places are mobilizing to increase the role of nonviolence in the resolution of disputes. There is a powerful world-wide movement in that direction. A: Sure, fair enough. You always try. Go on. D: That is not separate from this. A: But then, until you have a situation where everyone accepts this principle, you have concrete situations. In the mother's presence, the small child is put in hot boiling water. Then cold water, go on doing this, to extract something out of you. We should note that Sanjeev is not saying, I'm for nonviolence. D: No. A: If all I have taught is violence, then what have I taught. This is what Sanjeev has said. We have to teach something more. That is...and I might say, my interpretation of that is, if you have to do violence, do it with love. You have to teach that also. I'm just saying, Sanjeev has still left it open. He has not said, I am against violence.

Autonomy, Rights, Nonviolence
A: We raised the question of scale. A valid question: from the small to the big. That brought in the possibility of violence. K: I think the question of scale is from the few to the many, not just the big. A: Yes. D: So maybe the question of scale is the one that's most relevant for what we're trying to talk about at the moment. A: Yes, we come up against this question, and we're torn and agonized.

D: With particular reference to scale. The authors, the people who came together, represent a considerable diversity of situations, a plurality of forces. The book has an intent of helping these people—ourselves—connect their forces, communicate, work synergistically, so that from this diversity both inspiration, example, encouragement, and some specific techniques become more apparent. I believe that synergistic process can happen without violating the intrinsic importance of face-to-face in community. Scale efforts on a face-to-face basis. I also agree there would be tracks that might become counterproductive. You always have the danger that some of the synergy might either get directed toward contradictory aims, or might be used by some groups in a way that is really oppressive to other groups. It's important to be wary of those potentials. That essentially says to me that scale in itself is a phenomenon that we can approach in ways that enable it to be constructively used, rather than detrimentally used.

K: Anis, how does your point of view contrast? A: Well, I have no problem with the way you're putting it, except I still insist you haven't given me a strategy that will assure there will not be need for violence. D: I haven't undertaken to do that.

A: Quite so. So my point remains, that as we move toward scale, the possibility of violence may be increasing. K: Even without that, the possibility of violence exists at any scale. A: At smaller scales. D: That's exactly my point. A: In a small village, you start with something. Violence may happen. D: I think the possibility that violence may increase because of scale is a specific condition. I don't think one can generalize about that. One knows that violence is happening in many, many small scales. One is really trying for some forms of enlightenment, personality awakening, and change that, in all dimensions... K: Transform. D: Transform.

A: Yes. Mind you, I was saying the possibility of violence *may* increase. D: Right. A: I did not say, it *will* increase. D: Yes. A: All I'm saying is, I think I will stick to that statement. D: I think that's a good one. That would be a good thing to have stated. K: Well, I don't know if it's all that relevant to worry about whether it will increase or not, because it already exists. The dilemma of how to respond to it exists at any scale. I think what's really underlying this argument, is our response to it at any scale. Let's agree, it will exist. We already are that far. Sister Tan. I'm sure her comments reflected these concerns.

D: Well, I have a particular notion of a way to move toward a principle of action that would be renewing and have an inbuilt tendency to avoid violence. This notion can connect the insider/outsider question and the questions of scale and structural transformation. It's enlightened by what you say, Anis, when you say, "I have every right to speak to you as my equal." The United Nations Charter speaks of "the principle of equal rights and self-determination of peoples." It uses both phrases: equal rights, and self-determination. The perception that gives me is that if I am striving for my self-determination, it can only be legitimate if I combine it with respect for your equal rights.

A: Yes. D: Any assertion I make of expanding my identity or territory or prerogatives that reduces your rights to the same identity, language, religion, territory, or prerogatives, is not a defensible assertion for me to make. K: It might reduce your existing level of power, but would not reduce, shouldn't reduce, your ultimate, relative rights. D: In fact, maybe my self-determination has already impinged on other peoples' rights, just by the amount I consume. That principle, to my knowledge, has never been used by the United Nations in the resolution of any dispute. But if built into negotiating processes, perhaps it could have a very powerful leavening effect. Because it forces each party to look at herself or himself and say, am I respecting that other person's equal rights in how far I'm pushing my self-determination? In that sense this is an insider/outsider relationship.

K: In fact it's that very argument of self-determination that the U.S. constantly uses to interfere with other people's rights. D: Exactly. While we don't apply the other dimension of it. This principle has never been used in even approaching the setting of an agenda on how people see these rights. Now, in a particular sense that's been inspired by your saying "I have every right to speak to you as an equal," if we have this underlying respect for the other's autonomy, that person's autonomy can only in very rare instances be worked out in isolation from others. If each of us as individuals became more aware that our autonomy should include an appreciation of the boundaries where we're hurting somebody else, that would be a richer sense of autonomy. I think the ways dialogues go, as groups face the issue of how they're going to organize their program, how they're going to decide what risks to take, you begin to increase the decision capacity to use these aspects of equality, dignity, and justice as cornerstones on which you make decisions.

K: That's a personality change. D: Yes. But it's not a personality change that's impossible. K: How do you decide that? How did you decide that? I would love to decide that. D: That it's not impossible? K: That it's not impossible. I mean, on the scale of one individual with all resource supplied to it, perhaps that's true, but socially...

D: Yeah, but socially we have institutions which we just allow to go fumbling along without conscious thought. When you look at schools where some conscious thought has gone into ways in which teachers and parents in the community can really enrich the curriculum, lots of changes happen. K: Well, people pull together when there's a positive outcome like that. People don't seem to pull together well when what they believe is personal sacrifice is involved. D: There are examples, in the environment movement, where people certainly learn to sacrifice what they thought before was necessary. Perhaps they've changed only because they've had a realization that what they were doing was harmful.

K: I don't mean to say all people, I mean that there's just this sort of momentum of self interest, a basic quality that I consider healing, but it's just too forceful. D. I'm not winking an eye at that.

A: If you're asking what I was thinking. I was thinking, that you could not stop the violence in the Gulf. I wonder if there could have been a strategy to avoid the violence in Bangladesh. I don't see that. No matter how smart you are in devising ways.

K: It occurs to me that perhaps the only line of action against potential violence that would work, is to pursue nonviolence with as much passion and, shall I say, strategy, as people who prefer violent action. Because people who have a tendency to believe in nonviolence also tend to sit around a lot until it's too late. It probably takes much more early thinking, much more early on with very deliberate action.

D: You're right, absolutely right. We need to develop these strategies long in advance. K: You need to see the patterns. A: But with no effect. D: Kersten's right. You see these patterns, then you can organize in those contexts. K: If the causes of those ultimate conditions are addressed in time, you have some basis for hope.

IV

TRANSFORMATIONS THE COMPASS ROUND

Preface to Part IV

Four of the authors of Part IV attended the Global Forum of grassroots, non-governmental organizations at the Earth Summit, the United Nations Conference on Environment and Development, in Rio de Janeiro in July, 1992. They participated actively in drafting NGO treaties on Sustainable Agriculture, Biodiversity Conservation, Forestry, Consumption and Lifestyle, Environmental Education, and Indigenous Peoples' Rights. New associations were formed with grassroots activists working in these arenas in Brazil, the Philippines, Thailand, the United States, and elsewhere. The participants joined in significantly expanding the meeting's focus on environmental conservation to issues of resource distribution and control, and in widening discussion to north-south perspectives beyond the earlier west-east emphasis.

Part IV builds directly on issues advanced at the Rio summit. In the preceding months, members of the *People's Initiatives* workshop had participated together in international agency meetings oriented in part to the Rio issues. The editors also concluded their discussions at this time, raising issues of global equity in resource distribution, relationships west and east, north and south, and connections among grassroots groups. These editorial considerations appear ahead of the chapters in Part IV, so that the authors' chapters may set the book's closing tones.

Then, in Chapter 11, Khushi Kabir brings farmers' and women's experiences and critique to bear on internationally-sponsored development projects that result in major changes in water and land use, usually launched without local planning inputs but often with serious negative effects. In contrast, she tells how grassroots workshops in 23 regions of Bangladesh, organized with NGO support, took leadership in forming the country's National Environment Management Action Plan, identifying major environmental issues, causes, potential solutions and local action, and recommended government action. Through cohesive cooperation of this kind, NGOs in Bangladesh are coming to be looked on as crucial parts of civil society, advancing democracy.

Khushi Kabir goes on to analyze connections—or lack thereof—among environment, population, and health concerns, and priorities, particularly of women, among these concerns. She assesses recent attacks by politically motivated religious groups on women, symbolized by a noted woman author, and on grassroots movements in general. Every act of destruction by fundamentalist groups, she reports, has been met by peoples' rebuilding of schools, replanting of trees, renewal of programs. She concludes with advocacy of greater progress in getting peoples' voices heard, through more open dialogue between people, governments, and multilateral agencies.

Exploring issues of "how we give voice and how we celebrate community," Penny Levin has chosen, in Chapter 12, to write "speaking outward" from the voices of village residents in watershed areas of southern Thailand in their efforts to restore and preserve the environment, and from other layers of this experience. Forest villagers and farmers tell of the decline in water levels in their streams and the destruction of the forest from monocrop rubber plantation over the last 15 years. With a profound respect for the wisdom of village mentors and what they have taught her, and in gaining their trust over these years, Penny joined village residents, grassroots teachers, researchers, and non-profit groups in evolving the "Forests for Life" project. She shows the several faces of the project: communities' intended regeneration of traditional forest agriculture and forest gathering practices and products, to restore choices in ecosystem and community health and sustainability; and the intent of donors, through the Biodiversity Support Program funded by the U.S. Agency for International Development, to identify and support new patterns of small-scale enterprise and economic returns based on incentives for the protection of biodiversity.

Adopting a participatory action and education approach from the start, the project set a precedent that this would be a learning process rather than strictly a mobilization effort, so that it could be repeated and adapted by other groups. So many community voices had shaped the project's design that when it was funded, it happened like a strong river—things just flowed. Penny shows how understandings provided by the villagers meant that the project sustained their ideas and communicated them to researchers, donor agencies, and conservation practitioners, "viewing the locally ordinary as globally extraordinary;" removing conservation from a focus mainly in the marketplace and placing it in the context of community.

In parallel vein, "the beauty of the commons" is affirmed by Arthur Getz in telling of innovative social and ecological advances through community supported agriculture (CSA), in Chapter 13. He describes these direct partnerships between farmer and consumer groups as expressions of various food safety, land-use protection, cultural restoration, and local economic self-reliance values in Information Age societies. Crises that face family farms both north and south in markets, scale, and technology prompt the search for commonalities in community support concepts and practices that may strengthen local agriculture in both settings.

The imperative in southern nations of creating greater local self-reliance in food production is a strong motivating factor. Grassroots organizations south and north are increasingly collaborating, through computer conferences and fax networks, in dialogues on sustainability, agricultural research, trade, and related policy agendas. Moving out from his firsthand experience with the Japan "*teikei*" innovations in CSA, and with Hawaii agriculture in transition from its plantation history, Arthur analyzes key attributes of community supported agriculture in Japan, Europe, and the United States for qualities that may be widely relevant in shifts to biologically based, information rich, locally and ecologically focused farming practices.

Giving personal voice to her learning experiences in working with communities in Bhutan, Hawaii, and Appalachia on paths of change, organization, and self-review, Kersten Johnson creates a vision of life-sustaining community harmony and renewal, in Chapter 14. This is both a conceptual and an ethical paradigm, for as she portrays core values and sustaining principles of community, she points to each person's individual decisions and acts as ultimately building the paradigms that can reconstruct society. Sustenance, she finds in her encounters with people in many circumstances, is both physical and of the spirit: of connectedness with others, sharing, honoring justice. She thereby presents a reply to questions she had posed in the editors' dialogues: of whether the affluent, the powerful—especially in northern nations—can find motivation and joy in reducing their excessive material consumption, and achieving greater balance and more humane values in the holding and exchange of resources.

This chapter is a self-study, learning vehicle. Qualities of partnership in a sustenance society include personal balance, sustaining community, environmental kinship, creative diversity, deep justice, and humane economy. The author portrays these as a symphony of design, then articulates in fine detail the particular elements of celebration and compassion called forth in each person to perform the music. You can take this music with you. Study the notes, the demands, improvise, and create. In this dance of life we can all connect.

Puanani Burgess, from her home watching the waves on the Hawaiian shore, brings the book back to the global waves where we started: the wave of grassroots peoples, locally defining and acting to create their own futures, and the wave of growing awareness by wider institutions, national and international, that participatory, connected action on people's own terms is the source of sustainable progress. Puanani does this by reconstructing the bridges formed in the *People's Initiatives* workshop, telling how her unexpected "learning by surprise" of kinship with people in Bangladesh and Appalachia, and their deep water connections with the Hawaiian people, has motivated and guided her in recent work and travels. Her chapter, like her life, is one of action and movement, serenity and poetry. As the volume's epilogue, it weaves the poem Puanani promised in the *lei*-making, giving rhythms to the waves each now rides with greater surety, and carrying us all forward together.

Editorial Openers

Equity Overcoming Deprivation: First Change the Discourse

A: The other most profound, most fulfilling moment I had was in Zimbabwe. I heard about the Organization of Rural Associations for Progress (ORAP) when I was with the ILO. Grassroot associations that had formed an apex body. I wrote to them, very careful not to trespass: I have heard about you. I'd be interested in knowing more about your work, and exchanging. I'm sending you our literature by way of introducing ourselves. If you would care to share yours with me, I'd be very happy. Just that. They wrote back. We never could imagine we could receive such literature from a UN agency. When are you coming to visit us? They sent some reports they had written for their donors.

Then I met some of them in a workshop in Germany. Sithembiso Nyoni is the name of the kind of leader, the principal animator. She was known to be a tough, assertive woman. Assertive of people. Their rights, and so on. If you say anything with arrogance, she will immediately finish you. In that workshop, someone pointed me out. She rushed to me and embraced me. She hugged me. "You are Anis? I've been dying to meet you." That was wonderful. We chatted and chatted. Every now and then she would say, Wait a minute, taking out her diary and writing a note. Then she said, Now you must come to Africa.

They invited me there. First they wrote, Will you come to our review seminar of donors? I wrote, I am not a donor, so how can I come? They wrote back, We consider you to be our most important donor. Because you are giving us ideas. That was also very nice. Very fulfilling. K: Very. A: So I said, OK. Then they asked me to write a paper for that seminar. The subject they decided: "The Role of Community Participation to Overcome the Vicious Circle of Hunger and Poverty." K: Oh, my!

A: You can see, I was viciously angry. I wrote the paper, but the first few paragraphs attacked the title. Why do you call this the vicious circle of hunger and poverty? You are doing such wonderful work. The whole world is coming to you, wants to learn from you. Your work is very famous. Very rich. Do you want to give this image of yourselves? I elaborated what kind of richness ORAP has: mobilization, innovating, technology, all this, very proud people. I sent the paper first. They wrote to me, they liked it very much, they're debating it, they had translated it into their native language.

I went there. There also, I challenged them. I went beyond my paper. I said, look here, your forefathers, the first communities. Think of the first human communities. They had nothing. K: Materially. A: No cloth to wear, no hut. Lived in caves. In the open. Would you call them poor? Or would you call it the beginning of life, to move forward? Now, you have had your freedom struggle. You have won, you have your independence. This is becoming a way of constructive life of the society to move forward. Why should you think of a vicious circle of poverty and hunger? K: Um, hm. A: I was mobbed. By people, all kinds. Initially a few groups, NGOs, kept coming to me. Mainly to say, You have hit us very hard. But we have appreciated it. K: Uh, huh.

A: Finally one night, we were camping in a field. We were strolling outside, it was dark. Then one fellow came to me. Mr. Rahman, can I talk to you? He introduced himself as a village blacksmith. He was in the ORAP movement. He talked about that. Then, patted me. I wanted to thank you, for telling us that we are not poor. K: Hm. A: He goes on talking, many things we talk. Again from time to time he comes back. Oh, thank you so much, telling us that we are not poor.

K: Another great moment. A: I had lifted a burden from his shoulders. K: Because then there was no feeling of Well, with me, there's something wrong. Not even questioning. A: A burden lifted. He's now proud. K: He's now a life interpreter. A: Life interpreter. It was a great moment. I can never forget it. This I narrate in Bangladesh, in many seminars.

K: Undoubtedly this person has also said the same thing to friends, children. A: Yes. K: You know, a phrase I like a lot. It's most likely that the most important things any of us do are things we never knew we did. There might be a lot of people who had that very same feeling, and they didn't pat you on the back and tell you. A: That is right. K: Probably hundreds of other people in that same moment. And all the other times people have heard things. I take a lot of strength from that, because it makes it easier to do things when they don't look like they're changing. They might be changing. No matter who's doing it. A: Quite so. K: You can't tell by looking at that person that his life has changed. Yet perhaps it's changed. A: It has changed.

K: This brings us again to talk about poverty. A: Yes. Why am I unable to communicate? That we should not talk about poverty. We should not call people poor. We should not talk of overcoming hunger. K: There's a point you raised. You've said, poverty in Bangladesh is not a solvable concern in the next many decades. A: Um. K: That the issue, if I got it right, was the fact that people are in relative disadvantaged positions, which creates a great deal of tension, justifiable anger, frustration. But if there were greater equity, equality in this case, the situation of having little would be a very different experience. A: Well, you have said it. K: I got it right? A: Yes.

K: Is it perhaps that people keep talking about poverty because what we all recognize at some level is that there is an issue of equity that's not being addressed. Instead of dealing with it as equity, which is really how we should deal with it, they're saying, Well, you poor folks who don't have enough, here, we need to help you. There's that patronizing kind of help. A: That is right.

K: As opposed to, we need to look at how our wealth is shared, which is my problem. In Bangladesh, it's your problem. A: Quite so. We will sacrifice a little, to make you a little better off. K: As opposed to recognizing that it's your right to have a share. A: That everything that we're enjoying, we have taken the bulk of this from you, unfairly. K: Even if we didn't know it at the time. Exactly. That's right. A: The process of transfer, the appropriation, is very clear in some societies. Every day it is happening. By power, by guile, they're taking away and showing the fellow. K: Literally, stealing the harvest from the field. A: Yes. So instead of talking of that, you say, we realize you are very poor, so we'll do something about it. K: Some technology transfer. A: Yes. K: Training programs, and human development.

A: It's very good you have brought this out. That's one aspect of this question of talking about poverty. It's a very important one, the question of equity, structural change, ownership over society's resources. Often when one does some poverty alleviation projects here and there, those processes of making you more poor continue. K: You still have the flow of wealth out of there. A: It goes on. K: That's very important.

A: We are not facing or attacking that question. That is one part of it. The other is what you said in the beginning. Even if there were total equity, a society may be very poor. That problem may not be solvable in 20-30 years. I think there are many societies in that phase. It's a question of your resource base, population, state of resource development, technology. The ability of the resources to meet the needs of the population, given the state of technology, social administration, possibilities. There also I have my argument. Economists seem to be satisfied, if the people under the poverty line today are 80 percent, and after 10 years they measure again it is 70 percent. K: Hm. A: Suppose it were to happen. They feel we are making great progress. We shall progressively come down. I ask them, first you have reduced it from 80 to 70 percent. Another 10 years, 60 percent; 20 years, 50 percent. Certainly great progress. No question. But the 50 percent who remain below. They have not gotten anything. Would they allow this to happen? Their misery is increasing, relative misery. They are seeing others going up. Their own brethren who were poor like them, going up.

K: Relative to the richest, they are not any different. But relative to the average, getting worse. A: Getting worse. That will make them more miserable. They may start doing the kind of things which will in the first place not make this possible. You know, turn into what may be called "anti-social" activities. K: Yes.

A: Therefore, the task is to find some strategy which will keep the whole society, small disturbances apart, engaged in constructive work. Not just think of reducing 10, 20 percent. K: Can you describe what that looks like in your mind? Constructive work. A: They're engaged in solving problems. In a relation of reasonable order, not destructive. K: What kind of problems? A: That is for them to decide. They will identify. Today I have a health problem, increase production, education. Whatever it is, they will all be engaged.

K: The distinction is not just engaging in some material benefits, but rather the point is to reach everyone in a particular kind of connection. A: Yes, that is right. K: How do you picture that process? Is it something you shouldn't do at all unless you do it completely? A: Well, I don't use that extreme, but this is the basic strategy. K: Right. A: My strategy would be to be able to stimulate the entire society. Not think of poverty alleviation here and there, reduce poverty in... K: Focal groups. A: Certain groups. Next decade I'll handle some others, and so on. This way we're making great progress. I don't think that's even possible. K: So this constructive involvement of the whole society. A: Try to stimulate them to get engaged.

Moving Inward West and East, North and South: Control of Assets

K: This relates to another question. Is the tendency of people not to be concerned with the well-being of other people an illness, which can be healed, or is it a trait, which simply has to be accepted or dealt with? A: I would not generalize. For some people you can heal it. For others, we may not know how to do it... K: It's relevant for me because in attempts to heal, even in some long time scale, I get so discouraged that I can't even proceed. A: No, but that is our inabilities. I'm not saying it cannot be healed. I do not know how to.

K: An illness might be healed. If it's a genetic trait, the only way to heal it is to...weed it out. This relates to deeper levels of social change, structural change. And to some of the reasons for my great concern over violence. What is it that can bring about those deep kind of changes we were talking about, those person changes, in people who are raised to believe that being more comfortable than everyone else is their right? The God-given way of life in America kind of feeling. We have no responsibility, we only have rights. I find compassion in all people, but I find some peoples' compassion is buried very deep. I really wonder what the modes for change are. We have talked about this a little, but to think about it in a broad, social way is just mind-boggling.

A: Well, you were saying that people are affluent. K: Um hm. Or powerful. A: Powerful. Consider it to be their right. K: And often are very arrogant about it. Feel they know better. A: Very arrogant. If they say it is their right to exercise their power, how did they become affluent in the first place? Had they become affluent by not exploiting, or appropriating, or abusing, oppressing, any other community or society? K: They often believe they did, even if they didn't. A: Hm. But you know that is not true. K: Yes. But there are a lot of Americans who don't know. A: That is true, yes. They don't know that. K: It's probably easier to talk to those people.

A: They took this land in the first instance from some other communities. By brute force. When you were asking that question I was remembering something I was shown in Ghana. Which completely dazed me. December 1990. We had our big meeting. K: Was that the finale workshop? A: That's right. My grand finale. Very fulfilling. On self-reliance. I decided to challenge everybody. K: Great. A: A picked group, all talking of self-reliance, and had some commitment. So we challenged them. That is another part.

In Ghana we were taken to a coastal city, a sight-seeing trip. We were taken to a castle. K: Hm. A castle. A: Yes. We were shown many rooms, torture chambers, kind of thing. K: How old was the castle? A: You will have to cry, you asked me that question. K: If you can stand it, I think crying is very important. A: That's true, that's true, to release. Then they took us to one room which was deep inside. No sunlight, just one entrance, no window, no other doors. Completely dark. They told us, You are standing on solidified human excretion, several centuries back. The Black traders, traders with Black slaves, would bring the slaves and put them there, many many in the same little room. Cut off from sunlight and everything, make them have their food and toilet there. In that small room. The idea was to see who survived this. Those who survived are the fittest. To be exported. K: How amazing. A: Yes. As I say, we all felt dazed.

K: Direct experience of these kinds of things creates such rage, the desire to be violent is very understandable. What isn't clear is how to deal with that. What other response is there but complete rage? A: Quite so. I don't know whether they were being exported to

America, or not. Somewhere in the West. French also had their colonies. Are you talking of that kind of right?

K: At the worst case, Yes. Because cases less than that are easier to understand. A: Quite so. K: Because if you still find heart in a person, if you touch it, it breaks. But what do you think allows people to do that? How do human beings maintain their humanness, and do these things? Of course, they haven't... A: They don't maintain their humanness. K: How do they even stay alive? How do they even live with themselves?

A: But in various ways this is going on even today. K: Yes, in different ways. A: In different types of ways. I mean, what happened in our independence. How could the people do that? It is possible that those who are saying, this is our right, we're affluent because we've been privileged to be born that way. Maybe they don't know some of the ways which have helped them become what they are today. K: Some don't.

A: Some of them would weep if they knew. It is possible. K: Many. A: Many. But possibly not all. K: No, not all. It's that "not all" that's driving me nuts. A: Quite so. Even those many, if they knew this history, what would they say? Would they still insist that... K: It wasn't my fault, that was someone else. A: That's right. K: What am I to do? A: Yes. Quite so. K: Most people, yes.

A: Quite so. That is the first part of your question. The claim that it is our right. To this I have this kind of response. This is my question to all those who are working to promote grassroots initiatives, participation. You gave me that book, yesterday, *Voluntary Simplicity*. I was glancing through it quickly. They're addressing the affluent: Be simple. K: Yes. A: But what about the appropriation they have done? How did they become affluent in the first place? How about the question of justice? Not now to just become simple. You have a responsibility to return the control over assets. That is what I mean by a structural transformation.

K: Right. A: There has to be a massive shift of control over assets. K: Um hm. A: To undo this injustice. This is happening every day. Even today. You may not be feeling it here anymore, but we are still going through that kind of continuous polarization process. In Bangladesh, in Indian villages. The small, marginal farmer is losing his assets. Those who are affluent and powerful, they are still appropriating. By cheating, by force, by all means. K: Um hm. A: This kind of violence is going on. So there is a question of justice. To return this. First to stop this process, and then to return. Otherwise, we just ask them to get mobilized, solidarity and everything. Their assets have been taken away. This question is not featuring in most discussions of grassroots work. It's all very fine, participatory development. But participatory with what? I'm giving the thesis, if poverty cannot be solved, that doesn't mean I'm being made more and more impoverished. K: Um hm. A: In that material sense. Whatever little I had is also taken now. I don't mean, don't recover that. That has to be returned. A basic question of justice. This is my question to the affluent.

K: My question also. And that is also my question to myself. I always have to ask, How do I come by whatever wealth I have, and how do I use that justly? A: Yes. But it is not a personal question I'm asking. It is a scale question. It is a structural change question. K: Yes it is. A: I'm not asking for return through charity. K: Of course not. A: That humiliates them even more. This is their right. I have to give them in a way that they can take it with dignity. K: Exactly. A: That means there has to be a social consensus, social agreement. That this belongs to them. This will be returned. K: Right. A: Then no one individually will feel humiliated. That I'm now subject to charity. K: Right. A: That is what revolutions are supposed to do. K: Supposed to do. A: That's right. It's a social decision. The new society decides that it is yours. All these grassroots initiatives, they don't address this question. Some are, say like Khushi's work in Bangladesh. They have this very much in view in what they're doing, little bit here and there. But it's not enough to get them anywhere.

K: My sense is that the affluent and powerful, including the bulk of people in the U.S., including people working in grassroots situations but who have a choice of different career paths, ultimately need to come to a feeling, a deep understanding, that it is not one's right to have whatever one can have. For instance, if I wanted I could be doing jobs where I might be earning $60,000 a year, having a home, all those things. Most people think because you can do it, you should do it, it's your right to have it. I don't think people should get away with that. Because you can do it, it doesn't mean you have any right to it. A: Yah.

K: My question then is, How do people come to ask that question? How do people come to feel that burden? Especially people who really do believe that somehow there's some birthright to be superior? A: Hm. K: Because unless people...if the revolution doesn't change that mindset, this is my premise, it seems like people have to change it themselves. Affluent people have to change their own minds. It might take the pressure of others to do it. But their minds have to change. Not necessarily through some sort of enlightenment, probably a person has a confrontation. But what is that confrontation, what is that process, that brings that different kind of awareness into a person? Maybe my premise is wrong. But that's what I'm seeing, eventually.

A: Well, you are answering that a revolution of some kind is needed. K: Um hm. A: To give justice back to the people. It is not an individual question. That I feel, even if I get this opportunity, I should not take it. K: Why isn't it an individual question? Isn't it both individual and social? A: That to me is irrelevant. I mean it's a personal matter. It doesn't help in any way. K: I guess I totally disagree, but go on. A: That doesn't help, unless these individuals add up to something significant. K: Of course. A: That's what I'm saying. K: But they can't add up unless there are also individual decisions. The individual decisions are very significant. And, there must be many many.

A: Sure. I still say, in the end it is a social question. It is the summation of individual questions. K: Right. A: Not one individual deciding, I want to live my life that way, because I don't think I have a right to that. That by itself has no significance, unless this can add up. K: Right. You can't stop at just the individual. A: And that individual has to not only do it for himself or herself, but link up. With others, to try to become a force. To change the whole society. That is what I was trying to say. K: I understand. You can't just say, once I do it in my own life, that's all you need to do. A: That's irrelevant. That's your personal thing. K: Right. A: You must be part of a social effort.

K: You see, I can see this happening all over this country. Small groups of people are sitting down, asking these kinds of questions of each other and themselves, and making changes. Then asking the questions of more people. But they seem like people who are predisposed to ask these questions. What about all the people who have no interest in asking these questions? What happens to these people? A: Quite so. And most will not ask this question. K: Even if you put it right in front of them. A: Yes. That's my feeling. I may be totally wrong. After one century or so, today I don't see that. K: No, I don't either.

A: And there will be some who will resist this. If this really grows into a force, then the structure, those at the top, will come and crack down heavily. K: I think that's true. A: No mistake about it. K: Because they feel it's not only their right, but somehow the world is better off if they continue exercising the power and privilege that they have. Because they have the right of expertise. It's really an insidious sickness. A: Quite so. That is why I don't see it easily happening in the United States in the foreseeable future. K: But isn't it imperative that it happen in the United States? If the United States doesn't change, it will continue to perpetuate this. A: That is true, but I don't see how. K: Yes, that's my problem.

A: Quite so. That's why my basic question is to God. Are you going to win over the Devil? And God says I am in no hurry.

K: How can you, how have you at some point learned to keep from being stopped by grief? A: Stopped by? K: Stopped by grief. If you feel the pain, it can be really devastating. There's got to be a way to move it, keep it flowing. I haven't learned that. I wonder how you have. Or what you do, to deal with it.

A: That's a much more difficult question. I haven't thought about it. Maybe in our societies, the struggle is more intense. Daily. K: Um hm. A: So we get involved. That may help. Something is happening somewhere. Though on a big scale, it's not. Still things are happening. On small scales, struggles are going on. You can easily get involved. Be useful. Be frustrated, but still feel involved. K: Right. A: So you are in that sense relaxed. From time to time even big upheavals are happening. Like our Ershad fell...every one is excited. Of course, we also know this is not going to give what we want, yet. Still we can see that as one step forward. It was very important for Ershad to go. The people have shown, once more, that no matter how oppressive, how dictatorial the government is, they can rise and bring you down. You are not having that kind of change even in the United States.

K: Yeah. The only thing I see happening, and I think increasingly, are some of these discussions. But the action, the political change is going in the other direction. Individuals actually are forming groups, finding deeper levels of thinking, deeper levels of awareness, but the social expression seems to be the opposite. That seems like a contradiction. One can see that this time is like many other times, when things were about to change. But every time things change, they seem to go back in the other direction. You wonder, is there any upward trend? Or is there just this circle that goes round and round? Do you think there's an upward trend? Or just trust in God?

A: Upward trend I don't see. I'm not hopeful. That in our lifetime we shall see something that will really make us happy. Even in the lifetime of our children. Except by historical accident. K: Um hm. A: Which is an accident. It doesn't give us any hope, by way of logic. Actually, the logic is the opposite. It is a frightening scenario that logic is showing. That kind of accident, whether it will come in my country, in 20, 30 years. Either the country will completely perish, or something good must happen. By accident. Suddenly some leadership will arise, which can mobilize people. Because apart from people being oppressed by people, the question of the survival of the land. Land to be able to sustain. The country remaining above water itself. K: Even that. A: Even that is being questioned. That possibly could be stopped by massive mobilization of the people to do something about it. But mobilization requires that kind of leadership which we don't yet have. Maybe some day it may come. Logic doesn't show it, but....

K: Maybe the stress itself will bring it. A: Quite so. Then I think, all right. Suppose we perish as a nation. Water comes and swallows us. What do we do? The analogous question I ask. Suppose the doctor certifies you have a terminal disease. Six months is your time. This happens to many, it may happen to me also. What do I do then? Well, my answer is, that I will try to be...up to the last minute I will try to live as a human being. With value, with creativity, with everything. That's my challenge. How much creativity and values I can show. I want the nation also to have such spirit. So that when it perishes, the whole world and history will say, Oh what·a nation it was! Perishing itself is not of much significance. It doesn't matter. We all perish.

K: We all perish. That's true. A: As long as we live, you know, we show our best. This is my desire. I am not worried about Bangladesh... K: Perishing. It's more, can we be human? A: Can we perish with that kind of courage, show the world that we are going down fighting. Fighting to keep asserting our human spirit. The water comes and swallows us. K: Maybe that would be the kind of thing it takes to change the United States. Someone else showing what it means to be human.

A: This is what I meant by those experiments, also. With the flood. No matter your situation. I'm treating you as human beings. So how would you respond with these people? Their children will die, you will die. Die bravely. Not surrendering to the anti-human vibes. K: Um. A: Then you know what sustains us. It's more difficult for you, I can see that. The struggle for us is very intense, daily. K: You have so many examples of people doing that. A: Many examples. A lot of people are in the struggle, with very positive hands. K: You can see them shoulder to shoulder. A: See them. I can decide, I want to spend my life with them. K: Yes. A: That is great. That is what sustains us. Sometimes it is still very frustrating, but then, again.

K: There's a lot of that goodness in people here. But simultaneously there's blindness. A: Hm. K: People who are quite happy to make their own fortunes. And in some ways exemplify a lot of these values while they do it, but are totally blind to the fact that their livelihood is itself killing someone. They just don't see that. Could I perhaps add another dimension to the question? A: Yes.

K: This might be a whole separate question in itself. There's some sense we have about a natural grouping in which self-determination by the group is an issue. There are boundaries across these groupings that we haven't talked about. For instance, the question of equity may be addressed internally in a context that is politically independent, ethnically and culturally a group, a natural group like Bangladesh. There's still the question of it not being equitable in comparison with, for instance, India, or the United States. Shouldn't we push that issue to be across our boundaries of these groupings. Especially when you think of groupings which have no clear, obvious natural boundaries. Then, who is they? There are always little pockets where people have their own desire for self-determination. Shouldn't we push our equity concerns way past every little grouping? When we talk about self-determination, who is this self, who is this group which is self-determining? Or is it just individuals we're talking about?

A: Well you can push this in a moral sense. But I don't see how you can push this in an operational sense. The nation-state exists, separately, that boundary between nations. One nation does not have jurisdiction over the resources of another. K: In reality, though, they have jurisdiction. The U.S. has a great jurisdiction over the resources of many other nations, by virtue of the way it's set up the economy. It pulls, it has an effect on the resources, that's what I'm saying. Economically, it's behaving as though that was its own resource.

A: Yes, but I'm looking from the other point of view, those who would want an equitable share across national boundaries. Say Bangladesh, it has no jurisdiction to tell the United States you should give those resources to us. K: What of the fact that the United States has managed to take the resources over long periods of time? Not just the U.S., but England... A: I'm talking of operational jurisdiction, I'm not talking of the moral question. Morally, Bangladesh, Africa, everyone have the right to say this is ours. But operationally, how does Bangladesh control resources that are today under control of the United States?

K: Is that fundamentally any different question than how people in a village gain access to resources which the wealthy in that village have control over? A: But then, people in a village, it is still the same nation. There is the theoretical possibility of their combining, confronting the elites of their society. Within a nation, people do feel that there is a kind of a sporting chance of the oppressed confronting the elites who are a minority. They are very powerful; it's a sporting chance; you may lose. But Bangladesh has no sporting chance to seize back the resources from the United States.

K: No, that's not how I would go about it. I'm not asking that question. I'm asking the question, how we can decide. For many countries, for many political groupings, it's not easy to decide what those boundaries are, what equity might mean. It's also not fair, in my opinion, to stop at whatever the current political boundary is and say as long as we're happy with each other, forget others. A: Okay. What

I'm trying to say is that if, operationally, there is a realistic possibility of winning that battle, then it makes sense to me to talk about.

K: Well, do you really think it's realistic to confront that battle— it's all a question of time, partly—even within a country like, within Bangladesh. How realistic is it to expect the equity struggles to bear fruit? A: Well, in some societies it has happened. There have been radical transformations. K: For example? A: For example, China. There was a very radical land reform. Land reform has happened even in other societies, even in non-revolutionary societies. Japan has had a land reform, Korea, Taiwan, the Soviet Union. K: Right. It hasn't created equity in their countries, though. It may have made a big difference, a push within part of their economic development, but the countries are still full of great inequities. Less so in China, perhaps, but Japan, Korea.

A: Possibly. If you're thinking of a lasting solution, I have none. That will not again create inequities. I have no such answer. I have been telling you, that the devil will keep operating. You face one major inequity, you struggle to correct that. You correct that, it doesn't last forever. That something will last for all times to come, no.

K: Let's take, for instance, that one accomplishes this restructuring, or some improvement of equity within a group, why should we be satisfied with stopping there? A: I'm not saying I'm satisfied, I'm just saying that operationally I cannot take on that task. I'll try to do something where I feel I have the possibility. There also I may be wrong. K: Perhaps this comes down to our questions of strategy, because there are still quite a lot of people, in the U.S. itself, who are challenging this way of life and its ethics. Just as in all these struggles, it's a small percentage. But it's being heard, the voice is being heeded, the discussions are occurring. It's not out of my imagination to see a time, not necessarily in my lifetime, when because of internal kinds of forces, even places like the U.S. might at least become less dominating. It may not be an issue of completely giving up privilege and wealth. A: Quite so. You were asking the question of equity. K: Right. A: You can be less dominating, but even then retain all the things you have appropriated. So that equity we don't get. K: No, I mean that materially, as well as politically. I mean economic domination, as well as every other kind of domination... A: There may be a desire not to dominate any more economically. But what we have taken from you we don't return.

K: I'm not convinced that that's not part of the dialogue. A: I don't know. I don't see that. K: It doesn't appear in the international arena. It's appearing in other forums. That's true in a lot of places. A: Now you are assessing that to be significant, I have my disbelief, you may be right. K: For instance in the debates among the invited NGO's in the UNCED conference, at least as an example, some were concerned with women's issues, some with agriculture, some with oceans, and what not, but the equity theme continues to come up, across all these task groups. A: Okay, I'm not challenging that, but I still think that if these movements, however strong, keep on moving, it will eventually confront the structure, the establishment, within the United States.

K: Right. That's why I'm not proposing that this is the task of Bangladesh or Africa. I'm saying that if the society is to transform itself, those who are in positions of wealth and power ultimately have to make some kind of change. They may make this change because they're forced to, they may make this change partly out of re-evaluating themselves. That is more rare, I realize, not to be naive in any way. But it does occur. And in my sense, the long run change is going to depend on that kind of change. If again it's just a struggle for power, the struggle just keeps going on. A: That I agree.

K: If in fact that is the case, if those who are in relative positions of wealth and power have the option to re-evaluate, then we don't have to take it as given that the organized demand of countries that have been sucked of resources is the only source of the change. It's the responsibility of the internal dialogue of people with power, who also can change. So without saying that it should be a current concern, say, of villagers in Bangladesh, it is a current concern in the world. On this people in societies like the U.S. can be at least working.

A: I think this is a very valuable concern. I would like to see this awareness and concern spread. That's very good. Where it will end up with I don't know. As I say, I'd be astonished if evil gives up without a fight. K: Yeah. A: Ultimately, the hard core...there are many who are soft, they may change...but there will be a hard core, with tremendous power in their hands. It may still be possible to neutralize them, but I won't say that inevitably we can neutralize them. K: Yes, I leave that question open. But then there's also the people who aren't quite so hard core. A: Quite so. They may go on increasing, that's very worthwhile.

Self and Other: When We Connect

A: I asked a group of landless in a Bangladesh village what it would be like being saved from drowning by a rescuer who dragged you to the shore as if you were an object. Would you only be grateful for your life having been saved, or would something hurt you also? One man replied, something would hurt very deeply. I said, what is it? He said, my dignity. Then he gave the example, how his dignity could be saved. By asking him not to save me just like that, but asking him to hold me with one hand, and swim with the other. After we discussed this, I was preparing to leave. Then he said, very intense, looking at me, telling me: We have not heard anyone talk to us like that. I request you to go on talking. That was, you know, a very great moment. Very fulfilled. That I was able to touch him. Something very deep, and human. By reaching. Again, you know, I don't feel like saying this kind of thing in public.

K: But it's a very important story. A: Yes, it is very important, as an observation. That you can touch the chord. It's possible. Everyone should try that. Not let go easily.

K: I have a question. A: Let's hear. K: It's something of a challenge. I don't know if there's any word... But let me give you the description. From time to time I experience one kind or another of distress. Maybe it's physical, maybe emotional, different kinds of things. And somebody who loves me will have something that could ease that distress. It might be, just brilliant compassion, it might be any... I've had to overcome the feeling of accepting love as kind of difficult. The act of accepting something which I need takes in myself a lot of courage. When I do it, I feel healed. A: Hm. K: I feel very tender, in a sense vulnerable. But this is when I'm receiving it from somebody who isn't trying... isn't feeling himself superior to me because he's doing it. A: Paternalistic. K: It's wonderful. A: Yes.

K: How does that differ from the pain a person might feel to accept help? You know, it's really important for us to accept even help from people who love us. Isn't it good to be able to do that with each other? To be able to give and take? A: Well, certainly. But what is the problem? You know, if it is genuine... K: Yes, yes. It has to be genuine. A: Of course. I'm looking for a word, how to explain it. If the person, if you sense that the person is not gaining anything from it. That's one way of putting it, I don't know if it's the best way. If I am patronizing, extending that kind of consideration and affection, then I am gaining something from it.

K: Well I think people do gain, always gain from giving something. It doesn't seem to be a problem... A: Well, that is different. My ego is gaining something. K: Oh, OK. It's which part of you gains. A: Yes. K: Do you feel superior because of it, or do you feel whole? A: That's right. K: So you're not talking about the kind of self-help which doesn't allow that help, that love.

A: No. But then one has to be very very careful. One has to be accepted in those terms. The receiver does not have any... He fully understands you. He accepts you. Accepts you in those terms. K: Yes. A: You have to break that barrier. Make yourself that transparent. So that he has no doubt. He may have reason to doubt, because of experiences with others. K: That's true. A: Even if you are genuine you still have to respect that doubt. Not trespass, making sure he doesn't feel you're trespassing.

K: Yes. Something I've noticed, that's different with men and women. Men are very reluctant to accept love. Especially certain kinds of love. Like when being sick, accepting wiping your brow, bringing food, these little things. Sometimes it's easier for women to accept love. A: Hm. That is because of culture, practice. Man dominates. K: I mean, I know why. A: Yes. K: But I guess I'd like them to get over it. A: Very true, very true. K: I'd like us all to get over it. I guess maybe it's because I know in myself that it is in my moments of greatest courage in which I can accept love. That I don't hate myself. A: Hm. K: Because I get pride from being courageous. I've been privileged to have people with me who aren't patronizing. A: Hm. K: I'm not afraid of that.

A: But it is very sensitive. Particularly, to extend that kind of consideration. When you can break that barrier, and make yourself that kind of acceptable. Then even when they accept financial help from you... K: Um, hm. A: Without feeling humiliated. That is possible, but it is very sensitive. I remember once in a seminar in Switzerland. We gave a panel presentation to NGOs, journalists, donors. There this question came up. Don't start by offering money. Then they asked me, But they seem to need money. What shall we do? (Both laugh). K: Good question.

A: I said, No. First they need friendship. Just to connect. What you should do is, first without talking of money at all, forgetting that you have money, tell them, We want to understand you. You came to share experiences with us. And you understand me. What I am. We become friends. Then, if they open up to you, if you can make that happen... At some point you see that they could use some money. You may just say, look, I have some money. If it is of any use to you. I don't want to impose it on you, but it's there. If he says, No, I don't want money, you should respect that. If he says, OK, I can take it but I want to return it, you should accept that. Then it's OK. Or, you may possibly suggest, Look, I have no way to take it back from you. There's no procedure, that is my mandate. Why don't you, after you have used it, if you get it back from the use, give it to somebody else.

K: Cascade. A: Yes, cascade. A: He may find that... K: Quite acceptable. A: Yes. So you work it out with them. Don't push. It's quite possible, if you've been able to break that barrier. K: Again it's the same thing we keep coming back to. It's not a question of the behaviour, not the transaction, not any of these things that is intrinsically a problem. It's an attitude... A: An attitude. Absolutely. K: The attitude of our relating. A: That's true. Patronizing attitude, that humiliates.

K: You were saying the other day how, if I got you right, it is the deepest nature of human beings to be able to experience the feeling of each other. That if I am contented but you're not contented, I'm also not contented, because I can feel that. A: Hm. K: Is that true, do you feel that's a basic quality?

A: Yes, I think that is a basic quality. But every quality exists with its opposite. So, I don't say that this will become, in the end... K: A prevalent quality. A: A prevalent quality for everybody. And if the opposite disappears, I also disappear. Then it is not a quality anymore. There is nothing left in it. It's a good quality because I put it against the other, the opposite. I think that is how life has been created. The opposite will stay. The opposite is also inside me. My ego is also with me. The other thing also is there. I try to bring out the good one, but that doesn't mean that the good will emerge and stay there and rule, ever after. Its opposite will also keep coming.

K: But do you see that it's possible for the balance to change? Say, in one person, for starters. A: Yes, certainly, balance will change, but not necessarily for all times to come. It may again turn. K: You don't think it's possible for a person, on balance, to cultivate that part to be more prominent, more often, than the other. A: Well, with individuals it's easier. We have seen individuals really transform. But for societies, I have not seen any. K: That's a good point. Though I tend to extrapolate from individuals to society. In terms at least of what might be possible.

A: Personally I don't know. It's desirable, possibly. Though whether it's desirable also I don't know. Whether we should all be good, everyone... should just be good.

K: But that raises an interesting question, worthy of debating. My theory at the moment is that people lust after things which are in the end harmful to others partly because something which is a deeper need is being ignored. This is my theory. It seems to me to make sense. Often I see people, I feel out of some inner insecurity, some inner sense of not knowing how to find affection in their life, doing things which are just oriented more toward consuming, having power over people, a lot of things which are sort of surrogate for a deeper way of reaching contentment. When people do finally grasp how to reach that deeper way of finding contentment, the surrogate is less important. So it's not a question of being good, and giving up things, but rather getting something that is more satisfying than what it was that was destructive to have. Am I communicating?

A: Yes, possibly with individuals, this kind of transformation may happen. But I don't think we know enough of even this kind of therapeutic approaches, to handle all the individuals' problems. Individuals come from all kinds of evolutions and experiences of their own. When you say people it's a big word, millions of people. If you're trying to say every individual I can transform... no one knows that. K: Especially if it's in an individual lifetime, because sometimes a lifetime has been so full of cruelty that it's impossible to change. A: Quite so. No psychotherapist will claim that she's been able to cure all her patients.

K: Again I keep thinking of this in the context of time. A: What time means to this, I don't know. Whether the problem stays at a stationary level, then you just apply time to progressively heal it. Those whom you have not been able to heal, at this time. What turns the problems take, you don't know. So it is more than time.

K: And where the waves go. Which wave is rolling faster. I guess the reason I keep asking these questions in the context of time is because to me it's an issue of what is a beneficial strategy, or path. It's partly what's theoretically possible, as well as what works. What is the best thing for the present moment? When it's theoretically impossible, there's no point in working on that in the present either. If it's theoretically possible, it might be appropriate to work on it in the present moment, or it just might not be the right time. That's why I keep thinking, is it possible? If it's not even possible, then just drop it. If it's possible, it's worth thinking about.

A: You know we're discussing philosophy again, not immediately relevant to this editorial work that we're doing. K: I don't know, I think philosophy is very relevant. To the editorial work. A: The way I see it, it is very difficult to claim that it is theoretically possible. You can make your assumptions, and give a tautological theory. K: Yes. That doesn't mean it's provable. A: That doesn't help me. I'm seeing the complexity of it. You can linearize it, make it simple, and say, then why should it not be possible? Well, in your model it is possible. I don't see reality like that. And I don't see the problem remaining stationary. So if it is a matter of one after the other, you apply time. No. The dynamics goes on. You work on some, and transform them. Others don't get transformed. They get even more furious. So you have an extra dimension of the problem. New dimensions coming up. K: Interesting.

A: You know. These guys have changed. They have become good. Oh? If they had not changed, I might have compromised a little. But now by their changing, I feel more insecure. K: Though perhaps their changing will make people feel more secure. A: It may. I'm not saying.

But which direction it will take, the complexity continues. I don't think time will be able to handle that.

K: Let's go back to working within a particular context. I keep coming back to what directions of change will support this whole quality of self-reliance, positive self-reliance perhaps I should call it, from within a country like mine. And from within a country like yours. The sets of questions, sets of actions at one level seem to be different. At another level I'm not so sure they're different. The question in both is, relating self and other, how do we connect?

CHAPTER 11

THE ENVIRONMENT AND DEMOCRATIC PROCESSES: NGO ROLES IN BANGLADESH

Khushi Kabir

I'll try to be provocative here, because after the debate that went on yesterday, we thought that the environment is going to be a topic that will not initiate much debate, or provocation. I'd like to start by saying that there are a lot of issues which are provocative, and need a lot of discussions.

THE ENVIRONMENT AND ECONOMIC DEVELOPMENT: ISSUES AFTER RIO

I want to start talking about the whole question of the environment as it concerns us in the NGO world in terms of development projects. Most of the development projects in Bangladesh are geared towards economic development and economic growth. This is at the cost, which the Asia Society mission report has mentioned, of environmental concerns. This is a debate that is going on within Bangladesh. Two major examples of water and land use will illustrate.

There is the whole question of prawns, which are being cultivated in certain areas of Bangladesh, because it is the third biggest export earner for Bangladesh, and it's bringing in a lot of revenue. There are two different areas of brackish water where black tiger prawns are being cultivated. One is in an area which is an agriculture area, and where people are living and subsisting on very small agricultural farms, and in agriculture. The advent of this cultivation for export is displacing the majority of the people, the sharecroppers, the farmers, and the landless peasants who work on the land, because of the shrimp.

What is also happening, because of the intrusion of the salt water, is that the quality of the soil is deteriorating. You can see top dying of trees, there is deforestation in that area, and it will soon lead to a total environmental concern. For this we will again need lots of money and foreign assistance, and new programs to try and put the balance back again. I think this is something that we need to look at, the question of economics vs. environment, vs. people, and vs. displacement.

There has to be a balance that one has to work out, and see. We are bringing in a lot of money, that is true. We need that finance. But at what cost? We need to do an economic analysis as to how many people are being displaced through these processes. And how many people are going below, falling much below the poverty line, because of the commercial interests of a few people. One has to look into that in this context. I'm not saying that there should not be any cultivation of prawns whatsoever. But one has to look at it in its totality.

There is another issue that was raised many times today and yesterday—the issue of water. Bangladesh is a flat plain. We are criss-crossed by a large network of rivers, some of the largest rivers within the region. These rivers are at the tail end of a huge river system, that traverses through Nepal, parts of China, Tibet, and India, and then comes on to Bangladesh, where it is a delta, and then goes into the sea. It carries with it huge silt, and is extremely fertile. During the monsoons, the flood waters go over the plains, leave behind silt. There's a lot of fish that go through this flooding into the rivers and ponds, and it's a natural cycle. It's ideal for paddy cultivation. Now in the name of increasing food production, and in the name of decreasing disasters and floods, there are plans being made, called the Flood Action Plan, of building embankments on the sides of all the rivers.

What does a farmer have to say to this? What does the woman who lives in the village have to say to this? She needs the flooding. She needs the flooding, she needs the water. Once there are embankments, she now has to start getting dependent on external sources and controlled sources of agriculture. She has to depend on getting water supplied through pumps, and other irrigation systems. She has to depend on getting external seeds, because the seeds that were natural and organic for that land are not being used any longer. You now need a high-yielding variety of seeds, because the whole thing is geared to a different kind of a system. And that is changing the entire pattern.

So yes, it is increasing food production— up to a point, because the International Rice Research Institute (IRRI) in the Philippines is now stating that after having reached a certain target, even with increase of inputs the yields are not maintaining the same levels. This is the report given by IRRI recently. Last year the FAO Regional Office had a seminar and a conference where they stated the same thing. That there is a peak when the production goes high, then after a while it starts tapering off slowly. There are short-term system gains, short term of maybe 15 years, but short term nevertheless in terms of whole centuries of agricultural production. One has to look into that, and see what is needed. Countries like ours are importing pesticides that are banned, or that WHO has claimed as being hazardous.

Environmental groups have been questioning these issues. But what I'm trying to put forward is the need for dialogue and discussion amongst policy makers, amongst people who are supporting projects, people like you among donors, and people like us who are on the ground, as to what kind of development programs need to take place, what affects whom, how it gets affected, and what needs to be done.

Democratic Processes

There are alternatives that we have tried to put forward. As the NGOs in Bangladesh we have not always been critiquing, not giving alternatives. The Bangladesh government had initiated a National Environment Management Action Plan (NEMAP), which I think most governments have to be placing, as part of their mandate after the Rio conference. What Bangladesh did was to make it a very proactive process of participation. We organized 23 grassroots workshops where women, peasants, fishermen, craft people, professionals, elected representatives, and government officials sat together and discussed. What are the major environment issues? What are its causes? How can it be solved? What can we do locally? What do we recommend to the government? That document is now becoming the national, the government's document. It's owned by the government, but it is a process that all of us have been involved in.

The finance of it is one question that keeps coming up. The finance was jointly shared through UNDP giving a large portion, but the NGOs giving their resources in terms of their structures, their facilities, their expertise in running these workshops, these consultative processes. Writing up the document. The government contributed with the publicity campaign through printing of questionnaires, leaflets, radio and television discussions, and so on. We all did it together. Because this was our national document, and we wanted the ownership of it, as people of the country.

That is extremely important. We look at it as a very important step, and an important document, in terms of providing a model for how development processes can take into account participation of the grassroots. The document is here, and it's very clear. It has really strategized many different issues. It has not left out any issues. Water, land, agriculture, population—different environmental issues, what it is, what causes it, who is responsible.

So this is something that we in Bangladesh are putting forward. I just want to add that this is important in the long debate about the whole issue of NGOs, and the role of NGOs. Within Bangladesh I think NGOs are a very vibrant sector. We have to realize that in Bangladesh the NGO sector grew out of a commitment of the people who are now the leaders of the NGO movement, who were active in the liberation movement of Bangladesh in 1971, or who as a result of the liberation movement felt the need to go back to the village and rebuild the wartorn country, especially at the village level. This commitment led to a different kind of situation for the Bangladeshi NGOs, who are looking at the NGO movement, and Bangladesh, as something that we have a stake in, in our country, and we have a role to play, in building up in some way our own country's economy and its policies.

The NGOs are an independent sector. What we discuss all the time, because now NGOs have become a buzzword, donors are always saying that there must be NGO involvement, we say we don't want to be just implementers of projects that you have designed. We are going to be partners, through our contact with the people that we are working with in the grassroots, in designing what the policies should be. In helping you develop your policy. And designing what projects should be. Then we will talk about the implementation of the projects. So it's not just that projects are designed, and then NGOs are searched out, saying, there's this much funding available if you will implement this project for us.

The NGOs in Bangladesh have come together as a cohesive force, and are now being in many ways looked on as a part of the civil society, which previously did not happen That is I think one of the major factors of democracy, and democratic systems. To be able to be open, and much more wide, in listening to views, differences, critiques, and then come out together with what is the best position and solution. For the environment issue, it is extremely crucial that we follow this process. Otherwise, I think the interests are so diverse, that instead of working towards a much better world, we will be at cross-purposes with each other.

ENVIRONMENTAL PRIORITIES AND CONNECTIONS

When I had the topics Environment, Population, and Health in front of me, the first question I asked myself was, Why are the three linked together? I think the three issues are independent and separate issues. And requiring separate attention, each having an importance of its own. They are very vast topics. And extremely important topics.

I don't know whether a rationale for bringing population and environment together, and population and health together, is the concern that overpopulation is one of the main causes of environmental degradation, and that is why population control policies and population control programs are extremely important. This rationale is sometimes used in many projects, programs, and analysis. When it becomes centered towards the whole population program as such, and population becomes the center figure, then everything else is fitting into that whole population concern. And health also follows, in terms of, again the population issue.

While I agree that one has to be concerned about population, I do not believe in a population control-centered analysis of development, or the world, or environment. Many of our reports even put in things like cyclones, floods, global warming, rise of sea level, everything in terms of overpopulation. One has to be clear that that's not one of the reasons. Talking about population as one of the main reasons for environmental degradation is taking away the debate from overconsumption. And away from the kind of ozone layer depletion that has been caused by industrial pollution. I think it's very important that one talks about it in its proper perspective. Not look at it only in terms of overpopulation. And overpopulation only in terms of the Third World, and overpopulation in terms of the poor in the Third World, and Third World women, because that's where the population targets are aimed at.

I won't go very deeply into the whole issue. My focus here is more on the environment aspect of it, and the institutionalization of how solutions can be made. But within Bangladesh, and the NGO community in Bangladesh, there's a great big debate on the whole issue of population. You have those who think that population control is the most important factor, and therefore all kinds of programs should be aimed at that. You have those women's organizations who talk about the need for women to have better, safer contraceptives for themselves, and the need to be able to make decisions. Several merge this with the question, within our own country, of the narrow confines of the land, and the state boundary that we have. What is the best policy for ourselves? But aimed at people, and more people-centered.

Talking about the kind of methodologies that are being introduced into our countries, and the effect it has on women. Looking at it from a woman's point of view. So you have that kind of organization, of which there are many.

You also have other debates with those who don't want to discuss the whole issue without looking at the issue of the politics of population control policies. Because the thrust of most development aid policies is deliberately tied to population control, and particularly targeted towards poor women, where health is only a secondary concern merely to augment population control policies and not looking at women's health needs. So there's a great debate within Bangladesh, within the whole NGO community, on the different aspects and different positions that the women's organizations and other organizations take on the population debate. I just want to state that it is not very uniform, that all organizations do not have a very similar viewpoint, or look at it all totally from only a population control-centered point of view.

Environment, Impoverishment, and Commercial Interests

I also do not agree that the reason for a lot of the deforestation, particularly in the case of Bangladesh, is because of the poor. The whole question is also to do with commercial interests. I think also that has to be clarified. The question of the degradation of the soil and land is also because of commercial interests. When you try to go into new varieties, high-yielding varieties of agriculture, you also need chemical fertilizers, you also need chemical pesticides, you also need a higher way of controlling the water and therefore more irrigation systems and pumps. This leads to total conversion of the land from one kind, the way it was, the natural flood plain. I'm speaking in the context of Bangladesh, because that's what I understand.

The questions and debates on that also are on the whole residue of the chemical fertilizers which is now moving off into the rivers, the ponds, the tanks, which is now affecting the fish population. The construction of embankments which is in many ways stopping the inflow of fish for spawning and breeding, so this is in many ways depleting the fish production, and the fish species, within Bangladesh.

Population Policy and Health Services

The whole question of looking at population services has to be seen in connection with what it is doing in the health sector, and the improvement of the general situation, particularly of women. Bangladesh has been cited as having brought down its population growth rate. I don't want to debate on either the importance or relevance of this issue. But along with the reduction of the population growth rate in Bangladesh from 3.3 in the '70s to 2.1 or 2.2 today, if you look at the mortality rate of women between the ages of 15 and 40 in Bangladesh, you'll find that there are more women dying than men in a similar age group. But at a later age the number of men dying is comparable to the trend in the rest of the world.

The reason I'm putting this forward is because one has to look at the issue also in the context of providing the right kind of safe health services and maternal care, along with responsible family planning services. One has to look not only in terms of numbers and figures, of how we've brought down our population growth rate, but also—which I think the mission report has also, in its summary, mentioned—look at it in terms of how it is affecting women and the health services provided to them.

Yesterday there was a lot of discussion about how improving the status of women, the education, the economic, and the social status of women is one of the main factors for development. I worry that if you only look at population statistics, we may give the whole question of women's status a secondary position to the one it deserves, and the concern for women's empowerment be viewed only as a response to the goal of bringing her fertility down.

Causes and Analysis of Family Planning Policies

The Bangladesh government has looked on family planning as a priority area for a long time. What many of us would critique is that it has given overemphasis on family planning and population control rather than the other social sectors, social disparity, poverty alleviation. The family planning workers are the only government workers who are found operating at the village level. The other departments stop at the thana or block level, which is much higher than the village level. Our critique is the quality of services and the type of methodologies and the message that is being promoted in family planning services, rather than availability of services. But our strongest critique is the inadequacies of all other types of efforts toward meeting basic needs and which are of much more importance to people.

OPPOSITION AND DIALOGUE

The human rights question that has recently centered on the writer and poet Taslima Nasrin has a wider significance than the issue of the individual. Her issue provided conservative groups and politically motivated religious groups an excuse to attack education of women, employment of women, and women's empowerment.

People's Response to Fundamentalist Attacks

There is a growing religious right movement in Bangladesh, as in, not only neighboring countries, but many parts of the world. These movements are built up on slogans. They have attacked a lot of the work that the NGOs have done, particularly because the NGOs have worked with women, and women's empowerment.

Bangladesh has had a lot of models in the NGO sector that other countries in the world are using. The Grameen Bank is the most famous, but there are other different models that are being used by many different organizations. The NGOs in Bangladesh are using popular theater, social mobilization, building peoples' awareness and decision making on issues that affect them. Women's empowerment is a very crucial element in this process.

There are more women coming out, working, women out in the field based and other agriculture sectors. Previously they were working within the confines of the home. Women are out in the workforce everywhere, in the nontraditional sector both in the rural areas and in the urban areas. They have been an easy target for the extreme Muslim fundamentalist groups. There have been attacks on women to deter their new found employment. Trees that were planted by women as a roadside tree planting program were cut down. Economic sources that she could earn money from were being affected. Schools that girls were going to, nonformal, primary education schools, were being burned down. The extremist groups were strategic in their attacks. The better known programmes, or where public mobilization was comparatively weaker, were selected.

But this is because, as we in the NGO sector in Bangladesh have analyzed it, it is because there has been an impact made. Women are coming out. And the anti progress groups are now deciding that it is these women who would take their movement forward, that would move towards progress and towards development, and are therefore a potential resistance factor.

I just want to state that for every attack that has been done on these women's groups, every school is once again running, every program is continuing. People themselves have reacted, and taken up the issue as their own. So for every article that has been published in the papers, there have been 10 more cases where people have resisted, and where the fundamentalists could not make any headway, but which have remained unpublicized.

about, I would like that all people, both the public, people who are concerned and involved in issues, and those who are making policy, the government or elected representatives, learn to understand and engage in a dialogue in a much more open situation. We have to work with our governments in getting the governments to be much more open, and much more understanding. Most governments are at best uncomfortable with this open process. They need to understand that critiquing does not mean that we are against any form of democratic systems. That democracy needs this dialogue. This is true within our own countries and also with Donors and Multilateral Bodies.

To bridge that situation, the vision of a much better world, in a sense it's only a dream, an utopia, and maybe we won't achieve it in our generation, but can we work towards getting people's voices heard? Getting people to talk, getting people to be able to articulate what they need, and what they don't need, instead of having planners sitting in their isolated towers decide for them, what is best. That's what I would most wish to happen.

END NOTE

This chapter has been adapted from my presentation at the South Asia Symposium, The Asia Society, Washington, D.C., September 22-23, 1994.

CHAPTER 12

A THAI COMMUNITY EXPERIENCE IN BIODIVERSITY CONSERVATION: DEFINITIONS FROM THE INSIDE

Penny Levin

Dick: It occurs to me that when practitioners and theorists get together they do little to allow the telling of experience to inform theoretical discussion which would arise from it. In doing this, practitioners would have a chance to articulate theory or tell theorists if they are off base or not.

Penny: That's the primary opportunity you have encouraged us in, through the years—to tell the stories. In a sense it's what this book is about.

A Many-layered Story

Dick, you suggested I start by telling how the Forests for Life project all got connected—the behind the scenes work—and the astonishing clarity of design by villagers and grassroots teachers and researchers at a time when granting organizations couldn't understand or visualize the connections we were making.

Since you asked me to write this I have struggled with how to get the chapter out of the "looking in" context into one of "speaking outward." So part of what follows is direct translations from community members themselves, while other parts are a "telling"— observations from other distances, like the layers of an onion.

Some historical context is also relevent, particularly to shed light on differences in how the picture (or vision) was contextualized by different parties in the process of achieving their desired outcomes. Since what is happening has evolved over several years, and I hope will continue to do so, it's also hard to talk about this as "a project" even-though we ended up with some funding for a specific period of time and accomplished part of the vision.

Part of the experience went on in grant circles, development dialogues, and learning institutions. We became translators for outcomes desired by communities, as well as facilitators and advocates in part of the ongoing educational process within these other circles. I think this is an experience we all share. This always raises questions in my mind too, about when or when not to take this role.

RESOURCE MANAGEMENT ISSUES: THE BACKGROUND

My participation with communities in this work began almost ten years ago when I was a student. My mentor and "uncle," a man with an intense knowledge of the forest, and many of my other teachers from the village felt that southern Thailand had come to a critical juncture in how people envisioned forest use, protection, and management. They were most concerned about the immediate future for other villages faced with the conflicts over resources they had faced more than 30 years ago. And they were greatly saddened by the quality of community which was being lost as forests disappeared and were replaced by rubber plantations, the major crop in the region.

Community Experiences with Monocrop Rubber

Rubber changed people's lives. "You get up at two or three in the morning to cut the rubber. Eat breakfast and send your children to school. Go back to tip the cups of latex, set it, and roll the sheets. By two in the afternoon you are just tired. Your children come home and you just want to sleep."

Very few young families had time for the gardens found around most older households which used to supply all the basic ingredients for curries, the mainstay of southern Thai food. Up until 1994 if a farmer had assistance from the government to plant and care for the rubber, nothing was allowed to grow in the understory after the third year (originally the rule was nothing at all from the beginning of planting). A fine was levied on any trees (useful or not) left standing in the plantation every year until the trees were removed.[1]

Where it rains ten months out of the year, the crop was a terrible recommendation since latex could only be collected three or four months out of the year, but it was endorsed anyway.[2] One NGO group stated "Rubber is not a forest and not sustainable. There is no diversity. Currently less than 40 species of plants are allowed to be planted with rubber. Not less than [350] species from indigenous sources are edible and can be planted among rubber. The cost of rubber plantation to the government is 3,500 million baht over 8 years for 300,000 families [because they do not give us the choice of alternative planting systems for rubber]."

Rubber plantation has also, according to farmers in the region, radically changed the environment. What was little more than ten years ago almost continuous tropical forest the length of the peninsula is now mainly single story, low level, monocrop plantation. The climate is hotter and drier. Rains are erratic and cause far more damage during monsoon seasons without the protection of multi-storied forest cover.

Resource Policy and Structures

Often national level policy or power struggles tie the hands of local level officials and create temporarily insurmountable hurdles, such as jurisdictions over land between departments or contradictions in policy from one agency to another. At one point a neighboring community was allocated "right to livelihood" land certificates under one of the many Land Department programs only to be told by the Forestry Department that the documents were negated by their jurisdiction over the land. This type of conflict at the national level has proven to be a frustrating process for villagers and often in the past resulted in violence and anger.

Land tenure policy also encouraged deforestation and monocrop agriculture practices. In many villages we visited farmers would have liked to have the choice to practice traditional forest gardening and other non-conventional agriculture patterns or leave their land partially forested, but proof of occupation was that you had cleared the land and planted x number of trees per rai of an economic crop suitable for generating taxable revenues. Claimed land which remained forested might also be taken back by the government as part of the forest resource base. Villagers were left with little choice.[3]

Origins of a Community-based Project

What eventually became the Forests for Life project (*Krong gan Bah Peuah Chiwit*) in southern Thailand in 1993 evolved out of the ideas of concerned villagers, grassroots teachers, researchers, and non-profits who were sharing ideas about self-determination, participatory development, indigenous knowledge, environmental conservation, and sustainable agriculture. The project had many faces. Under its funding the project was technically a community based biodiversity conservation project whose premise was that if small scale enterprise depended on the survival of biodiversity this would provide the impetus for villages to protect and conserve the forest. This is the face that belonged far more to the international community.

A second face more closely related to village perspectives was that conventional agriculture, agricultural markets, and land tenure policies held no alternatives for communities in forested areas *even if they wanted to conserve their forests*. Traditional forest agriculture and forest gathering practices and products, however, did provide a number of choices in ecosystem and community health and sustainability.

Villagers stated simply that water levels in their streams had declined radically in the last ten years and the *only* thing which would reverse the trend (and allow them to continue to practice agriculture and their preferred lifestyles at all) was to protect and regenerate the watershed forests. It would be most effective if they were given a major role in designing, carrying out, and monitoring such activities. One non-confrontational way to do that was to *revalue* forest products and forest garden practices, which villagers depended on for a significant amount of food and income and which also maintained an extraordinarily high degree of plant and ecosystem diversity compared to conventional agricultural patterns.

PARTICIPATORY PLANNING FOR RENEWAL AND SUSTAINABILITY

Initially it was important to act as a conduit and web point for many of the early exchanges between those who later became involved in the project. Many "seeds" were planted. We would feel our way, come back and meet with others going through similar experiences, read, listen. There were a lot of shared ideas within the Participatory Development Group network which helped validate what we were learning. The most important source of validation was of course, the villagers themselves—when the words became a graspable presence in the community and an aroma in the kitchen rather than just the spoken word.

As the threads connected and multiplied, village level dialogues took shape. Later, parallel networks of People's Organizations (POs), NGOs and researchers, and eventually some government officials emerged in the larger arena of sustainable agriculture, biodiversity conservation, and genetic resource dialogues occurring disjointedly within Thailand.

In 1989 when we first started to look for grants, funding agencies didn't understand what villagers were trying to accomplish. They asked us "What does agriculture have to do with forest conservation?" They didn't understand the connection between increasing agricultural lands and declining forest lands, or that forest gardens decrease the need for new land because of their multistory nature. Farmers knew monocrop agriculture and agroforestry were destroying the forest ten years ago. It was easily observable. We had watched it happen. Villagers saw it over 30 years ago when rubber started to come to the south as part of economic development packages, even before the macadam roads. The NGOs confirmed it in 1992 along with the Royal Forestry Department (RFD), two years after the 1989 logging concession ban in Thailand. It took donor agencies more than four years to come around to these ideas.

Community, Earth-based Perspectives

Several events affected the course of community-based conservation for the Forests for Life project. The decline of forests due to agricultural development was not just occurring in Thailand but globally as well. That was why at Rio in 1992 the outcome of treaties on biodiversity conservation, forestry, and sustainable agriculture was so important. Governments (and industry) sought to justify tree plantations as "rebuilding forests" and to define biodiversity conservation by the individual components of ecosystems and the plants themselves. Most northern nations, with limiting legalistic notions of ownership and responsibility, and with benefit demands for timber revenues and patents for genetic resources, particularly in the field of pharmaceuticals and industrial agriculture, did not recognize the conflicting time horizons or the ethical questions within and between these objectives. Nor did they challenge the assumptions of current models of renewable resources, selective harvesting, rates of return and discount: a perverse economic language in which the forest *pays* industry a "protection fee" not to cut it down.

That humans might need to define *their* value to the Earth and our own successive generations from the Earth's perspective to justify their own existence in a longer-than-you-or-I-can-imagine-into-the-future time frame was not a position which occurred to the heads of nations. Many individual, NGO, and indigenous voices talked about preserving complete ecosystems and larger tracts of land for the whole connection between people and forests: to maintain the structure, wellbeing, and survival of both.

In the aftermath of the Earth Summit, the Biodiversity Conservation Network was the first grant source we had come across which carried with it a set of ethical guidelines responsible to communities at the grassroots. That was important to us. There were and still are those who were critical of the grant and its origins because of the political climate surrounding biodiversity conservation. Maintaining a standard of ethics came down solely to the individual participants of a given project.

Integrating Local Knowledge and Control: A Public Forum

In 1993 the Thai Forestry Sector Master Plan was also a hot issue for communities in watershed areas of the south. A public forum was held in the south of Thailand in June of that year and a number of villagers attended to hear what the government had in mind, and to tell who they were.

> We aren't just farmers. We have to take care of the forest. We have to do it in all the ways the law will allow us...[the question is will the law allow us?]

> We are not *in situ* conservationists because the government says so but because we live close to the forest. We have said for a long time that '*amnat*' (power) must be defined too. If we don't protect the forest we lose.

> If we don't have this forest, there would be no water, no animals, no forest—we need it to survive. Our conservation projects should arise from this thought, this understanding. The primary factor is that there are still things in [the] forest that villagers need and depend on.

> In my life with the forest all these years a lot has been destroyed [by rubber, by logging, by corruption..]—and we are still poor. What I have lost, how do I know I can get it back? In our village we had a wide, large forest. [Our homes] were not close to each other. In there, more than 1,000 families practiced agriculture. When you came to develop us you split us into three villages, sprayed DDT, built roads... but once RFD came in the forest was lost. This month there was no rain at all—more than one month.

> In the south we are more independent. We are supposed to be democratic. Where is it? The choice for villages who lose out if the price drops in agriculture is to return to forest agriculture and choose food things first.

Farmers voiced their concerns and ideas about how and why forest conservation and management should be grounded in the village. What was said was so clear that it should be included here. (There are similar voices all over the world saying the same things. Part of why we are sharing this book is to give power.) It set the context for village action the following year. There were some far-sighted individuals within the forestry department who understood what was being said and supported community efforts later.

The government misses half the picture. It's not enough to protect 100 percent of the forest. The poor are able to save the forest as well in a way which benefits them too. We don't need to 'bragat kaet' (announce the boundaries) with the forestry department in order to make it 'official' and happen. In our eyes it's already a protected forest. I believe the villagers not only are capable of protection but will be very good at it!

The feeling of ownership is crucial [to us]. If we lease it who will care what condition we return it in? People would just use it up so there is none left for the next [user].

We would like to ask for support *from* the government but *we* will do it. In the future we would like to join with other villages in this effort... [because] we are 'pi nong gan' (siblings).

The government still feels it has to fight with us. They misunderstand us. If I speak too much I will start trouble but I have to ask if there are any RFD/government officials we can sit and talk with [trust]. We must build something new. We can 'nae num' (recommend/introduce them to) forest agriculture and conservation practices and this is a good thing they need to learn.

When the edges of the forest are cut, all near it dies. Forest fruits *have to have* the 'climate' of the inner forest to produce. We [would like to] create community forests for each village... We are asking the provincial authority for [this permission].

One farmer posed a very clear challenge to place and form for reforestation, conservation, and how we view the world in general. Who and what was the government planting trees and protecting forest for? "If you [want to] plant 3 million rai/year, that is easy to accomplish. Try it here first. See if it works. Plant it along rivers, streams. Plant it all. Solve the water problems. Every road, small or large."

He followed with a telling analogy: "A shoe factory sends two people to another country to assess the shoe market. The whole country doesn't wear shoes. They come back and one says, 'Don't make more shoes, they don't wear them.' The other man says, 'Quick make as many shoes as we can, they need shoes!' "

Finally, an open letter to the Master Plan committee regarding community participation in the plan was read by the NGOs stating: (1) The projects didn't fit with environment and community life and needs. (2) PO groups have protected forests for a long time. Give them direct right to continue. (3) The Plan needed real participation from communities. Plan with us not for us, and then expect our approval.

Launching a Life-renewing Effort

The Forests for Life project was very small (approximately 500 families) but affected and connected many more. It was designed entirely from the village (or rather from a history of village voices) as the vision evolved, including indigenous methods for verification of what was going on in the environment wherever we could. The goal of the communities was to gain the right to remain where they were, to earn a livelihood that maintained their definition of quality of life, *and* be recognized by the local government as legitimate caretakers of the watershed area where they lived, but which was soon to be gazetted as a national park. To a great degree this is happening—it is an ongoing process.

By adopting a participatory action and education approach we. set a precedent from the beginning that this would be a learning process rather than strictly a mobilization effort, so that it could be repeated and adapted by other groups. When the actual project got funded, it happened like a strong river—things just flowed. I think this was because there had been so much thought, so many voices from the communities which shaped the design of the project. The things that villagers had provided the understandings for meant that the project sustained those understandings locally and communicated those ideas, viewing the locally ordinary as globally extraordinary, to researchers, donor agencies, and conservation practitioners.[4]

Communities determined early on that they were tired of confrontation; they had been in that a long time and it hadn't gotten them what they had hoped for. This changed the entire approach of how they were thinking about what was going on. The assumption was that "it was possible." The primary questions became "How can we get where we want to be so that it educates and empowers all of us, so that it uses what we have rather than what we don't have, so that we can all contribute to it? What alternatives are there?" As information was gathered they asked "What is it we need to know [to show that this will work]?" and, "How can we document that in a way which validates how we know *and* stands on its own as well documented [so that our own research/knowledge cannot be ignored]?"

Along the way many meetings were held often at night or late in the day, in the backs of kitchens, at caves, along the stream, at the edge of the road or the house that sometimes sold goods like garlic, batteries, candles and soap but wasn't really a store. On survey trips to assess forest health and composition, stream health, and important gathering sites, villagers (men, women, and children), who despite living alongside the forest for ten years or more, were going into the forest for the first time. The very first village level meetings were attended by more than two hundred people and shocked the village headmen so much that once they realized the issue at hand and the level of interest, it galvanized them into action and they became some of the villagers' strongest supporters.

Building Regional Communication by Listening to Their Own Voices

A number of workshops also helped to connect village experience to a larger movement of community-based conservation that was gathering speed in the region. Villagers were interested in what was being achieved, who was and was not involved and what the outcomes were. The workshops provided an opportunity to connect earlier teachers, who traveled more than 350 kilometers to share their experiences, with the new communities. The exchange was electric and while some of their comments surprised people it also served to clarify what needed to be done.

> Nobody thought at the time [the loss of and struggle over forest resources and the right to protect it] would come to this. There are three things which have to happen. You have to have people who are good examples, good leaders in the village. You have to mark the [forest] boundaries clearly. And you can't let the benefits to the community from the forest be severed. If it's going to work it rests with you. You have to teach your children.

> We agreed before about the rules for hunting. We had to agree to arrest our own children if we caught them. Rich or poor you have to arrest them. It's whether they are wrong or not that is important [you have to set the examples].

> But, I have to say for those of us who have no money, some of us have to eat. What do we do [in that situation]? One man in our village has seven children to feed. When we saw how he lived we didn't know what to do. I was the one who wrote the rules and I didn't know what to do.

This is the hard thing. But if we don't everyone else will take liberties. So, we [had to rethink it, if we] needed to help feed a family I would give my own money even if I have to borrow money. We committed to it, [this strengthened the community]...a group of many people can be as one person...

You have to have a peaceful strategy. Use your traditional and cultural knowledge. Think about it. I leave it to you to think about.

The plan developed by communities in the Forests for Life project reflected this wisdom. They strategically questioned, gathered information, selected actions and outcomes which favored the community and the surrounding resource, and enhanced and clarified how they defined themselves and the notion of conservation.

Local forestry officials have been both supportive and excited by what villagers were doing but are often constrained by policy in explicitly supporting village efforts. One commented that he "wished this could happen in every district in the province". For the first time issues of ownership, sharing resources, tenure, conservation and management strategies are being worked out from a positive "what's possible" perspective rather than the typical confrontation format which occurs when government and villagers claim the same resources.

Definitions from the Inside

The communities chose several main objectives: to revitalize traditional forest gardens as the core of how they earned a livelihood and lived alongside the forest; to restore the stream edges as a lifeline between and within their villages; and later, in degraded forest areas [when jurisdictions over degraded lands could be more openly discussed] to define forest use precisely and mark the boundaries of the forest clearly in their own minds as major vehicles for change and interaction.

To understand these activities and objectives it is important to see the why and how of the alternatives they chose—the definitions from the inside.

We have to make sure everyone in the village understands what we are doing and why, what the goal is... Who are the 'nodes' to convince first? Who are the people who may be able to speed up the network? Teachers, wild edible plant buyers, health workers, people who 'kuay gaeng' (are good talkers), those who already buy into it.

We should continue to invite those with knowledge of this and who also see the importance of conservation to come and talk to the village.

We also have to ask ourselves, "Is how we live affecting the forest and our own families?"

Traditional forest gardens reflected a desire to live sustainably with the surrounding forest. In their complexity (the oldest gardens are almost indistinguishable from natural tropical forest to the untrained eye) they also reflected a number of core values which expressed how villagers were thinking about that relationship, about what had been lost and what they wished to restore.

Our generation has to learn all over again what is edible. From 1,000 or more plants in the first generation, the second knows only 300, and the third only 30.

We need to use some artistry. There are two goals here: new enterprise and to convince the unconvinced. We need to make examples of ourselves, especially for the forest garden and wild plant trade. They have to see it too, not just hear it.

We need to choose plants which grow fast as well as slow so in 3-6 months they will see your garden and say wow— see the rapid returns as well as the long term plan.

Other villages were surprised when they found out the villagers from the project were not in their area to visit "the waterfall" but to investigate old forest gardens. The response was a rapid volunteering of tours of each family's "*suan*" (garden) and the growth of a great sense of pride. It dawned on them that they still had something of value. One woman when asked what she would choose if she was forced to choose between a forest garden or a single species plantation for her survival, stated: "Yes, for sure, I would choose the forest garden". This was after she had indicated that the *cash* income from the forest garden she had inherited from her father was less than one quarter that of her rubber and fruit plantation annually. "I get everything from my father's garden."

The gardens expressed self-created opportunity. Villagers' research into garden structure and function and the forest plants which were reaching local markets indicated that each family could shape the composition to favor their own preferences and intuitions.

Each garden became unique and so stepped out of the framework of competition—for space, for market. It prioritized families feeding themselves first rather than chasing cash in order to buy back food. It reconnected and strengthened family, neighbor, community and environmental interaction. It redefined self-sufficiency and inter-dependence, how people sustained community (and included the natural environment in what was meant by community). It reconnected generations. And it educated. You had to think about what worked and didn't, what relationships the plants developed with each other and what relationships developed between the forest garden and individuals, how it carried the past into the future.

The degraded forests which were a result of logging concessions could barely be called forest. They were also the lands which immediately surrounded the villages. The desire to reforest this land hinged upon being able to select locally important (to those in the communities) indigenous species for the recovery process. Forest edge would rebuild itself if left alone but the concession areas would take generations to reforest because they had been too heavily cleared. By focusing mainly on food tree species the villages sought to reduce gathering pressures for non-timber forest products inside old forest in the watershed. This strategy would also reduce the distances people had to travel to collect forest products and would enhance the food resources available to the communities. Questions over jurisdiction arose over the degraded lands and what should be planted (timber species in particular). The same issue arose over marking the boundaries of what was to be protected. So what was to be protected was marked by the communities inside themselves:

> The people are the fence, we don't need to put in posts to mark the border.

> If today I talk about conservation and tomorrow I eat [monkey] who will listen to me?

> If I take a tree and you tell me it's illegal, that's a bad feeling. But if you have a reason I would listen.

> People always say the villagers destroy the forest, no one ever says the villagers care for the forest.

Villagers were clear they did not need to own the land but only wanted the right to restore it in a way which would benefit the local community and the watershed. Yet outside agendas could not be cleared and the issue became too sensitive to pursue. They will wait.

We will reforest the stream and build our forest gardens and they will see that we intend to make this happen. Then perhaps they will allow us to continue.

Restoring the stream was a lifeline as in a "line for saving lives." A lifeline as in the palm of the hand when one's future is read, and their lifeblood. "It is our '*sien leuat*' (the vessels that carry blood)." They read what was happening to the stream and saw that without action it held an impoverished future. The primary reason for their conservation efforts was to save their water resources from further deterioration. This could only be done by protecting the watershed.

Their relationships to the streams, described how closely bound their lives were to the environment. A significant portion of their protein food sources came from streams. It was their bathtub, laundry tub, the swimming hole for their children, the path into the forest, the connection between communities, a primary site for women gathering food, their drinking water, a cooling off spot, a meeting place, and the source for agriculture. The biodiversity of the forest did not exist without the context of water deeply embedded in it.

The idea of reforesting the stream brought the immediate response of *"hen duay hen duay"*—agreement and understanding. Each member of the community who held lands along the streams on either side of the banks would plant trees for their own future needs (food species for home and market, trees that would grow with their children and provide future homes, trees for holding the banks, bamboo for tools, etc.) and as deeply into their lands as possible. For some that meant only a few meters back from the stream edge, for others it meant 10 or 20 meters.

> We will do it with those who want to first. I think it could be as much as 70-80 percent [of us]. Those others will see what we have done when the river edge is thick and green. Maybe they will follow. We don't want to force anyone. If someone can only do a little that's okay.

> We agree that it's for the benefit of each family. We are not planting for the RFD or any other project or anyone else. If I plant trees I want to be sure I will be able to use them and I must be able to replace the ones I use. If I plant trees and use them to build a house [for my children] I have that right (on my own land) and I also have the responsibility to replace them again. We will all help find the trees to plant. This is for us.

I can close my eyes and imagine this—see this vision. The entire length of the river, 15 kms, green and healthy. It will be beautiful...

He leaned back against the house with his eyes closed, and smiled.

There is a point when people cross the threshold between talking about a vision and being in it and owning it—visualizing the possibilities rather than the obstacles.

Concluding Perspectives

Several important perspectives came out of this work which suggest a need to re-evaluate how we approach and define conservation and biodiversity conservation. That we start from a model of poverty instead of richness is to our detriment. Villagers ask, Why allow environmental, social, cultural, mental (monocultures of the mind)[5] poverty to be knowingly created? The south of Thailand is insistent that we should not wait until it is as impoverished and degraded as the northeast before we decide to act. Things are still 'doable' there. Less of the socio-environmental fabric has to be repaired, the threads and patterns are still discernible, and dignity in the practice of traditional gardens is still intact.

It is better to build from what you have and from a respect for each individual contribution. The outcomes mean a great deal to an individual who contributes 40 baht to make something happen when they earn only 100 baht per day. The complete exclusion of access to all forests by the creation of parks and reserves is a political control which can equal ecological and social poverty (especially food and health resources) to people living right in it (villagers). There are better, more inclusive and sustainable ways in which this can occur.

In the context of forest gardens and biodiversity conservation, richness takes on even more depth. Richness of structure, species, food, choices, and alternatives. The health of the forest is directly linked to the community's health and survival. Biodiversity is only one indicator out of many for this. It is only one entrance into issues of conservation, which is only one door into community and environmental well-being and survival. Knowledge surrounding each plant is located in ecosystem—how and where it grows, under what conditions, in relation to what plants. Biodiversity conservation cannot occur without stepping out of the framework of single species conservation (and trying to justify conservation by valuing single species) and stepping into the practice of connectedness.

Returning to traditional agricultural (and that did not mean that what existed in the past was mimicked in the present; it was adapted to context) restored a rich diversity of livelihood practices compared to the monotonous, destructive, impoverished version of livelihood created by conventional agriculture. Rarely does economics contend with the three-dimensional issue of sustaining community and life's diversity. Traditional forest gardens are a restorative practice for the environment and families—reconnective tissue.

One teacher commented: "These are the attempts/efforts from those [below—at the bottom] to create their own plan without getting pressured from above. We [farmers] are looking at a group who are on a beeline. They want to get rich, not just regular rich, but rich fast. This is on a collision course with what's natural, the environment, the earth. This 'line' is not going on forever. It has to turn back on itself."

It's time to bring the compass round.

END NOTES

[1] Dialogues between farmers, NGOs, and researchers, coupled with many years of poor prices and expensive supports for rubber at high cost to the government, have changed this. The government now recognizes the need for mixed plantation for farmer survival and as a way to hedge against the poor price of rubber on the international market.

[2] The loan system for rubber plantation provided support for purchase of seedlings, innoculum and fertilizer over a seven-year period, the length of time a family waited to be able to begin to harvest the latex. These seven years often placed families in poverty. There was no area set aside for other types of agriculture because the farmers were encouraged to clear all their land to plant the rubber. The loss of a diversity of at-home food resources was immediately noticeable. Agriculture extension agents were expected to fill quotas for the number of rai they could get under production of each cash crop to meet national goals and were judged accordingly. Some households for the first time found family members hiring out their labor to make ends meet during the long wait, something considered a last resort in the southern Thai context. The few who were lucky enough to live in or near forested areas and had the skills and knowledge (many did not) had some limited options to return to hunting and gathering food resources and products for sale from the forest.

[3] Not only does land reform policy often contradict forest policy but is also often unrelated to what happens in the field because of other circles of influence. For example, in the early 1970's NS3 land titles were issued to those who openly declared themselves living or holding lands in existing forest reserves, something most villagers could or would not do because of political circumstances at the time. While villagers have been systematically evicted from forest lands because of lack of title, large private landholdings with these "legal" NS3 documents inside deeply forested areas go unquestioned [although not unchallenged] in court even though the lands were acquired under disputable and inappropriate conditions. Without a reconciliation of such contradictions government conservation efforts have little meaning for villagers. The government, at this point, might encourage the return, purchase, or exchange of these lands so that further deterioration of already extremely weak watershed systems does

not occur, yet they continue to fault villagers for forest destruction and illegal logging. Flooding of increasingly rare intact watershed forests for power generation and water storage also indicates a short-term perspective for resource management rather than long-term conservation [making existing systems and system users more efficient].

[4] By this I do not mean that what was happening in village conservation was ordinary. Each village act by the power of what it achieved was extraordinary. In the individualized context of each community, each success was unique. But the way in which these successes were achieved was through traditional social practice and knowledge, commonly understood by some yet seemingly invisible to others.

[5] Vandana Shiva.

CHAPTER 13

LOCALLY BASED, ECOLOGICALLY SOUND, AND SOCIALLY INNOVATIVE DEVELOPMENT: THE CONTRIBUTIONS OF COMMUNITY SUPPORTED AGRICULTURE TO THE GLOBAL DIALOGUE

Arthur Getz

ABSTRACT

This chapter examines the concepts and practices of community supported agriculture—direct partnerships between farmer and consumer groups—as an expression of various food safety, cultural restoration, land-use protection, local economic self-reliance, and other values finding representation in Information Age Eastern and Western societies. These initiatives to develop local support for agriculture are portrayed as a counter-reaction to trends in several geographic contexts toward greater centralized control and globalization of the food system. Attempts are made to identify commonalities and potential links to developing world contexts of diminishing security for small scale agriculture enterprises.

COMMUNITY SUPPORTED AGRICULTURE: INNOVATING LOCALLY, RELATING GLOBALLY

Small farms the world over face tremendous difficulties when they attempt to compete in price-driven wholesale food marketing systems. In developing countries small scale food production is being replaced in many ecological regions by agro-export or other industrial scale farming economies. In developed countries where industrial farming practices and price-driven food marketing systems have been concentrated, entire regions of small farms have been replaced by large farms or other land uses. In all countries and regions, the economies of scale and land conversion for non-agricultural use have made it very difficult or impossible for small scale farms to survive economically.

Marketing cooperatives, farmers' markets, and other direct markets continue to provide outlets for small farmers in many regions. However, the long term prospect for regional agricultures based on a diversity of farm types and scales is not promising, unless social, economic, and organizational innovations are tested and achieved on a wide scale.

Sustainable farming practices such as organic and reduced chemical methods of farming have proven environmental benefits to soil and water resources. Environmentally sound farming is by nature more labor and information management intensive than conventional agrichemically based farming practices and therefore is generally suited to smaller scale farms. A trend in North American, East Asian, and Western European societies has been the increasing acceptance and adoption of ecological practices by many farms both large and small. However, as food grown with such practices enters the conventional food marketing system, small farms increasingly find that they cannot compete with larger farms.

In the face of these constraints, an alternative has evolved known as "community supported agriculture" or "CSA". "Subscription farming" in the United States, and the "teikei" or producer-consumer co-partnerships of Japan are versions of community supported agriculture. They have in common a motif of farmers and consumers entering into a variety of long term formal associations to market food directly. These relationships occasionally extend to joint ownership of land and joint arrangements for farm labor, recreation, education, research, and other agriculturally related endeavors.

Community supported agriculture typically embraces small diversified farming systems and ecologically safe practices. CSAs build long term loyalties between non-farming and farming populations, maintain fair prices for both farmers and consumers, and support fair labor practices.

While great variety exists in the specific shape that a CSA arrangement may take, a central theme is their origin in a community-based response to the need to address environmental, economic, and social needs simultaneously, and to create the conditions of sustainability by weaving together these values with balance, commitment, and flexibility.

Information Paths in Agricultural Production and Consumption

Production and consumption relationships in agriculture can be visualized as a web of economic relationships—strands entwining factors of marketing, credit, technology, distribution, and economy of scale. The predominant modern shape of this web is unlike that of a spiders making. Rather, it is pinched at the middle, and has two lobes like those of an hourglass. On one side are the producers, tending toward larger scales and larger spans between them. On the other lobe are the vertically integrated food transport and distribution systems, sending produce and processed foods to widely distant markets. At the tightly constricted center are massive and powerful decision-making forces: the centralized wholesale systems, the grain traders, the economic planners, agricultural research institutions, and lending support to many of these, the agricultural subsidy systems of national governments.

A diversity of farm sizes within this pattern of relationships appears at first sight to offer no advantage. Smaller farms could only lie at angles of friction with the dominant directions of flow and communication. It is a movement of forces which, without counter-vailing innovations, prevent small farms from appearing productive or efficient. Yet when questions of adaptibility arise, of ability to maneuver and respond to local conditions and preferences, with capabilities for timely and site sensitive planning, the measures of productivity and efficiency appear different.

The challenges to the sustainability of the food system are daunting. Beyond a constant of unpredictability in the weather, they include forecasts of structural climatic change, vulnerability to disease and pest infestation, and looming resource constraints. These will inevitably demand greater flexibility and adaptability in the food web, with corresponding requirements placed upon the information gathering ability, adaptability, and sensitivity of the system. A dynamic tension links soil, water, and fuel resource bases, population pressures, changing dietary patterns, and genetic diversity of food and fiber resources. Rising direct and indirect energy use and environmental costs will require constant attention to the longevity and renewal of the connections in the weavework. Yet growing doubts surround the question of whether large-scaled, corporate-owned and narrowly profit oriented agribusiness concerns will be capable and motivated to anticipate and respond to these challenges with ecologically sensitive planning and location-specific solutions.

It is with their ability to maintain rich information intensity at a human scale, and their power of organizing complex, often competing dimensions in the process of raising food sustainably, that community-based groups demonstrate their capacity to adapt and flourish. Here patterns of community support for small farms can create greater stability by weaving together these elements more tightly and at a greater level of detail, while achieving a variety of reinforcing social welfare goals.

The theme of information distribution and efficiency tempts a stretch of this metaphor of web connection into another analogy. Consider the emerging options in computer processor architecture. On the one hand, the development of increasingly powerful and complex processor chips to manage and control the coordinating functions of a computer. On the other, innovations toward massively parallel computing, wherein functions are divided and distributed widely across a multitude of smaller, simpler computing units to achieve extensive calculations simultaneously, culminating in a solution which might otherwise have required supercomputer power and enormous expense. Still another possible comparison lies at a larger order of magnitude. The forecast in the not too distant past was that we would all be served by centrally maintained and controlled mainframe computers. Instead, we have a proliferation of personal computers which daily transact millions of direct exchanges between both individual and networked microcomputers, to a degree of efficiency and particularity unimaginable as the activity of a single mainframe computer.

Decision Making At the Community Level: The Context for Sustainable Development

During the ongoing process of discussion over how to balance concerns over environment and development, much attention is necessarily drawn to issues of equity and control over resources. This discussion of equity and control often takes the form of national strategy and discussion between countries. Yet of at least equal importance is that this inquiry also entail a steady focus on what options exist at the local level, and what experience can serve to guide planning and action for those who hope to make changes for themselves in their immediate surroundings.

A locally controlled, participatory form of decision making over issues of economic, social, and ecological impact will ultimately be the only way that long term benefit and immediate needs can reach a balance, to an important degree because memory, hope for the future, and shared understanding of limits are our guardians from the "tragedy of the commons." This oft-discussed paradox surrounds the apparent rationality of individuals using the property and resources shared by all with incremental additions of burdensome use that, taken in sum lead to collapse, but seen from a limited individual perspective seem riskworthy in order to maximize individual gain.

There are at least two kinds of "commons." Transboundary phenomena such as ozone depletion, acid rain, greenhouse gases, and broadscale water and air pollution will draw large scale institutional responses and calls to strengthen legal frameworks and regulations related to development and protection of land and water resources, and improved enforcement procedures. But at the ground level, it is the multitude of communities that will have to reach internal agreement on how their commons will be managed, barring some totalitarian eco-cratic order being established, subsuming all local jurisdiction and policing over all of us.

In contrast to the legalistic and regulatory nature of large scale institutional controls, communities have demonstrated their capacity to be adaptive and to do their own environmental problem solving on the basis of covenants and non-legalistic principles. Participants in a community organized to support their local agriculture join in making choices that are at once ecologically sensitized, economically practical, and socially aware, because their structure and their covenants are integrally based upon serving all of these needs and their democratic decision making process is a constant weighing of their internal capacity to adapt to these pressures and choose the best possible balance among them. It may not be too much to assume that managing a locally self-reliant food supply provides an important vehicle for communities to deal with larger issues, including those which have ramifications beyond the food system.

The scope of decisions made in actual practice among CSA groups has exhibited great range and layers of detail. A short list of these reveals the *"beauty of the commons"* that is being expressed among practitioners:

Examples of Assistance and Reduction of Risks to Producers
   - providing compensation to farmers for crops lost in a monsoon;
   - extending material assistance in time of need, from assisting in their construction of a farmhouse burned down, or funds for a driver hurt in an accident during a delivery;
   - balancing convenience with practicality in delivery systems, reducing waste in packaging by recycling boxes and designing efficient distribution by coordinating drop-off zones and teaming of volunteers;
   - collective support on purchases of new equipment for storage or processing;

- coordinating the retrieval of organic resources from municipal leaf collection, local restaurant or home kitchen wastes;
- sharing concerns about production practices such as consumers insisting on chicken manure sourced only from organic henhouses, and making adjustments for the additional burden that might imply.

Additional Decisions Made in Collaboration between Producer and Consumer Partners Extend the Benefits to Members and Non-members Less Fortunate
- sending surplus food to a homeless shelter or community food shelf;
- making public pledges of support during the annual auctioning off of the annual farm budget, while taking into consideration the incomes and expenses of single parent households and others;
- weighing the social consequences of trading with other entities for products that cannot be produced locally;
- or even something as simple as accommodating the temporary transfer of a vacationing shareholder's food share to a potential new member.

Collective Decisions Reflect an Appropriation of Roles Conventionally Left to Others
- the practice of self-monitoring and testing to determine nitrate levels in produce;
- taking part in grassroots political activity, from protesting aerial pesticide spraying campaigns to land use issues such as protection of farmland from golf course development.

The CSA/*teikei* co-partnership experiences provide examples of communities grounded in decision-making processes that relate place to people and people to place—in a shared kinship with nature. They are capacity-building exercises in the mutual relations between producer and consumer with a unique combination of responsibility; directly arising from the matching of the physical cycling of resources to the cycle of decision making and the cycle of finance. They also represent the accumulation of experience and trust in the capacity for a community to act, both in its own interest, and toward goals that serve others, including future generations. The unfolding educational process is both one of learning how to farm ecologically and how to cooperate in a compassionate and trusting direction.

CRISES AND COMMONALITIES SOUTH AND NORTH

As the phenomena of community supported agriculture develop, and more experience is gained among groups in the north, they come to resemble elements of village based societies still remaining in parts of the developing world. The irony is that in the north, these innovations are attempting to recover from the socio-cultural, economic, and ecological hazards of industrial agriculture. In the south, the opposite process is underway. Those remaining community-based agriculture systems that survived the colonial era of plantations and the post-war export-driven agricultural sector development processes are dismantling and being integrated into the cash economy, where a redefinition of aims toward export markets and cash crops—and a de-localization of the food economy—are powerful tendencies.

Southern Food Imperatives

In the south, therefore, support is necessary for creating greater self-reliance in food production at the local level. The dominant thrust in agriculture of cash crop production for export has clearly undermined this important aim, and has led to a concentration of power and wealth that resembles the order in the Northern food system. Indeed the two are tightly linked, as low world market prices make it increasingly difficult for all but the wealthiest and largest agribusiness interests to survive in all regions. As control shifts from the local area, as decision making becomes less governed by concern over long term impact, and as ownership concentrates, so also local means to address the social implications of change tend to disappear. Small scale farmers become entrapped in cycles of debt that are not unfamiliar to their northern counterparts. Often greater hardships are experienced at the hands of local elites charging usurious rates for loans to purchase fertilizer and pesticides, while the cost for chemical inputs continues to increase. Typically the result is the farmers' loss of their lands, and deprivation of their membership in their local community—they may be forced to migrate and attempt to survive in increasingly overcrowded and infrastructurally inadequate urban settings.

Those fortunate enough to be able to remain in their communities see the traditional variety of foods no longer available in the local markets, and cannot communicate their dietary wishes through local markets to farmers who are instead increasingly locked into cropping and pesticide regimes dictated by lenders and processing houses. As the local pallete of food choices dwindles, the biodiversity of traditional cultivars is diminished, and in turn, so is local food culture.

Local needs for new vegetable species and other nutritionally beneficial foods are not adequately met by market information regimes driven by export crop incentives.

Processing facilities collecting produce for export are as wasteful as their northern counterparts. Increasing centralization and control leads to tightening of crop standards, and the refusal of large amounts of fresh product. No longer sellable at promised prices, they are sold at farmers' expense to lower paying canners and processors. The collecting, moving, and storing of huge amounts of food results in situations where post-harvest losses are staggering.

Bridges between Communities and Across Continents

Many of the issues surrounding sustainable agriculture and rural development have stimulated community level groups to connect with regional, national, and international networks in a positive trend toward forming greater consensus for environmentally sound food growing and handling practices, and create some structure of support for local agriculture.

While international pressures toward trade liberalization have succeeded in reinforcing major trade regimes such as the GATT, these have on the other hand mobilized farming and other grassroots organizations in various countries and have drawn them into international dialogues on policy and information exchange. Under the current trade policy climate, many of the regulatory impositions of the Bretton Woods era are being modified, and the lifting of protections and quotas are clearing some markets. Greater quantities of food and fiber products are likely to move on the international trading platforms. Yet what constitute *fair* and *effective* trade practices are still very much under negotiation.

In this context of moving, not static, structures of trade relationships and resource allocations, the possibility emerges of re-writing the premises of food and fiber distribution on a global scale. Much of the critique of the multilateral development banks' approach to rural development, of creating excessive export dependency among developing nations agricultural sectors, is shifting policy emphasis toward greater food self-reliance. While the themes of equity and control over resource access have had little influence on the subject of sustainability in agriculture until recently, there are clear signs that this is not likely to remain a permanent condition.

Within the larger context of international food trade, safe food as a concept is tending to be channeled into market niche development in the northern hemisphere, with southern producers being brought once again into roles that are subservient to northern standards and techniques of production. The pressure to reduce chemical use in the south, while certainly strong from a human health and safety perspective, has more to do with the high costs of artificial inputs, and the growing costs of dislocation of small farming interests and landless laborers, in physical, political and cultural terms.

Northern advocates of farmland preservation, rural cultural revival, wildlife protection, water and other resource conservation have traditionally carried this broader basket of values, in addition to food safety, into their work of restoring sustainable forms of agriculture. They have recently found themselves increasingly edged out of the organic food market while agricultural production and trading enterprises of middle and large scale have arrived to capture and dominate the specialty markets for organic foods where previously they were alone. Some of these are enterprises sourcing organic foods from Latin America, Southeast Asia, and other regions in the south. Farmer organizations and consumer networks in southern hemisphere arenas are witnessing their social justice and land reform goals challenged by commercial trading interests connected to Northern markets, who while promoting cleaner production systems, retain the inequitable patterns of ownership and decision-making of their past.

These gaps across contexts in the north and south are being spanned with the increasing contacts grassroots organizations are experiencing through their participation in policy arenas such as the United Nations Conference on Environment and Development (UNCED), in regional dialogues on sustainability, and through direct exchanges promoted through electronic communications tools such as computer and fax networks. Through these channels, collaborative policy formulation among grassroots, non-governmental groups has taken new turns toward influencing broad development agendas, incorporating participation of local interests as a key fulcrum and measure of sustainability in project design and policy implementation.

Conferences which focus on alternative marketing and production techniques have become more numerous and directed at how to survive in the face of growing pressures toward disassociation of place and products. Participation has expanded to include a variety of new interests. Among these are food professionals from the hotel and restaurant industry, with interest in the re-regionalization of diet and the promotion of regional cuisine. These food service groups have taken interest in patterns of coordinated production between local farmers and consumers, and have brought local chefs and food buyers into the constellation. Additional experimentation is leading toward institutional buying and cooperative arrangments between public schools, hospitals, prisons, and the local farming community.

Among innovative regional initiatives to build capacity for farmer and grassroot community participation in the south-north dialogue is coordination in the southern cone of the Americas in developing a locally-based policy and research framework for ecological/sustainable agriculture. A two-focus work plan is underway: (1) to encourage development of community based indicators of social, environmental, and economic sustainability on a region-by-region and country-by-country basis; and (2) to encourage elaboration of principles, practices, and case studies of fair trade in agricultural products on local, country, regional, and international levels.

This initiative, and international conferences that will communicate progress on these issues in 1995, build on the wisdom of shifting toward biologically based, information rich, locally and ecologically focused farming practices and community support.

CENTRAL QUALITIES OF COMMUNITY SUPPORTED AGRICULTURE

Community supported agriculture has been the most sought after topic at major alternative farm conferences around the United States in the recent past. Yet it is not without an initial frustration that new farmers coming in, seeking to understand how they work, find that there is a lack of recipes or "cookie cutter formulas." Every group turns out to be different. Yet this diversity can be seen as a necessary quality of community based responses to local problems and opportunities, particularly when comparisons of these responses reach across geographic and cultural boundaries. Some prior examination of the contexts giving birth to the CSA phenomenon may provide a basis for extracting common attributes and identifying implications for their evolution elsewhere.

Community Support Structures in Asia: Japan's Experience

The post-World War II era in Japan has often been noted for how Japanese citizens have responded creatively to the conditions prevailing in their changing culture. Out of their postwar experiences of agricultural land reform emerged a relatively stable form of rural development which maintained large rural populations dispersed widely as small scale farming households. Production was coordinated by a highly centralized agricultural system of bureaucratic controls, a hierarchy of farmer's unions, and a tightly knit distribution system.

Accompanying Japan's rapid industrial growth was a parallel mechanization of agriculture, which enabled large numbers of farmers to devote less time to farming and be capable of filling on demand the growing but erratic labor needs of industry. This was achieved through reliance upon increasing application of off-farm inputs, ranging from capitalization incentives for machinery and infrastructure to pesticides and chemical fertilizers. Still insufficient to meet the changing dietary requirements of the rapidly industrializing nation, the volume and ratio of imports steadily rose to fill the gap in the food production and consumption system.

This body of expanding economic activity began to develop scars with incidents of industrial poisonings and urban air pollution. Place names like Minamata became imbedded in the national and international conscience as warnings of the exclusive focus on industrial development and the excesses of profit-seeking over health and safety. These episodes have their lesser known parallels in the Japanese food system's experiences with pesticide poisonings.

Both trends bred mistrust of government claims to safety. In the absence of an alternative food marketing system, and lacking a tradition of public interest consumer activism which could generate the political pressure to demand one, a housewife-based grassroots movement formed in search of a safe food supply. The result has been the creation of consumers' own locally based direct distribution systems, ranging widely in both in character and size. Some have taken the form of buyers clubs and cooperatives, and have grown large enough to amass collective buying power capable of shaping product lines in the household products industry for items such as soaps, oils, and laundry detergents. Some have taken a further step, and connected the consumer to the producer directly, in a co-partnership relationship known in Japanese as 'teikei'.

Teikei Co-partnerships in Japan: The Wakabakai Group in Tokyo

One such example lies near the heart of Tokyo, and links 14 farmer households to 400 consumer households. In the Setagaya Ward, not far from the Tama river, the Ohira family farm serves as the distribution and information hub for the group. The Ohira farm doubles as both a place where produce is brought in from outlying farms and sorted into shipments for groups of urban households, as well as functioning as the focal center of community-making, a meeting place for members to regularly discuss, reach compromises, and share in the results.

Wakabakai, as the group is known, formed after one farmer, Mr. Ohira, made the difficult decision to abandon the use of chemicals because of chronic illness in his family stemming from the use of agricultural chemicals. His ensuing struggle to develop a safer form of cultivation based on composting and other traditional techniques was rewarded by local housewives who appreciated the freshness and superior taste of his produce.

As more local residents, particularly young mothers, discovered this farmer's commitment to safer food production, they sought to create a permanent relationship with the farm. As numbers grew, their needs expanded to encompass more farming land and farmers. Their trust in the direct knowledge of the farmer and his methods led them to seek similar relationships with farmers who lived elsewhere, so they invented a social solution which would build this familiarity.

The central importance of creating the opportunity for farmers and consumers to meet regularly face to face is often emphasized. Over time, the developing personal relationships and trust form the basis for managing the complexity of sustaining both fertile soils and souls. Over their 20 year experience, families have worked and celebrated together in a marriage of personal concerns for safety and commitment to principles of mutual assistance, and have shared the risks and benefits inherent in ecologically-oriented farming.

The European Context: Common Agricultural Policy and the Unsettling of Rural Community

The European context bears some resemblance to the Japanese, in that the pressures of industrialization have had their impact on the environment and have decisively affected agriculture in particular. A diversity of farm sizes distinguishes Europe from those of the mountainous Japanese archipelago, however, where all farms are small and the protection of agriculture is synonymous with protecting small farms. Geological history has endowed regions of Europe with wider plains and fertile valleys with long, slow moving rivers, as well as high mountainous terrain. Farm scale varies accordingly.

The postwar burst in industrialization of European agriculture has meant considerable dismantling of the small farm landscape. Larger scaled and specialized monocrop production has taken root in particular regions, connected by rail and trucking transport systems which must stretch considerable distances to supply the necessary variety of food to large urban centers. Accompanying these dramatic changes in the visual landscape, the adoption of chemically intensive and mechanized production techniques has resulted in a variety of environmental ills, including tremendous soil loss and a nitrogen fertilizer pollution problem with general surface and groundwater concentrations unmatched in the industrialized world.

Popular reaction to the growing evidence of damage these changes were bringing has taken a variety of forms. Some have included personal changes of lifestyle, and public health related concerns over safe water, food, and the adequacy of physical exercise and open space. Political parties have formed to advance ecological goals, and achieved legislative responses to broad based political campaigns in defense of the environment.

The relatively greater mobility and availability of space in European society enabled a small portion of the population to reconsider their choices of work and domicile, and relocate in rural areas, at times in numbers large enough as to constitute a 'back to the land' movement. France, Germany, and the British Isles all experienced a degree of these changes together with a revival and deepening interest in rural culture, local self-sufficiency, and the protection of the natural environment.

Land and other costs in Europe have been too high relative to incomes gained from agriculture for most newcomers. While rural farming classes have been able to demonstrate sufficient power to maintain public subsidies under the Common Agriculture Policy, this has come under considerable internal and external pressure for change, particularly with economic unification and the General Agreement on Tariffs and Trade (GATT) trend toward liberalization of trade barriers. A clear possibility with the trend toward rationalizing production is that those farming in marginal areas will be unable to compete with those fortunate enough to be producing in areas of higher fertility, transport access, and other resource endowments.

Mounting public consensus on needing to clean up agriculture's impact on the environment has produced support for subsidizing the reduced use of chemical fertilizer inputs and has stimulated the expansion of research in biological means of improving productivity.

A marketplace solution to the supply of certified organic foods has been developing in advance of these policy trends over the past decade, with the lead in creating a private, nonprofit certification system being taken by IFOAM, the International Federation of Organic Agriculture Movements. At the outset a primarily European organization, IFOAM evolved out of a concern that the heterogeneous and factional alternative food producing scene would need to unify standards and support research collectively in order to advance the cause of a reliable and credibly safe food system.

Yet some of this factionalism has persisted. This has complicated consumer choices as to what is being offered by competing labels which claim to be organic. While these differences may become resolved by the forging of an European Community wide standard, competition has intensified between organic producers. It is not clear that the smaller producers, particularly those farming in areas of marginal productivity, will be able to survive.

The absence of social justice and ethical concerns within the core definitions of existing organic labeling schemes has prompted an evolution of systems aimed at deeper philosophical concerns. Areas gaining attention include priority assigned to food adequacy, security and nutrition especially for children and women, third world equity issues, social welfare, work place democracy, and animal rights. These criteria act as screens filtering consumption decisions and have led to the emergence of an ethical consumer movement which seeks to co-ordinate the evaluation of products and disseminate this information through subscriber networks and periodicals aimed at the consumer public.

Wirtschaftgemainschaft: Community Supported Agriculture in Germany

At the community level, efforts motivated by deeply philosophi-cal beliefs encompassing environmental, social justice, and animal welfare concerns have taken the form of creating direct support for farms and farmers. One example comes from Buschberghof in the north of Germany, not far from Hamburg. With the stated goals of seeking "to eliminate personal profit as the principal motive behind the farm and to use the land instead as a healthy base for people, animals and plants," this farming community embarked on its path.

The Buschberghof farm was established under a charitable land trust named *Landbauforschungsgesellschaft*, which owns the farm, its capital equipment, and livestock. With a core of three families, a second layer association, *Arbeitsgemainschaft*, was created to give farmers management responsibilities and the ability to choose their successors. Free from having to buy the land or pay any costs beyond property maintenance for using its resources, the families could begin by devoting their attention to restoring the fertility of the land and harvesting healthful foods.

The initial marketing of the farm's produce combined direct sales through a store, delivery by truck to individual homes, and sales to a wholesale outlet. In the last six years, the organization has evolved to distribute the responsibility of supporting the overall operation of the farm among its friends and customers. The 80 participating house-holds are clustered into nine distinct areas. Each area sends at least one representative to a regular monthly meeting to communicate needs, problems, and new ideas.

This is the third layer of association which members regard as the "*Wirtschaftgemainshaft*" or "extended farm community." This embraces the concept of the farm operating in all its functions as a farm organism and striving to support the whole of its activity by equitably sharing the cost. Each member contributes in accordance with their ability to pay or in some cases provide services to the farm. Collectively the membership gathers funds to meet an annual budget which has been drawn up by a core of farm members.

Like several farms inspired by the Camphill farm in England, Buschberghof's residents also include several who are mentally handicapped. The farm's broader social responsibilities include this function as a healing center, a place of meaningful and therapeutic work and recreation for participants of varying ability, age, and background.

In addition to this innovative social experience, the specific educational function of training interns in the techniques of biodynamic farming is served by the Buschberghof experiment. These interns have membership in the group, provide their labor in the farm operations, and are provided lodging and meals.

A number of other approaches to community supported agriculture have taken root in Europe, with the most apparent variety and experience originating in Swiss urban-rural partnerships in Basel, Zurich, Geneva and in Vaduz, Liechtenstein. In England as well, the CSA concept is being promoted by organizations of ecological farmers, as well as environmental groups.

The Postwar Era in the United States: Get Big or Get Out

What can be said of European availability of space and mobility needs to be expanded to sketch out the American background to the appearance of community supported agriculture. The nation's population has since the second world war distributed itself relatively evenly across the continent, moving in large numbers from rural areas and concentrating in a few megalopolises and a greater number of medium sized urban centers and surrounding "metropolitan areas." It is in the latter category that large areas of land have been consumed under the lawns, shopping malls, and pavement of suburban development.

A consequence of this movement, indeed the cause and effect of this migration, was an industrialization of agriculture which has created the greatest concentration of farmer numbers over the widest area in human history. Fewer than 2 percent of the US population can be described as farmers. An average farm size of over 600 acres conceals the actual trend of polarization toward larger, corporate-owned farms of the several thousand acre variety, and micro-farms with fewer than 25 acres. The mid-sized American farm has disappeared with the families that made them their livelihood leaving to fill the newly defined hybrid of rural and urban parentage: the American Suburb.

In tandem with this process of polarizing farm scales and suburban expansion into rural areas came the rise of land prices at the outer lying edges of metropolitan areas. This placed increasing pressure on diversified small scale agriculture in regions where terrain and tradition had established this pattern. It left regions such as the New England region of the northeastern United States unable to compete economically with the large scale monocrop farming operations typical of the central plains and western states.

Beginning with public subsidy for construction funding and continuing as subsidy for agricultural water use, massive irrigation schemes in the arid Southwest have been the undoing of other regional diversified agricultures. Massive transport and distribution chains operate coast-to-coast and rely on high fossil fuel, highway infrastructure, and other rates of inputs of questionable sustainability to link this region, where conditions permit year-round cropping of fruits and vegetables and migrant labor availability is high, to the rest of the country. Together with longstanding U.S. Department of Agriculture policy bias towards high input broadscale agricultural production systems, the infrastructure building, research agenda and extension efforts over the postwar period have been unfavorable to small scale diversified farming. The unofficial policy line was Get Big, or Get Out.

Not to be lost in obscurity, the New England region has also been the scene of rising community-based environmental activism, including resistance to nuclear power plant construction, protests over hazardous waste dumping, and the acid rain destruction of forest and lakes. Farmland preservation efforts, "Buy Local Products" campaigns, historic preservation trusts, and nature conservation groups have been born here. It may not a coincidence that New England currently also enjoys the greatest concentration of community supported agriculture groups.

Over the last two decades concern over health and food safety has led many Americans to make changes in their diets and place greater attention on food ingredient labeling. By consuming lower levels of fats and a greater number of fresh fruits and vegetables, consumers felt they were eating healthier, safer meals. Consumer demand led to the proliferation of small health food stores and food buying cooperatives which provided bulk foods, vitamins, and information about nutrition. Eventually mainstream supermarkets adopted an approach toward labeling and packaging which emphasized "natural," "high-fiber," or "reduced sugar" in order to recapture markets being lost to these smaller operations.

Events such as the 1989 release of reports on Alar residues on apples and proportionately greater exposure risks to schoolchildren consuming fruits and juices led to a greater concern not just over food categories and level of processing, but more specifically over chemical residues and production practices.

The ensuing boom in interest in organically produced food led to many retail and wholesale buyers providing products which could not always be certified as organic, until standards at the national level could define what organic meant and who would decide the details. These came in 1990 with the Organic Foods Act, which by 1994 provides for a definition and a National Organic Standards Board composed of representatives from consumer, environmental, organic farmer, processor, and retailer interests.

CSA comes to the USA

It has been only in the last eight years that CSA as a concept has taken hold in the USA. Most of the 500 or more groups have formed within the past five years, a period which has witnessed the availability of organic foods through more conventional channels steadily increase. Obviously if it were just for safe food, community support would not be needed or sought after for agriculture.

In this light, the Temple-Wilton Community farm can be seen as an American example of the upwelling desire to restore a spirit of community, in reaction to the haphazard development and anonymity in the landscape. It is also a turning away from the mode of relationship where legalistic and contractual forms predominate, where the "strictly business," "bottom line" mentality has dominated in recent times. Members speak of the farm being formed to "provide the opportunity to donate labor," and to remove land from speculation.

Temple-Wilton is actually a combination of two southern New Hampshire properties, one being a parcel under a land trust, and the other privately owned and loaned to the community for use along the principles that the 75 member households have chosen to guide their actions. The farms have been a magnet for social experiment and are the scene of considerable vitality and participation. Farm tours regularly attract local schoolchildren, while community celebrations of harvest and other festivals combine music and discussion, and inspire the making of handicrafts.

The operating costs of the farm are entirely supported by pledges from its members, in an annual ritual where the budget is "auctioned" through an open process. Contained within this budget is an estimate of what it would cost to support the farmers in the group, an element that many CSA groups point to in order to distinguish their approach to the food system.

Some Concluding Comparisons: Community Supported Agriculture in a Cross-cultural Perspective

Resistance among farmers to cut back their use of chemicals and adopt more organic farming methods often stems from the disbelief that there are consumers willing to pay sufficient prices for food which, while free from harmful chemicals, doesn't always look as picture perfect as the conventional marketing standards have contrived. Equally rare are consumers who believe they can find farmers still willing to commit themselves to full time farming and who will keep honest and responsible care of food they grow for others.

Yet it is in the example of the Japanese *teikei* groups that credibility is built for both producers' and consumers' concerns. They have created the opening for a simple and powerful idea of mutual adoption to take root. In each of the co-partnership groups, annual meetings between all concerned are held to decide which crops to plant, the price to be paid, and how to the divide the responsibility for distribution. The certainty of demand from the farmers' perspective enables them to plan, and gain a fair price for their produce, while the certainty of supply assures the consumers of the safety of the source of what they are consuming, and provides food at a reasonable and stable price. What nature does or doesn't produce one season is a boon or a burden shared by both partners, because an essential quality of the long term relationship is that it creates the certainty that over time this will reach a balance.

Many of these qualities apply to other forms of community supported agriculture elsewhere. Yet two features still seem to be unique to the Japanese experience. One is the diversity of co-partnership scale, ranging from single farm household relationships with a dozen consumer households, to an entire farming village's arrangement with a thousand consumer families. The second is that their growth has been fostered by a national umbrella organization, the Japan Organic Agriculture Association (Yukinogyo Kenkyukai). The Association links the 10,000 plus membership in groups from throughout the Japanese archipelago through a monthly journal, regular regional meetings, and an annual voting general assembly.

In the Western examples of Wilton and Buschberghof, distinguishing elements are the degree of commitment to the farms themselves, the inter-penetration of responsibilities, and the intensity and scope of the social contracts surrounding the farmers and the shareholders.

In both of these examples, they are attempting with their support to share the risk of farming across all of the families that are fed and fostered by the community farm, and to ensure that a fair livelihood can be gained by those who are entrusted with the focal task of farming the land. While labor is donated by many of the members during the year, there are several individuals for whom this must be a full time effort. It is in the valuing of their skills and devotion to this that the community strives to meet their needs.

At the Wilton farm, in the process of auctioning the budget it is common that the target is not met in the first round. The shortfall is auctioned again. In successive rounds after budget scrutiny and revision, those with higher incomes and other means to provide further support eventually come forward and pledge the additional amount. In these respects, in sharing the risk of running the farm, in striving to find a way to support all costs including a fair wage for the farmers, and in equitably and voluntarily dividing those costs, the exchange clearly means more than safe food. Compassion and a sense of fairness fill the process.

What meets at moments like these, and throughout the functioning experiment of community support for a farm, are the balancing of elements and the making of choices in weaving together economic, environmental, and social values. The process in action is a loom for authentic expressions of commitment, a practicing of equitable compromise and mutual support, a willingness to share in the risks and benefits in a system that strives to understand and enhance its relationship within the farm ecology and the eco-region. As patterns emerge from this loom, they represent a progressive refinement of management and technical considerations toward these goals, and a democratic process of learning how this is accomplished.

CHAPTER 14

SUSTENANCE AND SUSTAINABILITY: SOME VALUES AND PRINCIPLES UNDERLYING SOCIALLY-JUST, SUSTAINABLE DEVELOPMENT

Kersten L. Johnson

Sustainability... and Sustenance

Sustainability is life in balance. The inner and the outer, the ebb and the flow, the giving and the taking. It is not a static thing, unchanging or stagnant. A sustainable future is, at its best, life filled with vibrancy and renewal, growing in ways that create and deepen meaning and satisfaction, while opening the way for expressing the creative drama of the human spirit.

Sustainability is built on renewal: physical and environmental, social and spiritual.

It grows from integrity of relationship; connectedness—personal, and interpersonal—nurtured and sustained by a living relationship with the land.

It is built upon community: of place and of heart.

It is maintained by reciprocity, rooted in a deep sense of justice.

Sustainability has many facets. But ever at the core is a sense of renewal, fulfillment—sustenance. *Sustenance* refers in part to physical means of survival, to that which keeps our bodies whole and well. But the concept of sustenance also alludes to deeper forms of nourishment: succor for our inner well-being, draughts to quench inner thirst. Sustenance is food; food also for the human spirit. Without attending to our deeper needs as human beings, I believe that our reckless drives toward producing and consuming more and more will never be gentled. And without taming these drives, we have no hope of attaining lives of true balance and renewability, environmentally or socially.

A Matter of Balance: Connection, Reciprocity, Renewal

Sustainability, at heart, is much more than a physical concern. It is an expression of balance and renewal, within and without. But what could such a "balanced" society look like? What qualities might be expressed in a deeply renewing, sustainable society?

In this paper, I have drawn a simple composite—a floral design of values and principles that may underlie social and environmental renewability. The images are drawn from experiments in community renewal all over the globe, gleaned from over ten years of observation and involvement with movements relating to community-based participatory development. Still, this picture does not represent any one movement, or any one group. Virtually every effort I have observed toward social change and environmental renewal has exhibited only a few of the characteristics drawn in this picture. But together, the images add up to a certain kind of symphony: themes and variations that, taken together, may dance society toward balance.

This picture of sustainability is a paradigm that turns the classic "hierarchy of needs" on its head—or, more appropriately, curled up on its side. For I believe that our needs for sustenance, physical, social and spiritual, exist on a circle; we must constantly attend to all of these facets of our being. We can not wait to reach "completeness" in one area before we can touch upon the next; even those who are hungry feel some comfort from loving compassion. And those whose bellies are full continue to ache with emptiness unless their "deeper" human needs are also met.

On the following pages are sketched six clusters of values and principles which I believe to be at the heart of a sustainable future. They represent both goals and doorways—moments of inspiration and energy that describe some facets of balance which might drive and describe a sustainable future.

Many of the points in each cluster are inter-related, and themes repeat. Several fundamental themes are woven throughout:

- Getting what we need physically for basic health and comfort—without "excessive" consumption—and within the limits of being able to renew that which is consumed;
- Feeding our non-material needs for inner harmony; needs such as contribution, connection, integrity, compassionate relationship, personal dignity, and creative expression;

• Living in mutually-nurturing "webs" of reciprocal relationship (especially reflected under the clusters of *sustaining community*,
and *environmental kinship*);

• Maintaining a devotion to social justice, in both material
(economic) realms and in terms of social relationships and political
power;

• Attending to the impacts of our choices on the "seventh
generation" of our children.

Figure 1, *Overview: Partnership in a Sustenance Society*, presents
an overview of the six clusters of values and principles. Each cluster
represents a different entry point or gateway to a life process which
is deeply self-renewing, internally and externally. For any individual,
one point of entry will seem more natural, more compelling than
another; it really doesn't matter where one begins. Being of Western
origin I often begin with self, looking within for personal balance, and
then alternate among the other centering points. Others might be
more drawn to begin this exploration from interconnection—*sustaining
community*—or from points of action, relating to the external through
economy or environment. Creative, artistic, intuitive minds might
start from self-expression—*creative diversity*—while others are focused
on their passion to bring society into balance through issues of justice.

Wherever one might start, these clusters represent strong points
of impulse or identity which provide motivations for action and profound change. The descriptions can be approached in any order, and
build from one to the next through many diverse paths. As presently
mapped, they appear as follows:

Figure 1) Overview: Partnership in a Sustenance Society;
Sustaining values and principles
Figure 2) Personal Balance
Figure 3) Sustaining Community
Figure 4) Environmental Kinship
Figure 5) Creative Diversity
Figure 6) Deep Justice
Figure 7) Humane Economy

PERSONAL BALANCE—FINDING HARMONY WITHIN

Sustaining our inner life—the dramatic, dynamic boundary of
self—is an ongoing process of centering, healing, and building reflective awareness. The point of inner stillness is a place of personal
refuge. Yet it is also the place from which pulses of creative action
burst forth, and from which we can reach out with strength toward
others, to build mutually supportive connections.

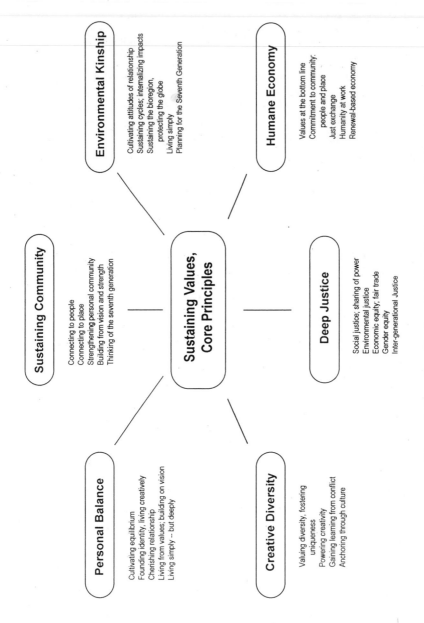

Figure 1. Overview: Partnership[1] in a Sustenance Society

For many decades, a predominant development model has enjoyed popularity—"Maslow's hierarchy of needs"—which maintains that people address various levels of basic human needs in a ladder-like fashion, focusing first on such needs as physical sustenance, security, and health. Emotional needs such as those for connectedness and love come later, and only once such needs are met does the individual proceed to "self-actualization," to develop higher levels of creative personal expression and integration. Yet there are many life experiences which run counter to this conventional theory. It often seems as though our many levels of sustenance are addressed in rhythmic, flowing cycles, sometimes even simultaneously.

To find balance within, perhaps we must at last learn to recognize, respect, and respond to our own deeper needs: our needs to make a contribution; our needs to feel connected, safe, and secure; to know that our lives are worthwhile; that our dreams are not without merit. Our needs to be creative, and to feel appreciated, and to give our love to others. We must address these needs in ways that truly fulfill us, finding an inner balance that allows our lives to move forward from a sense of deep, creative well-being. This type of well-being can lead us back to our inner wellsprings of passionate creativity.

There are many starting points in this dance of personal balance. Figure 2 describes some notions that underlie this balance:

- **Cultivating equilibrium**. Finding our intuitive inner points of balance and clear, reflective awareness. Healing, in body and mind.
- **Forging identity, living creatively**. Becoming aware of that which defines who we are, involving our personal connections to place, culture, history, and our immediate society. Learning to act from our sense of shared identity in a way that also reflects the deep impulses of our uniqueness.
- **Cherishing relationship**. Nurturing our many interconnections; weaving strong the threads that link us, one to another. Discovering sympathetic joy.
- **Living from values, building on vision**. Building clarity about our own life-sustaining values, living lives that reflect and express those values, and taking actions which allow the positive impacts of our choices to ripple through time, moving society step-by-step toward our long-term visions of a sustainable world.
- **Living simply, but deeply**. Learning the gentle, powerful art of voluntary simplicity.

Neglecting to nurture our own inner life can have profound negative consequences—not only upon ourselves, but for the world.

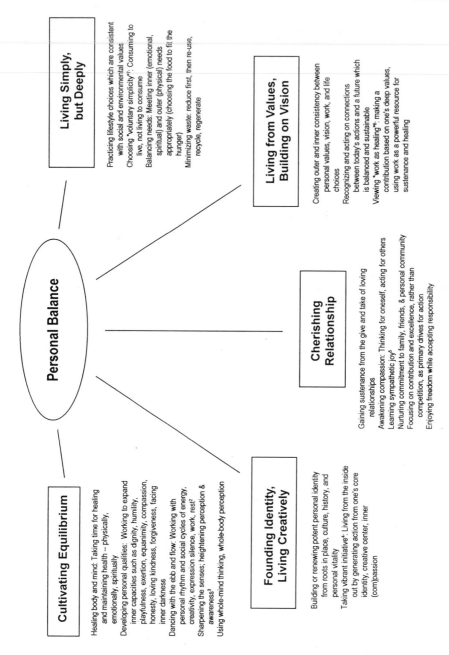

Figure 2. Some Principles of Personal Balance

Habitual starvation from inner sustenance may lead us to look outside ourselves, unsuccessfully, for fulfillment. The concept of "enoughness" then seems like a foreign notion, beyond our reach, because we are consuming not only to satisfy our natural physical appetites, but to fill an inner emptiness. This may distract us temporarily from our pain. But ultimately, I believe it is the unfilled heart which craves unceasingly for more: more comfort, more thrills, more flash, sparkle, speed. When we try to feed our deeper longings by purely physical means it is not surprising that our wants then seem insatiable. Even in the midst of abundance there is a nagging sense that something is missing—an emptiness that echoes hollowly within even while our bellies are full and our bodies safe and warm.

In this connection it is worth looking again at the story told by Anisur Rahman in Chapter 6, of his work in disaster relief in Bangladesh during several episodes of catastrophic flooding. At such times he would gather a group of his students and whatever food, medicine, and supplies they could collect, and travel by boat deep into regions untouched by governmental relief efforts. Although they brought as many supplies as possible, their resources were always but the tiniest fraction of the most urgent needs in the villages they encountered. When the villagers first saw the boats, they would rush to the riverside, jostling and clambering for prime positions, and pleading for aid. But Anis would stop them, and say, "The resources we can offer are but little compared to your great need. We can see that you are suffering intensely, but are there not some in your village with an even greater need? Seeing how little we have to give you, how would you decide to distribute what we have brought?" In much dismay, those at the riverbanks would argue for a while, disappointed that so little was available to relieve their immense pain. But in each village, a resolution would be reached, and they would eventually step forward and say something like, "Yes, you are right. There are some within the village who are not even present here, for they are too sick to walk. And over the hill lives a girl who cannot leave her home, for lack of even a sari to cover her. We will bring your gifts to them. It is a blessing that you have come."

Anis found that even those in the immediate agony of extreme crisis were quick to orient themselves to the needs of the worst among them. This experience is dramatic and in some ways unique, occurring during a time of intense physical distress. Sometimes the best in people emerges during times of crisis. But there are many variations on experiences such as these, which serve to remind us that the human spirit somehow weighs choices on a very different scale than a simple prioritizing of personal physical needs over our commitment to others. We often place self before others, it is true. But it is also true that expressions of loving compassion—even when it appears that we are giving up something that is valuable to us—fulfill a profound and fundamental human drive. This drive is indeed so basic to our identity as human beings that we can give it priority even when our very lives are at risk.

The quest for inner balance must acknowledge and respect impulses such as these, as well as our purely personal drives for satisfaction. We may start from anywhere, but working with focus and consistency toward personal balance may re-create our lives around healing and wholeness, toward lives which alternate action and re-flection, solitude and social connection, giving out and taking in. And our personal balance, in turn, may help to create a life-sustaining way of being, for both self and society... from the inside out.

SUSTAINING COMMUNITY—BUILDING RENEWAL FROM CONNECTION

Related to the ecology of our inner life is our network of connec-tions and core relationships with others. At heart, we may be alone, but our connections with others sustain us—and in turn, sustain those with whom we are connected.

In one of his poems, Robert Frost compares a person with a "Silken Tent:"

And its supporting central cedar pole
that is its pinnacle to heavenward
and signifies the sureness of the soul
though strictly held by none is loosely bound
by countless silken ties of love and thought
to everything on earth, the compass round
and only by one's going slightly taut
in the capriciousness of summer air,
is of the slightest bondage made aware.

The image of self as a wide, graceful, tent, supported by "count-less silken ties of love and thought" can symbolize the fundamental nature of community. While our individual integrity remains intact— a "strong, supporting, central cedar pole... that signifies the sureness of the soul"— our stability against the wind is assured through the many loving ties we have with others, which hold us against the wind and help give to us much of our shape. And the place on which our tent is rooted—the connection to the earth which brings our soul to ground—forms the relationship to place that expresses another level of identity and personal commitment.

Five qualities of sustaining community are sketched in Figure 3, "Principles of Sustaining Community,"— qualities which again form nuclei around which to build the vibrant, living web of interconnectedness that helps to keep us alive. They describe qualities of connection and commitment to others and the land, recognizing the dynamics of community change through time:

• **Connecting to people**. Learning to know the people in our community of place, and coming to a deep understanding of what moves them to be who and what they are.

• **Connecting to place**. Recognizing at a deep level "where we are." Learning and living by the rhythms of the place in which we live.

• **Strengthening personal community**. Realizing that our personal web of community—family, friends and loved ones—may stretch well beyond our geographic place. Sustaining these connections can provide a vibrancy and potency to our personal sense of community which deepens our commitment to nurture the place in which we live.

• **Building from vision and strength**. Being aware that we are creating our future, at every moment, by our deeds, attitudes, and expectations. This requires a deep clarity about one's own values, and a practice of choosing our directions and actions based clearly on those values. This approach moves continuously toward a desired outcome, building from resources at hand. It is an "assets" approach, distinctly different from the classic "problem-solving" approach which focuses primarily on "needs" and on struggling to acquire resources which are presently lacking.

• **Thinking of the seventh generation**. Extending an awareness of the impact of our choices upon a distant but tangible future, linked to our own community and kin, perhaps inspiring us to take responsibility for the future at a more profound level.

There is legendary folk hero in the United States: —the *rugged individualist*, or the *self-made man*. This hero has many faces, many names, but his core qualities of independence, strength, tenacity, and persistent fortitude remain the romantic ideal of many. Much can be achieved through such qualities. Yet, a powerful misconception lies behind this image: one is led to believe that a person can succeed entirely through the brute force of individualistic effort, relying on no contribution from others to make one's path open. There may indeed be times when it seems that we are totally alone, making it by ourselves, "pulling ourselves up by our own bootstraps." But even the briefest examination of the constant exchange of resources among us

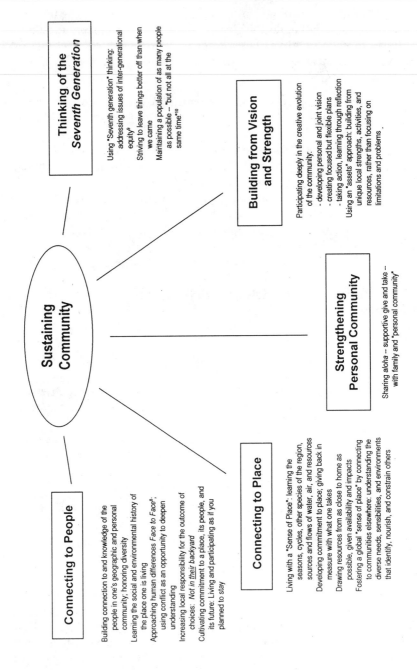

Figure 3. Principles of Sustaining Community

will reveal that we are constantly relying upon the creativity, productivity, and power of others. And even one who lives alone, entirely "off the land," is indebted for survival to the generosity of nature herself. Truly, no-one is an island.

At heart, sustaining community starts from recognizing, cherishing, and building upon connections to others and to the land in which we are rooted:

> *From connection is born compassion*
> *From compassion, commitment*
> *From commitment, responsibility*
> *From responsibility, reciprocity*
> *From reciprocity, renewal*
> *From renewal, the sustaining of community.*

ENVIRONMENTAL KINSHIP—A MATTER OF RELATIONSHIP; A BALANCE OF GIVE AND TAKE

In native Hawaiian tradition there is an approach to relating to the natural world and to one another which is tangibly, palpably different from the Western thinking in which I was raised. It is the view that people are not *stewards* of the natural world—but much more profoundly than this, we are *sister and brother* to all living things, and to the land, water, and ocean in which we all live.[11]

The Hawaiian creation myth illustrates the root of this kinship perspective through the kalo, or taro plant, traditional staple food of the Hawaiian people.[12] *Kalo* is said to have been born of the same parents as the progenitor of the human race, thus making humans and *kalo* siblings in the same spiritual family. *Kalo* and its derivative, *poi*, were therefore traditionally treated as sacred. Poi was *never* wasted. It was believed that when the *poi* bowl was uncovered, the family was in the presence of their gods. It was a sacred moment, and no harsh language or arguments were permitted, no quarreling was to be heard.

The Hawaiian view of *kalo* as kin to humankind extends to the entire natural world. As in many indigenous cultures, the trees, birds, animals, fish, and the land and ocean themselves are felt to be alive with *mana*—spiritual life force—never to be abused. This sense of kinship implies a very different approach toward the natural world than the scientific/industrial era has tended to promote. An attitude of kinship demands humility, responsibility, reciprocity, restraint, using only what you need, and replenishing what you have taken by nurturing the land and oceans to bring forth new life.

The concept of stewardship—a popular Western model of harmony between humans and the environment—has elements of the kinship attitude, but also contains significant differences. The stewardship model calls people to take seriously the husbandry of the natural world, defined as "the control or judicious use of resources." Yet the stewardship perspective still sees humans as the ordained "masters" of all life, with a right to make use of any resource or living creature for which we feel we have a need. Kinship, on the other hand, does not assume "rights" over other living and non-living things, but instead suggests that humans accept the responsibility of our place in the living family through practicing a thoughtful relationship of *give and take*.

Related to and building from this sense of kinship, one can build several principles for living with the natural world, as summarized in Figure 4, "Principles of Environmental Kinship," including:

- **Actively cultivating attitudes of relationship**. Relating to nature with a sense of reverence and connectedness, seeing ourselves as one element in a rich complex of life. Treating other creatures, the land and oceans with respect, rather than simply as a lode of resources of which we must make efficient use.
- **Sustaining cycles and internalizing impacts**. Taking responsibility for the life-cycle costs and impacts of everything we consume. Not being willing to export the impacts of production to distant places, to be borne by other people.
- **Sustaining the bioregion**. Cultivating a "sense of place," a deep understanding of the place where we live. Developing greater local self-reliance, learning to regenerate and replenish what we use. Working within the limits of environmental "cleansing" functions. Leaving some "untrammeled" spaces for other species to survive and thrive.
- **Living simply**. Getting back to basics, living comfortably without excess.
- **Planning for the seventh generation**. Solving the environmental problems we create; not deferring the cleaning up of our messes for another generation. Using non-renewables, if we must, at very conservative rates, not assuming (as in classical economics models) that substitutes will always become available as a result of scarcity. This just pushes the burden of risk and higher costs to our children's grandchildren.

A vibrant sense of kinship with nature provides a subjective, relational perspective in deciding what actions to take or not to take in relation to nature. Kinship embraces emotional, connecting,

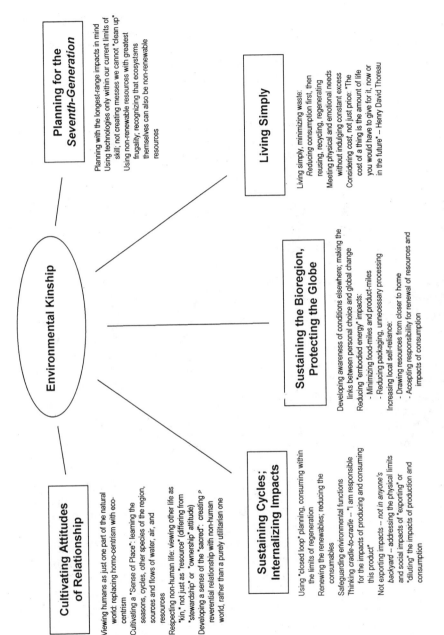

Figure 4. Principles of Environmental Kinship

aesthetic motivations and purposes. To include these qualities, a profound change will be necessary in modes of analysis and decision-making which are primarily quantitative and non-subjective. This is one of the types of shifts toward "people-based" knowledge generation and control advocated in earlier chapters.

We are perhaps now just at the threshold of such creative paradigm changes. This will have profound implications for policy dialogues and academic endeavors, and the re-visioning of "fields" and "disciplines." In moving into this era, we will need motivations and intellectual resources that draw upon other core values and principles—Creative Diversity and Deep Justice—and that guide the evolution of a Humane Economy.

CREATIVE DIVERSITY—CONNECTING TO THE LIFE-BRINGING IMPULSE

Reciprocal, just relationships with others and to the land lie at the heart of sustaining community and the future, as summarized later in the value/principle of "Deep Justice." Such connections are a common element of certain eastern and indigenous modes of thought. At the same time, there is a potent energy of creativity that has fueled many of the accomplishments of western culture, and which underlies the burning passion for "freedom" so often expressed by Americans. Such freedom is often at odds with justice and environmental renewability—since freedom is often equated with *carte blanche* to take as much as one can, and do whatever one pleases.

But there is another notion of freedom: a creative principle which allows for individuality and personal expression, but which does not intrude on the well-being of that which lies beyond the self, both human and environmental. It is fueled by a connection to the "life-enhancing" impulse—perhaps the same type of energy that brings an ear of corn to its fullness, or causes a baby to form and spring forth from the womb. It is a creative freedom which contributes to the world, on balance, more than it takes away.

This type of personal freedom and creativity allows for expression of the individual, but also understands that society is like a human organism, built as if from millions of cells that function on their own, yet bathed in the nutrients and communications of a larger body of life. It is this connection to the larger body that allows the cells of an organism to function independently, yet never in isolation. Analogously, a human being can be self-expressive while staying deeply connected to the body of human society, supported and nourished by the bones and blood of the earth itself. The difference between life-enhancing self-expression and that which is destructively out of hand is like the difference between a well-functioning cell and one turned cancerous, in which the individual impulse to expand has overwhelmed the balance of the body. Life-enhancing creativity strikes a balance between cell and body, person and society, humankind and the natural world.

The principle of "creative diversity" also acknowledges that our many human cultures, born in part from the deep richness of spirit of humankind, are a resource to celebrate, as well as a challenge. To bond as communities and "tribes," to share mutual identity, to work in cooperation with others, gives us a sense of unity which we deeply need. Still, the denial of the personal, unique creative nature in each person, which at times occurs as the result of our need to share identity with others, is a point of stifling and loss that many can not bear. The challenge, then, is to allow for seemingly exclusive qualities to co-exist and find harmony, such as:

•the pulses of creativity that individuals and small cooperative clusters of people can generate

•the joy of identity born of membership in a potent culture

•the ability to appreciate and support the diversity of cultures, without falling prey to the struggles for power that diversity can sometimes create.

This, then, means blending qualities of impulse, identity, and harmonious resolution of differences, without losing the unique sources of beauty that diversity creates. As summarized in Figure 5, among the principles involved in such creative diversity are:

•**Powering creativity.** Allowing, supporting the creative impulse of the individual.

•**Anchoring through culture.** Recognizing and nurturing identity through belonging.

•**Valuing diversity, fostering uniqueness.** Supporting the creative existence of individuality within cultures, and diversity among cultures.

•**Gaining learning from conflict.** Using conflict as an opportunity to deepen understanding about what is uniquely valuable about others, individually and collectively.

DEEP JUSTICE—THE BALANCE OF I AND THOU

Justice, deep justice, is not limited to issues of legal rights.

In the words of Richard Morse, "If I am concerned for my freedom, I must commit to your equal rights." This is a matter of

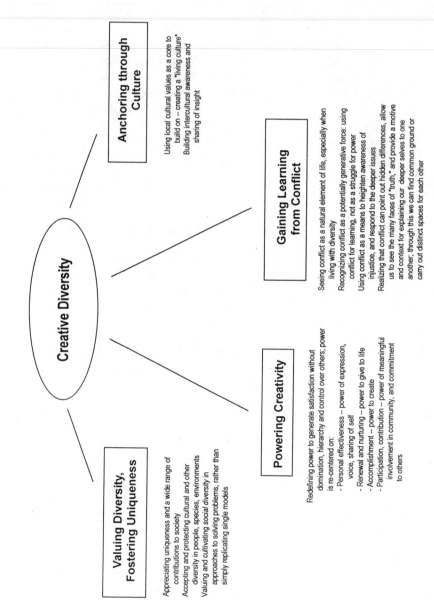

Figure 5. Principles of Creativity Diversity

Creative Diversity

Anchoring through Culture

Using local cultural values as a core to build on – creating a "living culture"
Building intercultural awareness and sharing of insight

Gaining Learning from Conflict

Seeing conflict as a natural element of life, especially when living with diversity
Recognizing conflict as a potentially generative force: using conflict for learning, not as a struggle for power
Using conflict as a means to heighten awareness of injustice, and respond to the deeper issues
Realizing that conflict can point out hidden differences, allow us to see the many faces of "truth," and provide a motive and context for explaining our deeper selves to one another; through this we can find common ground or carry out distinct spaces for each other

Powering Creativity

Redefining power to generate satisfaction without domination, hierarchy and control over others; power is re-centered on:
- Personal effectiveness – power of expression, voice, sharing of self
- Renewal and nurturing – power to give to life
- Accomplishment – power to create
- Participation, contribution – power of meaningful involvement in community, and commitment to others

Valuing Diversity, Fostering Uniqueness

Appreciating uniqueness and a wide range of contributions to society
Accepting and protecting cultural and other diversity in people, species, environments
Valuing and cultivating social diversity in approaches to solving problems, rather than simply replicating single models

whether and how my actions affect your life, and yours mine. A commitment to deep justice acknowledges that our decisions for personal well-being affect the well-being of others, and does not wait for others to protest injustice before we seek fairness. This requires a profound personal commitment to reciprocity, to take no more than we give, to refuse unfair shares of power, income, or wealth. It is, at its core, a principle of profound nonviolence.

To commit to deep issues of justice is, among other things, to fight for the dignity and rights of others: such rights as to be economically and socially valued, to be safe, to make a contribution, and to exercise responsibilities to others. At the same time, to act out of a commitment to deep justice requires a naked degree of self-inspection. Those of us in positions of privilege may need to learn how to say some "outrageous" things, like:

• I do not want this hazardous activity in my neighborhood, but neither will I accept shifting the burden of this risk to others. How can we reduce the activity that created this problem in the first place?

• Though I am the official leader of my organization, I do not claim the right to speak on major matters for my group. I must consult with the others before making this decision on their behalf.

• The wage you have offered me is too high relative to my co-workers; let us redefine the distribution of profits to create more balance among us.

Is this a pipe dream? It depends, perhaps, on the place and time. Have such things occurred before? Yes, and they happen all the time—they simply do not make the front-page. Indeed, entire societies have been built on such principles, to greater or lesser success. In Riane Eisler's *The Chalice and the Blade*, such notions of justice are framed in terms of a "partnership society," built upon mutual dignity and balanced power relationships. She traces the history of partnership societies, and projects this notion as a viable vision for the future.

Among the principles which might be embraced in deep justice, as sketched in Figure 6, are:

• **Social justice; sharing power.** Being willing to share the practice and fruits of power equally with others; not engaging in control games and power struggles with others.

• **Environmental justice; sharing resources and impacts.** Taking full responsibility for the environmental impacts of our actions. Sharing the fruits of the land and sea fairly with others.

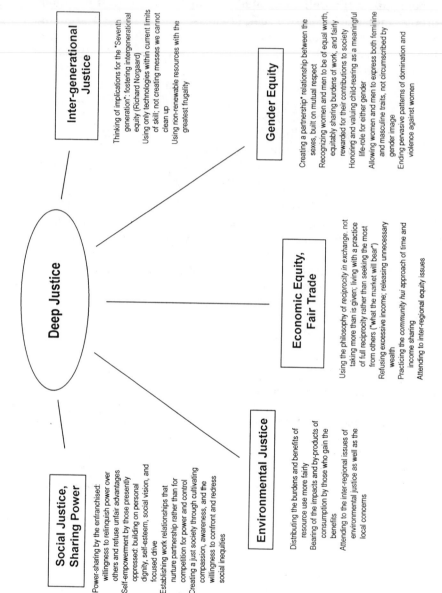

Figure 6. Principles of Deep Justice

• **Economic equity, fair trade.** Recognizing that the ability to gain advantages in trade relationships does not imply the moral right to do so. Reducing the disparity in the valuing of people's time across national, race, ethnic, and gender barriers.

• **Gender equity.** Finding a balance between the sexes which may allow for differences in style and preference, but which does not institutionalize unequal power relationships.

• **Inter-generational justice.** Not mortgaging our children's children's lives through selfish excesses today.

We know that passions for this type of justice have existed in the breast of humankind for millennia, and yet we seem only a hairsbreadth closer to realizing such dreams. Still, I suggest that a sustainable future must be built around such notions, and we must courageously discover how to practice them, even against great odds. For without voluntary social justice, the innate indominability of the human spirit will rise up and take action—perhaps even in violence—against the wrongs society perpetrates. A future society which is physically in balance but socially unjust not only will not thrive, it is unlikely even to survive.

HUMANE ECONOMY—A NEW SCALE IN THE BALANCE OF TRADE

In sharing, everyone has enough.
—Puanani Burgess, speaking of traditional Hawaiian values

A concept has been explained to me regarding the traditional Hawaiian view of trade within an "*ahupua'a* economy." The *ahupua'a* was a land division extending from the mountains to the sea, in which clusters of families lived: some in the upland areas near the forests, growing upland taro and gathering wild foods and medicinals; some in the middle lands, farming all manner of things, like taro, sweet potato, banana, breadfruit, and the like; and some in the coastal lands, spending time in the husbandry and collection of fish, the gathering of *opihi* and seaweed, and other activities of the coast and ocean. The fruits and products of the entire *ahupua'a* were needed by each family to survive, though any given family would specialize based on its location. It is only natural, therefore, that trade would be needed to bring a balance of goods to each family. Yet while the *ali'i* (rulers) were charged in part with the regulation of the *ahupua'a*, ensuring that all members the area received what they needed to survive, there was also a unique attitude that permeated this "trade" relationship unlike any common "market model." Since often there was a surplus of any given harvestable resource—whether fish from a co-operative netting endeavor, or fruit from a tree in full bearing—families often brought this surplus to one another freely as a gift, not as an item to barter in trade. A deep personal and social sense of commitment and reciprocity ensured that gifts from others did not go unreturned. This "surplus" style of exchanging the fruits of the land and sea apparently played a major role in balancing needs and re-sources among those in any given *ahupua'a*.

This trade system might be termed an "abundance model," in which those with more than they needed of any particular "good" would make certain that the surplus was shared with others. The practice was reinforced by the perspective that no-one owned the land—and therefore the fruits of the land were seen as a common resource—even though great individual effort may have been used to bring them forth. Remnants of this style of trade are still very visible in "local style" generosity... one does not visit a friend empty-handed. In some regions, such as the island of Moloka'i, gifting and barter still play a major role in the subsistence of local families.

There are many models for a more humane economy, one built around the deep rhythms of being human, rather than on the drive to produce more and more goods for less and less money. These experiments and principles are being practiced around the world, in large and small ways. As sketched in Figure 7, "Principles of Humane Economy," some of the directions and principles include:

- **Values at the bottom line.** Redefining the core values of economic decision making to place emphasis on personal, social, and environmental renewal and reciprocity.
- **Commitment to community: people and place.** Developing businesses with substantive roots in community, demonstrating concern for and commitment to both the people and the place in which the businesses are based.
- **Just exchange.** An economic corollary to Deep Justice, promoting the notion of "fair trade" rather than "free trade."
- **Humanity at work.** Creating humane workplaces which recognize the individual contribution, creativity, and importance of each person, and which support the many, sometimes conflicting, roles each person leads in their lives.
- **Renewal-based economy.** Shifting to a "life-sustaining" economy rather than a "consumptive" one.

None of these ideas are new. Increasingly, "rational" economic choices are being seen as those which also attempt to account for those intangible costs which do not appear in the price of a good.

Humane Economy

Renewal-Based Economy

Shifting to a "life-sustaining" economy rather than a "consumptive" economy (a contrast with both subsistence and consumerism):
- Developing industries based on resource renewal, "cyclism," and closed-loop materials use (cradle-to-cradle resource management and full-cycle costing)
- Including more environmental "externalities" in prices, and/or full cost-benefit comparisons
- Valuing simplicity

Encouraging "bioregional business" based on renewable resources common to the region, emphasizing local/regional loops of production and consumption that reduce "embodied mileage" in products

Re-evaluating the true indicators of poverty and wealth

Humanity at Work

Working with meaningful participation, encouraging:
- Worker participation in visioning, planning and decision-making
- Worker ownership and co-management models
- Emphasis on the dignity of work

Working with a balanced life, involving:
- Support for family responsibilities
- Job-sharing, flexible hours, or shorter workweek
- Extra leave time when needed for personal balance and healing

Working with a wider contribution to society and environment, including:
- Selling products or services that make a positive contribution to social and environmental concerns
- Paid community service time

Just Exchange

Attending to the *equity bottom-line*:
- Building *no poverty-no affluence*[14] wage structures
- Considering intergenerational equity issues
- Refusing unfair advantage

Basing exchange principles on *mutual sustenance*, not on maximizing personal profit

Promoting *fair trade* (as distinct from simple "free trade")

Increasing recognition, social status and concrete support for presently "unpaid" contributions to society

Values at the Bottom Line

Transforming consumerism:
- Learning a new definition of "rational economic choice": consumer support of "regenerative" or "lowest-impact" goods rather than "lowest-cost" goods (*sustainable sustenance*)
- Developing easily-accessible information sources for finding sources of *sustainable sustenance*

Expanding "Enviro-Social enterprises"

Emphasizing socially-conscious and local investment and banking practices

Practicing *voluntary equity*: reducing luxury income; focusing more on non-monetary, non-material factors of well-being

Using "work as healing"

Seeing the value of a life not in one's earning (consuming) power, but in one's power to sustain oneself while giving back to the land and to others

Commitment to Community: People and Place

Focusing on business that builds community (*workers, neighborhood,* and *environment*), through:
- "People-centered" productivity emphasizing worker co-creation in business
- Using the "community asset approach" – building upon local strengths, especially human resources
- Using appropriate scales (large or small) which reduce social and environmental costs
- Encouraging commitment to place instead of unbridled mobility

Moving from "simple profit-maximization" to "enhancing socio-environmental well-being" as preferred rationale for investment choices
- Incorporating subjective, qualitative measures of well-being into decision-making and evaluation processes
- Involving the community in developing business directions, based on local visions, strengths, and concerns

Figure 7. Principles of Humane Economy

Social and environmental impacts and benefits are increasingly included on the scales when we weigh economic choices. Long-accepted practices such as "charging what the market will bear" are making way for new decision making paradigms.

An elegant description of using inner scales of just exchange was once presented by Kahlil Gibran in his statement "On Buying and Selling":

...To you the earth yields her fruit, and you shall not want if you but know how to fill your hands.

It is in exchanging the gifts of the earth that you shall find abundance and be satisfied.

Yet unless the exchange be in love and kindly justice, it will but lead some to greed and others to hunger.

When in the market place you toilers of the sea and fields and vineyards meet the weavers and the potters and the gatherers of spices,

Invoke then the master spirit of the earth, to come into your midst and sanctify the scales and the reckoning that weighs value against value...

And before you leave the market place, see that no one has gone his way with empty hands.

For the master spirit of the earth shall not sleep peacefully upon the wind till the needs of the least of you are satisfied.

The Prophet

If, instead of relentlessly pursuing the "best deal" for ourselves alone, we learn increasingly to ask "the master spirit of the earth...to sanctify the scales and the reckoning that weighs value against value," the impacts of our lives and livelihoods will weigh less heavily upon the earth and one another.

CONCLUSION

The cost of a thing is the amount of life you must give for it, now or in the future.

—Henry David Thoreau

To sustain ourselves, the earth, the people and the creatures upon it, the amount of "life" we take must somehow be balanced with the amount that we give back to life in return. Deep, renewing sustenance based upon principles of simplicity, connectedness, reciprocity, and regeneration can naturally permeate our every act and decision. This way of living need not be driven from a feeling of gloomy self-deprivation, but can generate spontaneously from the sense of completeness and celebration that comes from profound connectedness with all living things.

Our lives and life choices are like raindrops falling on the ocean. The waters are vast, but still the impacts of our lives send ripples in all directions. And the cumulative waves of change that result may have effects we might never have imagined. It is important that we take our choices seriously. As once expressed by Mohandas Gandhi, what we do may seem insignificant, but it is imperative that we do it. The acts and choices that make up our daily lives eventually build the paradigms which can reconstruct society. Reflecting our deepest values in every act is ultimately our greatest gift to ourselves, to our children, and to life itself.

END NOTES

[1] Partnership terminology from Riane Eisler, *The Chalice and the Blade*.

[2] Concepts from Clarissa Pinkola Estes, *Women who Run with the Wolves*.

[3] Concepts from Clarissa Pinkola Estes, *Women who Run with the Wolves*.

[4] Terminology from First Nations Institute.

[5] From A.T. Aryaratne, founder of the Sarvodaya movement in Sri Lanka.

[6] Concept promoted by Puanani Burgess of the Wai'anae Coast Community Alternative Development Corporation.

[7] Idea outlined by Duane Elgin in *Voluntary Simplicity: Toward a Way of Life that's Outwardly Simple, Inwardly Rich*.

[8] From poem by Puanani Burgess, *He Alo a He Alo* (Face to Face).

[9] Issues of intergenerational economic justice have been developed in some detail by Richard Norgaard of the University of California at Berkeley.

[10] Concept as described by Herman Daly.

[11] The distinction between kinship and stewardship was originally described to me by Puanani Burgess of the Wai'anae Coast Community Alternative Development Corporation.

[12] As explained by Eric Enos, of the Cultural Learning Center at Ka'ala, in Wai'anae, Hawaii.

[13] *The Merriam-Webster Concise School and Office Dictionary*. Springfield: Merriam-Webster, Inc. 1991.

[14] The idea of a "no poverty - no affluence" society is used by A.T. Ariyaratne, founder of the Sarvodaya Movement in Sri Lanka.

CHAPTER 15

THE WORKSHOP AS A BRIDGE

Puanani Burgess

Bridging

Being together is knowing
even if what we know
is that we cannot really be together
caught in the teeth of the machinery
of the wrong moments of our lives.

A clear umbilicus
goes out invisibly between,
thread we spin fluid and finer than hair
but strong enough to hang a bridge on.

That bridge will be there
a blacklight rainbow arching out of your skull
whenever you need
whenever you can open your eyes and want
to walk upon it.

Nobody can live on a bridge
or plant potatoes
but it is fine for comings and goings,
meetings, partings and long view
and a real connection to someplace else
where you may
in the crazy weathers of struggle
now and again want to be.

Marge Piercy
From *To Be of Use*

It is November, 1994, a full five years and seven months since the 40-something of us gathered at the East-West Center for the Workshop on *People's Initiatives to Overcome Poverty*. We were each a separate system of class, experiences, work, traditions, spirituality, values, stories, abilities, world views, opinions, biases, successes, failures, hopes, dreams, and songs.

We were each separate streams, some flowing parallel to each other, others criss-crossing in several spots along the way—each with its own beginnings, unique from all others. There had not yet been created a place, an environment, or a bridge which could connect the streams flowing from Bangladesh, India, Philippines, United States, Thailand, Papua New Guinea, Canada, Japan, and Hawaii.

At the outset, there was discomfort; no one was quite sure why they were at this particular place at this particular time and for what particular reason. Many of us, indeed all of us, held the ideals of "participatory democracy" and "participatory development" in great esteem as part of our approach in working with clients/participants/villagers/beneficiaries/people. However, when it came to participating democratically in this newly formed group to develop goals, agendas, work plans, and outcomes for this ten day conference, we hit a wall.

Some were frustrated, expecting the organizers of the conference to have specific agendas, outcomes, etc., ready to be passed out and worked on. Some were intrigued by the opportunity to struggle through and develop the process and outcomes for the entire conference; this workshop presented a rare opportunity to "walk our talk." And others were simply confused.

But most of us agreed to struggle, just as we had to struggle in our daily work and in our lives, having to make up the "agenda" as we went along. It was hard work to come to agreement. We spent many hours in plenary sessions and small groups in discussion; at times it felt as though we were part of peace negotiations between long-warring countries or engaged in international debates at the United Nations over significant international issues.

This experience, because of its difficulty and complexity, has been invaluable in my growing work at helping to mediate complex public issues. Learning to see different points of view, helping the parties find common ground and being able to understand where people may never meet in agreement or cannot reach agreement at this particular stage of their maturity were essential lessons learned through this process.

In reflecting back upon those days, I have concluded that there is a deep place, where we seldom visit and are seldom asked to visit or act out of within the context of a conference or workshop, where we as participants in this workshop had to go in order to find common ground and to be able to be productive during these days we had to be together. This is the place where our true values live, where our good will resides.

The struggles in this workshop forced us below the surface, and sometimes it felt as if some of us were drowning. And when you find yourself in that kind of situation, you can fight the current, fight the rhythm of the flow, or you can go with the current, which may take you to a place you've never been before and to sights you've never seen before. At some point, impossible for me to say when that happened or how it happened, most of us decided to enter the current, which was both of our making and not of our making. A few members struggled against the current and remained frustrated throughout the conference and beyond, but that too was part of the fabric of this workshop and their challenges to what happened throughout the workshop were valuable in that they forced each of us to clarify and test our assumptions, beliefs, and actions constantly.

One of the most powerful insights for me was the contributions of the culture of my people, the *Po'e Hawai'i* (the indigenous people of Hawaii) with its traditions of *Aloha* (to Love), *Kokua* (to Help), and *Lokahi* (to Work Together) as a critical part of the process which allowed us to come *he alo a he alo* (face to face) with each other, to recognize our commonalities, to reconcile our differences, to create accommodation for different Ways, and to create new work for ourselves and with each other.

One of the most powerful experiences of the workshop was the visit to the sacred learning place of my people located in the foothills of the Ka'ala Mountain range. Ka'ala is the oldest place on my island of O'ahu, indeed it is the birthplace of this island. At Ka'ala, children from my island visit and work in the *lo'i kalo* (taro paddies) so that they can meet their ancestor, the Taro, care for it, and practice their culture.

The workshop participants came to our sacred place, many of them recognized the taro as a food that they ate, recognized the paddies as a way of growing, connected with the various trees and plants that they too had in their homelands. At Ka'ala, they met the *Po'e Hawai'i* (indigenous people), and *kuka kuka* (talked story) with the *kapuna* (our elders). For many of them, they felt as though they had come home.

The Bangladeshi, as their *ho'okupu* (offering) to the Land and to her people, sang the most beautiful song about their Motherland which connected our peoples at the marrow. We shared food and shared stories of struggle and dignity. We became *hoa'aina*, friends through the Land.

I often look at the photograph of most of the participants in that workshop which was taken and given to each of us by the East-West Center; it amazes me that I still remember each person's name and where they came from and what they brought with them from their countries and communities to share.

The deepest connections for me and my work came from the most unexpected places: Bangladesh, Appalachia, and home—Hawaii. Until that workshop Bangladesh and Appalachia were only names of places I would never visit—they were bits of exotica. These places were invisible to me; I knew nothing about them and was content to know nothing. In my entire run of life, I had spent no more than five minutes considering either of these places.

That soon changed.

On the first day of the workshop I sat next to Khushi Kabir from Bangladesh. She was exhausted from traveling; there were no direct routes between Bangladesh and Hawaii. Wrapped in a traditional sari, she looked like a butterfly emerging from her cocoon. In the center of her forehead was a red dot; this was something that had fascinated me for a long time. I knew it meant something spiritual and my eyes were always drawn to it.

Except for the minute it took to say her name, her country, and give a brief description of her work with women, she was quiet and gave no clues to the lively, passionate, and spiritual being I was to come to know.

Over the next ten days Khushi awakened my spirit as a woman; she told me stories of the women she worked with in the villages; she talked to me about their struggles for dignity for themselves and their families; how they suffered under the yoke of poverty which was not of their making; how they worked and worked and worked with so little; how stories of their courage would never appear in a book; how they fought for education for themselves and their children; how they shared and made do; how they loved their children. She sang songs of her Motherland softly in my ear, like a lullaby; although younger than me, she became my mother, teaching me lessons of compassion and simple courage through these stories of the women of Bangladesh. Through her I became whole again; my work reconnected to the feminine spirit in me and in the Land.

On the visit to Ka'ala, we sat next to each other on the bus and I told her stories of the communities through which we were passing. During the ride, she took that red dot from the center of her forehead and placed it on mine. She whispered to me that this was the *tikka*, the third eye; that which sees the unseeable. And she called me "sister." Even now as I sit at my computer composing these thoughts, I am transported to that journey and my face is wet.

The second person who was to profoundly affect my life was Anisur Rahman, also from Bangladesh; he became for me the philosophical center of the workshop. Whenever I felt uncertain about where the workshop was headed or should be headed, I conferred with him. I felt that his knowledge and wisdom came from a deep place—unknown to me, but to be trusted.

My first encounter with him was the night before the workshop at a cultural event sponsored by the East-West Center. He sang songs from the Motherland and of the famous Bangladesh poet, Tagore. Consistently throughout the workshop Anis introduced the concept of finding common ground through sharing poetry, song, dance, and story. Each day began with a different person from a different country sharing a part of his/her heart. From this experience I began to understand the role of art and culture to peoples' struggles and their liberation.

My own work as a poet in the struggle for independence for Hawaii from the United States took on new and greater meaning. From Anis, who had participated in the independence struggle of Bangladesh, I learned about the role of poetry and music in that struggle. Over the next five years, Anis, his wife Dora, my husband, Poka Laenui, who is one of the leaders in the struggle for Hawaii's independence from the United States, and I, have had several discussions about the Bangladesh revolution and the lessons applicable to Hawaii's struggle for independence. Whenever the road to independence gets rocky or I become uncertain, I remember the stories, and especially the songs which gave the Bangladeshi people courage, patience, and spirit to continue.

The third person who profoundly affected me and continues to affect my work is John Gaventa from Tennessee, part of the Appalachian region of the United States. At the time of the conference he was still the Director of the Highlander Research and Education Center in New Market, Tennessee. Highlander and one of its founders, Myles Horton, had been in the forefront of social and political change in the United States. It was through the courage and wisdom of those who created Highlander that major changes in civil rights for African-Americans and by extension, other minorities, were won.

Highlander also fought against the economic and environmental terrorism practiced by the coal mine companies which commodified, exploited, and used up the human spirit and the spirit of the land for enormous financial gains for the owners and stockholders of the mines. Over their 60 plus years of existence, Highlander helped organize the coal miners into unions; conducted literacy campaigns as part of qualifying people to vote for the first time in the South; did research into the GATT and other international trade agreements and treaties; created educational opportunities and curriculum around community-based economic development; and has been a residential retreat center for established and emerging leadership from Appalachian communities to meet with each other and learn from each other.

Of critical importance to me was hearing John talk about the research he did which he wrote about in his book, *Power and Powerlessness: Quiescence and Rebellion in an Appalachian Valley*. In his presentation to the plenary he explored the relationship between power and powerlessness and how the understanding of these relationships resulted in people in Appalachia deciding not to participate. He verified for me a belief that people chose not to participate because of their understanding of power, not because they were ignorant or apathetic. Too often, apathy and ignorance of the grassroots people have been the reasons articulated by academics, social scientists, and politicians for people not participating in voting or protests or filing class action suits. He asked us the following critical questions and challenged us to answer them from our own contexts: "Why, in an oppressed community where one might intuitively expect upheaval, does one instead find, or appear to find, quiescence? Under what conditions and against what obstacles does rebellion begin to emerge?"

These questions forced me to look again at what people understood about Power, their relationship to Power, and their ability to challenge that Power in order to change their lives in peaceful and positive ways. Seeking answers to these powerful questions has shaped our programs and the ways we use people's curiosity and desire to keep learning as ways of gently pulling them into an empowerment and development process.

For example, for years we had been challenging, as a community, the kinds of resort and luxury residential developments that are being built in and near our community. We did the usual "activist" types of activities: petitions to protest the development, blockades, picket lines, being arrested, and filing for temporary restraining orders or injunctions. To some degree we were successful in keeping these developments at bay and reducing the size of the developments. While many community residents were concerned about the impact these kinds of developments would have on our rural, multi-cultural community, most felt helpless to stop it. They had seen over the last 20 years many unsuccessful attempts other community residents had made to stop these types of developments, and instead felt that their energies would be better invested in recreational activities with their families, or working at another job, or doing community service.

We decided that rather than organizing people around crisis and negative issues, we would organize around something positive—learning to grow food fish for their families and their neighbors. Families learn to build these small wooden tanks, 12 feet in diameter, and to stock, maintain, and harvest the fresh water tilapia they grow in these tanks. By being community food producers, families begin to feel responsible for and able to shape things that affect the community at large. At the last Water Commission hearing on revisions to the State of Hawaii's Water Code, more than 13 families turned out to give input about how the water code should be changed to include community development usage as opposed to concerning itself merely with the water needs of agro-businesses like sugar and pineapple, resort/golf course developers, and housing developers.

We believe that the high level of participation of families in the hearings was due to their viewing themselves as powerful, as having something important to say and to contribute, and confident because of the important role they play in the health and well-being of their community. It was clear that these families did not feel powerless. Meeting John Gaventa, Highlander, and these critical ideas at that precise moment contributed, in a most profound way, to the success and empowerment of our families, thousands and thousands of miles away from the source of these gifts—the struggles and victories of the people of Appalachia.

One of the most precious gifts I received from this workshop was the ability to work with Richard Morse, Kersten Johnson, and Arthur Getz. Often, you will hear community people, and I have been one of them, say about "university-types" that they live in ivory towers and don't know what is really happening at the grassroots. The relationship between the community and the intelligentsia has been sporadic and often adversarial.

Participation in this workshop, however, helped me look at scholars, researchers, and intellectuals in new light. It helped me look at myself and my community in new light. These three scholars treated the knowledge that I brought from my community and my experiences in working within the community, with honor and dignity. I have relied upon advice from them in creating partnerships between my community and faculty within the university and East-West Center systems. Richard, Kersten, and Arthur have been honored guests and workers in my community, have assisted in planning programs and approaches to development with my organization, and offered encouragement at appropriate moments.

In recognition of the many *hoa'aina* (friends through the Land) that came from participation in this conference, who had the courage to come face to face, I dedicate the following poem. It is in this willingness to come *he alo a he alo* that needed changes in how we relate to ourselves, to each other, and to our Mother, the 'Aina, will emerge.

To each of my *hoa'aina*, known and to be known, mahalo for your gifts of Spirit, Humor, and Love.

HE ALO A HE ALO
(Face to Face)

He alo a he alo,
(Face to face)

That's how you learn about what makes us weep.

He alo a he alo,
(Face to face)

That's how you learn about what makes us bleed.

He alo a he alo,
(Face to face)

That's how you learn about what makes us feel.
  what makes us work.
  what makes us sing.
  what makes us bitter.
  what makes us fight.
  what makes us stand against the wind.
  what makes us sit in the flow of power.
  what makes us, us.

Not from a distance.
Not from miles away.
Not from a book.
Not from an article you read.
Not from the newspaper.
Not from what somebody told you.
Not from a "reliable source."
Not from what you think.
Not from a cliff.
Not from a cave.
Not from your reality.
Not from your darkness.

But,

He alo a he alo
(Face to face)

Or,
else,

Pa'a ka waha. (Shut tight, your mouth)

'A'ohe o kahi nana o luna o ka pali;
iho mai a lalo nei;
'ike i ke au nui ke au iki;
he alo a he alo.
(The top of the cliff isn't the place to look at us;
come down here and learn of the big and little current,
face to face.)

And come and help us dig, the lo'i, deep.